第二版

MongoDB权威指南（影印版）

MongoDB: The Definitive Guide

Kristina Chodorow 著

O'REILLY®

Beijing · Cambridge · Farnham · Köln · Sebastopol · Tokyo

O'Reilly Media, Inc.授权东南大学出版社出版

南京 东南大学出版社

图书在版编目（CIP）数据

MongoDB 权威指南：第 2 版：英文 /（美）霍多罗夫（Chodorow, K.）著 .—影印本 .—南京：东南大学出版社，2014.1

书名原文：MongoDB: The Definitive Guide, 2E

ISBN 978-7-5641-4602-3

I. ① M… II. ①霍… III. ①关系数据库系统－英文 IV. ① TP311.138

中国版本图书馆 CIP 数据核字（2013）第 246107 号

江苏省版权局著作权合同登记

图字：10-2013-375 号

MongoDB 权威指南 第二版（影印版）

出版发行：东南大学出版社

地　　址：南京四牌楼 2 号　　邮编：210096

出 版 人：江建中

网　　址：http://www.seupress.com

电子邮件：press@seupress.com

印　　刷：扬中市印刷有限公司

开　　本：787 毫米 × 980 毫米　16 开本

印　　张：27

字　　数：529 千字

版　　次：2014 年 1 月第 1 版

印　　次：2014 年 1 月第 1 次印刷

书　　号：ISBN 978-7-5641-4602-3

定　　价：64.00 元（册）

本社图书若有印装质量问题，请直接与营销部联系。电话（传真）：025-83791830

Table of Contents

Foreword

In the last 10 years, the Internet has challenged relational databases in ways nobody could have foreseen. Having used MySQL at large and growing Internet companies during this time, I've seen this happen firsthand. First you have a single server with a small data set. Then you find yourself setting up replication so you can scale out reads and deal with potential failures. And, before too long, you've added a caching layer, tuned all the queries, and thrown even more hardware at the problem.

Eventually you arrive at the point when you need to shard the data across multiple clusters and rebuild a ton of application logic to deal with it. And soon after that you realize that you're locked into the schema you modeled so many months before.

Why? Because there's so much data in your clusters now that altering the schema will take a long time and involve a lot of precious DBA time. It's easier just to work around it in code. This can keep a small team of developers busy for many months. In the end, you'll always find yourself wondering if there's a better way—or why more of these features are not built into the core database server.

Keeping with tradition, the Open Source community has created a plethora of "better ways" in response to the ballooning data needs of modern web applications. They span the spectrum from simple in-memory key/value stores to complicated SQL-speaking MySQL/InnoDB derivatives. But the sheer number of choices has made finding the right solution more difficult. I've looked at many of them.

I was drawn to MongoDB by its pragmatic approach. MongoDB doesn't try to be everything to everyone. Instead it strikes the right balance between features and complexity, with a clear bias toward making previously difficult tasks far easier. In other words, it has the features that really matter to the vast majority of today's web applications: indexes, replication, sharding, a rich query syntax, and a very flexible data model. All of this comes without sacrificing speed.

Like MongoDB itself, this book is very straightforward and approachable. New MongoDB users can start with Chapter 1 and be up and running in no time. Experienced users will appreciate this book's breadth and authority. It's a solid reference for advanced administrative topics such as replication, backups, and sharding, as well as popular client APIs.

Having recently started to use MongoDB in my day job, I have no doubt that this book will be at my side for the entire journey—from the first install to production deployment of a sharded and replicated cluster. It's an essential reference to anyone seriously looking at using MongoDB.

—Jeremy Zawodny
Craigslist Software Engineer
August 2010

Preface

How This Book Is Organized

This book is split up into six sections, covering development, administration, and deployment information.

Getting Started with MongoDB

In Chapter 1 we provide background about MongoDB: why it was created, the goals it is trying to accomplish, and why you might choose to use it for a project. We go into more detail in Chapter 2, which provides an introduction to the core concepts and vocabulary of MongoDB. Chapter 2 also provides a first look at working with MongoDB, getting you started with the database and the shell. The next two chapters cover the basic material that developers need to know to work with MongoDB. In Chapter 3, we describe how to perform those basic write operations, including how to do them with different levels of safety and speed. Chapter 4 explains how to find documents and create complex queries. This chapter also covers how to iterate through results and gives options for limiting, skipping, and sorting results.

Developing with MongoDB

Chapter 5 covers what indexing is and how to index your MongoDB collections. Chapter 6 explains how to use several special types of indexes and collections. Chapter 7 covers a number of techniques for aggregating data with MongoDB, including counting, finding distinct values, grouping documents, the aggregation framework, and using MapReduce. Finally, this section finishes with a chapter on designing your application: Chapter 8 goes over tips for writing an application that works well with MongoDB.

Replication

The replication section starts with Chapter 9, which gives you a quick way to set up a replica set locally and covers many of the available configuration options. Chapter 10 then covers the various concepts related to replication. Chapter 11 shows how replication interacts with your application and Chapter 12 covers the administrative aspects of running a replica set.

Sharding

The sharding section starts in Chapter 13 with a quick local setup. Chapter 14 then gives an overview of the components of the cluster and how to set them up. Chapter 15 has advice on choosing a shard key for a variety of application. Finally, Chapter 16 covers administering a sharded cluster.

Application Administration

The next two chapters cover many aspects of MongoDB administration from the perspective of your application. Chapter 17 discusses how to introspect what MongoDB is doing. Chapter 18 covers administrative tasks such as building indexes, and moving and compacting data. Chapter 19 explains how MongoDB stores data durably.

Server Administration

The final section is focused on server administration. Chapter 20 covers common options when starting and stopping MongoDB. Chapter 21 discusses what to look for and how to read stats when monitoring. Chapter 22 describes how to take and restore backups for each type of deployment. Finally, Chapter 23 discusses a number of system settings to keep in mind when deploying MongoDB.

Appendixes

Appendix A explains MongoDB's versioning scheme and how to install it on Windows, OS X, and Linux. Appendix B details ow MongoDB works internally: its storage engine, data format, and wire protocol.

Conventions Used in This Book

The following typographical conventions are used in this book:

Italic

Indicates new terms, URLs, email addresses, collection names, database names, filenames, and file extensions.

`Constant width`
: Used for program listings, as well as within paragraphs to refer to program elements such as variable or function names, command-line utilities, environment variables, statements, and keywords.

`Constant width bold`
: Shows commands or other text that should be typed literally by the user.

`Constant width italic`
: Shows text that should be replaced with user-supplied values or by values determined by context.

This icon signifies a tip, suggestion, or general note.

This icon indicates a warning or caution.

Using Code Examples

This book can help you get your job done. In general, you may use the code in this book in your programs and documentation. You do not need to contact us for permission unless you're reproducing a significant portion of the code. For example, writing a program that uses several chunks of code from this book does not require permission. Selling or distributing a CD-ROM of examples from O'Reilly books does require permission. Answering a question by citing this book and quoting example code does not require permission. Incorporating a significant amount of example code from this book into your product's documentation does require permission.

We appreciate, but do not require, attribution. An attribution usually includes the title, author, publisher, and ISBN. For example: "*MongoDB: The Definitive Guide, Second Edition* by Kristina Chodorow (O'Reilly). Copyright 2013 Kristina Chodorow, 978-1-449-34468-9."

If you feel your use of code examples falls outside fair use or the permission given here, feel free to contact us at *permissions@oreilly.com*.

Safari® Books Online

Safari Books Online (*www.safaribooksonline.com*) is an on-demand digital library that delivers expert content in both book and video form from the world's leading authors in technology and business.

Technology professionals, software developers, web designers, and business and creative professionals use Safari Books Online as their primary resource for research, problem solving, learning, and certification training.

Safari Books Online offers a range of product mixes and pricing programs for organizations, government agencies, and individuals. Subscribers have access to thousands of books, training videos, and prepublication manuscripts in one fully searchable database from publishers like O'Reilly Media, Prentice Hall Professional, Addison-Wesley Professional, Microsoft Press, Sams, Que, Peachpit Press, Focal Press, Cisco Press, John Wiley & Sons, Syngress, Morgan Kaufmann, IBM Redbooks, Packt, Adobe Press, FT Press, Apress, Manning, New Riders, McGraw-Hill, Jones & Bartlett, Course Technology, and dozens more. For more information about Safari Books Online, please visit us online.

How to Contact Us

Please address comments and questions concerning this book to the publisher:

O'Reilly Media, Inc.
1005 Gravenstein Highway North
Sebastopol, CA 95472
800-998-9938 (in the United States or Canada)
707-829-0515 (international or local)
707 829-0104 (fax)

We have a web page for this book, where we list errata, examples, and any additional information. You can access this page at:

http://oreil.ly/mongodb-2e

To comment or ask technical questions about this book, send email to:

bookquestions@oreilly.com

For more information about our books, conferences, Resource Centers, and the O'Reilly Network, see our website at:

http://www.oreilly.com

Acknowledgments

I would like to thank my tech reviewers, Adam Comerford, Eric Milke, and Greg Studer. You guys made this book immeasurably better (and more correct). Thank you, Ann Spencer, for being such a terrific editor and for helping me every step of the way. Thanks to all of my coworkers at 10gen for sharing your knowledge and advice on MongoDB as well as Eliot Horowitz and Dwight Merriman, for starting the MongoDB project. And thank you, Andrew, for all of your support and suggestions.

PART I
Introduction to MongoDB

CHAPTER 1

Introduction

MongoDB is a powerful, flexible, and scalable general-purpose database. It combines the ability to scale out with features such as secondary indexes, range queries, sorting, aggregations, and geospatial indexes. This chapter covers the major design decisions that made MongoDB what it is.

Ease of Use

MongoDB is a *document-oriented* database, not a relational one. The primary reason for moving away from the relational model is to make scaling out easier, but there are some other advantages as well.

A document-oriented database replaces the concept of a "row" with a more flexible model, the "document." By allowing embedded documents and arrays, the document-oriented approach makes it possible to represent complex hierarchical relationships with a single record. This fits naturally into the way developers in modern object-oriented languages think about their data.

There are also no predefined schemas: a document's keys and values are not of fixed types or sizes. Without a fixed schema, adding or removing fields as needed becomes easier. Generally, this makes development faster as developers can quickly iterate. It is also easier to experiment. Developers can try dozens of models for the data and then choose the best one to pursue.

Easy Scaling

Data set sizes for applications are growing at an incredible pace. Increases in available bandwidth and cheap storage have created an environment where even small-scale applications need to store more data than many databases were meant to handle. A terabyte of data, once an unheard-of amount of information, is now commonplace.

As the amount of data that developers need to store grows, developers face a difficult decision: how should they scale their databases? Scaling a database comes down to the choice between scaling up (getting a bigger machine) or scaling out (partitioning data across more machines). Scaling up is often the path of least resistance, but it has drawbacks: large machines are often very expensive, and eventually a physical limit is reached where a more powerful machine cannot be purchased at any cost. The alternative is to scale *out*: to add storage space or increase performance, buy another commodity server and add it to your cluster. This is both cheaper and more scalable; however, it is more difficult to administer a thousand machines than it is to care for one.

MongoDB was designed to scale out. Its document-oriented data model makes it easier for it to split up data across multiple servers. MongoDB automatically takes care of balancing data and load across a cluster, redistributing documents automatically and routing user requests to the correct machines. This allows developers to focus on programming the application, not scaling it. When a cluster need more capacity, new machines can be added and MongoDB will figure out how the existing data should be spread to them.

Tons of Features…

MongoDB is intended to be a general-purpose database, so aside from creating, reading, updating, and deleting data, it provides an ever-growing list of unique features:

Indexing
: MongoDB supports generic secondary indexes, allowing a variety of fast queries, and provides unique, compound, geospatial, and full-text indexing capabilities as well.

Aggregation
: MongoDB supports an "aggregation pipeline" that allows you to build complex aggregations from simple pieces and allow the database to optimize it.

Special collection types
: MongoDB supports time-to-live collections for data that should expire at a certain time, such as sessions. It also supports fixed-size collections, which are useful for holding recent data, such as logs.

File storage
: MongoDB supports an easy-to-use protocol for storing large files and file metadata.

Some features common to relational databases are not present in MongoDB, notably joins and complex multirow transactions. Omitting these was an architectural decision to allow for greater scalability, as both of those features are difficult to provide efficiently in a distributed system.

...Without Sacrificing Speed

Incredible performance is a major goal for MongoDB and has shaped much of its design. MongoDB adds dynamic padding to documents and preallocates data files to trade extra space usage for consistent performance. It uses as much of RAM as it can as its cache and attempts to automatically choose the correct indexes for queries. In short, almost every aspect of MongoDB was designed to maintain high performance.

Although MongoDB is powerful and attempts to keep many features from relational systems, it is not intended to do everything that a relational database does. Whenever possible, the database server offloads processing and logic to the client side (handled either by the drivers or by a user's application code). Maintaining this streamlined design is one of the reasons MongoDB can achieve such high performance.

Let's Get Started

Throughout the course of the book, we will take the time to note the reasoning or motivation behind particular decisions made in the development of MongoDB. Through those notes we hope to share the philosophy behind MongoDB. The best way to summarize the MongoDB project, however, is through its main focus—to create a full-featured data store that is scalable, flexible, and fast.

CHAPTER 2

Getting Started

MongoDB is powerful but easy to get started with. In this chapter we'll introduce some of the basic concepts of MongoDB:

- A *document* is the basic unit of data for MongoDB and is roughly equivalent to a row in a relational database management system (but much more expressive).
- Similarly, a *collection* can be thought of as a table with a dynamic schema.
- A single instance of MongoDB can host multiple independent *databases*, each of which can have its own collections.
- Every document has a special key, `"_id"`, that is unique within a collection.
- MongoDB comes with a simple but powerful JavaScript *shell*, which is useful for the administration of MongoDB instances and data manipulation.

Documents

At the heart of MongoDB is the *document*: an ordered set of keys with associated values. The representation of a document varies by programming language, but most languages have a data structure that is a natural fit, such as a map, hash, or dictionary. In JavaScript, for example, documents are represented as objects:

```
{"greeting" : "Hello, world!"}
```

This simple document contains a single key, `"greeting"`, with a value of `"Hello, world!"`. Most documents will be more complex than this simple one and often will contain multiple key/value pairs:

```
{"greeting" : "Hello, world!", "foo" : 3}
```

As you can see from the example above, values in documents are not just "blobs." They can be one of several different data types (or even an entire embedded document—see

"Embedded Documents" on page 19). In this example the value for "greeting" is a string, whereas the value for "foo" is an integer.

The keys in a document are strings. Any UTF-8 character is allowed in a key, with a few notable exceptions:

- Keys must not contain the character \0 (the null character). This character is used to signify the end of a key.
- The . and $ characters have some special properties and should be used only in certain circumstances, as described in later chapters. In general, they should be considered reserved, and drivers will complain if they are used inappropriately.

MongoDB is type-sensitive and case-sensitive. For example, these documents are distinct:

```
{"foo" : 3}
{"foo" : "3"}
```

as are as these:

```
{"foo" : 3}
{"Foo" : 3}
```

A final important thing to note is that documents in MongoDB cannot contain duplicate keys. For example, the following is not a legal document:

```
{"greeting" : "Hello, world!", "greeting" : "Hello, MongoDB!"}
```

Key/value pairs in documents are ordered: `{"x" : 1, "y" : 2}` is not the same as `{"y" : 2, "x" : 1}`. Field order does not usually matter and you should not design your schema to depend on a certain ordering of fields (MongoDB may reorder them). This text will note the special cases where field order is important.

In some programming languages the default representation of a document does not even maintain ordering (e.g., dictionaries in Python and hashes in Perl or Ruby 1.8). Drivers for those languages usually have some mechanism for specifying documents with ordering, when necessary.

Collections

A *collection* is a group of documents. If a document is the MongoDB analog of a row in a relational database, then a collection can be thought of as the analog to a table.

Dynamic Schemas

Collections have *dynamic schemas*. This means that the documents within a single collection can have any number of different "shapes." For example, both of the following documents could be stored in a single collection:

```
{"greeting" : "Hello, world!"}
{"foo" : 5}
```

Note that the previous documents not only have different types for their values (string versus integer) but also have entirely different keys. Because any document can be put into any collection, the question often arises: "Why do we need separate collections at all?" It's a good question—with no need for separate schemas for different kinds of documents, why *should* we use more than one collection? There are several good reasons:

- Keeping different kinds of documents in the same collection can be a nightmare for developers and admins. Developers need to make sure that each query is only returning documents of a certain type or that the application code performing a query can handle documents of different shapes. If we're querying for blog posts, it's a hassle to weed out documents containing author data.
- It is much faster to get a list of collections than to extract a list of the types in a collection. For example, if we had a `"type"` field in each document that specified whether the document was a "skim," "whole," or "chunky monkey," it would be much slower to find those three values in a single collection than to have three separate collections and query the correct collection.
- Grouping documents of the same kind together in the same collection allows for data locality. Getting several blog posts from a collection containing only posts will likely require fewer disk seeks than getting the same posts from a collection containing posts and author data.
- We begin to impose some structure on our documents when we create indexes. (This is especially true in the case of unique indexes.) These indexes are defined per collection. By putting only documents of a single type into the same collection, we can index our collections more efficiently.

As you can see, there are sound reasons for creating a schema and for grouping related types of documents together, even though MongoDB does not enforce it.

Naming

A collection is identified by its name. Collection names can be any UTF-8 string, with a few restrictions:

- The empty string (`""`) is not a valid collection name.
- Collection names may not contain the character \0 (the `null` character) because this delineates the end of a collection name.
- You should not create any collections that start with *system.*, a prefix reserved for internal collections. For example, the *system.users* collection contains the database's

users, and the *system.namespaces* collection contains information about all of the database's collections.

- User-created collections should not contain the reserved character $ in the name. The various drivers available for the database do support using $ in collection names because some system-generated collections contain it. You should not use $ in a name unless you are accessing one of these collections.

Subcollections

One convention for organizing collections is to use namespaced subcollections separated by the . character. For example, an application containing a blog might have a collection named *blog.posts* and a separate collection named *blog.authors*. This is for organizational purposes only—there is no relationship between the *blog* collection (it doesn't even have to exist) and its "children."

Although subcollections do not have any special properties, they are useful and incorporated into many MongoDB tools:

- GridFS, a protocol for storing large files, uses subcollections to store file metadata separately from content chunks (see Chapter 6 for more information about GridFS).
- Most drivers provide some syntactic sugar for accessing a subcollection of a given collection. For example, in the database shell, `db.blog` will give you the *blog* collection, and `db.blog.posts` will give you the *blog.posts* collection.

Subcollections are a great way to organize data in MongoDB, and their use is highly recommended.

Databases

In addition to grouping documents by collection, MongoDB groups collections into *databases*. A single instance of MongoDB can host several databases, each grouping together zero or more collections. A database has its own permissions, and each database is stored in separate files on disk. A good rule of thumb is to store all data for a single application in the same database. Separate databases are useful when storing data for several application or users on the same MongoDB server.

Like collections, databases are identified by name. Database names can be any UTF-8 string, with the following restrictions:

- The empty string ("") is not a valid database name.
- A database name cannot contain any of these characters: /, \, ., ", *, <, >, :, |, ?, $, (a single space), or \0 (the null character). Basically, stick with alphanumeric ASCII.

- Database names are case-sensitive, even on non-case-sensitive filesystems. To keep things simple, try to just use lowercase characters.
- Database names are limited to a maximum of 64 bytes.

One thing to remember about database names is that they will actually end up as files on your filesystem. This explains why many of the previous restrictions exist in the first place.

There are also several reserved database names, which you can access but which have special semantics. These are as follows:

admin
: This is the "root" database, in terms of authentication. If a user is added to the *admin* database, the user automatically inherits permissions for all databases. There are also certain server-wide commands that can be run only from the *admin* database, such as listing all of the databases or shutting down the server.

local
: This database will never be replicated and can be used to store any collections that should be local to a single server (see Chapter 9 for more information about replication and the local database).

config
: When MongoDB is being used in a sharded setup (see Chapter 13), it uses the *config* database to store information about the shards.

By concatenating a database name with a collection in that database you can get a fully qualified collection name called a *namespace*. For instance, if you are using the *blog.posts* collection in the *cms* database, the namespace of that collection would be `cms.blog.posts`. Namespaces are limited to 121 bytes in length and, in practice, should be fewer than 100 bytes long. For more on namespaces and the internal representation of collections in MongoDB, see Appendix B.

Getting and Starting MongoDB

MongoDB is almost always run as a network server that clients can connect to and perform operations on. Download MongoDB and decompress it. To start the server, run the `mongod` executable:

```
$ mongod
mongod --help for help and startup options
Thu Oct 11 12:36:48 [initandlisten] MongoDB starting : pid=2425 port=27017
    dbpath=/data/db/ 64-bit host=spock
Thu Oct 11 12:36:48 [initandlisten] db version v2.4.0, pdfile version 4.5
Thu Oct 11 12:36:48 [initandlisten] git version:
    3aaea5262d761e0bb6bfef5351cfbfca7af06ec2
Thu Oct 11 12:36:48 [initandlisten] build info: Darwin spock 11.2.0 Darwin Kernel
```

```
    Version 11.2.0: Tue Aug 9 20:54:00 PDT 2011;
    root:xnu-1699.24.8~1/RELEASE_X86_64 x86_64 BOOST_LIB_VERSION=1_48
Thu Oct 11 12:36:48 [initandlisten] options: {}
Thu Oct 11 12:36:48 [initandlisten] journal dir=/data/db/journal
Thu Oct 11 12:36:48 [initandlisten] recover : no journal files present, no
    recovery needed
Thu Oct 11 12:36:48 [websvr] admin web console waiting for connections on
    port 28017
Thu Oct 11 12:36:48 [initandlisten] waiting for connections on port 27017
```

Or if you're on Windows, run this:

```
$ mongod.exe
```

> For detailed information on installing MongoDB on your system, see Appendix A.

When run with no arguments, `mongod` will use the default data directory, */data/db/* (or *\data\db* on the current volume on Windows). If the data directory does not already exist or is not writable, the server will fail to start. It is important to create the data directory (e.g., *mkdir -p /data/db/*) and to make sure your user has permission to write to the directory before starting MongoDB.

On startup, the server will print some version and system information and then begin waiting for connections. By default MongoDB listens for socket connections on port 27017. The server will fail to start if the port is not available—the most common cause of this is another instance of MongoDB that is already running.

`mongod` also sets up a very basic HTTP server that listens on a port 1,000 higher than the main port, in this case 28017. This means that you can get some administrative information about your database by opening a web browser and going to *http://localhost:28017*.

You can safely stop `mongod` by typing Ctrl-C in the shell that is running the server.

> For more information on starting or stopping MongoDB, see Chapter 20.

Introduction to the MongoDB Shell

MongoDB comes with a JavaScript shell that allows interaction with a MongoDB instance from the command line. The shell is useful for performing administrative functions, inspecting a running instance, or just playing around. The mongo shell is a crucial tool for using MongoDB and is used extensively throughout the rest of the text.

Running the Shell

To start the shell, run the mongo executable:

```
$ mongo
MongoDB shell version: 2.4.0
connecting to: test
>
```

The shell automatically attempts to connect to a MongoDB server on startup, so make sure you start mongod before starting the shell.

The shell is a full-featured JavaScript interpreter, capable of running arbitrary JavaScript programs. To illustrate this, let's perform some basic math:

```
> x = 200
200
> x / 5;
40
```

We can also leverage all of the standard JavaScript libraries:

```
> Math.sin(Math.PI / 2);
1
> new Date("2010/1/1");
"Fri Jan 01 2010 00:00:00 GMT-0500 (EST)"
> "Hello, World!".replace("World", "MongoDB");
Hello, MongoDB!
```

We can even define and call JavaScript functions:

```
> function factorial (n) {
... if (n <= 1) return 1;
... return n * factorial(n - 1);
... }
> factorial(5);
120
```

Note that you can create multiline commands. The shell will detect whether the JavaScript statement is complete when you press Enter. If the statement is not complete, the shell will allow you to continue writing it on the next line. Pressing Enter three times in a row will cancel the half-formed command and get you back to the >-prompt.

A MongoDB Client

Although the ability to execute arbitrary JavaScript is cool, the real power of the shell lies in the fact that it is also a standalone MongoDB client. On startup, the shell connects to the *test* database on a MongoDB server and assigns this database connection to the global variable db. This variable is the primary access point to your MongoDB server through the shell.

To see the database db is currently assigned to, type in db and hit Enter:

```
> db
test
```

The shell contains some add-ons that are not valid JavaScript syntax but were implemented because of their familiarity to users of SQL shells. The add-ons do not provide any extra functionality, but they are nice syntactic sugar. For instance, one of the most important operations is selecting which database to use:

```
> use foobar
switched to db foobar
```

Now if you look at the db variable, you can see that it refers to the *foobar* database:

```
> db
foobar
```

Because this is a JavaScript shell, typing a variable will convert the variable to a string (in this case, the database name) and print it.

Collections can be accessed from the db variable. For example, `db.baz` returns the *baz* collection in the current database. Now that we can access a collection in the shell, we can perform almost any database operation.

Basic Operations with the Shell

We can use the four basic operations, create, read, update, and delete (CRUD) to manipulate and view data in the shell.

Create

The `insert` function adds a document to a collection. For example, suppose we want to store a blog post. First, we'll create a local variable called `post` that is a JavaScript object representing our document. It will have the keys `"title"`, `"content"`, and `"date"` (the date that it was published):

```
> post = {"title" : "My Blog Post",
... "content" : "Here's my blog post.",
... "date" : new Date()}
{
    "title" : "My Blog Post",
    "content" : "Here's my blog post.",
    "date" : ISODate("2012-08-24T21:12:09.982Z")
}
```

This object is a valid MongoDB document, so we can save it to the *blog* collection using the `insert` method:

```
> db.blog.insert(post)
```

The blog post has been saved to the database. We can see it by calling `find` on the collection:

```
> db.blog.find()
{
    "_id" : ObjectId("5037ee4a1084eb3ffeef7228"),
    "title" : "My Blog Post",
    "content" : "Here's my blog post.",
    "date" : ISODate("2012-08-24T21:12:09.982Z")
}
```

You can see that an `"_id"` key was added and that the other key/value pairs were saved as we entered them. The reason for the sudden appearance of the `"_id"` field is explained at the end of this chapter.

Read

`find` and `findOne` can be used to query a collection. If we just want to see one document from a collection, we can use `findOne`:

```
> db.blog.findOne()
{
    "_id" : ObjectId("5037ee4a1084eb3ffeef7228"),
    "title" : "My Blog Post",
    "content" : "Here's my blog post.",
    "date" : ISODate("2012-08-24T21:12:09.982Z")
}
```

`find` and `findOne` can also be passed criteria in the form of a *query document*. This will restrict the documents matched by the query. The shell will automatically display up to 20 documents matching a `find`, but more can be fetched. See Chapter 4 for more information on querying.

Update

If we would like to modify our post, we can use `update`. `update` takes (at least) two parameters: the first is the criteria to find which document to update, and the second is the new document. Suppose we decide to enable comments on the blog post we created earlier. We'll need to add an array of comments as the value for a new key in our document.

The first step is to modify the variable `post` and add a `"comments"` key:

```
> post.comments = []
[ ]
```

Then we perform the update, replacing the post titled "My Blog Post" with our new version of the document:

```
> db.blog.update({title : "My Blog Post"}, post)
```

Now the document has a "comments" key. If we call find again, we can see the new key:

```
> db.blog.find()
{
    "_id" : ObjectId("5037ee4a1084eb3ffeef7228"),
    "title" : "My Blog Post",
    "content" : "Here's my blog post.",
    "date" : ISODate("2012-08-24T21:12:09.982Z"),
    "comments" : [ ]
}
```

Delete

remove permanently deletes documents from the database. Called with no parameters, it removes all documents from a collection. It can also take a document specifying criteria for removal. For example, this would remove the post we just created:

```
> db.blog.remove({title : "My Blog Post"})
```

Now the collection will be empty again.

Data Types

The beginning of this chapter covered the basics of what a document is. Now that you are up and running with MongoDB and can try things on the shell, this section will dive a little deeper. MongoDB supports a wide range of data types as values in documents. In this section, we'll outline all the supported types.

Basic Data Types

Documents in MongoDB can be thought of as "JSON-like" in that they are conceptually similar to objects in JavaScript. JSON is a simple representation of data: the specification can be described in about one paragraph (their website proves it) and lists only six data types. This is a good thing in many ways: it's easy to understand, parse, and remember. On the other hand, JSON's expressive capabilities are limited because the only types are null, boolean, numeric, string, array, and object.

Although these types allow for an impressive amount of expressivity, there are a couple of additional types that are crucial for most applications, especially when working with a database. For example, JSON has no date type, which makes working with dates even more annoying than it usually is. There is a number type, but only one—there is no way to differentiate floats and integers, never mind any distinction between 32-bit and 64-bit numbers. There is no way to represent other commonly used types, either, such as regular expressions or functions.

MongoDB adds support for a number of additional data types while keeping JSON's essential key/value pair nature. Exactly how values of each type are represented varies by language, but this is a list of the commonly supported types and how they are represented as part of a document in the shell. The most common types are:

null
: Null can be used to represent both a null value and a nonexistent field:

```
{"x" : null}
```

boolean
: There is a boolean type, which can be used for the values `true` and `false`:

```
{"x" : true}
```

number
: The shell defaults to using 64-bit floating point numbers. Thus, these numbers look "normal" in the shell:

```
{"x" : 3.14}
```

or:

```
{"x" : 3}
```

For integers, use the `NumberInt` or `NumberLong` classes, which represent 4-byte or 8-byte signed integers, respectively.

```
{"x" : NumberInt("3")}
{"x" : NumberLong("3")}
```

string
: Any string of UTF-8 characters can be represented using the string type:

```
{"x" : "foobar"}
```

date
: Dates are stored as milliseconds since the epoch. The time zone is not stored:

```
{"x" : new Date()}
```

regular expression
: Queries can use regular expressions using JavaScript's regular expression syntax:

```
{"x" : /foobar/i}
```

array
: Sets or lists of values can be represented as arrays:

```
{"x" : ["a", "b", "c"]}
```

embedded document
: Documents can contain entire documents embedded as values in a parent document:

```
{"x" : {"foo" : "bar"}}
```

object id

An object id is a 12-byte ID for documents. See the section "_id and ObjectIds" on page 20 for details:

```
{"x" : ObjectId()}
```

There are also a few less common types that you may need, including:

binary data

Binary data is a string of arbitrary bytes. It cannot be manipulated from the shell. Binary data is the only way to save non-UTF-8 strings to the database.

code

Queries and documents can also contain arbitrary JavaScript code:

```
{"x" : function() { /* ... */ }}
```

There are a few types that are mostly used internally (or superseded by other types). These will be described in the text as needed.

For more information on MongoDB's data format, see Appendix B.

Dates

In JavaScript, the `Date` class is used for MongoDB's date type. When creating a new `Date` object, always call `new Date(...)`, not just `Date(...)`. Calling the constructor as a function (that is, not including `new`) returns a string representation of the date, not an actual `Date` object. This is not MongoDB's choice; it is how JavaScript works. If you are not careful to always use the `Date` constructor, you can end up with a mishmash of strings and dates. Strings do not match dates and vice versa, so this can cause problems with removing, updating, querying...pretty much everything.

For a full explanation of JavaScript's `Date` class and acceptable formats for the constructor, see ECMAScript specification section 15.9.

Dates in the shell are displayed using local time zone settings. However, dates in the database are just stored as milliseconds since the epoch, so they have no time zone information associated with them. (Time zone information could, of course, be stored as the value for another key.)

Arrays

Arrays are values that can be interchangeably used for both ordered operations (as though they were lists, stacks, or queues) and unordered operations (as though they were sets).

In the following document, the key `"things"` has an array value:

```
{"things" : ["pie", 3.14]}
```

As we can see from the example, arrays can contain different data types as values (in this case, a string and a floating-point number). In fact, array values can be any of the supported values for normal key/value pairs, even nested arrays.

One of the great things about arrays in documents is that MongoDB "understands" their structure and knows how to reach inside of arrays to perform operations on their contents. This allows us to query on arrays and build indexes using their contents. For instance, in the previous example, MongoDB can query for all documents where 3.14 is an element of the `"things"` array. If this is a common query, you can even create an index on the `"things"` key to improve the query's speed.

MongoDB also allows atomic updates that modify the contents of arrays, such as reaching into the array and changing the value *pie* to *pi*. We'll see more examples of these types of operations throughout the text.

Embedded Documents

Documents can be used as the *value* for a key. This is called an *embedded document*. Embedded documents can be used to organize data in a more natural way than just a flat structure of key/value pairs.

For example, if we have a document representing a person and want to store his address, we can nest this information in an embedded `"address"` document:

```
{
    "name" : "John Doe",
    "address" : {
        "street" : "123 Park Street",
        "city" : "Anytown",
        "state" : "NY"
    }
}
```

The value for the `"address"` key in the previous example is an embedded document with its own key/value pairs for `"street"`, `"city"`, and `"state"`.

As with arrays, MongoDB "understands" the structure of embedded documents and is able to reach inside them to build indexes, perform queries, or make updates.

We'll discuss schema design in depth later, but even from this basic example we can begin to see how embedded documents can change the way we work with data. In a relational database, the previous document would probably be modeled as two separate rows in two different tables (one for "people" and one for "addresses"). With MongoDB we can embed the address document directly within the person document. When used properly, embedded documents can provide a more natural representation of information.

The flip side of this is that there can be more data repetition with MongoDB. Suppose "addresses" were a separate table in a relational database and we needed to fix a typo in an address. When we did a join with "people" and "addresses," we'd get the updated address for everyone who shares it. With MongoDB, we'd need to fix the typo in each person's document.

_id and ObjectIds

Every document stored in MongoDB must have an `"_id"` key. The `"_id"` key's value can be any type, but it defaults to an `ObjectId`. In a single collection, every document must have a unique value for `"_id"`, which ensures that every document in a collection can be uniquely identified. That is, if you had two collections, each one could have a document where the value for `"_id"` was 123. However, neither collection could contain more than one document with an `"_id"` of 123.

ObjectIds

`ObjectId` is the default type for `"_id"`. The `ObjectId` class is designed to be lightweight, while still being easy to generate in a globally unique way across different machines. MongoDB's distributed nature is the main reason why it uses `ObjectId`s as opposed to something more traditional, like an autoincrementing primary key: it is difficult and time-consuming to synchronize autoincrementing primary keys across multiple servers. Because MongoDB was designed to be a distributed database, it was important to be able to generate unique identifiers in a sharded environment.

`ObjectId`s use 12 bytes of storage, which gives them a string representation that is 24 hexadecimal digits: 2 digits for each byte. This causes them to appear larger than they are, which makes some people nervous. It's important to note that even though an `ObjectId` is often represented as a giant hexadecimal string, the string is actually twice as long as the data being stored.

If you create multiple new `ObjectId`s in rapid succession, you can see that only the last few digits change each time. In addition, a couple of digits in the middle of the `ObjectId` will change (if you space the creations out by a couple of seconds). This is because of the manner in which `ObjectId`s are created. The 12 bytes of an `ObjectId` are generated as follows:

0	1	2	3	4	5	6	7	8	9	10	11
Timestamp				Machine			PID		Increment		

The first four bytes of an `ObjectId` are a timestamp in seconds since the epoch. This provides a couple of useful properties:

- The timestamp, when combined with the next five bytes (which will be described in a moment), provides uniqueness at the granularity of a second.

- Because the timestamp comes first, it means that `ObjectId`s will sort in *roughly* insertion order. This is not a strong guarantee but does have some nice properties, such as making `ObjectId`s efficient to index.
- In these four bytes exists an implicit timestamp of when each document was created. Most drivers expose a method for extracting this information from an `ObjectId`.

Because the current time is used in `ObjectId`s, some users worry that their servers will need to have synchronized clocks. Although synchronized clocks are a good idea for other reasons (see "Synchronizing Clocks" on page 383), the actual timestamp doesn't matter to ObjectIds, only that it is often new (once per second) and increasing.

The next three bytes of an `ObjectId` are a unique identifier of the machine on which it was generated. This is usually a hash of the machine's hostname. By including these bytes, we guarantee that different machines will not generate colliding `ObjectId`s.

To provide uniqueness among different processes generating `ObjectId`s concurrently on a single machine, the next two bytes are taken from the process identifier (PID) of the `ObjectId`-generating process.

These first nine bytes of an `ObjectId` guarantee its uniqueness across machines and processes for a single second. The last three bytes are simply an incrementing counter that is responsible for uniqueness within a second in a single process. This allows for up to 256^3 (16,777,216) unique `ObjectId`s to be generated *per process* in a single second.

Autogeneration of _id

As stated previously, if there is no `"_id"` key present when a document is inserted, one will be automatically added to the inserted document. This can be handled by the MongoDB server but will generally be done by the driver on the client side. The decision to generate them on the client side reflects an overall philosophy of MongoDB: work should be pushed out of the server and to the drivers whenever possible. This philosophy reflects the fact that, even with scalable databases like MongoDB, it is easier to scale out at the application layer than at the database layer. Moving work to the client side reduces the burden requiring the database to scale.

Using the MongoDB Shell

This section covers how to use the shell as part of your command line toolkit, customize it, and use some of its more advanced functionality.

Although we connected to a local *mongod* instance above, you can connect your shell to any MongoDB instance that your machine can reach. To connect to a *mongod* on a different machine or port, specify the hostname, port, and database when starting the shell:

```
$ mongo some-host:30000/myDB
MongoDB shell version: 2.4.0
connecting to: some-host:30000/myDB
>
```

db will now refer to *some-host:30000*'s myDB database.

Sometimes it is handy to not connect to a *mongod* at all when starting the *mongo* shell. If you start the shell with --nodb, it will start up without attempting to connect to anything:

```
$ mongo --nodb
MongoDB shell version: 2.4.0
>
```

Once started, you can connect to a *mongod* at your leisure by running new Mongo(*hostname*):

```
> conn = new Mongo("some-host:30000")
connection to some-host:30000
> db = conn.getDB("myDB")
myDB
```

After these two commands, you can use db normally. You can use these commands to connect to a different database or server at any time.

Tips for Using the Shell

Because mongo is simply a JavaScript shell, you can get a great deal of help for it by simply looking up JavaScript documentation online. For MongoDB-specific functionality, the shell includes built-in help that can be accessed by typing **help**:

```
> help
    db.help()                    help on db methods
    db.mycoll.help()             help on collection methods
    sh.help()                    sharding helpers
    ...

    show dbs                     show database names
    show collections             show collections in current database
    show users                   show users in current database
    ...
```

Database-level help is provided by db.help() and collection-level help by db.foo.help().

A good way of figuring out what a function is doing is to type it without the parentheses. This will print the JavaScript source code for the function. For example, if we are curious about how the update function works or cannot remember the order of parameters, we can do the following:

```
> db.foo.update
function (query, obj, upsert, multi) {
    assert(query, "need a query");
    assert(obj, "need an object");
    this._validateObject(obj);
    this._mongo.update(this._fullName, query, obj,
                       upsert ? true : false, multi ? true : false);
}
```

Running Scripts with the Shell

Other chapters have used the shell interactively, but you can also pass the shell JavaScript files to execute. Simply pass in your scripts at the command line:

```
$ mongo script1.js script2.js script3.js
MongoDB shell version: 2.4.0
connecting to: test
I am script1.js
I am script2.js
I am script3.js
$
```

The *mongo* shell will execute each script listed and exit.

If you want to run a script using a connection to a non-default host/port *mongod*, specify the address first, then the script(s):

```
$ mongo --quiet server-1:30000/foo script1.js script2.js script3.js
```

This would execute the three scripts with `db` set to the *foo* database on *server-1:30000*. As shown above, any command line options for running the shell go before the address.

You can print to stdout in scripts (as the scripts above did) using the `print()` function. This allows you to use the shell as part of a pipeline of commands. If you're planning to pipe the output of a shell script to another command use the `--quiet` option to prevent the "MongoDB shell version..." banner from printing.

You can also run scripts from within the interactive shell using the `load()` function:

```
> load("script1.js")
I am script1.js
>
```

Scripts have access to the `db` variable (as well as any other globals). However, shell helpers such as "`use db`" or "`show collections`" do not work from files. There are valid JavaScript equivalents to each of these, as shown in Table 2-1.

Table 2-1. JavaScript equivalents to shell helpers

Helper	Equivalent
`use foo`	`db.getSisterDB("foo")`
`show dbs`	`db.getMongo().getDBs()`
`show collections`	`db.getCollectionNames()`

You can also use scripts to inject variables into the shell. For example, we could have a script that simply initializes helper functions that you commonly use. The script below, for instance, may be helpful for the replication and sharding sections of the book. It defines a function, `connectTo()`, that connects to the locally-running database on the given port and sets `db` to that connection:

```
// defineConnectTo.js

/**
 * Connect to a database and set db.
 */
var connectTo = function(port, dbname) {
    if (!port) {
        port = 27017;
    }

    if (!dbname) {
        dbname = "test";
    }

    db = connect("localhost:"+port+"/"+dbname);
    return db;
};
```

If we load this script in the shell, `connectTo` is now defined:

```
> typeof connectTo
undefined
> load('defineConnectTo.js')
> typeof connectTo
function
```

In addition to adding helper functions, you can use scripts to automate common tasks and administrative activities.

By default, the shell will look in the directory that you started the shell in (use `run("pwd")` to see what directory that is). If the script is not in your current directory, you can give the shell a relative or absolute path to it. For example, if you wanted to put your shell scripts in *~/my-scripts*, you could load *defineConnectTo.js* with `load("/home/myUser/my-scripts/defineConnectTo.js")`. Note that `load` cannot resolve ~.

You can use `run()` to run command-line programs from the shell. Pass arguments to the function as parameters:

```
> run("ls", "-l", "/home/myUser/my-scripts/")
sh70352| -rw-r--r--  1 myUser myUser 2012-12-13 13:15 defineConnectTo.js
sh70532| -rw-r--r--  1 myUser myUser 2013-02-22 15:10 script1.js
sh70532| -rw-r--r--  1 myUser myUser 2013-02-22 15:12 script2.js
sh70532| -rw-r--r--  1 myUser myUser 2013-02-22 15:13 script3.js
```

This is of limited use, generally, as the output is formatted oddly and it doesn't support pipes.

Creating a .mongorc.js

If you have frequently-loaded scripts you might want to put them in your *mongorc.js* file. This file is run whenever you start up the shell.

For example, suppose we would like the shell to greet us when we log in. Create a file called *.mongorc.js* in your home directory, and then add the following lines to it:

```
// mongorc.js

var compliment = ["attractive", "intelligent", "like Batman"];
var index = Math.floor(Math.random()*3);

print("Hello, you're looking particularly "+compliment[index]+" today!");
```

Then, when you start the shell, you'll see something like:

```
$ mongo
MongoDB shell version: 2.4.0-pre-
connecting to: test
Hello, you're looking particularly like Batman today!
>
```

More practically, you can use this script to set up any global variables you'd like to use, alias long names to shorter ones, and override built-in functions. One of the most common uses for *.mongorc.js* is remove some of the more "dangerous" shell helpers. You can override functions like `dropDatabase` or `deleteIndexes` with no-ops or undefine them altogether:

```
var no = function() {
    print("Not on my watch.");
};

// Prevent dropping databases
db.dropDatabase = DB.prototype.dropDatabase = no;

// Prevent dropping collections
DBCollection.prototype.drop = no;

// Prevent dropping indexes
DBCollection.prototype.dropIndex = no;
```

Make sure that, if you change any database functions, you do so on both the db variable and the DB prototype (as shown in the example above). If you change only one, either the db variable won't see the change or all new databases you use (when you run use anotherDB) won't see your change.

Now if you try to call any of these functions, it will simply print an error message. Note that this technique does not protect you against malicious users; it can only help with fat-fingering.

You can disable loading your *.mongorc.js* by using the --norc option when starting the shell.

Customizing Your Prompt

The default shell prompt can be overridden by setting the prompt variable to either a string or a function. For example, if you are running a query that takes minutes to complete, you may want to have a prompt that prints the current time when it is drawn so you can see when the last operation finished:

```
prompt = function() {
    return (new Date())+"> ";
};
```

Another handy prompt might show the current database you're using:

```
prompt = function() {
    if (typeof db == 'undefined') {
        return '(nodb)> ';
    }

    // Check the last db operation
    try {
        db.runCommand({getLastError:1});
    }
    catch (e) {
        print(e);
    }

    return db+"> ";
};
```

Note that prompt functions should return strings and be very cautious about catching exceptions: it can be very confusing if your prompt turns into an exception!

In general, your prompt function should include a call to getLastError. This catches errors on writes and reconnects you "automatically" if the shell gets disconnected (e.g., if you restart *mongod*).

The *.mongorc.js* file is a good place to set your prompt if you want to always use a custom one (or set up a couple of custom prompts that you can switch between in the shell).

Editing Complex Variables

The multiline support in the shell is somewhat limited: you cannot edit previous lines, which can be annoying when you realize that the first line has a typo and you're currently working on line 15. Thus, for larger blocks of code or objects, you may want to edit them in an editor. To do so, set the `EDITOR` variable in the shell (or in your environment, but since you're already in the shell):

```
> EDITOR="/usr/bin/emacs"
```

Now, if you want to edit a variable, you can say `"edit varname"`, for example:

```
> var wap = db.books.findOne({title: "War and Peace"})
> edit wap
```

When you're done making changes, save and exit the editor. The variable will be parsed and loaded back into the shell.

Add `EDITOR="/path/to/editor";` to your *.mongorc.js* file and you won't have to worry about setting it again.

Inconvenient Collection Names

Fetching a collection with the `db.collectionName` syntax almost always works, unless the collection name a reserved word or is an invalid JavaScript property name.

For example, suppose we are trying to access the *version* collection. We cannot say `db.version` because `db.version` is a method on `db` (it returns the version of the running MongoDB server):

```
> db.version
function () {
    return this.serverBuildInfo().version;
}
```

To actually access the version collection, you must use the `getCollection` function:

```
> db.getCollection("version");
test.version
```

This can also be used for collection names with characters that aren't valid in JavaScript property names, such as *foo-bar-baz* and *123abc* (JavaScript property names can only contain letters, numbers, "$" and "_" and cannot start with a number).

Another way of getting around invalid properties is to use array-access syntax: in JavaScript, `x.y` is identical to `x['y']`. This means that subcollections can be accessed using variables, not just literal names. Thus, if you needed to perform some operation on every *blog* subcollection, you could iterate through them with something like this:

```
var collections = ["posts", "comments", "authors"];
```

```
for (var i in collections) {
    print(db.blog[collections[i]]);
}
```

instead of this:

```
print(db.blog.posts);
print(db.blog.comments);
print(db.blog.authors);
```

Note that you cannot do *db.blog.i*, which would be interpreted as *test.blog.i*, not *test.blog.posts*. You must use the `db.blog[i]` syntax for `i` to be interpreted as a variable.

You can use this technique to access awkwardly-named collections:

```
> var name = "@#&!"
> db[name].find()
```

Attempting to query `db.@#&!` would be illegal, but `db[name]` would work.

CHAPTER 3

Creating, Updating, and Deleting Documents

This chapter covers the basics of moving data in and out of the database, including the following:

- Adding new documents to a collection
- Removing documents from a collection
- Updating existing documents
- Choosing the correct level of safety versus speed for all of these operations

Inserting and Saving Documents

Inserts are the basic method for adding data to MongoDB. To insert a document into a collection, use the collection's `insert` method:

```
> db.foo.insert({"bar" : "baz"})
```

This will add an `"_id"` key to the document (if one does not already exist) and store it in MongoDB.

Batch Insert

If you have a situation where you are inserting multiple documents into a collection, you can make the insert faster by using batch inserts. Batch inserts allow you to pass an array of documents to the database.

In the shell, you can try this out using the `batchInsert` function, which is similar to insert except that it takes an array of documents to insert:

```
> db.foo.batchInsert([{"_id" : 0}, {"_id" : 1}, {"_id" : 2}])
> db.foo.find()
{ "_id" : 0 }
{ "_id" : 1 }
{ "_id" : 2 }
```

Sending dozens, hundreds, or even thousands of documents at a time can make inserts significantly faster.

Batch inserts are only useful if you are inserting multiple documents into a single collection: you cannot use batch inserts to insert into multiple collections with a single request. If you are just importing raw data (for example, from a data feed or MySQL), there are command-line tools like `mongoimport` that can be used instead of batch insert. On the other hand, it is often handy to munge data before saving it to MongoDB (converting dates to the date type or adding a custom `"_id"`) so batch inserts can be used for importing data, as well.

Current versions of MongoDB do not accept messages longer than 48 MB, so there is a limit to how much can be inserted in a single batch insert. If you attempt to insert more than 48 MB, many drivers will split up the batch insert into multiple 48 MB batch inserts. Check your driver documentation for details.

If you are importing a batch and a document halfway through the batch fails to be inserted, the documents up to that document will be inserted and everything after that document will not:

```
> db.foo.batchInsert([{"_id" : 0}, {"_id" : 1}, {"_id" : 1}, {"_id" : 2}])
```

Only the first two documents will be inserted, as the third will produce an error: you cannot insert two documents with the same `"_id"`.

If you want to ignore errors and make `batchInsert` attempt to insert the rest of the batch, you can use the `continueOnError` option to continue after an insert failure. This would insert the first, second, and fourth documents above. The shell does not support this option, but all the drivers do.

Insert Validation

MongoDB does minimal checks on data being inserted: it check's the document's basic structure and adds an `"_id"` field if one does not exist. One of the basic structure checks is size: all documents must be smaller than 16 MB. This is a somewhat arbitrary limit (and may be raised in the future); it is mostly to prevent bad schema design and ensure consistent performance. To see the BSON size (in bytes) of the document *doc*, run `Object.bsonsize(`*`doc`*`)` from the shell.

To give you an idea of how much data 16 MB is, the entire text of *War and Peace* is just 3.14 MB.

These minimal checks also mean that it is fairly easy to insert invalid data (if you are trying to). Thus, you should only allow trusted sources, such as your application servers, to connect to the database. All of the drivers for major languages (and most of the minor ones, too) do check for a variety of invalid data (documents that are too large, contain non-UTF-8 strings, or use unrecognized types) before sending anything to the database.

Removing Documents

Now that there's data in our database, let's delete it:

```
> db.foo.remove()
```

This will remove all of the documents in the *foo* collection. This doesn't actually remove the collection, and any meta information about it will still exist.

The `remove` function optionally takes a query document as a parameter. When it's given, only documents that match the criteria will be removed. Suppose, for instance, that we want to remove everyone from the *mailing.list* collection where the value for `"opt-out"` is `true`:

```
> db.mailing.list.remove({"opt-out" : true})
```

Once data has been removed, it is gone forever. There is no way to undo the remove or recover deleted documents.

Remove Speed

Removing documents is usually a fairly quick operation, but if you want to clear an entire collection, it is faster to *drop* it (and then recreate any indexes on the empty collection).

For example, suppose we insert a million dummy elements with the following:

```
> for (var i = 0; i < 1000000; i++) {
... db.tester.insert({"foo": "bar", "baz": i, "z": 10 - i})
... }
```

Now we'll try to remove all of the documents we just inserted, measuring the time it takes. First, here's a simple `remove`:

```
> var timeRemoves = function() {
... var start = (new Date()).getTime();
...
... db.tester.remove();
... db.findOne(); // makes sure the remove finishes before continuing
...
... var timeDiff = (new Date()).getTime() - start;
... print("Remove took: "+timeDiff+"ms");
... }
> timeRemoves()
```

On a MacBook Air, this script prints "Remove took: 9676ms".

If the `remove` and `findOne` are replaced by `db.tester.drop()`, the time drops to one millisecond! This is obviously a vast improvement, but it comes at the expense of granularity: we cannot specify any criteria. The whole collection is dropped, and all of its metadata is deleted.

Updating Documents

Once a document is stored in the database, it can be changed using the `update` method. `update` takes two parameters: a query document, which locates documents to update, and a modifier document, which describes the changes to make to the documents found.

Updating a document is atomic: if two updates happen at the same time, whichever one reaches the server first will be applied, and then the next one will be applied. Thus, conflicting updates can safely be sent in rapid-fire succession without any documents being corrupted: the last update will "win."

Document Replacement

The simplest type of update fully replaces a matching document with a new one. This can be useful to do a dramatic schema migration. For example, suppose we are making major changes to a user document, which looks like the following:

```
{
    "_id" : ObjectId("4b2b9f67a1f631733d917a7a"),
    "name" : "joe",
    "friends" : 32,
    "enemies" : 2
}
```

We want to move the `"friends"` and `"enemies"` fields to a `"relationships"` subdocument. We can change the structure of the document in the shell and then replace the database's version with an `update`:

```
> var joe = db.users.findOne({"name" : "joe"});
> joe.relationships = {"friends" : joe.friends, "enemies" : joe.enemies};
{
    "friends" : 32,
    "enemies" : 2
}> joe.username = joe.name;
"joe"
> delete joe.friends;
true
> delete joe.enemies;
true
> delete joe.name;
true
> db.users.update({"name" : "joe"}, joe);
```

Now, doing a `findOne` shows that the structure of the document has been updated:

```
{
    "_id" : ObjectId("4b2b9f67a1f631733d917a7a"),
    "username" : "joe",
    "relationships" : {
        "friends" : 32,
        "enemies" : 2
    }
}
```

A common mistake is matching more than one document with the criteria and then creating a duplicate `"_id"` value with the second parameter. The database will throw an error for this, and no documents will be updated.

For example, suppose we create several documents with the same value for `"name"`, but we don't realize it:

```
> db.people.find()
{"_id" : ObjectId("4b2b9f67a1f631733d917a7b"), "name" : "joe", "age" : 65},
{"_id" : ObjectId("4b2b9f67a1f631733d917a7c"), "name" : "joe", "age" : 20},
{"_id" : ObjectId("4b2b9f67a1f631733d917a7d"), "name" : "joe", "age" : 49},
```

Now, if it's Joe #2's birthday, we want to increment the value of his `"age"` key, so we might say this:

```
> joe = db.people.findOne({"name" : "joe", "age" : 20});
{
    "_id" : ObjectId("4b2b9f67a1f631733d917a7c"),
    "name" : "joe",
    "age" : 20
}
> joe.age++;
> db.people.update({"name" : "joe"}, joe);
E11001 duplicate key on update
```

What happened? When you call update, the database will look for a document matching `{"name" : "joe"}`. The first one it finds will be the 65-year-old Joe. It will attempt to replace that document with the one in the `joe` variable, but there's already a document in this collection with the same `"_id"`. Thus, the update will fail, because `"_id"` values must be unique. The best way to avoid this situation is to make sure that your update always specifies a unique document, perhaps by matching on a key like `"_id"`. For the example above, this would be the correct update to use:

```
> db.people.update({"_id" : ObjectId("4b2b9f67a1f631733d917a7c")}, joe)
```

Using `"_id"` for the criteria will also be faster than querying on random fields, as `"_id"` is indexed. We'll cover how indexing effects updates and other operations more in Chapter 5.

Using Modifiers

Usually only certain portions of a document need to be updated. You can update specific fields in a document using atomic *update modifiers*. Update modifiers are special keys that can be used to specify complex update operations, such as altering, adding, or removing keys, and even manipulating arrays and embedded documents.

Suppose we were keeping website analytics in a collection and wanted to increment a counter each time someone visited a page. We can use update modifiers to do this increment atomically. Each URL and its number of page views is stored in a document that looks like this:

```
{
    "_id" : ObjectId("4b253b067525f35f94b60a31"),
    "url" : "www.example.com",
    "pageviews" : 52
}
```

Every time someone visits a page, we can find the page by its URL and use the `"$inc"` modifier to increment the value of the `"pageviews"` key:

```
> db.analytics.update({"url" : "www.example.com"},
... {"$inc" : {"pageviews" : 1}})
```

Now, if we do a `find`, we see that `"pageviews"` has increased by one:

```
> db.analytics.find()
{
    "_id" : ObjectId("4b253b067525f35f94b60a31"),
    "url" : "www.example.com",
    "pageviews" : 53
}
```

When using modifiers, the value of `"_id"` cannot be changed. (Note that `"_id"` *can* be changed by using whole-document replacement.) Values for any other key, including other uniquely indexed keys, can be modified.

Getting started with the "$set" modifier

`"$set"` sets the value of a field. If the field does not yet exist, it will be created. This can be handy for updating schema or adding user-defined keys. For example, suppose you have a simple user profile stored as a document that looks something like the following:

```
> db.users.findOne()
{
    "_id" : ObjectId("4b253b067525f35f94b60a31"),
    "name" : "joe",
    "age" : 30,
    "sex" : "male",
    "location" : "Wisconsin"
}
```

This is a pretty bare-bones user profile. If the user wanted to store his favorite book in his profile, he could add it using "$set":

```
> db.users.update({"_id" : ObjectId("4b253b067525f35f94b60a31")},
... {"$set" : {"favorite book" : "War and Peace"}})
```

Now the document will have a "favorite book" key:

```
> db.users.findOne()
{
    "_id" : ObjectId("4b253b067525f35f94b60a31"),
    "name" : "joe",
    "age" : 30,
    "sex" : "male",
    "location" : "Wisconsin",
    "favorite book" : "War and Peace"
}
```

If the user decides that he actually enjoys a different book, "$set" can be used again to change the value:

```
> db.users.update({"name" : "joe"},
... {"$set" : {"favorite book" : "Green Eggs and Ham"}})
```

"$set" can even change the type of the key it modifies. For instance, if our fickle user decides that he actually likes quite a few books, he can change the value of the "favorite book" key into an array:

```
> db.users.update({"name" : "joe"},
... {"$set" : {"favorite book" :
...     ["Cat's Cradle", "Foundation Trilogy", "Ender's Game"]}})
```

If the user realizes that he actually doesn't like reading, he can remove the key altogether with "$unset":

```
> db.users.update({"name" : "joe"},
... {"$unset" : {"favorite book" : 1}})
```

Now the document will be the same as it was at the beginning of this example.

You can also use "$set" to reach in and change embedded documents:

```
> db.blog.posts.findOne()
{
    "_id" : ObjectId("4b253b067525f35f94b60a31"),
    "title" : "A Blog Post",
    "content" : "...",
    "author" : {
        "name" : "joe",
        "email" : "joe@example.com"
    }
}
> db.blog.posts.update({"author.name" : "joe"},
... {"$set" : {"author.name" : "joe schmoe"}})
```

```
> db.blog.posts.findOne()
{
    "_id" : ObjectId("4b253b067525f35f94b60a31"),
    "title" : "A Blog Post",
    "content" : "...",
    "author" : {
        "name" : "joe schmoe",
        "email" : "joe@example.com"
    }
}
```

You must always use a $-modifier for adding, changing, or removing keys. A common error people make when starting out is to try to set the value of `"foo"` to `"bar"` by doing an update that looks like this:

```
> db.coll.update(criteria, {"foo" : "bar"})
```

This will not function as intended. It actually does a full-document replacement, replacing the matched document with `{"foo" : "bar"}`. Always use $ operators for modifying individual key/value pairs.

Incrementing and decrementing

The `"$inc"` modifier can be used to change the value for an existing key or to create a new key if it does not already exist. It is very useful for updating analytics, karma, votes, or anything else that has a changeable, numeric value.

Suppose we are creating a game collection where we want to save games and update scores as they change. When a user starts playing, say, a game of pinball, we can insert a document that identifies the game by name and user playing it:

```
> db.games.insert({"game" : "pinball", "user" : "joe"})
```

When the ball hits a bumper, the game should increment the player's score. As points in pinball are given out pretty freely, let's say that the base unit of points a player can earn is 50. We can use the `"$inc"` modifier to add 50 to the player's score:

```
> db.games.update({"game" : "pinball", "user" : "joe"},
... {"$inc" : {"score" : 50}})
```

If we look at the document after this update, we'll see the following:

```
> db.games.findOne()
{
     "_id" : ObjectId("4b2d75476cc613d5ee930164"),
     "game" : "pinball",
     "user" : "joe",
     "score" : 50
}
```

The score key did not already exist, so it was created by "$inc" and set to the increment amount: 50.

If the ball lands in a "bonus" slot, we want to add 10,000 to the score. This can be accomplished by passing a different value to "$inc":

```
> db.games.update({"game" : "pinball", "user" : "joe"},
... {"$inc" : {"score" : 10000}})
```

Now if we look at the game, we'll see the following:

```
> db.games.find()
{
        "_id" : ObjectId("4b2d75476cc613d5ee930164"),
        "game" : "pinball",
        "user" : "joe",
        "score" : 10050
}
```

The "score" key existed and had a numeric value, so the server added 10,000 to it.

"$inc" is similar to "$set", but it is designed for incrementing (and decrementing) numbers. "$inc" can be used only on values of type integer, long, or double. If it is used on any other type of value, it will fail. This includes types that many languages will automatically cast into numbers, like nulls, booleans, or strings of numeric characters:

```
> db.foo.insert({"count" : "1"})
> db.foo.update({}, {"$inc" : {"count" : 1}})
Cannot apply $inc modifier to non-number
```

Also, the value of the "$inc" key must be a number. You cannot increment by a string, array, or other non-numeric value. Doing so will give a "Modifier "$inc" allowed for numbers only" error message. To modify other types, use "$set" or one of the following array operations.

Array modifiers

An extensive class of modifiers exists for manipulating arrays. Arrays are common and powerful data structures: not only are they lists that can be referenced by index, but they can also double as sets.

Adding elements

"$push" adds elements to the end of an array if the array exists and creates a new array if it does not. For example, suppose that we are storing blog posts and want to add a "comments" key containing an array. We can push a comment onto the nonexistent "comments" array, which will create the array and add the comment:

```
> db.blog.posts.findOne()
{
      "_id" : ObjectId("4b2d75476cc613d5ee930164"),
```

```
        "title" : "A blog post",
        "content" : "..."
}
> db.blog.posts.update({"title" : "A blog post"},
... {"$push" : {"comments" :
...     {"name" : "joe", "email" : "joe@example.com",
...     "content" : "nice post."}}})
> db.blog.posts.findOne()
{
    "_id" : ObjectId("4b2d75476cc613d5ee930164"),
    "title" : "A blog post",
    "content" : "...",
    "comments" : [
        {
            "name" : "joe",
            "email" : "joe@example.com",
            "content" : "nice post."
        }
    ]
}
```

Now, if we want to add another comment, we can simply use "`$push`" again:

```
> db.blog.posts.update({"title" : "A blog post"},
... {"$push" : {"comments" :
...     {"name" : "bob", "email" : "bob@example.com",
...     "content" : "good post."}}})
> db.blog.posts.findOne()
{
    "_id" : ObjectId("4b2d75476cc613d5ee930164"),
    "title" : "A blog post",
    "content" : "...",
    "comments" : [
        {
            "name" : "joe",
            "email" : "joe@example.com",
            "content" : "nice post."
        },
        {
            "name" : "bob",
            "email" : "bob@example.com",
            "content" : "good post."
        }
    ]
}
```

This is the "simple" form of push, but you can use it for more complex array operations as well. You can push multiple values in one operation using the "`$each`" suboperator:

```
> db.stock.ticker.update({"_id" : "GOOG"},
... {"$push" : {"hourly" : {"$each" : [562.776, 562.790, 559.123]}}})
```

This would push three new elements onto the array. Specify a single-element array to get equivalent behavior to the non-$each form of "$push".

If you only want the array to grow to a certain length, you can also use the "$slice" operator in conjunction with "$push" to prevent an array from growing beyond a certain size, effectively making a "top N" list of items:

```
> db.movies.find({"genre" : "horror"},
... {"$push" : {"top10" : {
...     "$each" : ["Nightmare on Elm Street", "Saw"],
...     "$slice" : -10}}})
```

This example would limit the array to the last 10 elements pushed. Slices must always be negative numbers.

If the array was smaller than 10 elements (after the push), all elements would be kept. If the array was larger than 10 elements, only the last 10 elements would be kept. Thus, "$slice" can be used to create a queue in a document.

Finally, you can "$sort" before trimming, so long as you are pushing subobjects onto the array:

```
> db.movies.find({"genre" : "horror"},
... {"$push" : {"top10" : {
...     "$each" : [{"name" : "Nightmare on Elm Street", "rating" : 6.6},
...                {"name" : "Saw", "rating" : 4.3}],
...     "$slice" : -10,
...     "$sort" : {"rating" : -1}}}})
```

This will sort all of the objects in the array by their "rating" field and then keep the first 10. Note that you must include "$each"; you cannot just "$slice" or "$sort" an array with "$push".

Using arrays as sets

You might want to treat an array as a set, only adding values if they are not present. This can be done using a "$ne" in the query document. For example, to push an author onto a list of citations, but only if he isn't already there, use the following:

```
> db.papers.update({"authors cited" : {"$ne" : "Richie"}},
... {$push : {"authors cited" : "Richie"}})
```

This can also be done with "$addToSet", which is useful for cases where "$ne" won't work or where "$addToSet" describes what is happening better.

For instance, suppose you have a document that represents a user. You might have a set of email addresses that they have added:

```
> db.users.findOne({"_id" : ObjectId("4b2d75476cc613d5ee930164")})
{
    "_id" : ObjectId("4b2d75476cc613d5ee930164"),
    "username" : "joe",
```

```
    "emails" : [
        "joe@example.com",
        "joe@gmail.com",
        "joe@yahoo.com"
    ]
}
```

When adding another address, you can use "$addToSet" to prevent duplicates:

```
> db.users.update({"_id" : ObjectId("4b2d75476cc613d5ee930164")},
... {"$addToSet" : {"emails" : "joe@gmail.com"}})
> db.users.findOne({"_id" : ObjectId("4b2d75476cc613d5ee930164")})
{
    "_id" : ObjectId("4b2d75476cc613d5ee930164"),
    "username" : "joe",
    "emails" : [
        "joe@example.com",
        "joe@gmail.com",
        "joe@yahoo.com",
    ]
}
> db.users.update({"_id" : ObjectId("4b2d75476cc613d5ee930164")},
... {"$addToSet" : {"emails" : "joe@hotmail.com"}})
> db.users.findOne({"_id" : ObjectId("4b2d75476cc613d5ee930164")})
{
    "_id" : ObjectId("4b2d75476cc613d5ee930164"),
    "username" : "joe",
    "emails" : [
        "joe@example.com",
        "joe@gmail.com",
        "joe@yahoo.com",
        "joe@hotmail.com"
    ]
}
```

You can also use "$addToSet" in conjunction with "$each" to add multiple unique values, which cannot be done with the "$ne"/"$push" combination. For instance, we could use these modifiers if the user wanted to add more than one email address:

```
> db.users.update({"_id" : ObjectId("4b2d75476cc613d5ee930164")}, {"$addToSet" :
... {"emails" : {"$each" :
...     ["joe@php.net", "joe@example.com", "joe@python.org"]}}})
> db.users.findOne({"_id" : ObjectId("4b2d75476cc613d5ee930164")})
{
    "_id" : ObjectId("4b2d75476cc613d5ee930164"),
    "username" : "joe",
    "emails" : [
        "joe@example.com",
        "joe@gmail.com",
        "joe@yahoo.com",
        "joe@hotmail.com"
        "joe@php.net"
        "joe@python.org"
```

```
    ]
}
```

Removing elements

There are a few ways to remove elements from an array. If you want to treat the array like a queue or a stack, you can use "$pop", which can remove elements from either end. {"$pop" : {"*key*" : 1}} removes an element from the end of the array. {"$pop" : {"*key*" : -1}} removes it from the beginning.

Sometimes an element should be removed based on specific criteria, rather than its position in the array. "$pull" is used to remove elements of an array that match the given criteria. For example, suppose we have a list of things that need to be done but not in any specific order:

```
> db.lists.insert({"todo" : ["dishes", "laundry", "dry cleaning"]})
```

If we do the laundry first, we can remove it from the list with the following:

```
> db.lists.update({}, {"$pull" : {"todo" : "laundry"}})
```

Now if we do a find, we'll see that there are only two elements remaining in the array:

```
> db.lists.find()
{
    "_id" : ObjectId("4b2d75476cc613d5ee930164"),
    "todo" : [
        "dishes",
        "dry cleaning"
    ]
}
```

Pulling removes all matching documents, not just a single match. If you have an array that looks like [1, 1, 2, 1] and pull 1, you'll end up with a single-element array, [2].

Array operators can be used only on keys with array values. For example, you cannot push on to an integer or pop off of a string, for example. Use "$set" or "$inc" to modify scalar values.

Positional array modifications

Array manipulation becomes a little trickier when we have multiple values in an array and want to modify some of them. There are two ways to manipulate values in arrays: by position or by using the position operator (the "$" character).

Arrays use 0-based indexing, and elements can be selected as though their index were a document key. For example, suppose we have a document containing an array with a few embedded documents, such as a blog post with comments:

```
> db.blog.posts.findOne()
{
    "_id" : ObjectId("4b329a216cc613d5ee930192"),
```

```
        "content" : "...",
        "comments" : [
            {
                "comment" : "good post",
                "author" : "John",
                "votes" : 0
            },
            {
                "comment" : "i thought it was too short",
                "author" : "Claire",
                "votes" : 3
            },
            {
                "comment" : "free watches",
                "author" : "Alice",
                "votes" : -1
            }
        ]
    }
```

If we want to increment the number of votes for the first comment, we can say the following:

```
> db.blog.update({"post" : post_id},
... {"$inc" : {"comments.0.votes" : 1}})
```

In many cases, though, we don't know what index of the array to modify without querying for the document first and examining it. To get around this, MongoDB has a positional operator, "$", that figures out which element of the array the query document matched and updates that element. For example, if we have a user named John who updates his name to Jim, we can replace it in the comments by using the positional operator:

```
db.blog.update({"comments.author" : "John"},
... {"$set" : {"comments.$.author" : "Jim"}})
```

The positional operator updates only the first match. Thus, if John had left more than one comment, his name would be changed only for the first comment he left.

Modifier speed

Some modifiers are faster than others. `$inc` modifies a document *in place*: it does not have to change the size of a document, only a couple of bytes, so it is very efficient. On the other hand, array modifiers might change the size of a document and can be slow. (`"$set"` can modify documents in place if the size isn't changing but otherwise is subject to the same performance limitations as array operators.)

When you start inserting documents into MongoDB, it puts each document right next to the previous one on disk. Thus, if a document gets bigger, it will no longer fit in the space it was originally written to and will be moved to another part of the collection.

You can see this in action by creating a new collection with just a few documents and then making a document that is sandwiched between two other documents larger. It will be bumped to the end of the collection:

```
> db.coll.insert({"x" :"a"})
> db.coll.insert({"x" :"b"})
> db.coll.insert({"x" :"c"})
> db.coll.find()
{ "_id" : ObjectId("5e7c3581d87d6a342e1c81d3"), "x" : "a" }
{ "_id" : ObjectId("5e7c3583d87d6a342e1c81d4"), "x" : "b" }
{ "_id" : ObjectId("5e7c3585d87d6a342e1c81d5"), "x" : "c" }
> db.coll.update({"x" : "b"}, {$set: {"x" : "bbb"}})
> db.coll.find()
{ "_id" : ObjectId("5e7c3581d87d6a342e1c81d3"), "x" : "a" }
{ "_id" : ObjectId("5e7c3585d87d6a342e1c81d5"), "x" : "c" }
{ "_id" : ObjectId("5e7c3583d87d6a342e1c81d4"), "x" : "bbb" }
```

When MongoDB has to move a document, it bumps the collection's *padding factor*, which is the amount of extra space MongoDB leaves around new documents to give them room to grow. You can see the padding factor by running `db.coll.stats()`. Before doing the update above, the `"paddingFactor"` field will be 1: allocate exactly the size of the document for each new document, as shown in Figure 3-1. If you run it again after making one of the documents larger (as shown in Figure 3-2), you'll see that it has grown to around 1.5: each new document will be given half of its size in free space to grow. If subsequent updates cause more moves, the padding factor will continue to grow (although not as dramatically as it did on the first move). If there aren't more moves, the padding factor will slowly go down, as shown in Figure 3-3.

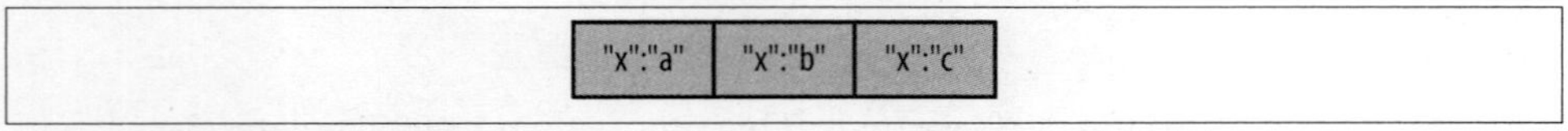

Figure 3-1. Initially, documents are inserted with no space between them

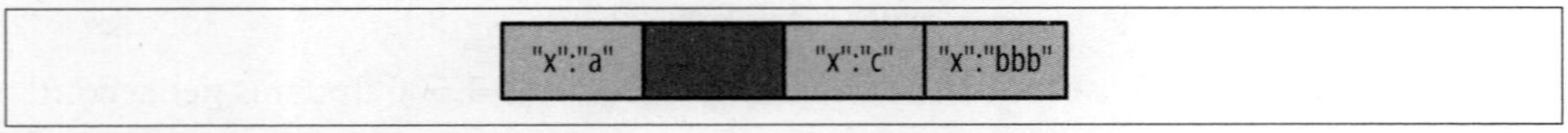

Figure 3-2. If a document grows and must be moved, free space is left behind and the padding size in increased

Figure 3-3. Subsequent documents are inserted with the padding factor in free space between them. If moves do not occur on subsequent inserts, this padding factor will decrease.

Moving documents is slow. MongoDB has to free the space the document was in and write the document somewhere else. Thus, you should try to keep the padding factor as close to 1 as possible. You cannot manually set the padding factor (unless you're compacting the collection: see "Compacting Data" on page 320), but you can design a schema that does not depend on documents growing arbitrarily large. See Chapter 8 for more advice on schema design.

A simple program demonstrates the speed difference between in-place updates and moves. The program below inserts a single key and increments its value 100,000 times:

```
> db.tester.insert({"x" : 1})
> var timeInc = function() {
... var start = (new Date()).getTime();
...
... for (var i=0; i<100000; i++) {
...     db.tester.update({}, {"$inc" : {"x" : 1}});
...     db.getLastError();
... }
...
... var timeDiff = (new Date()).getTime() - start;
... print("Updates took: "+timeDiff+"ms");
... }
> timeInc()
```

On a MacBook Air this took 7.33 seconds. That's more than 13,000 updates per second. Now, let's try it with a document with a single array key, pushing new values onto that array 100,000 times. Change the update call to this:

```
...     db.tester.update({}, {"$push" : {"x" : 1}})
```

This program took 67.58 seconds to run, which is less than 1,500 updates per second.

Using `"$push"` and other array modifiers is encouraged and often necessary, but it is good to keep in mind the trade-offs of such updates. If `"$push"` becomes a bottleneck, it may be worth pulling an embedded array out into a separate collection, manually padding, or using one of the other techniques discussed in Chapter 8.

As of this writing, MongoDB is not great at reusing empty space, so moving documents around a lot can result in large swaths of empty data file. If you have a lot of empty space, you'll start seeing messages that look like this in the logs:

```
Thu Apr  5 01:12:28 [conn124727] info DFM::findAll(): extent a:7f18dc00 was
    empty, skipping ahead
```

That means that, while querying, MongoDB looked through an entire extent (see Appendix B for a definition but it's basically a subset of your collection) without finding any documents: it was just empty space. The message itself is harmless, but it indicates that you have fragmentation and may wish to perform a compact.

If your schema requires lots of moves or lots of churn through inserts and deletes, you can improve disk reuse by using the `usePowerOf2Sizes` option. You can set this with the `collMod` command:

```
> db.runCommand({"collMod" : collectionName, "usePowerOf2Sizes" : true})
```

All subsequent allocations made by the collection will be in power-of-two-sized blocks. Only use this option on high-churn collections, though, as this makes initial space allocation less efficient. Setting this on an insert- or in-place-update-only collection will make writes slower.

Running this command with `"usePowerOf2Sizes" : false` turns off the special allocation. The option only affects newly allocated records, so there is no harm in running it on an existing collection or toggling the value.

Upserts

An *upsert* is a special type of update. If no document is found that matches the update criteria, a new document will be created by combining the criteria and updated documents. If a matching document is found, it will be updated normally. Upserts can be handy because they can eliminate the need to "seed" your collection: you can often have the same code create and update documents.

Let's go back to our example that records the number of views for each page of a website. Without an upsert, we might try to find the URL and increment the number of views or create a new document if the URL doesn't exist. If we were to write this out as a JavaScript program it might look something like the following:

```
// check if we have an entry for this page
blog = db.analytics.findOne({url : "/blog"})

// if we do, add one to the number of views and save
if (blog) {
  blog.pageviews++;
  db.analytics.save(blog);
}
// otherwise, create a new document for this page
else {
  db.analytics.save({url : "/blog", pageviews : 1})
}
```

This means we are making a round trip to the database, plus sending an update or insert, every time someone visits a page. If we are running this code in multiple processes, we are also subject to a race condition where more than one document can be inserted for a given URL.

We can eliminate the race condition and cut down on the amount of code by just sending an upsert (the third parameter to `update` specifies that this should be an upsert):

```
db.analytics.update({"url" : "/blog"}, {"$inc" : {"pageviews" : 1}}, true)
```

This line does exactly what the previous code block does, except it's faster and atomic! The new document is created using the criteria document as a base and applying any modifier documents to it.

For example, if you do an upsert that matches a key and has an increment to the value of that key, the increment will be applied to the match:

```
> db.users.update({"rep" : 25}, {"$inc" : {"rep" : 3}}, true)
> db.users.findOne()
{
    "_id" : ObjectId("4b3295f26cc613d5ee93018f"),
    "rep" : 28
}
```

The upsert creates a new document with a `"rep"` of 25 and then increments that by 3, giving us a document where `"rep"` is 28. If the upsert option were not specified, `{"rep" : 25}` would not match any documents, so nothing would happen.

If we run the upsert again (with the criteria `{"rep" : 25}`), it will create another new document. This is because the criteria does not match the only document in the collection. (Its `"rep"` is 28.)

Sometimes a field needs to be seeded when a document is created, but not changed on subsequent updates. This is what `"$setOnInsert"` is for. `"$setOnInsert"` is a modifier that only sets the value of a field when the document is being inserted. Thus, we could do something like this:

```
> db.users.update({}, {"$setOnInsert" : {"createdAt" : new Date()}}, true)
> db.users.findOne()
{
    "_id" : ObjectId("512b8aefae74c67969e404ca"),
    "createdAt" : ISODate("2013-02-25T16:01:50.742Z")
}
```

If we run this update again, it will match the existing document, nothing will be inserted, and so the `"createdAt"` field will not be changed:

```
> db.users.update({}, {"$setOnInsert" : {"createdAt" : new Date()}}, true)
> db.users.findOne()
{
    "_id" : ObjectId("512b8aefae74c67969e404ca"),
    "createdAt" : ISODate("2013-02-25T16:01:50.742Z")
}
```

Note that you generally do not need to keep a "createdAt" field, as ObjectIds contain a timestamp of when the document was created. However, "$setOnInsert" can be useful for creating padding, initializing counters, and for collections that do not use ObjectIds.

The save shell helper

`save` is a shell function that lets you insert a document if it doesn't exist and update it if it does. It takes one argument: a document. If the document contains an "_id" key, `save` will do an upsert. Otherwise, it will do an insert. `save` is really just a convenience function so that programmers can quickly modify documents in the shell:

```
> var x = db.foo.findOne()
> x.num = 42
42
> db.foo.save(x)
```

Without `save`, the last line would have been a more cumbersome `db.foo.update({"_id" : x._id}, x)`.

Updating Multiple Documents

Updates, by default, update only the first document found that matches the criteria. If there are more matching documents, they will remain unchanged. To modify all of the documents matching the criteria, you can pass `true` as the fourth parameter to `update`.

> `update`'s behavior may be changed in the future (the server may update all matching documents by default and update one only if `false` is passed as the fourth parameter), so it is recommended that you always specify whether you want a multiple update.
>
> Not only is it more obvious what the update should be doing, but your program also won't break if the default is ever changed.

Multiupdates are a great way of performing schema migrations or rolling out new features to certain users. Suppose, for example, we want to give a gift to every user who has a birthday on a certain day. We can use multiupdate to add a "gift" to their account:

```
> db.users.update({"birthday" : "10/13/1978"},
... {"$set" : {"gift" : "Happy Birthday!"}}, false, true)
```

This would add the "gift' field to all user documents with birthdays on October 13, 1978.

To see the number of documents updated by a multiupdate, you can run the `getLastError` database command (which you can think of as "return information about the last operation"). The "n" key will contain the number of documents affected by the update:

```
> db.count.update({x : 1}, {$inc : {x : 1}}, false, true)
> db.runCommand({getLastError : 1})
{
    "err" : null,
    "updatedExisting" : true,
    "n" : 5,
    "ok" : true
}
```

"n" is 5, meaning that five documents were affected by the update. "updatedExisting" is true, meaning that the update modified existing documents.

Returning Updated Documents

You can get some limited information about what was updated by calling getLastError, but it does not actually return the updated document. For that, you'll need the findAndModify command. It is handy for manipulating queues and performing other operations that need get-and-set style atomicity.

Suppose we have a collection of processes run in a certain order. Each is represented with a document that has the following form:

```
{
    "_id" : ObjectId(),
    "status" : state,
    "priority" : N
}
```

"status" is a string that can be "READY", "RUNNING", or "DONE". We need to find the job with the highest priority in the "READY" state, run the process function, and then update the status to "DONE". We might try querying for the ready processes, sorting by priority, and updating the status of the highest-priority process to mark it is "RUNNING". Once we have processed it, we update the status to "DONE". This looks something like the following:

```
var cursor = db.processes.find({"status" : "READY"});
ps = cursor.sort({"priority" : -1}).limit(1).next();
db.processes.update({"_id" : ps._id}, {"$set" : {"status" : "RUNNING"}});
do_something(ps);
db.processes.update({"_id" : ps._id}, {"$set" : {"status" : "DONE"}});
```

This algorithm isn't great because it is subject to a race condition. Suppose we have two threads running. If one thread (call it A) retrieved the document and another thread (call it B) retrieved the same document before A had updated its status to "RUNNING", then both threads would be running the same process. We can avoid this by checking the status as part of the update query, but this becomes complex:

```
var cursor = db.processes.find({"status" : "READY"});
cursor.sort({"priority" : -1}).limit(1);
while ((ps = cursor.next()) != null) {
    ps.update({"_id" : ps._id, "status" : "READY"},
              {"$set" : {"status" : "RUNNING"}});

    var lastOp = db.runCommand({getlasterror : 1});
    if (lastOp.n == 1) {
        do_something(ps);
        db.processes.update({"_id" : ps._id}, {"$set" : {"status" : "DONE"}})
        break;
    }
    cursor = db.processes.find({"status" : "READY"});
    cursor.sort({"priority" : -1}).limit(1);
}
```

Also, depending on timing, one thread may end up doing all the work while another thread uselessly trails it. Thread A could always grab the process, and then B would try to get the same process, fail, and leave A to do all the work.

Situations like this are perfect for `findAndModify`. `findAndModify` can return the item and update it in a single operation. In this case, it looks like the following:

```
> ps = db.runCommand({"findAndModify" : "processes",
... "query" : {"status" : "READY"},
... "sort" : {"priority" : -1},
... "update" : {"$set" : {"status" : "RUNNING"}})
{
    "ok" : 1,
    "value" : {
        "_id" : ObjectId("4b3e7a18005cab32be6291f7"),
        "priority" : 1,
        "status" : "READY"
    }
}
```

Notice that the status is still `"READY"` in the returned document as `findAndModify` defaults to returning the document in its pre-modified state. If you do a find on the collection, though, you can see that the document's `"status"` has been updated to `"RUNNING"`:

```
> db.processes.findOne({"_id" : ps.value._id})
{
    "_id" : ObjectId("4b3e7a18005cab32be6291f7"),
    "priority" : 1,
    "status" : "RUNNING"
}
```

Thus, the program becomes the following:

```
ps = db.runCommand({"findAndModify" : "processes",
    "query" : {"status" : "READY"},
    "sort" : {"priority" : -1},
```

```
        "update" : {"$set" : {"status" : "RUNNING"}}}).value
    do_something(ps)
    db.process.update({"_id" : ps._id}, {"$set" : {"status" : "DONE"}})
```

findAndModify can have either an "update" key or a "remove" key. A "remove" key indicates that the matching document should be removed from the collection. For instance, if we wanted to simply remove the job instead of updating its status, we could run the following:

```
ps = db.runCommand({"findAndModify" : "processes",
    "query" : {"status" : "READY"},
    "sort" : {"priority" : -1},
    "remove" : true}).value
do_something(ps)
```

The findAndModify command has the following fields:

findAndModify
: A string, the collection name

query
: A query document; the criteria with which to search for documents

sort
: Criteria by which to sort results (optional)

update
: A modifier document; the update to perform on the document found (either this or "remove" must be specified)

remove
: Boolean specifying whether the document should be removed (either this or "update" must be specified)

new
: Boolean specifying whether the document returned should be the updated document or the pre-update document, to which it defaults

fields
: The fields of the document to return (optional)

upsert
: Boolean specifying whether or not this should be an upsert, and which defaults to false

Either "update" or "remove" must be included, but not both. If no matching document is found, the command will return an error.

Setting a Write Concern

Write concern is a client setting used to describe how safely a write should be stored before the application continues. By default, inserts, removes, and updates wait for a database response—did the write succeed or not?—before continuing. Generally, clients will throw an exception (or whatever the language's version of an exception is) on failure.

There are a number of options available to tune exactly what you want the application to wait for. The two basic write concerns are *acknowledged* or *unacknowledged* writes. Acknowledged writes are the default: you get a response that tells you whether or not the database successfully processed your write. Unacknowledged writes do not return any response, so you do not know if the write succeeded or not.

In general, applications should stick with acknowledged writes. However, for low-value data (e.g., logs or bulk data loading), you may not want to wait for a response you don't care about. In these situations, use unacknowledged writes.

Although unacknowledged writes will not return database errors, they do not eliminate the need for error checking in your application. If the socket was closed or there was an error writing to it, attempting a write will cause an exception.

One type of error that is easy to miss when using unacknowledged writes is inserting invalid data. For example, if we attempt to insert two documents with the same `"_id"`, the shell will throw an exception:

```
> db.foo.insert({"_id" : 1})
> db.foo.insert({"_id" : 1})
E11000 duplicate key error index: test.foo.$_id_  dup key: { : 1.0 }
```

Were the second write sent with "unacknowledged" write concern, the second insert would not throw an exception. Duplicate key exceptions are a common source of errors, but there are many others, from invalid $-modifiers to running out of disk space.

The shell does not actually support write concerns in the same way that the client libraries do: it does unacknowledged writes and then checks that the last operation was successful before drawing the prompt. Thus, if you do a series of invalid operations on a collection, finishing with a valid operation, the shell will not complain:

```
> db.foo.insert({"_id" : 1}); db.foo.insert({"_id" : 1}); db.foo.count()
1
```

You can manually force a check in the shell by calling *getLastError*, which checks for an error on the last operation:

```
> db.foo.insert({"_id" : 1}); db.foo.insert({"_id" : 1}); print(
... db.getLastError()); db.foo.count()
E11000 duplicate key error index: test.foo.$_id_  dup key: { : 1.0 }
1
```

This can be helpful when scripting for the shell.

There are actually several other write concern options that are covered in later chapters: Chapter 11 covers write concern for multiple servers and Chapter 19 covers committing to disk on a per-write basis.

> The default write concern was changed in 2012, so legacy code may behave differently. Prior to the change, writes were unacknowledged by default.
>
> Fortunately, there is an easy way to tell if you're using code written before or after the write concern switch: all of the drivers began using a class called `MongoClient` when they began defaulting to safe writes. If your program is using a connection object called `Mongo` or `Connection` or something else, you are using the old, default-unsafe API. No language used `MongoClient` as a class name prior to the switch, so if your code is using that, your writes are safe.
>
> If you are using non-`MongoClient` connections, you should changed unacknowledged writes to acknowledged writes wherever possible in old code.

CHAPTER 4

Querying

This chapter looks at querying in detail. The main areas covered are as follows:

- You can perform ad hoc queries on the database using the `find` or `findOne` functions and a query document.
- You can query for ranges, set inclusion, inequalities, and more by using `$`-conditionals.
- Queries return a database cursor, which lazily returns batches of documents as you need them.
- There are a lot of metaoperations you can perform on a cursor, including skipping a certain number of results, limiting the number of results returned, and sorting results.

Introduction to find

The `find` method is used to perform queries in MongoDB. Querying returns a subset of documents in a collection, from no documents at all to the entire collection. Which documents get returned is determined by the first argument to `find`, which is a document specifying the query criteria.

An empty query document (i.e., `{}`) matches everything in the collection. If `find` isn't given a query document, it defaults to `{}`. For example, the following:

```
> db.c.find()
```

matches every document in the collection *c* (and returns these documents in batches).

When we start adding key/value pairs to the query document, we begin restricting our search. This works in a straightforward way for most types: numbers match numbers, booleans match booleans, and strings match strings. Querying for a simple type is as easy as specifying the value that you are looking for. For example, to find all documents where the value for "age" is 27, we can add that key/value pair to the query document:

```
> db.users.find({"age" : 27})
```

If we have a string we want to match, such as a "username" key with the value "joe", we use that key/value pair instead:

```
> db.users.find({"username" : "joe"})
```

Multiple conditions can be strung together by adding more key/value pairs to the query document, which gets interpreted as "*condition1* AND *condition2* AND … AND *conditionN*." For instance, to get all users who are 27-year-olds with the username "joe," we can query for the following:

```
> db.users.find({"username" : "joe", "age" : 27})
```

Specifying Which Keys to Return

Sometimes you do not need all of the key/value pairs in a document returned. If this is the case, you can pass a second argument to find (or findOne) specifying the keys you want. This reduces both the amount of data sent over the wire and the time and memory used to decode documents on the client side.

For example, if you have a user collection and you are interested only in the "username" and "email" keys, you could return just those keys with the following query:

```
> db.users.find({}, {"username" : 1, "email" : 1})
{
    "_id" : ObjectId("4ba0f0dfd22aa494fd523620"),
    "username" : "joe",
    "email" : "joe@example.com"
}
```

As you can see from the previous output, the "_id" key is returned by default, even if it isn't specifically requested.

You can also use this second parameter to exclude specific key/value pairs from the results of a query. For instance, you may have documents with a variety of keys, and the only thing you know is that you never want to return the "fatal_weakness" key:

```
> db.users.find({}, {"fatal_weakness" : 0})
```

This can also prevent "_id" from being returned:

```
> db.users.find({}, {"username" : 1, "_id" : 0})
{
    "username" : "joe",
}
```

Limitations

There are some restrictions on queries. The value of a query document must be a constant as far as the database is concerned. (It can be a normal variable in your own code.) That is, it cannot refer to the value of another key in the document. For example, if we were keeping inventory and we had both "in_stock" and "num_sold" keys, we couldn't compare their values by querying the following:

```
> db.stock.find({"in_stock" : "this.num_sold"}) // doesn't work
```

There are ways to do this (see "$where Queries" on page 65), but you will usually get better performance by restructuring your document slightly, such that a "normal" query will suffice. In this example, we could instead use the keys "initial_stock" and "in_stock". Then, every time someone buys an item, we decrement the value of the "in_stock" key by one. Finally, we can do a simple query to check which items are out of stock:

```
> db.stock.find({"in_stock" : 0})
```

Query Criteria

Queries can go beyond the exact matching described in the previous section; they can match more complex criteria, such as ranges, OR-clauses, and negation.

Query Conditionals

"$lt", "$lte", "$gt", and "$gte" are all comparison operators, corresponding to <, <=, >, and >=, respectively. They can be combined to look for a range of values. For example, to look for users who are between the ages of 18 and 30, we can do this:

```
> db.users.find({"age" : {"$gte" : 18, "$lte" : 30}})
```

This would find all documents where the "age" field was greater than or equal to 18 AND less than or equal to 30.

These types of range queries are often useful for dates. For example, to find people who registered before January 1, 2007, we can do this:

```
> start = new Date("01/01/2007")
> db.users.find({"registered" : {"$lt" : start}})
```

An exact match on a date is less useful, since dates are only stored with millisecond precision. Often you want a whole day, week, or month, making a range query necessary.

To query for documents where a key's value is not equal to a certain value, you must use another conditional operator, "$ne", which stands for "not equal." If you want to find all users who do not have the username "joe," you can query for them using this:

```
> db.users.find({"username" : {"$ne" : "joe"}})
```

"$ne" can be used with any type.

OR Queries

There are two ways to do an OR query in MongoDB. "$in" can be used to query for a variety of values for a single key. "$or" is more general; it can be used to query for any of the given values across multiple keys.

If you have more than one possible value to match for a single key, use an array of criteria with "$in". For instance, suppose we were running a raffle and the winning ticket numbers were 725, 542, and 390. To find all three of these documents, we can construct the following query:

```
> db.raffle.find({"ticket_no" : {"$in" : [725, 542, 390]}})
```

"$in" is very flexible and allows you to specify criteria of different types as well as values. For example, if we are gradually migrating our schema to use usernames instead of user ID numbers, we can query for either by using this:

```
> db.users.find({"user_id" : {"$in" : [12345, "joe"]})
```

This matches documents with a "user_id" equal to 12345, and documents with a "user_id" equal to "joe".

If "$in" is given an array with a single value, it behaves the same as directly matching the value. For instance, {ticket_no : {$in : [725]}} matches the same documents as {ticket_no : 725}.

The opposite of "$in" is "$nin", which returns documents that don't match any of the criteria in the array. If we want to return all of the people who didn't win anything in the raffle, we can query for them with this:

```
> db.raffle.find({"ticket_no" : {"$nin" : [725, 542, 390]}})
```

This query returns everyone who did not have tickets with those numbers.

"$in" gives you an OR query for a single key, but what if we need to find documents where "ticket_no" is 725 or "winner" is true? For this type of query, we'll need to use the "$or" conditional. "$or" takes an array of possible criteria. In the raffle case, using "$or" would look like this:

```
> db.raffle.find({"$or" : [{"ticket_no" : 725}, {"winner" : true}]})
```

"$or" can contain other conditionals. If, for example, we want to match any of the three "ticket_no" values or the "winner" key, we can use this:

```
> db.raffle.find({"$or" : [{"ticket_no" : {"$in" : [725, 542, 390]}},
                           {"winner" : true}]})
```

With a normal AND-type query, you want to narrow down your results as far as possible in as few arguments as possible. OR-type queries are the opposite: they are most efficient if the first arguments match as many documents as possible.

While "$or" will always work, use "$in" whenever possible as the query optimizer handles it more efficiently.

$not

"$not" is a metaconditional: it can be applied on top of any other criteria. As an example, let's consider the modulus operator, "$mod". "$mod" queries for keys whose values, when divided by the first value given, have a remainder of the second value:

```
> db.users.find({"id_num" : {"$mod" : [5, 1]}})
```

The previous query returns users with "id_num"s of 1, 6, 11, 16, and so on. If we want, instead, to return users with "id_num"s of 2, 3, 4, 5, 7, 8, 9, 10, 12, etc., we can use "$not":

```
> db.users.find({"id_num" : {"$not" : {"$mod" : [5, 1]}}})
```

"$not" can be particularly useful in conjunction with regular expressions to find all documents that don't match a given pattern (regular expression usage is described in the section "Regular Expressions" on page 58).

Conditional Semantics

If you look at the update modifiers in the previous chapter and previous query documents, you'll notice that the $-prefixed keys are in different positions. In the query, "$lt" is in the inner document; in the update, "$inc" is the key for the outer document. This generally holds true: conditionals are an inner document key, and modifiers are always a key in the outer document.

Multiple conditions can be put on a single key. For example, to find all users between the ages of 20 and 30, we can query for both "$gt" and "$lt" on the "age" key:

```
> db.users.find({"age" : {"$lt" : 30, "$gt" : 20}})
```

Any number of conditionals can be used with a single key. Multiple update modifiers *cannot* be used on a single key, however. For example, you cannot have a modifier document such as {"$inc" : {"age" : 1}, "$set" : {age : 40}} because it modifies "age" twice. With query conditionals, no such rule applies.

There are a few "meta-operators" that go in the outer document: "$and“, "$or“, and "$nor“. They all have a similar form:

```
> db.users.find({"$and" : [{"x" : {"$lt" : 1}}, {"x" : 4}]})
```

This query would match documents with an "x" field both less than 1 and equal to 4. Although these seem like contradictory conditions, it is possible to fulfill if the "x" field is an array: {"x" : [0, 4]} would match. Note that the query optimizer does not optimize "$and" as well as other operators. This query would be more efficient to structure as:

```
> db.users.find({"x" : {"$lt" : 1, "$in" : [4]}})
```

Type-Specific Queries

As covered in Chapter 2, MongoDB has a wide variety of types that can be used in a document. Some of these types have special behavior when querying.

null

`null` behaves a bit strangely. It does match itself, so if we have a collection with the following documents:

```
> db.c.find()
{ "_id" : ObjectId("4ba0f0dfd22aa494fd523621"), "y" : null }
{ "_id" : ObjectId("4ba0f0dfd22aa494fd523622"), "y" : 1 }
{ "_id" : ObjectId("4ba0f148d22aa494fd523623"), "y" : 2 }
```

we can query for documents whose "y" key is `null` in the expected way:

```
> db.c.find({"y" : null})
{ "_id" : ObjectId("4ba0f0dfd22aa494fd523621"), "y" : null }
```

However, `null` not only matches itself but also matches "does not exist." Thus, querying for a key with the value `null` will return all documents lacking that key:

```
> db.c.find({"z" : null})
{ "_id" : ObjectId("4ba0f0dfd22aa494fd523621"), "y" : null }
{ "_id" : ObjectId("4ba0f0dfd22aa494fd523622"), "y" : 1 }
{ "_id" : ObjectId("4ba0f148d22aa494fd523623"), "y" : 2 }
```

If we only want to find keys whose value is `null`, we can check that the key is `null` and exists using the "`$exists`" conditional:

```
> db.c.find({"z" : {"$in" : [null], "$exists" : true}})
```

Unfortunately, there is no "`$eq`" operator, which makes this a little awkward, but "`$in`" with one element is equivalent.

Regular Expressions

Regular expressions are useful for flexible string matching. For example, if we want to find all users with the name Joe or joe, we can use a regular expression to do case-insensitive matching:

```
> db.users.find({"name" : /joe/i})
```

Regular expression flags (for example, `i`) are allowed but not required. If we want to match not only various capitalizations of joe, but also joey, we can continue to improve our regular expression:

```
> db.users.find({"name" : /joey?/i})
```

MongoDB uses the Perl Compatible Regular Expression (PCRE) library to match regular expressions; any regular expression syntax allowed by PCRE is allowed in MongoDB. It is a good idea to check your syntax with the JavaScript shell before using it in a query to make sure it matches what you think it matches.

> MongoDB can leverage an index for queries on prefix regular expressions (e.g., `/^joey/`). Indexes *cannot* be used for case-insensitive searches (`/^joey/i`).

Regular expressions can also match themselves. Very few people insert regular expressions into the database, but if you insert one, you can match it with itself:

```
> db.foo.insert({"bar" : /baz/})
> db.foo.find({"bar" : /baz/})
{
    "_id" : ObjectId("4b23c3ca7525f35f94b60a2d"),
    "bar" : /baz/
}
```

Querying Arrays

Querying for elements of an array is designed to behave the way querying for scalars does. For example, if the array is a list of fruits, like this:

```
> db.food.insert({"fruit" : ["apple", "banana", "peach"]})
```

the following query:

```
> db.food.find({"fruit" : "banana"})
```

will successfully match the document. We can query for it in much the same way as we would if we had a document that looked like the (illegal) document: `{"fruit" : "apple", "fruit" : "banana", "fruit" : "peach"}`.

$all

If you need to match arrays by more than one element, you can use `"$all"`. This allows you to match a list of elements. For example, suppose we created a collection with three elements:

```
> db.food.insert({"_id" : 1, "fruit" : ["apple", "banana", "peach"]})
> db.food.insert({"_id" : 2, "fruit" : ["apple", "kumquat", "orange"]})
> db.food.insert({"_id" : 3, "fruit" : ["cherry", "banana", "apple"]})
```

Then we can find all documents with both "apple" and "banana" elements by querying with "$all":

```
> db.food.find({fruit : {$all : ["apple", "banana"]}})
    {"_id" : 1, "fruit" : ["apple", "banana", "peach"]}
    {"_id" : 3, "fruit" : ["cherry", "banana", "apple"]}
```

Order does not matter. Notice "banana" comes before "apple" in the second result. Using a one-element array with "$all" is equivalent to not using "$all". For instance, {fruit : {$all : ['apple']}} will match the same documents as {fruit : 'apple'}.

You can also query by exact match using the entire array. However, exact match will not match a document if any elements are missing or superfluous. For example, this will match the first document above:

```
> db.food.find({"fruit" : ["apple", "banana", "peach"]})
```

But this will not:

```
> db.food.find({"fruit" : ["apple", "banana"]})
```

and neither will this:

```
> db.food.find({"fruit" : ["banana", "apple", "peach"]})
```

If you want to query for a specific element of an array, you can specify an index using the syntax *key.index*:

```
> db.food.find({"fruit.2" : "peach"})
```

Arrays are always 0-indexed, so this would match the third array element against the string "peach".

$size

A useful conditional for querying arrays is "$size", which allows you to query for arrays of a given size. Here's an example:

```
> db.food.find({"fruit" : {"$size" : 3}})
```

One common query is to get a range of sizes. "$size" cannot be combined with another $ conditional (in this example, "$gt"), but this query can be accomplished by adding a "size" key to the document. Then, every time you add an element to the array, increment the value of "size". If the original update looked like this:

```
> db.food.update(criteria, {"$push" : {"fruit" : "strawberry"}})
```

it can simply be changed to this:

```
> db.food.update(criteria,
... {"$push" : {"fruit" : "strawberry"}, "$inc" : {"size" : 1}})
```

Incrementing is extremely fast, so any performance penalty is negligible. Storing documents like this allows you to do queries such as this:

```
> db.food.find({"size" : {"$gt" : 3}})
```

Unfortunately, this technique doesn't work as well with the "$addToSet" operator.

The $slice operator

As mentioned earlier in this chapter, the optional second argument to find specifies the keys to be returned. The special "$slice" operator can be used to return a subset of elements for an array key.

For example, suppose we had a blog post document and we wanted to return the first 10 comments:

```
> db.blog.posts.findOne(criteria, {"comments" : {"$slice" : 10}})
```

Alternatively, if we wanted the last 10 comments, we could use −10:

```
> db.blog.posts.findOne(criteria, {"comments" : {"$slice" : -10}})
```

"$slice" can also return pages in the middle of the results by taking an offset and the number of elements to return:

```
> db.blog.posts.findOne(criteria, {"comments" : {"$slice" : [23, 10]}})
```

This would skip the first 23 elements and return the 24th through 33th. If there were fewer than 33 elements in the array, it would return as many as possible.

Unless otherwise specified, all keys in a document are returned when "$slice" is used. This is unlike the other key specifiers, which suppress unmentioned keys from being returned. For instance, if we had a blog post document that looked like this:

```
{
    "_id" : ObjectId("4b2d75476cc613d5ee930164"),
    "title" : "A blog post",
    "content" : "...",
    "comments" : [
        {
            "name" : "joe",
            "email" : "joe@example.com",
            "content" : "nice post."
        },
        {
            "name" : "bob",
            "email" : "bob@example.com",
            "content" : "good post."
        }
    ]
}
```

and we did a "$slice" to get the last comment, we'd get this:

```
> db.blog.posts.findOne(criteria, {"comments" : {"$slice" : -1}})
{
    "_id" : ObjectId("4b2d75476cc613d5ee930164"),
```

```
    "title" : "A blog post",
    "content" : "...",
    "comments" : [
        {
            "name" : "bob",
            "email" : "bob@example.com",
            "content" : "good post."
        }
    ]
}
```

Both "title" and "content" are still returned, even though they weren't explicitly included in the key specifier.

Returning a matching array element

"$slice" is helpful when you know the index of the element, but sometimes you want whichever array element matched your criteria. You can return the matching element with the $-operator. Given the blog example above, you could get Bob's comment back with:

```
> db.blog.posts.find({"comments.name" : "bob"}, {"comments.$" : 1})
{
    "_id" : ObjectId("4b2d75476cc613d5ee930164"),
    "comments" : [
        {
            "name" : "bob",
            "email" : "bob@example.com",
            "content" : "good post."
        }
    ]
}
```

Note that this only returns the first match for each document: if Bob had left multiple comments on this post, only the first one in the "comments" array would be returned.

Array and range query interactions

Scalars (non-array elements) in documents must match each clause of a query's criteria. For example, if you queried for `{"x" : {"$gt" : 10, "$lt" : 20}}`, "x" would have to be both greater than 10 and less than 20. However, if a document's "x" field is an array, the document matches if there is an element of "x" that matches each part of the criteria *but each query clause can match a different array element.*

The best way to understand this behavior is to see an example. Suppose we have the following documents:

```
{"x" : 5}
{"x" : 15}
{"x" : 25}
{"x" : [5, 25]}
```

If we wanted to find all documents where "x" is between 10 and 20, one might naively structure a query as `db.test.find({"x" : {"$gt" : 10, "$lt" : 20}})` and expect to get back one document: `{"x" : 15}`. However, running this, we get two:

```
> db.test.find({"x" : {"$gt" : 10, "$lt" : 20}})
{"x" : 15}
{"x" : [5, 25]}
```

Neither 5 nor 25 is between 10 and 20, but the document is returned because 25 matches the first clause (it is greater than 25) and 5 matches the second clause (it is less than 20).

This makes range queries against arrays essentially useless: a range will match any multi-element array. There are a couple of ways to get the expected behavior.

First, you can use "`$elemMatch`" to force MongoDB to compare both clauses with a single array element. However, the catch is that "`$elemMatch`" won't match non-array elements:

```
> db.test.find({"x" : {"$elemMatch" : {"$gt" : 10, "$lt" : 20}})
> // no results
```

The document `{"x" : 15}` no longer matches the query, because the "x" field is not an array.

If you have an index over the field that you're querying on (see Chapter 5), you can use `min()` and `max()` to limit the index range traversed by the query to your "`$gt`" and "`$lt`" values:

```
> db.test.find({"x" : {"$gt" : 10, "$lt" : 20}}).min({"x" : 10}).max({"x" : 20})
{"x" : 15}
```

Now this will only traverse the index from 10 to 20, missing the 5 and 25 entries. You can only use `min()` and `max()` when you have an index on the field you are querying for, though, and you must pass all fields of the index to `min()` and `max()`.

Using `min()` and `max()` when querying for ranges over documents that may include arrays is generally a good idea: if you look at the index bounds for a "`$gt`"/"`$lt`" query over an array, you can see that it's horribly inefficient. It basically accepts any value, so it will search every index entry, not just those in the range.

Querying on Embedded Documents

There are two ways of querying for an embedded document: querying for the whole document or querying for its individual key/value pairs.

Querying for an entire embedded document works identically to a normal query. For example, if we have a document that looks like this:

```
{
    "name" : {
        "first" : "Joe",
        "last" : "Schmoe"
```

```
    },
    "age" : 45
}
```

we can query for someone named Joe Schmoe with the following:

```
> db.people.find({"name" : {"first" : "Joe", "last" : "Schmoe"}})
```

However, a query for a full subdocument must exactly match the subdocument. If Joe decides to add a middle name field, suddenly this query won't work anymore; it doesn't match the entire embedded document! This type of query is also order-sensitive: `{"last" : "Schmoe", "first" : "Joe"}` would not be a match.

If possible, it's usually a good idea to query for just a specific key or keys of an embedded document. Then, if your schema changes, all of your queries won't suddenly break because they're no longer exact matches. You can query for embedded keys using dot-notation:

```
> db.people.find({"name.first" : "Joe", "name.last" : "Schmoe"})
```

Now, if Joe adds more keys, this query will still match his first and last names.

This dot notation is the main difference between query documents and other document types. Query documents can contain dots, which mean "reach into an embedded document." Dot notation is also the reason that documents to be inserted cannot contain the . character. Oftentimes people run into this limitation when trying to save URLs as keys. One way to get around it is to always perform a global replace before inserting or after retrieving, substituting a character that isn't legal in URLs for the dot character.

Embedded document matches can get a little tricky as the document structure gets more complicated. For example, suppose we are storing blog posts and we want to find comments by Joe that were scored at least a 5. We could model the post as follows:

```
> db.blog.find()
{
    "content" : "...",
    "comments" : [
        {
            "author" : "joe",
            "score" : 3,
            "comment" : "nice post"
        },
        {
            "author" : "mary",
            "score" : 6,
            "comment" : "terrible post"
        }
    ]
}
```

Now, we can't query using `db.blog.find({"comments" : {"author" : "joe", "score" : {"$gte" : 5}}})`. Embedded document matches have to match the whole document, and this doesn't match the `"comment"` key. It also wouldn't work to do `db.blog.find({"comments.author" : "joe", "comments.score" : {"$gte" : 5}})`, because the author criteria could match a different comment than the score criteria. That is, it would return the document shown above: it would match `"author" : "joe"` in the first comment and `"score" : 6` in the second comment.

To correctly group criteria without needing to specify every key, use `"$elemMatch"`. This vaguely-named conditional allows you to partially specify criteria to match a single embedded document in an array. The correct query looks like this:

```
> db.blog.find({"comments" : {"$elemMatch" : {"author" : "joe",
                                              "score" : {"$gte" : 5}}}})
```

`"$elemMatch"` allows us to "group" our criteria. As such, it's only needed when you have more than one key you want to match on in an embedded document.

$where Queries

Key/value pairs are a fairly expressive way to query, but there are some queries that they cannot represent. For queries that cannot be done any other way, there are `"$where"` clauses, which allow you to execute arbitrary JavaScript as part of your query. This allows you to do (almost) anything within a query. For security, use of `"$where"` clauses should be highly restricted or eliminated. End users should never be allowed to execute arbitrary `"$where"` clauses.

The most common case for using `"$where"` is to compare the values for two keys in a document. For instance, suppose we have documents that look like this:

```
> db.foo.insert({"apple" : 1, "banana" : 6, "peach" : 3})
> db.foo.insert({"apple" : 8, "spinach" : 4, "watermelon" : 4})
```

We'd like to return documents where any two of the fields are equal. For example, in the second document, `"spinach"` and `"watermelon"` have the same value, so we'd like that document returned. It's unlikely MongoDB will ever have a $-conditional for this, so we can use a `"$where"` clause to do it with JavaScript:

```
> db.foo.find({"$where" : function () {
... for (var current in this) {
...     for (var other in this) {
...         if (current != other && this[current] == this[other]) {
...             return true;
...         }
...     }
... }
... return false;
... }});
```

If the function returns `true`, the document will be part of the result set; if it returns `false`, it won't be.

`"$where"` queries should not be used unless strictly necessary: they are much slower than regular queries. Each document has to be converted from BSON to a JavaScript object and then run through the `"$where"` expression. Indexes cannot be used to satisfy a `"$where"`, either. Hence, you should use `"$where"` only when there is no other way of doing the query. You can cut down on the penalty by using other query filters in combination with `"$where"`. If possible, an index will be used to filter based on the non-`$where` clauses; the `"$where"` expression will be used only to fine-tune the results.

Another way of doing complex queries is to use one of the aggregation tools, which are covered in Chapter 7.

Server-Side Scripting

You must be very careful with security when executing JavaScript on the server. If done incorrectly, server-side JavaScript is susceptible to injection attacks similar to those that occur in a relational database. However, by following certain rules around accepting input, you can use JavaScript safely. Alternatively, you can turn off JavaScript execution altogether by running *mongod* with the `--noscripting` option.

The security issues with JavaScript are all related to executing user-provided programs on the server. You want to avoid doing that, so make sure you aren't accepting user input and passing it directly to *mongod*. For example, suppose you want to print "Hello, *name*!", where `name` is provided by the user. A naive approach might be to write a JavaScript function such as the following:

```
> func = "function() { print('Hello, "+name+"!'); }"
```

If `name` is a user-defined variable, it could be the string `"'); db.dropDatabase(); print('"`, which would turn the code into this:

```
> func = "function() { print('Hello, '); db.dropDatabase(); print('!'); }"
```

Now, if you run this code, your entire database will be dropped!

To prevent this, you should use a *scope* to pass in the name. In Python, for example, this looks like this:

```
func = pymongo.code.Code("function() { print('Hello, '+username+'!'); }",
           {"username": name})
```

Now the database will harmlessly print this:

```
Hello, '); db.dropDatabase(); print('!
```

Most drivers have a special type for sending code to the database, since code can actually be a composite of a string and a *scope*. A scope is a document that maps variable names to values. This mapping becomes a local scope for the JavaScript function being executed. Thus, in the example above, the function would have access to a variable called `username`, whose value would be the string that the user gave.

> The shell does not have a code type that includes scope; you can only use strings or JavaScript functions with it.

Cursors

The database returns results from `find` using a *cursor*. The client-side implementations of cursors generally allow you to control a great deal about the eventual output of a query. You can limit the number of results, skip over some number of results, sort results by any combination of keys in any direction, and perform a number of other powerful operations.

To create a cursor with the shell, put some documents into a collection, do a query on them, and assign the results to a local variable (variables defined with `"var"` are local). Here, we create a very simple collection and query it, storing the results in the `cursor` variable:

```
> for(i=0; i<100; i++) {
...     db.collection.insert({x : i});
... }
> var cursor = db.collection.find();
```

The advantage of doing this is that you can look at one result at a time. If you store the results in a global variable or no variable at all, the MongoDB shell will automatically iterate through and display the first couple of documents. This is what we've been seeing up until this point, and it is often the behavior you want for seeing what's in a collection but not for doing actual programming with the shell.

To iterate through the results, you can use the `next` method on the cursor. You can use `hasNext` to check whether there is another result. A typical loop through results looks like the following:

```
> while (cursor.hasNext()) {
...     obj = cursor.next();
...     // do stuff
... }
```

`cursor.hasNext()` checks that the next result exists, and `cursor.next()` fetches it.

The `cursor` class also implements JavaScript's iterator interface, so you can use it in a `forEach` loop:

```
> var cursor = db.people.find();
> cursor.forEach(function(x) {
...     print(x.name);
```

```
... });
adam
matt
zak
```

When you call `find`, the shell does not query the database immediately. It waits until you start requesting results to send the query, which allows you to chain additional options onto a query before it is performed. Almost every method on a cursor object returns the cursor itself so that you can chain options in any order. For instance, all of the following are equivalent:

```
> var cursor = db.foo.find().sort({"x" : 1}).limit(1).skip(10);
> var cursor = db.foo.find().limit(1).sort({"x" : 1}).skip(10);
> var cursor = db.foo.find().skip(10).limit(1).sort({"x" : 1});
```

At this point, the query has not been executed yet. All of these functions merely build the query. Now, suppose we call the following:

```
> cursor.hasNext()
```

At this point, the query will be sent to the server. The shell fetches the first 100 results or first 4 MB of results (whichever is smaller) at once so that the next calls to `next` or `hasNext` will not have to make trips to the server. After the client has run through the first set of results, the shell will again contact the database and ask for more results with a *getMore* request. getMore requests basically contain an identifier for the query and ask the database if there are any more results, returning the next batch if there are. This process continues until the cursor is exhausted and all results have been returned.

Limits, Skips, and Sorts

The most common query options are limiting the number of results returned, skipping a number of results, and sorting. All these options must be added before a query is sent to the database.

To set a limit, chain the `limit` function onto your call to `find`. For example, to only return three results, use this:

```
> db.c.find().limit(3)
```

If there are fewer than three documents matching your query in the collection, only the number of matching documents will be returned; `limit` sets an upper limit, not a lower limit.

`skip` works similarly to `limit`:

```
> db.c.find().skip(3)
```

This will skip the first three matching documents and return the rest of the matches. If there are fewer than three documents in your collection, it will not return any documents.

`sort` takes an object: a set of key/value pairs where the keys are key names and the values are the sort directions. Sort direction can be 1 (ascending) or −1 (descending). If multiple keys are given, the results will be sorted in that order. For instance, to sort the results by `"username"` ascending and `"age"` descending, we do the following:

```
> db.c.find().sort({username : 1, age : -1})
```

These three methods can be combined. This is often handy for pagination. For example, suppose that you are running an online store and someone searches for *mp3*. If you want 50 results per page sorted by price from high to low, you can do the following:

```
> db.stock.find({"desc" : "mp3"}).limit(50).sort({"price" : -1})
```

If that person clicks Next Page to see more results, you can simply add a skip to the query, which will skip over the first 50 matches (which the user already saw on page 1):

```
> db.stock.find({"desc" : "mp3"}).limit(50).skip(50).sort({"price" : -1})
```

However, large skips are not very performant; there are suggestions for how to avoid them in the next section.

Comparison order

MongoDB has a hierarchy as to how types compare. Sometimes you will have a single key with multiple types: for instance, integers and booleans, or strings and nulls. If you do a sort on a key with a mix of types, there is a predefined order that they will be sorted in. From least to greatest value, this ordering is as follows:

1. Minimum value
2. `null`
3. Numbers (integers, longs, doubles)
4. Strings
5. Object/document
6. Array
7. Binary data
8. Object ID
9. Boolean
10. Date
11. Timestamp
12. Regular expression
13. Maximum value

Avoiding Large Skips

Using `skip` for a small number of documents is fine. For a large number of results, `skip` can be slow, since it has to find and then discard all the skipped results. Most databases keep more metadata in the index to help with skips, but MongoDB does not yet support this, so large skips should be avoided. Often you can calculate the next query based on the result from the previous one.

Paginating results without skip

The easiest way to do pagination is to return the first page of results using limit and then return each subsequent page as an offset from the beginning:

```
> // do not use: slow for large skips
> var page1 = db.foo.find(criteria).limit(100)
> var page2 = db.foo.find(criteria).skip(100).limit(100)
> var page3 = db.foo.find(criteria).skip(200).limit(100)
...
```

However, depending on your query, you can usually find a way to paginate without `skip`s. For example, suppose we want to display documents in descending order based on `"date"`. We can get the first page of results with the following:

```
> var page1 = db.foo.find().sort({"date" : -1}).limit(100)
```

Then, we can use the `"date"` value of the last document as the criteria for fetching the next page:

```
var latest = null;

// display first page
while (page1.hasNext()) {
   latest = page1.next();
   display(latest);
}

// get next page
var page2 = db.foo.find({"date" : {"$gt" : latest.date}});
page2.sort({"date" : -1}).limit(100);
```

Now the query does not need to include a `skip`.

Finding a random document

One fairly common problem is how to get a random document from a collection. The naive (and slow) solution is to count the number of documents and then do a `find`, skipping a random number of documents between 0 and the size of the collection:

```
> // do not use
> var total = db.foo.count()
> var random = Math.floor(Math.random()*total)
> db.foo.find().skip(random).limit(1)
```

It is actually highly inefficient to get a random element this way: you have to do a count (which can be expensive if you are using criteria), and skipping large numbers of elements can be time-consuming.

It takes a little forethought, but if you know you'll be looking up a random element on a collection, there's a much more efficient way to do so. The trick is to add an extra random key to each document when it is inserted. For instance, if we're using the shell, we could use the `Math.random()` function (which creates a random number between 0 and 1):

```
> db.people.insert({"name" : "joe", "random" : Math.random()})
> db.people.insert({"name" : "john", "random" : Math.random()})
> db.people.insert({"name" : "jim", "random" : Math.random()})
```

Now, when we want to find a random document from the collection, we can calculate a random number and use that as query criteria, instead of doing a `skip`:

```
> var random = Math.random()
> result = db.foo.findOne({"random" : {"$gt" : random}})
```

There is a slight chance that `random` will be greater than any of the `"random"` values in the collection, and no results will be returned. We can guard against this by simply returning a document in the other direction:

```
> if (result == null) {
...     result = db.foo.findOne({"random" : {"$lt" : random}})
... }
```

If there aren't any documents in the collection, this technique will end up returning `null`, which makes sense.

This technique can be used with arbitrarily complex queries; just make sure to have an index that includes the random key. For example, if we want to find a random plumber in California, we can create an index on `"profession"`, `"state"`, and `"random"`:

```
> db.people.ensureIndex({"profession" : 1, "state" : 1, "random" : 1})
```

This allows us to quickly find a random result (see Chapter 5 for more information on indexing).

Advanced Query Options

There are two types of queries: *wrapped* and *plain*. A plain query is something like this:

```
> var cursor = db.foo.find({"foo" : "bar"})
```

There are a couple options that "wrap" the query. For example, suppose we perform a sort:

```
> var cursor = db.foo.find({"foo" : "bar"}).sort({"x" : 1})
```

Instead of sending `{"foo" : "bar"}` to the database as the query, the query gets wrapped in a larger document. The shell converts the query from `{"foo" : "bar"}` to `{"$query" : {"foo" : "bar"}, "$orderby" : {"x" : 1}}`.

Most drivers provide helpers for adding arbitrary options to queries. Other helpful options include the following:

`$maxscan : integer`
: Specify the maximum number of documents that should be scanned for the query.

```
> db.foo.find(criteria)._addSpecial("$maxscan", 20)
```

This can be useful if you want a query to not to take too long but are not sure how much of a collection will need to be scanned. This will limit your results to whatever was found in the part of the collection that was scanned (i.e., you may miss other documents that match).

`$min : document`
: Start criteria for querying. *`document`* must exactly match the keys of an index used for the query. This forces the given index to be used for the query.

This is used internally and you should generally use `"$gt"` instead of `"$min"`. You can use `"$min"` to force the lower bound on an index scan, which may be helpful for complex queries.

`$max : document`
: End criteria for querying. *`document`* must exactly match the keys of an index used for the query. This forces the given index to be used for the query.

If this is used internally, you should generally use `"$lt"` instead of `"$max"`. You can use `"$max"` to force bounds on an index scan, which may be helpful for complex queries.

`$showDiskLoc : true`
: Adds a `"$diskLoc"` field to the results that shows where on disk that particular result lives. For example:

```
> db.foo.find()._addSpecial('$showDiskLoc',true)
{ "_id" : 0, "$diskLoc" : { "file" : 2, "offset" : 154812592 } }
{ "_id" : 1, "$diskLoc" : { "file" : 2, "offset" : 154812628 } }
```

The file number shows which file the document is in. In this case, if we're using the *test* database, the document is in *test.2*. The second field gives the byte offset of each document within the file.

Getting Consistent Results

A fairly common way of processing data is to pull it out of MongoDB, change it in some way, and then save it again:

```
cursor = db.foo.find();

while (cursor.hasNext()) {
    var doc = cursor.next();
    doc = process(doc);
    db.foo.save(doc);
}
```

This is fine for a small number of results, but MongoDB can return the same result multiple times for a large result set. To see why, imagine how the documents are being stored. You can picture a collection as a list of documents that looks something like Figure 4-1. Snowflakes represent documents, since every document is beautiful and unique.

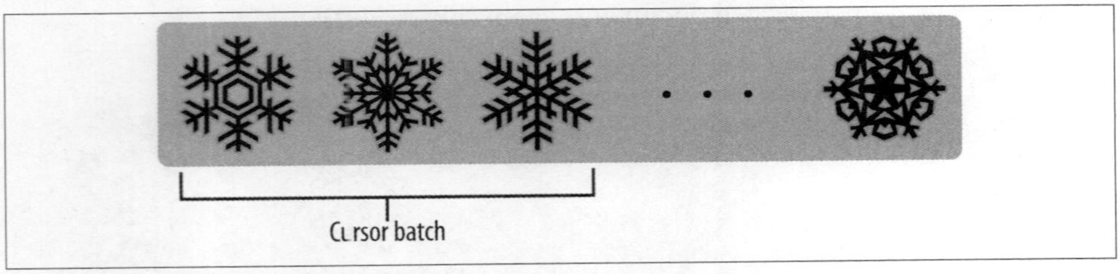

Figure 4-1. A collection being queried

Now, when we do a `find`, the cursor starts returning results from the beginning of the collection and moves right. Your program grabs the first 100 documents and processes them. When you save them back to the database, if a document does not have the padding available to grow to its new size, like in Figure 4-2, it needs to be relocated. Usually, a document will be relocated to the end of a collection (Figure 4-3).

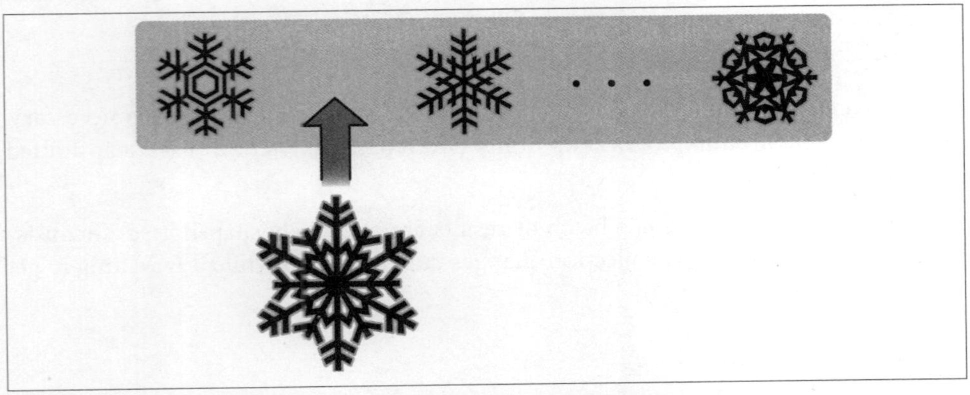

Figure 4-2. An enlarged document may not fit where it did before

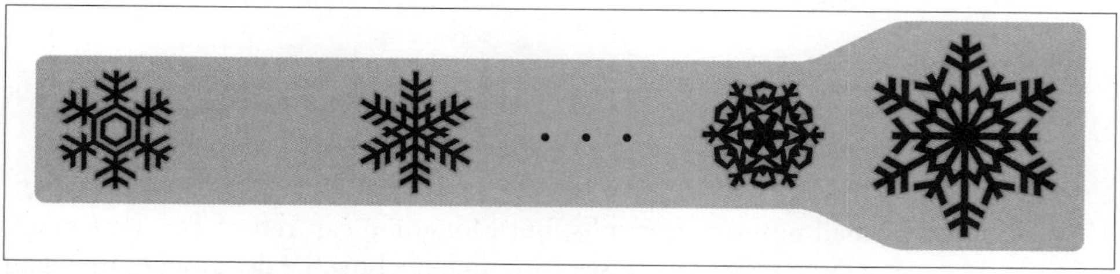

Figure 4-3. MongoDB relocates updated documents that don't fit in their original position

Now our program continues to fetch batches of documents. When it gets toward the end, it will return the relocated documents again (Figure 4-4)!

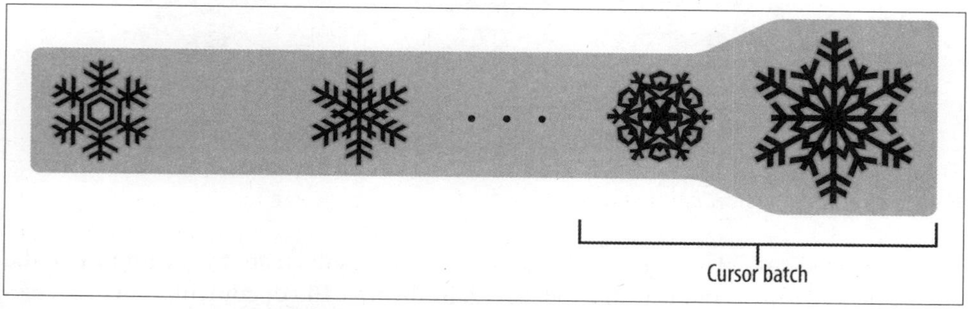

Figure 4-4. A cursor may return these relocated documents again in a later batch

The solution to this problem is to *snapshot* your query. If you add the option, the query will be run by traversing the "_id" index, which guarantees that you'll only return each document once. For example, instead of `db.foo.find()`, you'd run:

```
> db.foo.find().snapshot()
```

Snapshotting makes queries slower, so only use snapshotted queries when necessary. For example, *mongodump* (a backup utility covered in Chapter 22) uses snapshotted queries by default.

All queries that return a single batch of results are effectively snapshotted. Inconsistencies arise only when the collection changes under a cursor while it is waiting to get another batch of results.

Immortal Cursors

There are two sides to a cursor: the client-facing cursor and the database cursor that the client-side one represents. We have been talking about the client-side one up until now, but we are going to take a brief look at what's happening on the server.

On the server side, a cursor takes up memory and resources. Once a cursor runs out of results or the client sends a message telling it to die, the database can free the resources it was using. Freeing these resources lets the database use them for other things, which is good, so we want to make sure that cursors can be freed quickly (within reason).

There are a couple of conditions that can cause the death (and subsequent cleanup) of a cursor. First, when a cursor finishes iterating through the matching results, it will clean itself up. Another way is that, when a cursor goes out of scope on the client side, the drivers send the database a special message to let it know that it can kill that cursor. Finally, even if the user hasn't iterated through all the results and the cursor is still in scope, after 10 minutes of inactivity, a database cursor will automatically "die." This way, if a client crashes or is buggy, MongoDB will not be left with thousands of open cursors.

This "death by timeout" is usually the desired behavior: very few applications expect their users to sit around for minutes at a time waiting for results. However, sometimes you might know that you need a cursor to last for a long time. In that case, many drivers have implemented a function called `immortal`, or a similar mechanism, which tells the database not to time out the cursor. If you turn off a cursor's timeout, you must iterate through all of its results or kill it to make sure it gets closed. Otherwise, it will sit around in the database hogging resources until the server is restarted.

Database Commands

There is one very special type of query called a *database command*. We've covered creating, updating, deleting, and finding documents. Database commands do "everything else," from administrative tasks like shutting down the server and cloning databases to counting documents in a collection and performing aggregations.

Commands are mentioned throughout this text, as they are useful for data manipulation, administration, and monitoring. For example, dropping a collection is done via the `"drop"` database command:

```
> db.runCommand({"drop" : "test"});
{
    "nIndexesWas" : 1,
    "msg" : "indexes dropped for collection",
    "ns" : "test.test",
    "ok" : true
}
```

You might be more familiar with the *shell helper*, which wraps the command and provides a simpler interface:

```
> db.test.drop()
```

Often you can just use the shell helpers, but knowing the underlying commands can be helpful if you're stuck on a box with an old version of the shell and connected to a new version of the database: the shell might not have the wrappers for new database commands, but you can still run them with `runCommand()`.

We've already seen a couple of commands in the previous chapters; for instance, we used the `getLastError` command in Chapter 3 to check the number of documents affected by an update:

```
> db.count.update({x : 1}, {$inc : {x : 1}}, false, true)
> db.runCommand({getLastError : 1})
{
    "err" : null,
    "updatedExisting" : true,
    "n" : 5,
    "ok" : true
}
```

In this section, we'll take a closer look at commands to see exactly what they are and how they're implemented. We'll also describe some of the most useful commands that are supported by MongoDB. You can see all commands by running the `db.listCommands()` command.

How Commands Work

A database command always returns a document containing the key `"ok"`. If `"ok"` is `1`, the command was successful; and if it is `0`, the command failed for some reason.

If `"ok"` is `0` then an additional key will be present, `"errmsg"`. The value of `"errmsg"` is a string explaining why the command failed. As an example, let's try running the `drop` command again, on the collection that was dropped in the previous section:

```
> db.runCommand({"drop" : "test"});
{ "errmsg" : "ns not found", "ok" : false }
```

Commands in MongoDB are implemented as a special type of query that gets performed on the *$cmd* collection. `runCommand` just takes a command document and performs the equivalent query, so our drop call becomes the following:

```
db.$cmd.findOne({"drop" : "test"});
```

When the MongoDB server gets a query on the *$cmd* collection, it handles it using special logic, rather than the normal code for handling queries. Almost all MongoDB drivers provide a helper method like `runCommand` for running commands, but commands can always be run using a simple query.

Some commands require administrator access and must be run on the *admin* database. If such a command is run on any other database, it will return an "access denied" error. If you're working on another database and you need to run an admin command, you can use the adminCommand function, instead of runCommand:

```
> use temp
switched to db temp
> db.runCommand({shutdown:1})
{ "errmsg" : "access denied; use admin db", "ok" : 0 }
> db.adminCommand({"shutdown" : 1})
```

Commands are one of the few places that are field-order-sensitive: the command name must always be the first field in the command. Thus, {"getLastError" : 1, "w" : 2} will work, but {"w" : 2, "getLastError" : 1} will not.

PART II

Designing Your Application

CHAPTER 5
Indexing

This chapter introduces MongoDB's indexing, which allows you to optimize your queries and is even required for certain types of queries:

- What indexing is and why you'd want to use it
- How to choose which fields to index
- How to enforce and evaluate index usage
- Administrative details on creating and removing indexes

Choosing the right indexes for your collections is critical to performance.

Introduction to Indexing

A database index is similar to a book's index. Instead of looking through the whole book, the database takes a shortcut and just looks at an ordered list that points to the content, which allows it to query orders of magnitude faster.

A query that does not use an index is called a *table scan* (a term inherited from relational databases), which means that the server has to "look through the whole book" to find a query's results. This process is basically what you'd do if you were looking for information in a book without an index: you start at page 1 and read through the whole thing. In general, you want to avoid making the server do table scans because it is very slow for large collections.

For example, let's create a collection with 1 million documents in it (or 10 million or 100 million, if you have the patience):

```
> for (i=0; i<1000000; i++) {
...     db.users.insert(
...         {
...             "i" : i,
```

```
...                     "username" : "user"+i,
...                     "age" : Math.floor(Math.random()*120),
...                     "created" : new Date()
...             }
...         );
... }
```

If we do a query on this collection, we can use the explain() function to see what MongoDB is doing when it executes the query. Try querying on a random username to see an example.

```
> db.users.find({username: "user101"}).explain()
{
    "cursor" : "BasicCursor",
    "nscanned" : 1000000,
    "nscannedObjects" : 1000000,
    "n" : 1,
    "millis" : 721,
    "nYields" : 0,
    "nChunkSkips" : 0,
    "isMultiKey" : false,
    "indexOnly" : false,
    "indexBounds" : {

    }
}
```

"Using explain() and hint()" on page 98 will explain the output fields; for now you can ignore almost all of them. "nscanned" is the number of documents MongoDB looked at while trying to satisfy the query, which, as you can see, is every document in the collection. That is, MongoDB had to look through every field in every document. This took nearly a second to accomplish: the "millis" field shows the number of milliseconds it took to execute the query.

The "n" field shows the number of results returned: 1, which makes sense because there is only one user with the username "user101". Note that MongoDB had to look through every document in the collection for matches because it did not know that usernames are unique. To optimize this query, we could limit it to one result so that MongoDB would stop looking after it found user101:

```
> db.users.find({username: "user101"}).limit(1).explain()
{
    "cursor" : "BasicCursor",
    "nscanned" : 102,
    "nscannedObjects" : 102,
    "n" : 1,
    "millis" : 2,
    "nYields" : 0,
    "nChunkSkips" : 0,
    "isMultiKey" : false,
    "indexOnly" : false,
```

```
        "indexBounds" : {

        }
}
```

The number scanned has now been cut way down and the query is almost instantaneous. However, this is an impractical solution in general: what if we were looking for user999999? Then we'd still have to traverse the entire collection and our service would just get slower and slower as we added users.

Indexes are a great way to fix queries like this because they organize data by a given field to let MongoDB find it quickly. Try creating an index on the username field:

```
> db.users.ensureIndex({"username" : 1})
```

Depending on your machine and how large you made the collection, creating an index may take a few minutes. If the `ensureIndex` call does not return after a few seconds, run `db.currentOp()` (in a different shell) or check your *mongod*'s log to see the index build's progress.

Once the index build is complete, try repeating the original query:

```
> db.users.find({"username" : "user101"}).explain()
{
        "cursor" : "BtreeCursor username_1",
        "nscanned" : 1,
        "nscannedObjects" : 1,
        "n" : 1,
        "millis" : 3,
        "nYields" : 0,
        "nChunkSkips" : 0,
        "isMultiKey" : false,
        "indexOnly" : false,
        "indexBounds" : {
            "username" : [
                [
                    "user101",
                    "user101"
                ]
            ]
        }
}
```

This `explain()` output is more complex, but continue to ignore all the fields other than `"n"`, `"nscanned"`, and `"millis"` for now. As you can see, the query is now almost instantaneous and, even better, has a similar runtime when querying for any username:

```
> db.users.find({username: "user999999"}).explain().millis
1
```

As you can see, an index can make a dramatic difference in query times. However, indexes have their price: every write (insert, update, or delete) will take longer for every index you add. This is because MongoDB has to update all your indexes whenever your data changes, as well as the document itself. Thus, MongoDB limits you to 64 indexes per collection. Generally you should not have more than a couple of indexes on any given collection. The tricky part becomes figuring out which fields to index.

> MongoDB's indexes work almost identically to typical relational database indexes, so if you are familiar with those, you can skim this section for syntax specifics. We'll go over some indexing basics, but keep in mind that it's an extensive topic and most of the material out there on indexing for MySQL/Oracle/SQLite will apply equally well to MongoDB [such as the "Use the Index, Luke!" tutorial].

To choose which fields to create indexes for, look through your common queries and queries that need to be fast and try to find a common set of keys from those. For instance, in the example above, we were querying on `"username"`. If that was a particularly common query or was becoming a bottleneck, indexing `"username"` would be a good choice. However, if this was an unusual query or one that was only done by administrators who didn't care how long it took, it would not be a good choice of index.

Introduction to Compound Indexes

An index keeps all of its values in a sorted order so it makes sorting documents by the indexed key much faster. However, an index can only help with sorting if it is a prefix of the sort. For example, the index on `"username"` wouldn't help much for this sort:

```
> db.users.find().sort({"age" : 1, "username" : 1})
```

This sorts by `"age"` and then `"username"`, so a strict sorting by `"username"` isn't terribly helpful. To optimize this sort, you could make an index on `"age"` *and* `"username"`:

```
> db.users.ensureIndex({"age" : 1, "username" : 1})
```

This is called a *compound index* and is useful if your query has multiple sort directions or multiple keys in the criteria. A compound index is an index on more than one field.

Suppose we have a *users* collection that looks something like this, if we run a query with no sorting (called *natural order*):

```
> db.users.find({}, {"_id" : 0, "i" : 0, "created" : 0})
{ "username" : "user0", "age" : 69 }
{ "username" : "user1", "age" : 50 }
{ "username" : "user2", "age" : 88 }
{ "username" : "user3", "age" : 52 }
{ "username" : "user4", "age" : 74 }
{ "username" : "user5", "age" : 104 }
{ "username" : "user6", "age" : 59 }
{ "username" : "user7", "age" : 102 }
```

```
{ "username" : "user8", "age" : 94 }
{ "username" : "user9", "age" : 7 }
{ "username" : "user10", "age" : 80 }
...
```

If we index this collection by `{"age" : 1, "username" : 1}`, the index will look roughly like this:

```
[0, "user100309"] -> 0x0c965148
[0, "user100334"] -> 0xf51f818e
[0, "user100479"] -> 0x00fd7934
...
[0, "user99985" ] -> 0xd246648f
[1, "user100156"] -> 0xf78d5bdd
[1, "user100187"] -> 0x68ab28bd
[1, "user100192"] -> 0x5c7fb621
...
[1, "user999920"] -> 0x67ded4b7
[2, "user100141"] -> 0x3996dd46
[2, "user100149"] -> 0xfce68412
[2, "user100223"] -> 0x91106e23
...
```

Each index entry contains an age and a username and points to the location of a document on disk (represented by the hexadecimal numbers, which can be ignored). Note that `"age"` fields are ordered to be strictly ascending and, within each age, `"username"`s are also in ascending order. As each age has approximately 8,000 usernames associated with it, only those necessary to convey the general idea have been included.

The way MongoDB uses this index depends on the type of query you're doing. These are the three most common ways:

`db.users.find({"age" : 21}).sort({"username" : -1})`

This is a *point query*, which searches for a single value (although there may be multiple documents with that value). Due to the second field in the index, the results are already in the correct order for the sort: MongoDB can start with the last match for `{"age" : 21}` and traverse the index in order:

```
[21, "user999977"] -> 0x9b3160cf
[21, "user999954"] -> 0xfe039231
[21, "user999902"] -> 0x719996aa
...
```

This type of query is very efficient: MongoDB can jump directly to the correct age and doesn't need to sort the results as traversing the index returns the data in the correct order.

Note that sort direction doesn't matter: MongoDB is comfortable traversing the index in either direction.

`db.users.find({"age" : {"$gte" : 21, "$lte" : 30}})`

This is a *multi-value query*, which looks for documents matching multiple values (in this case, all ages between 21 and 30). MongoDB will use the first key in the index, "age", to return the matching documents, like so:

```
[21, "user100000"] -> 0x37555a81
[21, "user100069"] -> 0x6951d16f
[21, "user1001"]   -> 0x9a1f5e0c
[21, "user100253"] -> 0xd54bd959
[21, "user100409"] -> 0x824fef6c
[21, "user100469"] -> 0x5fba778b
...
[30, "user999775"] -> 0x45182d8c
[30, "user999850"] -> 0x1df279e9
[30, "user999936"] -> 0x525caa57
```

In general, if MongoDB uses an index for a query it will return the resulting documents in index order.

`db.users.find({"age" : {"$gte" : 21, "$lte" : 30}}).sort({"username" : 1})`

This is a multi-value query, like the previous one, but this time it has a sort. As before, MongoDB will use the index to match the criteria:

```
[21, "user100000"] -> 0x37555a81
[21, "user100069"] -> 0x6951d16f
[21, "user1001"]   -> 0x9a1f5e0c
[21, "user100253"] -> 0xd54bd959
...
[22, "user100004"] -> 0x81e862c5
[22, "user100328"] -> 0x83376384
[22, "user100335"] -> 0x55932943
[22, "user100405"] -> 0x20e7e664
...
```

However, the index doesn't return the usernames in sorted order and the query requested that the results be sorted by username, so MongoDB has to sort the results in memory before returning them. Thus, this query is usually less efficient than the queries above.

Of course, the speed depends on how many results match your criteria: if your result set is only a couple of documents, MongoDB won't have much work to do to sort them. If there are more results, it will be slower or may not work at all: if you have more than 32 MB of results MongoDB will just error out, refusing to sort that much data:

```
Mon Oct 29 16:25:26 uncaught exception: error: {
    "$err" : "too much data for sort() with no index.  add an index or
        specify a smaller limit",
    "code" : 10128
}
```

One other index you can use in the last example is the same keys in reverse order: `{"username" : 1, "age" : 1}`. MongoDB will then traverse all the index entries, but in the order you want them back in. It will pick out the matching documents using the "age" part of the index:

```
["user0", 69]
["user1", 50]
["user10", 80]
["user100", 48]
["user1000", 111]
["user10000", 98]
["user100000", 21] -> 0x73f0b48d
["user100001", 60]
["user100002", 82]
["user100003", 27] -> 0x0078f55f
["user100004", 22] -> 0x5f0d3088
["user100005", 95]
...
```

This is good in that it does not require any giant in-memory sorts. However, it does have to scan the entire index to find all matches. Thus, putting the sort key first is generally a good strategy when you're using a limit so MongoDB can stop scanning the index after a couple of matches.

You can diagnose how MongoDB defaults to processing `db.users.find({"age" : {"$gte" : 21, "$lte" : 30}}).sort({"username" : 1})` by using `explain()`:

```
> db.users.find({"age" : {"$gte" : 21, "$lte" : 30}}).
... sort({"username" : 1}).
... explain()
{
    "cursor" : "BtreeCursor age_1_username_1",
    "isMultiKey" : false,
    "n" : 83484,
    "nscannedObjects" : 83484,
    "nscanned" : 83484,
    "nscannedObjectsAllPlans" : 83484,
    "nscannedAllPlans" : 83484,
    "scanAndOrder" : true,
    "indexOnly" : false,
    "nYields" : 0,
    "nChunkSkips" : 0,
    "millis" : 2766,
    "indexBounds" : {
        "age" : [
            [
                21,
                30
            ]
        ],
        "username" : [
            [
```

```
                    {
                        "$minElement" : 1
                    },
                    {
                        "$maxElement" : 1
                    }
                ]
            ]
        },
        "server" : "spock:27017"
}
```

You can ignore most of these fields; they will be covered later in this chapter. For now, note that the `"cursor"` field indicates that this query would use the `{"age" : 1, "username" : 1}` index and looks at less than a tenth of the documents (`"nscanned"` is only 83484), but takes nearly three seconds to execute (the `"millis"` field). The `"scanAndOrder"` field is `true`: this indicates that MongoDB had to sort the data in memory, as mentioned above.

We can use a *hint* to force MongoDB to use a certain index, so try the same query again using the `{"username" : 1, "age" : 1}` index, instead. This query scans more documents, but does not have to do an in-memory sort:

```
> db.users.find({"age" : {"$gte" : 21, "$lte" : 30}}).
... sort({"username" : 1}).
... hint({"username" : 1, "age" : 1}).
... explain()
{
        "cursor" : "BtreeCursor username_1_age_1",
        "isMultiKey" : false,
        "n" : 83484,
        "nscannedObjects" : 83484,
        "nscanned" : 984434,
        "nscannedObjectsAllPlans" : 83484,
        "nscannedAllPlans" : 984434,
        "scanAndOrder" : false,
        "indexOnly" : false,
        "nYields" : 0,
        "nChunkSkips" : 0,
        "millis" : 14820,
        "indexBounds" : {
            "username" : [
                [
                    {
                        "$minElement" : 1
                    },
                    {
                        "$maxElement" : 1
                    }
                ]
            ],
```

```
            "age" : [
                [
                    21,
                    30
                ]
            ]
        },
        "server" : "spock:27017"
}
```

Note that this took nearly 15 seconds to run, making the first index the clear winner. However, if we limit the number of results for each query, a new winner emerges:

```
> db.users.find({"age" : {"$gte" : 21, "$lte" : 30}}).
... sort({"username" : 1}).
... limit(1000).
... hint({"age" : 1, "username" : 1}).
... explain()['millis']
2031
> db.users.find({"age" : {"$gte" : 21, "$lte" : 30}}).
... sort({"username" : 1}).
... limit(1000).
... hint({"username" : 1, "age" : 1}).
... explain()['millis']
181
```

The first query is still hovering between two and three seconds, but the second query now takes less than a fifth of a second! Thus, you should always run `explain()`s on *exactly* the queries that your application is running. Excluding any options could make the `explain()` output misleading.

The index pattern of `{"sortKey" : 1, "queryCriteria" : 1}` often works well in applications, as most application do not want all possible results for a query but only the first few. It also scales well because of the way indexes are organized internally. Indexes are basically trees, with the smallest value on the leftmost leaf and the greatest on the rightmost. If you have a "`sortKey`" that is a date (or any value that increases over time) then as you traverse the tree from left to right, you're basically travelling forward in time. Thus, for applications that tend to use recent data more than older data, MongoDB only has to keep the rightmost (most recent) branches of the tree in memory, not the whole thing. An index like this is called *right-balanced* and, whenever possible, you should make your indexes right-balanced. The "`_id`" index is an example of a right-balanced index.

Using Compound Indexes

In the section above, we've been using *compound indexes*, which are indexes with more than one key in them. Compound indexes are a little more complicated to think about than single-key indexes, but they are very powerful. This section covers them in more depth.

Choosing key directions

So far, all of our index entries have been sorted in *ascending*, or least-to-greatest, order. However, if you need to sort on two (or more) criteria, you may need to have index keys go in different directions. For example, suppose we want to sort the collection above by youngest to oldest and usernames from Z-A. Our previous indexes would not be very efficient for this problem: within each age group users were sorted by `"username"` ascending A-Z, not Z-A. The compound indexes above do not hold the values in any useful order for getting `"age"` ascending and `"username"` descending.

To optimize compound sorts in different directions, use an index with matching directions. In this example, we could use `{"age" : 1, "username" : -1}`, which would organize the data as follows:

```
[21, "user999977"] -> 0xe57bf737
[21, "user999954"] -> 0x8bffa512
[21, "user999902"] -> 0x9e1447d1
[21, "user999900"] -> 0x3a6a8426
[21, "user999874"] -> 0xc353ee06
...
[30, "user999936"] -> 0x7f39a81a
[30, "user999850"] -> 0xa979e136
[30, "user999775"] -> 0x5de6b77a
...
[30, "user100324"] -> 0xe14f8e4d
[30, "user100140"] -> 0x0f34d446
[30, "user100050"] -> 0x223c35b1
```

The ages are arranged from youngest to oldest and, within each age, usernames are sorted from Z to A (or, rather, "9" to "0", given our usernames).

If our application also needed to optimize sorting by `{"age" : 1, "username" : 1}`, we would have to create a second index with those directions. To figure out which directions to use for an index, simply match the directions your sort is using. Note that inverse indexes (multiplying each direction by -1) are equivalent: `{"age" : 1, "username" : -1}` suits the same queries that `{"age" : -1, "username" : 1}` does.

Index direction only really matters when you're sorting based on multiple criteria. If you're only sorting by a single key, MongoDB can just as easily read the index in the opposite order. For example, if you had a sort on `{"age" : -1}` and an index on `{"age" : 1}`, MongoDB could optimize it just as well as if you had an index on `{"age" : -1}` (so don't create both!). The direction only matters for multikey sorts.

Using covered indexes

In the examples above, the query was always used to find the correct document, and then follow a pointer back to fetch the actual document. However, if your query is only looking for the fields that are included in the index, it does not need to fetch the document. When an index contains all the values requested by the user, it is considered to be *covering* a query. Whenever practical, use covered indexes in preference to going back to documents. You can make your working set much smaller that way, especially if you can combine this with a right-balanced index.

To make sure a query can use the index only, you should use projections (see "Specifying Which Keys to Return" on page 54) to not return the `"_id"` field (unless it is part of the index). You may also have to index fields that you aren't querying on, so you should balance your need for faster queries with the overhead this will add on writes.

If you run an `explain` on a covered query, the `"indexOnly"` field will be true.

If you index a field containing arrays, that index can never cover a query (due to the way arrays are stored in indexes, this is covered in more depth in "Indexing Objects and Arrays" on page 95). Even if you exclude the array field from the fields returned, you cannot cover a query using such an index.

Implicit indexes

Compound index can do "double duty" and act like different indexes for different queries. If we have an index on `{"age" : 1, "username" : 1}`, the `"age"` field is sorted identically to the way it would be if you had an index on just `{"age" : 1}`. Thus, the compound index can be used the way an index on `{"age" : 1}` by itself would be.

This can be generalized to as many keys as necessary: if an index has N keys, you get a "free" index on any prefix of those keys. For example, if we have an index that looks like `{"a": 1, "b": 1, "c": 1, ..., "z": 1}`, we effectively have indexes on `{"a": 1}`, `{"a": 1, "b" : 1}`, `{"a": 1, "b": 1, "c": 1}`, and so on.

Note that this doesn't hold for *any* subset of keys: queries that would use the index `{"b": 1}` or `{"a": 1, "c": 1}` (for example) will not be optimized: only queries that can use a prefix of the index can take advantage of it.

How $-Operators Use Indexes

Some queries can use indexes more efficiently than others; some queries cannot using indexes at all. This section covers how various query operators are handled by MongoDB.

Inefficient operators

There are a few queries that cannot use an index at all, such as "`$where`" queries and checking if a key exists (`{"key" : {"$exists" : true}}`). There are several other operators that use indexes but not very efficiently.

If there is a "vanilla" index on `"x"`, querying for documents where `"x"` does not exist can use the index (`{"x" : {"$exists" : false}}`). However, as nonexistent fields are stored the same way as `null` fields in the index, the query must visit each document to check if the value is actually null or nonexistent. If you use a sparse index, it cannot be used for either `{"$exists" : true}` nor `{"$exists" : false}`.

In general, negation is inefficient. `"$ne"` queries can use an index, but not very well. They must look at all the index entries other than the one specified by the `"$ne"`, so it basically has to scan the entire index. For example, here are the index ranges traversed for such a query:

```
> db.example.find({"i" : {"$ne" : 3}}).explain()
{
    "cursor" : "BtreeCursor i_1 multi",
    ...,
    "indexBounds" : {
        "i" : [
            [
                {
                    "$minElement" : 1
                },
                3
            ],
            [
                3,
                {
                    "$maxElement" : 1
                }
            ]
        ]
    },
    ...
}
```

This query looks at all index entries less than 3 and all index entries greater than 3. This can be efficient if a large swath of your collection is 3, but otherwise it must check almost everything.

`"$not"` can sometimes use an index but often does not know how. It can reverse basic ranges (`{"`*`key`*`" : {"$lt" : 7}}` becomes `{"`*`key`*`" : {"$gte" : 7}}`) and regular expressions. However, most other queries with `"$not"` will fall back to doing a table scan. `"$nin"` always uses a table scan.

If you need to perform one of these types of queries quickly, figure out if there's another clause that you could add to the query that could use an index to filter the result set down to a small number of documents before MongoDB attempts to do non-indexed matching.

For example, suppose we were finding all users without a `"birthday"` field. If we knew that the application started adding a birthday field on March 20th, we could limit the query to users created before then:

```
> db.users.find({"birthday" : {"$exists" : false}, "_id" : {"$lt" : march20Id}})
```

The order of fields in a query is irrelevant: MongoDB will find which fields it can use indexes on regardless of ordering.

Ranges

Compound indexes can help MongoDB execute more effectively queries with multiple clauses. When designing an index with multiple fields, put fields that will be used in exact matches first (e.g., "x" : "foo") and ranges last (e.g., "y": {"$gt" : 3, "$lt" : 5}). This allows the query to find an exact value for the first index key and then search within that for a second index range. For example, suppose we were querying for a specific age and a range of usernames using an {"age" : 1, "username" : 1} index. We would get fairly exact index bounds:

```
> db.users.find({"age" : 47,
... "username" : {"$gt" : "user5", "$lt" : "user8"}}).explain()
{
    "cursor" : "BtreeCursor age_1_username_1",
    "n" : 2788,
    "nscanned" : 2788,
    ...,
    "indexBounds" : {
        "age" : [
            [
                47,
                47
            ]
        ],
        "username" : [
            [
                "user5",
                "user8"
            ]
        ]
    },
    ...
}
```

The query goes directly to "age" : 47 and then searches within that for usernames between "user5" and "user8".

Conversely, suppose we use an index on {"username" : 1, "age" : 1}. This changes the query plan, as the query must look at all users between "user5" and "user8" and pick out the ones with "age" : 47:

```
> db.users.find({"age" : 47,
... "username" : {"$gt" : "user5", "$lt" : "user8"}}).explain()
{
    "cursor" : "BtreeCursor username_1_age_1",
    "n" : 2788,
    "nscanned" : 319499,
    ...,
```

```
        "indexBounds" : {
            "username" : [
                [
                    "user5",
                    "user8"
                ]
            ],
            "age" : [
                [
                    47,
                    47
                ]
            ]
        },
        "server" : "spock:27017"
    }
```

This forces MongoDB to scan 10 times the number of index entries as using the previous index would. Using two ranges in a query basically always forces this less-efficient query plan.

OR queries

As of this writing, MongoDB can only use one index per query. That is, if you create one index on `{"x" : 1}` and another index on `{"y" : 1}` and then do a query on `{"x" : 123, "y" : 456}`, MongoDB will use one of the indexes you created, not use both. This only exception to this rule is `"$or"`. `"$or"` can use one index per `$or` clause, as `$or` preforms two queries and then merges the results:

```
> db.foo.find({"$or" : [{"x" : 123}, {"y" : 456}]}).explain()
{
    "clauses" : [
        {
            "cursor" : "BtreeCursor x_1",
            "isMultiKey" : false,
            "n" : 1,
            "nscannedObjects" : 1,
            "nscanned" : 1,
            "nscannedObjectsAllPlans" : 1,
            "nscannedAllPlans" : 1,
            "scanAndOrder" : false,
            "indexOnly" : false,
            "nYields" : 0,
            "nChunkSkips" : 0,
            "millis" : 0,
            "indexBounds" : {
                "x" : [
                    [
                        123,
                        123
                    ]
```

```
                ]
            }
        },
        {
            "cursor" : "BtreeCursor y_1",
            "isMultiKey" : false,
            "n" : 1,
            "nscannedObjects" : 1,
            "nscanned" : 1,
            "nscannedObjectsAllPlans" : 1,
            "nscannedAllPlans" : 1,
            "scanAndOrder" : false,
            "indexOnly" : false,
            "nYields" : 0,
            "nChunkSkips" : 0,
            "millis" : 0,
            "indexBounds" : {
                "y" : [
                    [
                        456,
                        456
                    ]
                ]
            }
        }
    ],
    "n" : 2,
    "nscannedObjects" : 2,
    "nscanned" : 2,
    "nscannedObjectsAllPlans" : 2,
    "nscannedAllPlans" : 2,
    "millis" : 0,
    "server" : "spock:27017"
}
```

As you can see, this explain is the conglomerate of two separate queries. In general, doing two queries and merging the results is much less efficient than doing a single query; thus, whenever possible, prefer "$in" to "$or".

If you must use an $or, keep in mind that MongoDB needs to look through the query results of both queries and remove any duplicates (documents that matched more than one $or clause).

When running "$in" queries there is no way, other than sorting, to control the order of documents returned. For example, {"x" : [1, 2, 3]} will return documents in the same order as {"x" : [3, 2, 1]}.

Indexing Objects and Arrays

MongoDB allows you to reach into your documents and create indexes on nested fields and arrays. Embedded object and array fields can be combined with top-level fields in compound indexes and although they are special in some ways, they mostly behave the way "normal" index fields behave.

Indexing embedded docs

Indexes can be created on keys in embedded documents in the same way that they are created on normal keys. If we had a collection where each document represented a user, we might have an embedded document that described each user's location:

```
{
    "username" : "sid",
    "loc" : {
        "ip" : "1.2.3.4",
        "city" : "Springfield",
        "state" : "NY"
    }
}
```

We could put an index on one of the subfields of `"loc"`, say `"loc.city"`, to speed up queries using that field:

```
> db.users.ensureIndex({"loc.city" : 1})
```

You can go as deep as you'd like with these: you could index `"x.y.z.w.a.b.c"` (and so on) if you wanted.

Note that indexing the embedded document itself (`"loc"`) has very different behavior than indexing a field of that embedded document (`"loc.city"`). Indexing the entire subdocument will only help queries that are querying for the entire subdocument. In the example above, the query optimizer could only use an index on `"loc"` for queries that described the whole subdocument with fields in the correct order (e.g., `db.users.find({"loc" : {"ip" : "123.456.789.000", "city" : "Shelbyville", "state" : "NY"}}})`). It could not use the index for queries that looked like `db.users.find({"loc.city" : "Shelbyville"})`.

Indexing arrays

You can also index arrays, which allows you to use the index to search for specific array elements efficiently.

Suppose we have a collection of blog posts where each document was a post. Each post has a `"comments"` field, which is an array of comment subdocuments. If we want to be able to find the most-recently-commented-on blog posts, we could create an index on the `"date"` key in the array of embedded `"comments"` documents of our blog post collection:

```
> db.blog.ensureIndex({"comments.date" : 1})
```

Indexing an array creates an index entry for each element of the array, so if a post had 20 comments, it would have 20 index entries. This makes array indexes more expensive than single-value ones: for a single insert, update, or remove, every array entry might have to be updated (potentially thousands of index entries).

Unlike the "loc" example in the previous section, you cannot index an entire array as a single entity: indexing an array field indexes each element of the array, not the array itself.

Indexes on array elements do not keep any notion of position: you cannot use an index for a query that is looking for a specific array element, such as "comments.4".

You can, incidentally, index a specific array entry, for example:

```
> db.blog.ensureIndex({"comments.10.votes": 1})
```

However, this index would only be useful for queries for exactly the 11th array element (arrays start at index 0).

Only one field in an index entry can be from an array. This is to avoid the explosive number of index entries you'd get from multiple multikey indexes: every possible pair of elements would have to be indexed, causing indexes to be $n*m$ entries per document. For example, suppose we had an index on {"x" : 1, "y" : 1}:

```
> // x is an array - legal
> db.multi.insert({"x" : [1, 2, 3], "y" : 1})
>
> // y is an array - still legal
> db.multi.insert({"x" : 1, "y" : [4, 5, 6]})
>
> // x and y are arrays - illegal!
> db.multi.insert({"x" : [1, 2, 3], "y" : [4, 5, 6]})
cannot index parallel arrays [y] [x]
```

Were MongoDB to index the final example, it would have to create index entries for {"x" : 1, "y" : 4}, {"x" : 1, "y" : 5}, {"x" : 1, "y" : 6}, {"x" : 2, "y" : 4}, {"x" : 2, "y" : 5}, {"x" : 2, "y" : 6}, {"x" : 3, "y" : 4}, {"x" : 3, "y" : 5}, and {"x" : 3, "y" : 6} (and these arrays are only three elements long).

Multikey index implications

If any document has an array field for the indexed key, the index immediately is flagged as a *multikey index*. You can see whether an index is multikey from explain()'s output: if a multikey index was used, the "isMultikey" field will be true. Once an index has been flagged as multikey, it can never be un-multikeyed, even if all of the documents containing arrays in that field are removed. The only way to un-multikey it is to drop and recreate it.

Multikey indexes may be a bit slower than non-multikey indexes. Many index entries can point at a single document so MongoDB may need to do some de-duping before returning results.

Index Cardinality

Cardinality refers to how many distinct values there are for a field in a collection. Some fields, such as `"gender"` or `"newsletter opt-out"`, might only have two possible values, which is considered a very low cardinality. Others, such as `"username"` or `"email"`, might have a unique value for every document in the collection, which is high cardinality. Still others fall somewhere in between, such as `"age"` or `"zip code"`.

In general, the greater the cardinality of a field, the more helpful an index on that field can be. This is because the index can quickly narrow the search space to a much smaller result set. For a low cardinality field, an index generally cannot eliminate as many possible matches.

For example, suppose we had an index on `"gender"` and were looking for women named Susan. We could only narrow down the result space by approximately 50% before referring to individual documents to look up `"name"`. Conversely, if we indexed by `"name"`, we could immediately narrow down our result set to the tiny fraction of users named Susan and then we could refer to those documents to check the gender.

As a rule of thumb, try to create indexes on high-cardinality keys or at least put high-cardinality keys first in compound indexes (before low-cardinality keys).

Using explain() and hint()

As you have seen above, `explain()` gives you lots of information about your queries. It is one of the most important diagnostic tools there is for slow queries. You can find out which indexes are being used and how by looking at a query's *explain*. For any query, you can add a call to `explain()` at the end (the way you would add a `sort()` or `limit()`, but `explain()` must be the last call).

There are two types of `explain()` output that you'll see most commonly: indexed and non-indexed queries. Special index types may create slightly different query plans, but most fields should be similar. Also, sharding returns a conglomerate of `explain()`s (as covered in Chapter 13), as it runs the query on multiple servers.

The most basic type of `explain()` is on a query that doesn't use an index. You can tell that a query doesn't use an index because it uses a `"BasicCursor"`. Conversely, most queries that use an index use a `BtreeCursor` (some special types of indexes, such as geospatial indexes, use their own type of cursor).

The output to an `explain()` on a query that uses an index varies, but in the simplest case, it looks something like this:

```
> db.users.find({"age" : 42}).explain()
{
    "cursor" : "BtreeCursor age_1_username_1",
    "isMultiKey" : false,
```

```
    "n" : 8332,
    "nscannedObjects" : 8332,
    "nscanned" : 8332,
    "nscannedObjectsAllPlans" : 8332,
    "nscannedAllPlans" : 8332,
    "scanAndOrder" : false,
    "indexOnly" : false,
    "nYields" : 0,
    "nChunkSkips" : 0,
    "millis" : 91,
    "indexBounds" : {
        "age" : [
            [
                42,
                42
            ]
        ],
        "username" : [
            [
                {
                    "$minElement" : 1
                },
                {
                    "$maxElement" : 1
                }
            ]
        ]
    },
    "server" : "ubuntu:27017"
}
```

This output first tells you what index was used: `age_1_username_1`. `"millis"` reports how fast the query was executed, from the server receiving the request to when it sent a response. However, it may not always be the number you are looking for. If MongoDB tried multiple query plans, `"millis"` will reflect how long it took all of them to run, not the one chosen as the best.

Next is how many documents were actually returned as a result: `"n"`. This doesn't reflect how much work MongoDB did to answer the query: how many index entries and documents did it have to search? Index entries are described by `"nscanned"`. The number of documents scanned is reflected in `"nscannedObjects"`. Finally, if you were using a sort and MongoDB could not use an index for it, `"scanAndOrder"` would be true. This means that MongoDB had to sort the results in memory, which is generally quite slow and limited to a small number of results.

Now that you know the basics, here is a breakdown of the all of the fields in more detail:

`"cursor" : "BtreeCursor age_1_username_1"`
: BtreeCursor means that an index was used, specifically, the index on age and username: `{"age" : 1, "username" : 1}`. You may also see `reverse` (if the query is

traversing the index in reverse direction—say for a sort) or `multi`, if it is using a multikey index.

`"isMultiKey" : false`
: If this query used a multikey index (see "Indexing Objects and Arrays" on page 95).

`"n" : 8332`
: This is the number of documents returned by the query.

`"nscannedObjects" : 8332`
: This is a count of the number of times MongoDB had to follow an index pointer to the actual document on disk. If the query contains criteria that is not part of the index or requests fields back that aren't contained in the index, MongoDB must look up the document each index entry points to.

`"nscanned" : 8332`
: The number of index entries looked at if an index was used. If this was a table scan, it is the number of documents examined.

`"scanAndOrder" : false`
: If MongoDB had to sort results in memory.

`"indexOnly" : false`
: If MongoDB was able to fulfill this query using only the index entries (as discussed in "Using covered indexes" on page 90).

  In this example, MongoDB found all matching documents using the index, which we know because `"nscanned"` is the same as `"n"`. However, the query was told to return every field in the matching documents and the index only contained the `"age"` and `"username"` fields. If we changed the query to have a second argument, `{"_id" : 0, "age" : 1, "username" : 1}`, then it would be covered by the index and `"indexOnly"` would be `true`.

`"nYields" : 0`
: The number of times this query yielded (paused) to allow a write request to proceed. If there are writes waiting to go, queries will periodically release their lock and allow them to do so. However, on this system, there were no writes waiting so the query never yielded.

`"millis" : 91`
: The number of milliseconds it took the database to execute the query. The lower this number is, the better.

`"indexBounds" : {...}`
: This field describes how the index was used, giving ranges of the index traversed. As the first clause in the query was an exact match, the index only needed to look at that value: 42. The second index key was a free variable, as the query didn't specify

any restrictions to it. Thus, the database looked for values between negative infinity ("$minElement" : 1) and infinity("$maxElement" : 1) for usernames within "age" : 42.

Let's take a slightly more complicated example: suppose you have an index on {"username" : 1, "age" : 1} and an index on {"age" : 1, "username" : 1}. What happens if you query for "username" and "age"? Well, it depends on the query:

```
> db.c.find({age : {$gt : 10}, username : "sally"}).explain()
{
    "cursor" : "BtreeCursor username_1_age_1",
    "indexBounds" : [
        [
            {
                "username" : "sally",
                "age" : 10
            },
            {
                "username" : "sally",
                "age" : 1.7976931348623157e+308
            }
        ]
    ],
    "nscanned" : 13,
    "nscannedObjects" : 13,
    "n" : 13,
    "millis" : 5
}
```

We are querying for an exact match on "username" and a range of values for "age", so the database chooses to use the {"username" : 1, "age" : 1} index, reversing the terms of the query. If, on the other hand, we query for an exact age and a range of names, MongoDB will use the other index:

```
> db.c.find({"age" : 14, "username" : /.*/}).explain()
{
    "cursor" : "BtreeCursor age_1_username_1 multi",
    "indexBounds" : [
        [
            {
                "age" : 14,
                "username" : ""
            },
            {
                "age" : 14,
                "username" : {

                }
            }
        ],
        [
            {
```

```
                    "age" : 14,
                    "username" : /.*/
                },
                {
                    "age" : 14,
                    "username" : /.*/
                }
            ]
        ],
        "nscanned" : 2,
        "nscannedObjects" : 2,
        "n" : 2,
        "millis" : 2
}
```

If you find that Mongo is using different indexes than you want it to for a query, you can force it to use a certain index by using `hint()`. For instance, if you want to make sure MongoDB uses the `{"username" : 1, "age" : 1}` index on the previous query, you could say the following:

```
> db.c.find({"age" : 14, "username" : /.*/}).hint({"username" : 1, "age" : 1})
```

If a query is not using the index that you want it to and you use a hint to change it, run an `explain()` on the hinted query before deploying. If you force MongoDB to use an index on a query that it does not know how to use an index for, you could end up making the query less efficient than it was without the index.

The Query Optimizer

MongoDB's query optimizer works a bit differently than any other database's. Basically, if an index exactly matches a query (you are querying for `"x"` and have an index on `"x"`), the query optimizer will use that index. Otherwise, there might be a few possible indexes that could work well for your query. MongoDB will select a subset of likely indexes and run the query once with each plan, in parallel. The first plan to return 100 results is the "winner" and the other plans' executions are halted.

This plan is cached and used subsequently for that query until the collection has seen a certain amount of churn. Once the collection has changed a certain amount since the initial plan evaluation, the query optimizer will re-race the possible plans. Plans will also be reevaluated after index creation or every 1,000 queries.

The `"allPlans"` field in `explain()`'s output shows each plan the query tried running.

When Not to Index

Indexes are most effective at retrieving small subsets of data and some types of queries are faster without indexes. Indexes become less and less efficient as you need to get larger percentages of a collection because using an index requires two lookups: one to look at the index entry and one following the index's pointer to the document. A table scan only requires one: looking at the document. In the worst case (returning all of the documents in a collection) using an index would take twice as many lookups and would generally be significantly slower than a table scan.

Unfortunately, there isn't a hard-and-fast rule about when an index helps and when it hinders as it really depends on the size of your data, size of your indexes, size of your documents, and the average result set size (Table 5-1). As a rule of thumb: if a query is returning 30% or more of the collection, start looking at whether indexes or table scans are faster. However, this number can vary from 2% to 60%.

Table 5-1. Properties that affect the effectiveness of indexes

Indexes often work well for	Table scans often work well for
Large collections	Small collections
Large documents	Small documents
Selective queries	Non-selective queries

Let's say we have an analytics system that collects statistics. Your application queries the system for all documents for a given account to generate a nice graph of all data from an hour ago to the beginning of time:

```
> db.entries.find({"created_at" : {"$lt" : hourAgo}})
```

We index `"created_at"` to speed up this query.

When we first launch, this is a tiny result set and returns instantly. But after a couple weeks, it starts being a lot of data, and after a month this query is already taking too long to run.

For most applications, this is probably the "wrong" query: do you really want a query that's returning most of your data set? Most applications, particularly those with large data sets, do not. However, there are some legitimate cases where you may want most or all of your data: you might be exporting this data to a reporting system or using it for a batch job. In these cases, you would like to return this large proportion of the data set as fast as possible.

You can force it to do a table scan by hinting `{"$natural" : 1}`. As described in "Capped Collections" on page 109, `$natural` specifies on-disk order when used in a sort. In particular, `$natural` forces MongoDB to do a table scan:

```
> db.entries.find({"created_at" : {"$lt" : hourAgo}}).hint({"$natural" : 1})
```

One side effect of sorting by `"$natural"` is that it gives you results in on-disk order. This is generally meaningless for an active collection: as documents grow and shrink they'll be moved around on disk and new documents will be written in the "holes" they left. However, for insert-only workloads, `$natural` can be useful for giving you the latest (or earliest) documents.

Types of Indexes

There are a few index options you can specify when building an index that change the way the index behaves. The most common variations are described in the following sections, and more advanced or special-case options are described in the next chapter.

Unique Indexes

Unique indexes guarantee that each value will appear at most once in the index. For example, if you want to make sure no two documents can have the same value in the `"username"` key, you can create a unique index:

```
> db.users.ensureIndex({"username" : 1}, {"unique" : true})
```

For example, suppose that we try to insert the following documents on the collection above:

```
> db.users.insert({username: "bob"})
> db.users.insert({username: "bob"})
E11000 duplicate key error index: test.users.$username_1  dup key: { : "bob" }
```

If you check the collection, you'll see that only the first "bob" was stored. Throwing duplicate key exceptions is not very efficient, so use the unique constraint for the occasional duplicate, not to filter out zillions of duplicates a second.

A unique index that you are probably already familiar with is the index on `"_id"`, which is automatically created whenever you create a collection. This is a normal unique index (aside from the fact that it cannot be dropped as other unique indexes can be).

> If a key does not exist, the index stores its value as `null` for that document. This means that if you create a unique index and try to insert more than one document that is missing the indexed field, the inserts will fail because you already have a document with a value of `null`. See "Sparse Indexes" on page 106 for advice on handling this.

In some cases a value won't be indexed. Index buckets are of limited size and if an index entry exceeds it, it just won't be included in the index. This can cause confusion as it makes a document "invisible" to queries that use the index. All fields must be smaller than 1024 bytes to be included in an index. MongoDB does not return any sort of error or warning if a document's fields cannot be indexed due to size. This means that keys longer than 8 KB will not be subject to the unique index constraints: you can insert identical 8 KB strings, for example.

Compound unique indexes

You can also create a compound unique index. If you do this, individual keys can have the same values, but the combination of values across all keys in an index entry can appear in the index at most once.

For example, if we had a unique index on `{"username" : 1, "age" : 1}`, the following inserts would be legal:

```
> db.users.insert({"username" : "bob"})
> db.users.insert({"username" : "bob", "age" : 23})
> db.users.insert({"username" : "fred", "age" : 23})
```

However, attempting to insert a second copy of any of these documents would cause a duplicate key exception.

GridFS, the standard method for storing large files in MongoDB (see "Storing Files with GridFS" on page 123), uses a compound unique index. The collection that holds the file content has a unique index on `{"files_id" : 1, "n" : 1}`, which allows documents that look like (in part) the following:

```
{"files_id" : ObjectId("4b23c3ca7525f35f94b60a2d"), "n" : 1}
{"files_id" : ObjectId("4b23c3ca7525f35f94b60a2d"), "n" : 2}
{"files_id" : ObjectId("4b23c3ca7525f35f94b60a2d"), "n" : 3}
{"files_id" : ObjectId("4b23c3ca7525f35f94b60a2d"), "n" : 4}
```

Note that all of the values for `"files_id"` are the same, but `"n"` is different.

Dropping duplicates

If you attempt to build a unique index on an existing collection, it will fail to build if there are any duplicate values:

```
> db.users.ensureIndex({"age" : 1}, {"unique" : true})
E11000 duplicate key error index: test.users.$age_1  dup key: { : 12 }
```

Generally, you'll need to process your data (the aggregation framework can help) and figure out where the duplicates are and what to do with them.

In a few rare cases, you may just want to delete documents with duplicate values. The `"dropDups"` option will save the first document found and remove any subsequent documents with duplicate values:

```
> db.people.ensureIndex({"username" : 1}, {"unique" : true, "dropDups" : true})
```

`"dropDups"` forces the unique index build, but it's a very drastic option; you have no control over which documents are dropped and which are kept (and MongoDB gives you no indication of which documents were dropped, if any). If your data is of any importance, do not use `"dropDups"`.

Sparse Indexes

As mentioned in an earlier section, unique indexes count `null` as a value, so you cannot have a unique index with more than one document missing the key. However, there are lots of cases where you may want the unique index to be enforced only if the key exists. If you have a field that may or may not exist but must be unique when it does, you can combine the unique option with the sparse option.

> If you are familiar with sparse indexes on relational databases, MongoDB's sparse indexes are a completely different concept. MongoDB sparse indexes are basically indexes that need not include every document as an entry.

To create a sparse index, include the `sparse` option. For example, if providing an email address was optional but, if provided, should be unique, we could do:

```
> db.ensureIndex({"email" : 1}, {"unique" : true, "sparse" : true})
```

Sparse indexes do not necessarily have to be unique. To make a non-unique sparse index, simply do not include the `unique` option.

One thing to be aware of is that the same query can return different results depending on whether or not it uses the sparse index. For example, suppose we had a collection where most of the documents had `"x"` fields, but one does not:

```
> db.foo.find()
{ "_id" : 0 }
{ "_id" : 1, "x" : 1 }
{ "_id" : 2, "x" : 2 }
{ "_id" : 3, "x" : 3 }
```

When we do a query on `"x"`, it will return all matching documents:

```
> db.foo.find({"x" : {"$ne" : 2}})
{ "_id" : 0 }
{ "_id" : 1, "x" : 1 }
{ "_id" : 3, "x" : 3 }
```

If we create a sparse index on `"x"`, the `"_id" : 0` document won't be included in the index. So now if we query on `"x"`, MongoDB will use the index and not return the `{"_id" : 0}` document:

```
> db.foo.find({"x" : {"$ne" : 2}})
{ "_id" : 1, "x" : 1 }
{ "_id" : 3, "x" : 3 }
```

You can use `hint()` to force it to do a table scan if you need documents with missing fields.

Index Administration

As shown in the previous section, you can create new indexes using the `ensureIndex` function. An index only needs to be created once per collection. If you try to create the same index again, nothing will happen.

All of the information about a database's indexes is stored in the *system.indexes* collection. This is a reserved collection, so you cannot modify its documents or remove documents from it. You can manipulate it only through `ensureIndex` and the `dropIndexes` database command.

When you create an index, you can see its meta information in *system.indexes*. You can also run `db.collectionName.getIndexes()` to see all index information about a given collection:

```
> db.foo.getIndexes()
[
    {
        "v" : 1,
        "key" : {
            "_id" : 1
        },
        "ns" : "test.foo",
        "name" : "_id_"
    },
    {
        "v" : 1,
        "key" : {
            "y" : 1
        },
        "ns" : "test.foo",
        "name" : "y_1"
    },
    {
        "v" : 1,
        "key" : {
            "x" : 1,
            "y" : 1
        },
        "ns" : "test.foo",
        "name" : "x_1_y_1"
    }
]
```

The important fields are the `"key"` and `"name"`. The key can be used for hinting, max, min, and other places where an index must be specified. This is a place where field order matters: an index on `{"x" : 1, "y" : 1}` is not the same as an index on `{"y" : 1, "x" : 1}`. The index name is used as identifier for a lot of administrative index operations, such as `dropIndex`. Whether or not the index is multikey is not specified in its spec.

The "v" field is used internally for index versioning. If you have any indexes that do not have a "v" : 1 field, they are being stored in an older, less efficient format. You can upgrade them by ensuring that you're running at least MongoDB version 2.0 and dropping and rebuilding the index.

Identifying Indexes

Each index in a collection has a name that uniquely identifies the index and is used by the server to delete or manipulate it. Index names are, by default, *keyname1_dir1_keyname2_dir2_..._keynameN_dirN*, where *keynameX* is the index's key and *dirX* is the index's direction (1 or -1). This can get unwieldy if indexes contain more than a couple keys, so you can specify your own name as one of the options to ensureIndex:

```
> db.foo.ensureIndex({"a" : 1, "b" : 1, "c" : 1, ..., "z" : 1},
... {"name" : "alphabet"})
```

There is a limit to the number of characters in an index name, so complex indexes may need custom names to be created. A call to getLastError will show if the index creation succeeded or why it didn't.

Changing Indexes

As your application grows and changes, you may find that your data or queries have changed and that indexes that used to work well no longer do. You can remove unneeded indexes using the dropIndex command:

```
> db.people.dropIndex("x_1_y_1")
{ "nIndexesWas" : 3, "ok" : 1 }
```

Use the "name" field from the index description to specify which index to drop.

Building new indexes is time-consuming and resource-intensive. By default, MongoDB will build an index as fast as possible, blocking all reads and writes on a database until the index build has finished. If you would like your database to remain somewhat responsive to reads and writes, use the background option when building an index. This forces the index build to occasionally yield to other operations, but may still have a severe impact on your application (see "Building Indexes" on page 222 for more information). Background indexing is also much slower than foreground indexing.

If you have the choice, creating indexes on existing documents is slightly faster than creating the index first and then inserting all documents.

There is more on the operational aspects of building indexes in Chapter 18.

CHAPTER 6

Special Index and Collection Types

This chapter covers the special collections and index types MongoDB has available, including:

- Capped collections for queue-like data
- TTL indexes for caches
- Full-text indexes for simple string searching
- Geospatial indexes for 2D and spherical geometries
- GridFS for storing large files

Capped Collections

"Normal" collections in MongoDB are created dynamically and automatically grow in size to fit additional data. MongoDB also supports a different type of collection, called a *capped collection*, which is created in advance and is fixed in size (see Figure 6-1). Having fixed-size collections brings up an interesting question: what happens when we try to insert into a capped collection that is already full? The answer is that capped collections behave like circular queues: if we're out of space, the oldest document will be deleted, and the new one will take its place (see Figure 6-2). This means that capped collections automatically age-out the oldest documents as new documents are inserted.

Certain operations are not allowed on capped collections. Documents cannot be removed or deleted (aside from the automatic age-out described earlier), and updates that would cause documents to grow in size are disallowed. By preventing these two operations, we guarantee that documents in a capped collection are stored in insertion order and that there is no need to maintain a free list for space from removed documents.

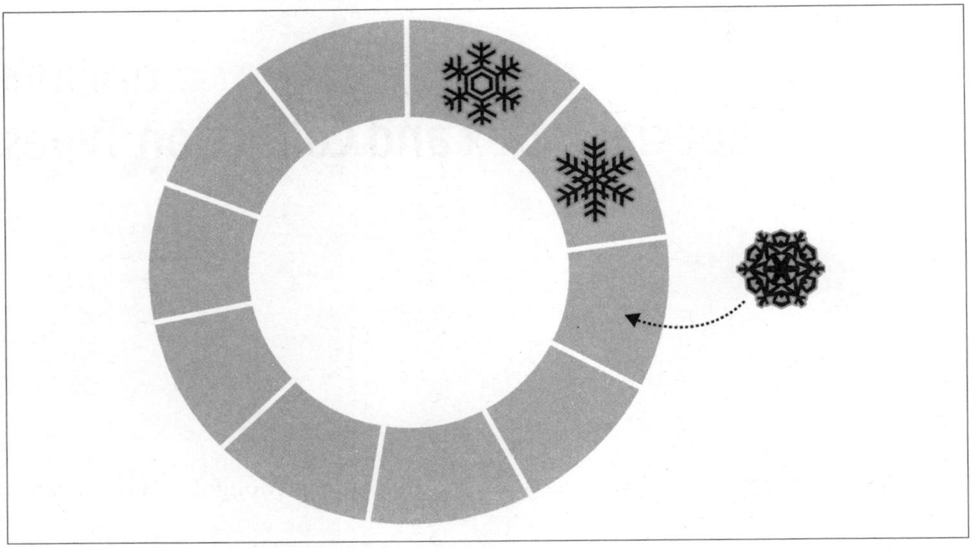

Figure 6-1. New documents are inserted at the end of the queue

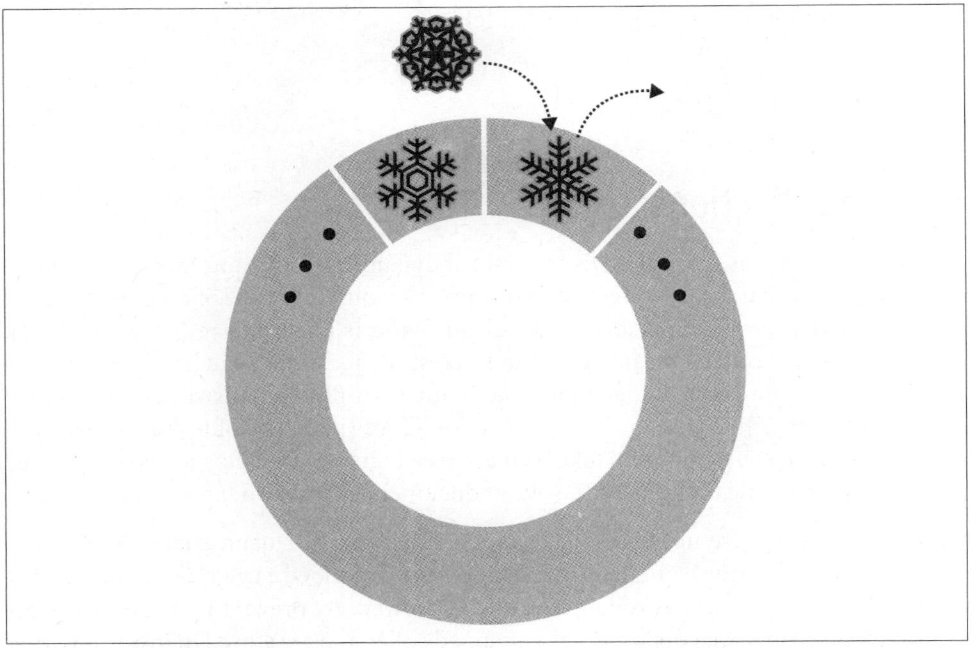

Figure 6-2. When the queue is full, the oldest element will be replaced by the newest

Capped collections have a different access pattern than most MongoDB collections: data is written sequentially over a fixed section of disk. This makes them tend to perform writes quickly on spinning disk, especially if they can be given their own disk (so as not to be "interrupted" by other collections' random writes).

> Capped collections cannot be sharded.

Capped collections tend to be useful for logging, although they lack flexibility: you cannot control when data ages out, other than setting a size when you create the collection.

Creating Capped Collections

Unlike normal collections, capped collections must be explicitly created before they are used. To create a capped collection, use the `create` command. From the shell, this can be done using `createCollection`:

```
> db.createCollection("my_collection", {"capped" : true, "size" : 100000});
{ "ok" : true }
```

The previous command creates a capped collection, *my_collection*, that is a fixed size of 100,000 bytes.

`createCollection` can also specify a limit on the number of documents in a capped collection in addition to the limit size:

```
> db.createCollection("my_collection2",
... {"capped" : true, "size" : 100000, "max" : 100});
{ "ok" : true }
```

You could use this to keep, say, the latest 10 news articles or limit a user to 1,000 documents.

Once a capped collection has been created, it cannot be changed (it must be dropped and recreated if you wish to change its properties). Thus, you should think carefully about the size of a large collection before creating it.

> When limiting the number of documents in a capped collection, you must specify a size limit as well. Age-out will be based on whichever limit is reached first: it cannot hold more than `"max"` documents nor take up more than `"size"` space.

Another option for creating a capped collection is to convert an existing, regular collection into a capped collection. This can be done using the `convertToCapped` command—in the following example, we convert the *test* collection to a capped collection of 10,000 bytes:

```
> db.runCommand({"convertToCapped" : "test", "size" : 10000});
{ "ok" : true }
```

There is no way to "uncap" a capped collection (other than dropping it).

Sorting Au Naturel

There is a special type of sort that you can do with capped collections, called a *natural sort*. A natural sort returns the documents in the order that they appear on disk (see Figure 6-3).

For most collections, this isn't a very useful sort because documents move around. However, documents in a capped collection are always kept in insertion order so that natural order is the same as insertion order. Thus, a natural sort gives you documents from oldest to newest. You can also sort from newest to oldest (see Figure 6-4):

```
> db.my_collection.find().sort({"$natural" : -1})
```

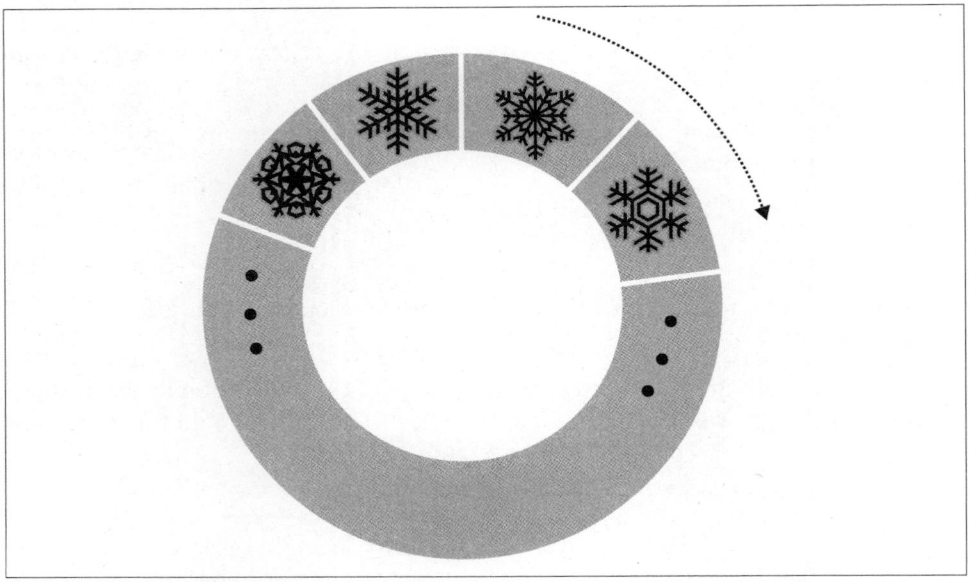

Figure 6-3. Sort by {"$natural" : 1}

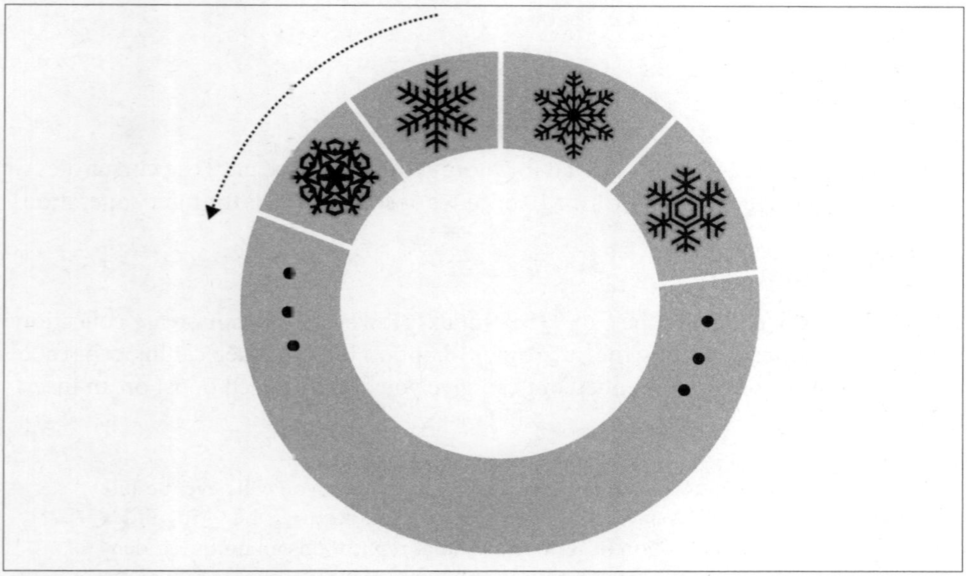

Figure 6-4. Sort by {"$natural" : -1}

Tailable Cursors

Tailable cursors are a special type of cursor that are not closed when their results are exhausted. They were inspired by the *tail -f* command and, similar to the command, will continue fetching output for as long as possible. Because the cursors do not die when they run out of results, they can continue to fetch new results as documents are added to the collection. Tailable cursors can be used only on capped collections, since insert order is not tracked for normal collections.

Tailable cursors are often used for processing documents as they are inserted onto a "work queue" (the capped collection). Because tailable cursors will time out after 10 minutes of no results, it is important to include logic to re-query the collection if they die. The *mongo* shell does not allow you to use tailable cursors, but using one in PHP looks something like the following:

```
$cursor = $collection->find()->tailable();

while (true) {
    if (!$cursor->hasNext()) {
        if ($cursor->dead()) {
            break;
        }
        sleep(1);
    }
    else {
        while ($cursor->hasNext()) {
```

```
                do_stuff($cursor->getNext());
            }
        }
    }
```

The cursor will process results or wait for more results to arrive until the cursor dies (it will time out if there are no inserts for 10 minutes or someone kills the query operation).

No-_id Collections

By default, every collection has an "_id" index. However, you can create collections with "_id" indexes by setting the `autoIndexId` option to false when calling `createCollection`. This is not recommended but can give you a slight speed boost on an insert-only collection.

> If you create a collection without an "_id" index, you will never be able replicate the *mongod* it lives on. Replication requires the "_id" index on every collection (it is important that replication can uniquely identify each document in a collection).

Capped collections prior to version 2.2 did not have an "_id" index unless `autoIndexId` was explicitly set to true. If you are working with an "old" capped collection, ensure that your application is populating the "_id" field (most drivers will do this automatically) and then create the "_id" index using `ensureIndex`.

Remember to make the "_id" index unique. Do a practice run before creating the index in production, as unlike other indexes, the "_id" index cannot be dropped once created. Thus, you must get it right the first time! If you do not, you cannot change it without dropping the collection and recreating it.

Time-To-Live Indexes

As mentioned in the previous section, capped collections give you limited control over when their contents are overwritten. If you need a more flexible age-out system, *time-to-live* (TTL) indexes allow you to set a timeout for each document. When a document reaches a preconfigured age, it will be deleted. This type of index is useful for caching problems like session storage.

You can create a TTL index by specifying the `expireAfterSecs` option in the second argument to `ensureIndex`:

```
> // 24-hour timeout
> db.foo.ensureIndex({"lastUpdated" : 1}, {"expireAfterSecs" : 60*60*24})
```

This creates a TTL index on the "lastUpdated" field. If a document's "lastUpdated" field exists and is a date, the document will be removed once the server time is expireAfterSecs seconds ahead of the document's time.

To prevent an active session from being removed, you can update the "lastUpdated" field to the current time whenever there is activity. Once "lastUpdated" is 24 hours old, the document will be removed.

MongoDB sweeps the TTL index once per minute, so you should not depend on to-the-second granularity. You can change the expireAfterSecs using the *collMod* command:

```
> db.runCommand({"collMod" : "someapp.cache", "expireAfterSecs" : 3600})
```

You can have multiple TTL indexes on a given collection. They cannot be compound indexes but can be used like "normal" indexes for the purposes of sorting and query optimization.

Full-Text Indexes

MongoDB has a special type of index for searching for text within documents. In previous chapters, we've queried for strings using exact matches and regular expressions, but these techniques have some limitations. Searching a large block of text for a regular expression is slow and it's tough to take linguistic issues into account (e.g., that "entry" should match "entries"). Full-text indexes give you the ability to search text quickly, as well as provide built-in support for multi-language stemming and stop words.

While all indexes are expensive to create, full-text indexes are particularly heavyweight. Creating a full-text index on a busy collection can overload MongoDB, so adding this type of index should always be done offline or at a time when performance does not matter. You should be wary of creating full-text indexes that will not fit in RAM (unless you have SSDs). See Chapter 18 for more information on creating indexes with minimal impact on your application.

Full-text search will also incur more severe performance penalties on writes than "normal" indexes, since all strings must be split, stemmed, and stored in a few places. Thus, you will tend to see poorer write performance on full-text-indexed collections than on others. It will also slow down data movement if you are sharding: all text must be reindexed when it is migrated to a new shard.

As of this writing, full text indexes are an "experimental" feature, so you must enable them specifically. You can either start MongoDB with the --setParameter textSearchEnabled=true option or set it at runtime by running the *setParameter* command:

```
> db.adminCommand({"setParameter" : 1, "textSearchEnabled" : true})
```

Suppose we use the unofficial Hacker News JSON API to load some recent stories into MongoDB.

To run a search over the text, we first need to create a "`text`" index:

```
> db.hn.ensureIndex({"title" : "text"})
```

Now, to use the index, we must use the *text* command (as of this writing, full text indexes cannot be used with "normal" queries):

```
test> db.runCommand({"text" : "hn", "search" : "ask hn"})
{
    "queryDebugString" : "ask|hn||||||",
    "language" : "english",
    "results" : [
        {
            "score" : 2.25,
            "obj" : {
                "_id" : ObjectId("50dcab296803fa7e4f000011"),
                "title" : "Ask HN: Most valuable skills you have?",
                "url" : "/comments/4974230",
                "id" : 4974230,
                "commentCount" : 37,
                "points" : 31,
                "postedAgo" : "2 hours ago",
                "postedBy" : "bavidar"
            }
        },
        {
            "score" : 0.5625,
            "obj" : {
                "_id" : ObjectId("50dcab296803fa7e4f000001"),
                 "title" : "Show HN: How I turned an old book...",
                 "url" : "http://www.howacarworks.com/about",
                 "id" : 4974055,
                 "commentCount" : 44,
                 "points" : 95,
                 "postedAgo" : "2 hours ago",
                 "postedBy" : "AlexMuir"
            }
        },
        {
            "score" : 0.5555555555555556,
            "obj" : {
                 "_id" : ObjectId("50dcab296803fa7e4f000010"),
                 "title" : "Show HN: ShotBlocker - iOS Screenshot detector...",
                 "url" : "https://github.com/clayallsopp/ShotBlocker",
                 "id" : 4973909,
                 "commentCount" : 10,
                 "points" : 17,
                 "postedAgo" : "3 hours ago",
                 "postedBy" : "10char"
            }
```

```
        }
    ],
    "stats" : {
        "nscanned" : 4,
        "nscannedObjects" : 0,
        "n" : 3,
        "timeMicros" : 89
    },
    "ok" : 1
}
```

The matching documents are returned in order of decreasing relevance: "Ask HN" is first, then two "Show HN" partial matches. The "score" field before each object describes how closely the result matched the query.

As you can see from the results, the search is case insensitive, at least for characters in [a-zA-Z]. Full-text indexes use toLower to lowercase words, which is locale-dependant, so users of other languages may find MongoDB unpredictably case sensitive, depending on how toLower behaves on their character set. Better collation support is in the works.

Full text indexes only index string data: other data types are ignored and not included in the index. Only one full-text index is allowed per collection, but it may contain multiple fields:

```
> db.blobs.ensureIndex({"title" : "text", "desc" : "text", "author" : "text"})
```

This is not like "nomal" multikey indexes where there is an ordering on the keys: each field is given equal consideration. You can control the relative importance MongoDB attaches to each field by specifying a weight:

```
> db.hn.ensureIndex({"title" : "text", "desc" : "text", "author" : "text"},
... {"weights" : {"title" : 3, "author" : 2}})
```

The default weight is 1, and you may use weights from 1 to 1 billion. The weights above would weight "title" fields the most, followed by "author" and then "desc" (not specified in the weight list, so given a default weight of 1).

You cannot change field weights after index creation (without dropping the index and recreating it), so you may want to play with weights on a sample data set before creating the index on your production data.

For some collections, you may not know which fields a document will contain. You can create a full-text index on all string fields in a document by creating an index on "$**": this not only indexes all top-level string fields, but also searches embedded documents and arrays for string fields:

```
> db.blobs.ensureIndex({"$**" : "text"})
```

You can also give "$**" a weight:

```
> db.hn.ensureIndex({"whatever" : "text"},
... {"weights" : {"title" : 3, "author" : 1, "$**" : 2}})
```

"whatever" can be anything since it is not used. As the weights specify that you're indexing all fields, MongoDB does not require you to give a field list.

Search Syntax

By default, MongoDB queries for an OR of all the words: "ask OR hn". This is the most efficient way to perform a full text query, but you can also do exact phrase searches and NOT. To search for the exact phrase "ask hn", you can query for that by including the query in quotes:

```
> db.runCommand({text: "hn", search: "\"ask hn\""})
{
    "queryDebugString" : "ask|hn|||ask hn||",
    "language" : "english",
    "results" : [
        {
            "score" : 2.25,
            "obj" : {
                "_id" : ObjectId("50dcab296803fa7e4f000011"),
                "title" : "Ask HN: Most valuable skills you have?",
                "url" : "/comments/4974230",
                "id" : 4974230,
                "commentCount" : 37,
                "points" : 31,
                "postedAgo" : "2 hours ago",
                "postedBy" : "bavidar"
            }
        }
    ],
    "stats" : {
        "nscanned" : 4,
        "nscannedObjects" : 0,
        "n" : 1,
        "nfound" : 1,
        "timeMicros" : 20392
    },
    "ok" : 1
}
```

This is slower than the OR-type match, since MongoDB first performs an OR match and then post-processes the documents to ensure that they are AND matches, as well.

You can also make part of a query literal and part not:

```
> db.runCommand({text: "hn", search: "\"ask hn\" ipod"})
```

This will search for exactly "ask hn" and, optionally, "ipod".

You can also search for *not* including a certain string by using "-":

```
> db.runCommand({text: "hn", search: "-startup vc"})
```

This will return results that match "vc" and don't include the word "startup".

Full-Text Search Optimization

There are a couple ways to optimize full text searches. If you can first narrow your search results by other criteria, you can create a compound index with a prefix of the other criteria and then the full-text fields:

```
> db.blog.ensureIndex({"date" : 1, "post" : "text"})
```

This is referred to as *partitioning* the full-text index, as it breaks it into several smaller trees based on "date" (in the example above). This makes full-text searches for a certain date much faster.

You can also use a postfix of other criteria to cover queries with the index. For example, if we were only returning the "author" and "post" fields, we could create a compound index on both:

```
> db.blog.ensureIndex({"post" : "text", "author" : 1})
```

These prefix and postfix forms can be combined:

```
> db.blog.ensureIndex({"date" : 1, "post" : "text", "author" : 1})
```

You cannot use a multikey field for any of the prefix or postfix index fields.

Creating a full-text index automatically enables the usePowerOf2Sizes option on the collection, which controls how space is allocated. Do not disable this option, since it should improve writes speed.

Searching in Other Languages

When a document is inserted (or the index is first created), MongoDB looks at the indexes fields and *stems* each word, reducing it to an essential unit. However, different languages stem words in different ways, so you must specify what language the index or document is. Thus, text-type indexes allow a "default_language" option to be specified, which defaults to "english" but can be set to a number of other languages (see the online documentation for an up-to-date list).

For example, to create a French-language index, we could say:

```
> db.users.ensureIndex({"profil" : "text", "intérêts" : "text"},
... {"default_language" : "french"})
```

Then French would be used for stemming, unless otherwise specified. You can, on a per-document basis, specify another stemming language by having a "language" field that describes the document's language:

```
> db.users.insert({"username" : "swedishChef",
... "profile" : "Bork de bork", language : "swedish"})
```

Geospatial Indexing

MongoDB has a few types of geospatial indexes. The most commonly used ones are `2dsphere`, for surface-of-the-earth-type maps, and `2d`, for flat maps (and time series data).

`2dsphere` allows you to specify points, lines, and polygons in GeoJSON format. A point is given by a two-element array, representing [*longitude*, *latitude*]:

```
{
    "name" : "New York City",
    "loc" : {
        "type" : "Point",
        "coordinates" : [50, 2]
    }
}
```

A line is given by an array of points:

```
{
    "name" : "Hudson River",
    "loc" : {
        "type" : "Line",
        "coordinates" : [[0,1], [0,2], [1,2]]
    }
}
```

A polygon is specified the same way a line is (an array of points), but with a different `"type"`:

```
{
    "name" : "New England",
    "loc" : {
        "type" : "Polygon",
        "coordinates" : [[0,1], [0,2], [1,2]]
    }
}
```

The `"loc"` field can be called anything, but the field names within its subobject are specified by GeoJSON and cannot be changed.

You can create a geospatial index using the `"2dsphere"` type with `ensureIndex`:

```
> db.world.ensureIndex({"loc" : "2dsphere"})
```

Types of Geospatial Queries

There are several types of geospatial query that you can perform: intersection, within, and nearness. To query, specify what you're looking for as a GeoJSON object that looks like `{"$geometry" : geoJsonDesc}`.

For example, you can find documents that intersect the query's location using the "$geoIntersects" operator:

```
> var eastVillage = {
... "type" : "Polygon",
... "coordinates" : [
...     [-73.9917900, 40.7264100],
...     [-73.9917900, 40.7321400],
...     [-73.9829300, 40.7321400],
...     [-73.9829300, 40.7264100]
... ]}
> db.open.street.map.find(
... {"loc" : {"$geoIntersects" : {"$geometry" : eastVillage}}})
```

This would find all point-, line-, and polygon-containing documents that had a point in the East Village.

You can use "$within" to query for things that are completely contained in an area, for instance: "What restaurants are in the East Village?"

```
> db.open.street.map.find({"loc" : {"$within" : {"$geometry" : eastVillage}}})
```

Unlike our first query, this would not return things that merely pass through the East Village (such as streets) or partially overlap it (such as a polygon describing Manhattan).

Finally, you can query for nearby locations with "$near":

```
> db.open.street.map.find({"loc" : {"$near" : {"$geometry" : eastVillage}}})
```

Note that $near is the only geospatial operator that implies a sort: results from "$near" are always returned in distance from closest to farthest.

One interesting thing about geospatial queries is that you do not need a geospatial index to use "$geoIntersects" or "$within" ("$near" requires an index). However, having an index on your geo field will speed up queries significantly, so it's usually recommended.

Compound Geospatial Indexes

As with other types of indexes, you can combine geospatial indexes with other fields to optimize more complex queries. A possible query mentioned above was: "What restaurants are in the East Village?" Using only a geospatial index, we could narrow the field to everything in the East Village, but narrowing it down to only "restaurants" or "pizza" would require another field in the index:

```
> db.open.street.map.ensureIndex({"tags" : 1, "location" : "2dsphere"})
```

Then we can quickly find a pizza place in the East Village:

```
> db.open.street.map.find({"loc" : {"$within" : {"$geometry" : eastVillage}},
... "tags" : "pizza"})
```

We can have the "vanilla" index field either before or after the "2dsphere" field, depending on whether we'd like to filter by the vanilla field or the location first. Choose whichever will filter out more results as the first index term.

2D Indexes

For non-spherical maps (video game maps, time series data, etc.) you can use a "2d" index, instead of "2dsphere":

```
> db.hyrule.ensureIndex({"tile" : "2d"})
```

"2d" indexes assume a perfectly flat surface, instead of a sphere. Thus, "2d" indexes should not be used with spheres unless you don't mind massive distortion around the poles.

Documents should use a two-element array for their 2d indexed field (which is *not* a GeoJSON document, as of this writing). A sample document might look like this:

```
{
    "name" : "Water Temple",
    "tile" : [ 32, 22 ]
}
```

"2d" indexes can only index points. You can store an array of points, but it will be stored as exactly that: an array of points, not a line. This is an important distinction for "$within" queries, in particular. If you store a street as an array of points, the document will match $within if one of those points is within the given shape. However, the line created by those points might not be wholly contained in the shape.

By default, geospatial indexing assumes that your values are going to range from -180 to 180. If you are expecting larger or smaller bounds, you can specify what the minimum and maximum values will be as options to ensureIndex:

```
> db.star.trek.ensureIndex({"light-years" : "2d"}, {"min" : -1000, "max" : 1000})
```

This will create a spatial index calibrated for a 2,000 × 2,000 square.

"2d" predates "2dsphere", so querying is a bit simpler. You can only use "$near" or "$within", and neither have a "$geometry" subobject. You just specify the coordinates:

```
> db.hyrule.find({"tile" : {"$near" : [20, 21]}})
```

This finds all of the documents in the *hyrule* collection, in order by distance from the point (20, 21). A default limit of 100 documents is applied if no limit is specified. If you don't need that many results, you should set a limit to conserve server resources. For example, the following code returns the 10 documents nearest to (20, 21):

```
> db.hyrule.find({"tile" : {"$near" : [20, 21]}}).limit(10)
```

"$within" can query for all points within a rectangle, circle, or polygon. To use a rectangle, use the "$box" option:

```
> db.hyrule.find({"tile" : {"$within" : {"$box" : [[10, 20], [15, 30]]}}})
```

"$box" takes a two-element array: the first element specifies the coordinates of the lower-left corner; the second element the upper right.

Similarly, you can find all points within a circle with "$center", which takes an array with the center point and then a radius:

```
> db.hyrule.find({"tile" : {"$within" : {"$center" : [[12, 25], 5]}}})
```

Finally, you can specify a polygon as an array of points.

```
> db.hyrule.find(
... {"tile" : {"$within" : {"$polygon" : [[0, 20], [10, 0], [-10, 0]]}}})
```

This example would locate all documents containing points within the given triangle. The final point in the list will be "connected to" the first point to form the polygon.

Storing Files with GridFS

GridFS is a mechanism for storing large binary files in MongoDB. There are several reasons why you might consider using GridFS for file storage:

- Using GridFS can simplify your stack. If you're already using MongoDB, you might be able to use GridFS instead of a separate tool for file storage.
- GridFS will leverage any existing replication or autosharding that you've set up for MongoDB, so getting failover and scale-out for file storage is easier.
- GridFS can alleviate some of the issues that certain filesystems can exhibit when being used to store user uploads. For example, GridFS does not have issues with storing large numbers of files in the same directory.
- You can get great disk locality with GridFS, because MongoDB allocates data files in 2 GB chunks.

There are some downsides, too:

- Slower performance: accessing files from MongoDB will not be as fast as going directly through the filesystem.
- You can only modify documents by deleting them and resaving the whole thing. MongoDB stores files as multiple documents so it cannot lock all of the chunks in a file at the same time.

GridFS is generally best when you have large files you'll be accessing in a sequential fashion that won't be changing much.

Getting Started with GridFS: mongofiles

The easiest way to try out GridFS is by using the `mongofiles` utility. `mongofiles` is included with all MongoDB distributions and can be used to upload, download, list, search for, or delete files in GridFS.

As with any of the other command-line tools, run `mongofiles --help` to see the options available for `mongofiles`.

The following session shows how to use `mongofiles` to upload a file from the filesystem to GridFS, list all of the files in GridFS, and download a file that we've previously uploaded:

```
$ echo "Hello, world" > foo.txt
$ ./mongofiles put foo.txt
connected to: 127.0.0.1
added file: { _id: ObjectId('4c0d2a6c3052c25545139b88'),
              filename: "foo.txt", length: 13, chunkSize: 262144,
              uploadDate: new Date(1275931244818),
              md5: "a7966bf58e23583c9a5a4059383ff850" }
done!
$ ./mongofiles list
connected to: 127.0.0.1
foo.txt 13
$ rm foo.txt
$ ./mongofiles get foo.txt
connected to: 127.0.0.1
done write to: foo.txt
$ cat foo.txt
Hello, world
```

In the previous example, we perform three basic operations using `mongofiles`: `put`, `list`, and `get`. The `put` operation takes a file in the filesystem and adds it to GridFS; `list` will list any files that have been added to GridFS; and `get` does the inverse of `put`: it takes a file from GridFS and writes it to the filesystem. `mongofiles` also supports two other operations: `search` for finding files in GridFS by filename and `delete` for removing a file from GridFS.

Working with GridFS from the MongoDB Drivers

All the client libraries have GridFS APIs. For example, with PyMongo (the Python driver for MongoDB) you can perform the same series of operations as we did with `mongofiles`:

```
>>> from pymongo import Connection
>>> import gridfs
>>> db = Connection().test
>>> fs = gridfs.GridFS(db)
>>> file_id = fs.put("Hello, world", filename="foo.txt")
>>> fs.list()
```

```
[u'foo.txt']
>>> fs.get(file_id).read()
'Hello, world'
```

The API for working with GridFS from PyMongo is very similar to that of `mongofiles`: we can easily perform the basic `put`, `get`, and `list` operations. Almost all the MongoDB drivers follow this basic pattern for working with GridFS, while often exposing more advanced functionality as well. For driver-specific information on GridFS, please check out the documentation for the specific driver you're using.

Under the Hood

GridFS is a lightweight specification for storing files that is built on top of normal MongoDB documents. The MongoDB server actually does almost nothing to "special-case" the handling of GridFS requests; all the work is handled by the client-side drivers and tools.

The basic idea behind GridFS is that we can store large files by splitting them up into *chunks* and storing each chunk as a separate document. Because MongoDB supports storing binary data in documents, we can keep storage overhead for chunks to a minimum. In addition to storing each chunk of a file, we store a single document that groups the chunks together and contains metadata about the file.

The chunks for GridFS are stored in their own collection. By default chunks will use the collection *fs.chunks*, but this can be overridden. Within the chunks collection the structure of the individual documents is pretty simple:

```
{
    "_id" : ObjectId("..."),
    "n" : 0,
    "data" : BinData("..."),
    "files_id" : ObjectId("...")
}
```

Like any other MongoDB document, the chunk has its own unique `"_id"`. In addition, it has a couple of other keys:

`"files_id"`
: The `"_id"` of the file document that contains the metadata for this chunk.

`"n"`
: The chunk's position in the file, relative to the other chunks.

`"data"`
: The bytes in this chunk of the file.

The metadata for each file is stored in a separate collection, which defaults to *fs.files*. Each document in the files collection represents a single file in GridFS and can contain any custom metadata that should be associated with that file. In addition to any user-defined keys, there are a couple of keys that are mandated by the GridFS specification:

`"_id"`
: A unique id for the file—this is what will be stored in each chunk as the value for the `"files_id"` key.

`"length"`
: The total number of bytes making up the content of the file.

`"chunkSize"`
: The size of each chunk comprising the file, in bytes. The default is 256K, but this can be adjusted if needed.

`"uploadDate"`
: A timestamp representing when this file was stored in GridFS.

`"md5"`
: An md5 checksum of this file's contents, generated on the server side.

Of all of the required keys, perhaps the most interesting (or least self-explanatory) is `"md5"`. The value for `"md5"` is generated by the MongoDB server using the `filemd5` command, which computes the md5 checksum of the uploaded chunks. This means that users can check the value of the `"md5"` key to ensure that a file was uploaded correctly.

As mentioned above, you are not limited to the required fields in *fs.files*: feel free to keep any other file metadata in this collection as well. You might want to keep information such as download count, mimetype, or user rating with a file's metadata.

Once you understand the underlying GridFS specification, it becomes trivial to implement features that the driver you're using might not provide helpers for. For example, you can use the `distinct` command to get a list of unique filenames stored in GridFS:

```
> db.fs.files.distinct("filename")
[ "foo.txt" , "bar.txt" , "baz.txt" ]
```

This allows your application a great deal of flexibility in loading and collecting information about files.

CHAPTER 7

Aggregation

Once you have data stored in MongoDB, you may want to do more than just retrieve it; you may want to analyze and crunch it in interesting ways. This chapter introduces the aggregation tools MongoDB provides:

- The aggregation framework
- MapReduce support
- Several simple aggregation commands: count, distinct, and group

The Aggregation Framework

The aggregation framework lets you transform and combine documents in a collection. Basically, you build a pipeline that processes a stream of documents through several building blocks: filtering, projecting, grouping, sorting, limiting, and skipping.

For example, if you had a collection of magazine articles, you might want find out who your most prolific authors were. Assuming that each article is stored as a document in MongoDB, you could create a pipeline with several steps:

1. Project the authors out of each article document.
2. Group the authors by name, counting the number of occurrences.
3. Sort the authors by the occurrence count, descending.
4. Limit results to the first five.

Each of these steps maps to a aggregation framework operator:

1. `{"$project" : {"author" : 1}}`

   This projects the author field in each document.

The syntax is similar to the field selector used in querying: you can select fields to project by specifying "*fieldname*" : 1 or exclude fields with "*fieldname*" : 0. After this operation, each document in the results looks like: {"_id" : *id*, "author" : "*authorName*"}. These resulting documents only exists in memory and are not written to disk anywhere.

2. {"$group" : {"_id" : "$author", "count" : {"$sum" : 1}}}

   This groups the authors by name and increments "count" for each document an author appears in.

   First, we specify the field we want to group by, which is "author". This is indicated by the "_id" : "$author" field. You can picture this as: after the group there will be one result document per author, so "author" becomes the unique identifier ("_id").

   The second field means to add 1 to a "count" field for each document in the group. Note that the incoming documents do not have a "count" field; this is a new field created by the "$group".

   At the end of this step, each document in the results looks like: {"_id" : "*authorName*", "count" : *articleCount*}.

3. {"$sort" : {"count" : -1}}

   This reorders the result documents by the "count" field from greatest to least.

4. {"$limit" : 5}

   This limits the result set to the first five result documents.

To actually run this in MongoDB, pass each operation to the aggregate() function:

```
> db.articles.aggregate({"$project" : {"author" : 1}},
... {"$group" : {"_id" : "$author", "count" : {"$sum" : 1}}},
... {"$sort" : {"count" : -1}},
... {"$limit" : 5})
{
    "result" : [
        {
            "_id" : "R. L. Stine",
            "count" : 430
        },
        {
            "_id" : "Edgar Wallace",
            "count" : 175
        },
        {
            "_id" : "Nora Roberts",
            "count" : 145
        },
        {
            "_id" : "Erle Stanley Gardner",
```

```
                "count" : 140
            },
            {
                "_id" : "Agatha Christie",
                "count" : 85
            }
        ],
        "ok" : 1
    }
```

`aggregate()` returns an array of result documents, showing the five most prolific authors.

> To debug a pipeline that's giving unexpected results, run the aggregation with just the first pipeline operator. If that gives the expected result, add the next. In the previous example, you'd first try aggregating with just the `"$project"`; if that works, add the `"$group"`; if that works, add the `"$sort"`; and finally add the `"$limit"`. This can help you narrow down which operator is causing issues.

As of this writing, the aggregation framework cannot write to collections, so all results must be returned to the client. Thus, aggregation results are limited to 16 MB of data (the maximum response size).

Pipeline Operations

Each operator receives a stream of documents, does some type of transformation on these documents, and then passes on the results of the transformation. If it is the last pipeline operator, these results are returned to the client. Otherwise, the results are streamed to the next operator as input.

Operators can be combined in any order and repeated as many times as necessary. For example, you could `"$match"`, `"$group"`, and then `"$match"` again with different criteria.

$match

`$match` filters documents so that you can run an aggregation on a subset of documents. For example, if you only want to find out stats about users in Oregon, you might add a `"$match"` expression such as `{$match : {"state" : "OR"}}`. `"$match"` can use all of the usual query operators (`"$gt"`, `"$lt"`, `"$in"`, etc.). One notable exception is that you cannot use geospatial operators in a `"$match"`.

Generally, good practice is to put `"$match"` expressions as early as possible in the pipeline. This has two benefits: it allows you to filter out unneeded documents quickly (lightening the work the pipeline has to perform) and the query can use indexes if it is run before any projections or groupings.

$project

Projection is much more powerful in the pipeline than it is in the "normal" query language. "`$project`" allows you to extract fields from subdocuments, rename fields, and perform interesting operations on them.

The simplest operation "`$project`" can perform is simply selecting fields from your incoming documents. To include or exclude a field, use the same syntax you would in the second argument of a query. The following would return a result document containing one field, "`author`", for each document in the original collection:

```
> db.articles.aggregate({"$project" : {"author" : 1, "_id" : 0}})
```

By default, "`_id`" is always returned if it exists in the incoming document (some pipeline operators remove the "`_id`" or it can be removed in a former projection). You can exclude it as above. Inclusion and exclusion rules in general work the same way that they do for "normal" queries.

You can also rename the projected field. For example, if you wanted to return the "`_id`" of each user as "`userId`", you could do:

```
> db.users.aggregate({"$project" : {"userId" : "$_id", "_id" : 0}})
{
    "result" : [
        {
            "userId" : ObjectId("50e4b32427b160e099ddbee7")
        },
        {
            "userId" : ObjectId("50e4b32527b160e099ddbee8")
        }
        ...
    ],
    "ok" : 1
}
```

The "`$fieldname`" syntax is used to refer to *fieldname*'s value in the aggregation framework. For example, "`$age`" would be replaced with the contents of the age field (and probably be a number, not a string) and "`$tags.3`" would be replaced with the fourth element of the tags array. Thus, "`$_id`" is replaced by the "`_id`" field of each document coming through the pipeline.

Note that you must specifically exclude "`_id`" to prevent it from returning the field twice, once labeled "`userId`" and once labelled "`_id`". You can use this technique to make multiple copies of a field for later use in a "`$group`", say.

MongoDB does not track field name history when fields are renamed. Thus, if you had an index on "originalFieldname", aggregation would be unable to use the index for the sort below, even though to a human eye it is obvious that "newFieldname" is the same field as "originalFieldname":

```
> db.articles.aggregate({"$project" : {"newFieldname" : "$originalFieldname"}},
... {"$sort" : {"newFieldname" : 1}})
```

Thus, try to utilize indexes before changing the names of fields.

Pipeline expressions

The simplest "$project" expressions are inclusion, exclusion, and field names ("$*fieldname*"). However, there are several other, more powerful options. You can also use *expressions*, which allow you to combine multiple literals and variables into a single value.

There are several expressions available with aggregation which you can combine and nest to any depth to create more complex expressions.

Mathematical expressions. Arithmetic expressions let you manipulate numeric values. You generally use these expressions by specifying an array of numbers to operate on. For example, the following expression would sum the "salary" and "bonus" fields:

```
> db.employees.aggregate(
... {
...     "$project" : {
...         "totalPay" : {
...             "$add" : ["$salary", "$bonus"]
...         }
...     }
... })
```

If we have a more complex expression, it can be nested. Suppose that we want to subtract 401k contributions from this total. We can add a "$subtract" expression:

```
> db.employees.aggregate(
... {
...     "$project" : {
...         "totalPay" : {
...             "$subtract" : [{"$add" : ["$salary", "$bonus"]}, "$401k"]
...         }
...     }
... })
```

Expressions may be nested arbitrarily deep.

Here's the syntax for each operator:

"$add" : [*expr1*[, *expr2*, ..., *exprN*]]
: Takes one or more expressions and adds them together.

`"$subtract" : [expr1, expr2]`
: Takes two expressions and subtracts the second from the first.

`"$multiply" : [expr1[, expr2, ..., exprN]]`
: Takes one or more expressions and multiplies them together.

`"$divide" : [expr1, expr2]`
: Takes two expressions and divides the first by the second.

`"$mod" : [expr1, expr2]`
: Takes two expressions and returns the remainder of dividing the first by the second.

Date expressions. Many aggregations are time-based: What was happening last week? Last month? Over the last year? Thus, aggregation has a set of expressions that can be used to extract date information in more useful ways: `"$year"`, `"$month"`, `"$week"`, `"$dayOfMonth"`, `"$dayOfWeek"`, `"$dayOfYear"`, `"$hour"`, `"$minute"`, and `"$second"`. You can only use date operations on fields stored with the date type, not numeric types.

Each of these date types is basically the same: it takes a date expression and returns a number. This would return the month that each employee was hired in:

```
> db.employees.aggregate(
... {
...     "$project" : {
...         "hiredIn" : {"$month" : "$hireDate"}
...     }
... })
```

You can also use literal dates. This would calculate many years each employee had worked at the company:

```
> db.employees.aggregate(
... {
...     "$project" : {
...         "tenure" : {
...             "$subtract" : [{"$year" : new Date()}, {"$year" : "$hireDate"}]
...         }
...     }
... })
```

String expressions. There are a few basic string operations you can do as well. Their signatures are:

`"$substr" : [expr, startOffset, numToReturn]`
: This returns a substring of the first argument, starting at the `startOffset`-th byte and including the next `numToReturn` bytes (note that this is measured in bytes, not characters, so multibytes encodings will have to be careful of this). `expr` must evaluate to a string.

`"$concat" : [expr1[, expr2, ..., exprN]]`
: Concatenates each string expression (or string) given.

`"$toLower" : expr`
: Returns the string in lower case. *expr* must evaluate to a string.

`"$toUpper" : expr`
: Returns the string in upper case. *expr* must evaluate to a string.

Case-affecting operations are only guaranteed to work on characters from the Roman alphabet.

Here is an example that generates email addresses of the format *j.doe@example.com*. It extracts the first initial and concatenates it with several constant strings and the `"lastName"` field:

```
> db.employees.aggregate(
... {
...     "$project" : {
...         "email" : {
...             "$concat" : [
...                 {"$substr" : ["$firstName", 0, 1]},
...                 ".",
...                 "$lastName",
...                 "@example.com"
...             ]
...         }
...     }
... })
```

Logical expressions. There are several operators that you can use for control statements.

There are several comparison expressions:

`"$cmp" : [expr1, expr2]`
: Compare *expr1* and *expr2*. Return 0 if the two expressions are equal, a negative number if *expr1* is less than *expr2*, and a positive number if *expr2* is less than *expr1*.

`"$strcasecmp" : [string1, string2]`
: Case insensitive comparison between *string1* and *string2*. Only works for Roman characters.

`"$eq"/"$ne"/"$gt"/"$gte"/"$lt"/"$lte" : [expr1, expr2]`
: Perform the comparison on *expr1* and *expr2*, returning whether it evaluates to true or false.

There are a few boolean expressions:

`"$and" : [expr1[, expr2, ..., exprN]]`
: Returns true if all expressions are true.

`"$or" : [expr1[, expr2, ..., exprN]]`
: Returns true if at least one expression is true.

`"$not" : expr`
: Returns the boolean opposite of *expr*.

Finally, there are two control statements:

`"$cond" : [booleanExpr, trueExpr, falseExpr]`
: If *booleanExpr* evaluates to `true`, *trueExpr* is returned; otherwise *falseExpr* is returned.

`"$ifNull" : [expr, replacementExpr]`
: If *expr* is `null` this returns *replacementExpr*; otherwise it returns *expr*.

These operators let you include more complex logic in your aggregations by following different "code paths" depending on the shape of your data.

Pipelines are particular about getting properly formed input, so these operators can be invaluable in filling in default values. The arithmetic operators will complain about non-numeric values, date operators will complain about non-dates, string operators will complain about non-strings, and everything will complain about missing fields. If your data set is inconsistent, you can use this conditionals to detect missing values and populate them.

A projection example

Suppose a professor wanted to generate grades using a somewhat complex calculation: the students are graded 10% on attendance, 30% on quizzes, and 60% on tests (unless the student is a teacher's pet, in which case the grade is set to 100). We could express these rules as follows:

```
> db.students.aggregate(
... {
...     "$project" : {
...         "grade" : {
...             "$cond" : [
...                 "$teachersPet",
...                 100, // if
...                 {    // else
...                     "$add" : [
...                         {"$multiply" : [.1, "$attendanceAvg"]},
...                         {"$multiply" : [.3, "$quizzAvg"]},
...                         {"$multiply" : [.6, "$testAvg"]}
...                     ]
...                 }
...             ]
...         }
...     }
... })
```

$group

Grouping allows you to group documents based on certain fields and combine their values. Some examples of groupings:

- If we had per-minute measurements and we wanted to find the average humidity per day, we would group by the "day" field.
- If we had a collection of students and we wanted to organize student into groups based on grade, we could group by their "grade" field.
- If we had a collection of users and we wanted to see how many users we had by city, we could group by both the "state" and "city" fields, creating one group per city/state pair. We wouldn't want to just group by city, as there are many cities with identical names in different states.

When you choose a field or fields to group by, you pass it to the "$group" function as the group's "_id" field. Thus, for the examples above, you'd have:

- `{"$group" : {"_id" : "$day"}}`
- `{"$group" : {"_id" : "$grade"}}`
- `{"$group" : {"_id" : {"state" : "$state", "city" : "$city"}}}`

As these stand now, the result would be a document for each group with a single field: the grouping key. For example, the grading result might look something like this: `{"result" : [{"_id" : "A+"}, {"_id" : "A"}, {"_id" : "A-"}, ..., {"_id" : "F"}], "ok" : 1}`. This does a nice job of getting all of the distinct values for a field, but all of the examples involve using these groups to calculate things. Thus, you can add fields that use grouping operators to make computations based on the documents in each group.

Grouping operators

These grouping operators allow you to compute results for each group. In the example in "The Aggregation Framework" on page 127, we saw "$sum" used as a grouping operator: it added 1 to a total for each document in the group.

Arithmetic operators. There are two operators that can be used to compute numeric values from fields: "$sum" and "$average".

`"$sum" : value`

This adds *value* for each document and returns the result. Note that, although the example above used a literal (1), this can also take more complex values. For example, if we had a collection of sales made in a variety of countries, this would find the total revenue by country:

```
> db.sales.aggregate(
... {
...     "$group" : {
...         "_id" : "$country",
...         "totalRevenue" : {"$sum" : "$revenue"}
...     }
... })
```

`"$avg" : value`
: Returns an average of all input values seen during the group.

For example, this would return the average revenue per country, plus the number of sales made:

```
> db.sales.aggregate(
... {
...     "$group" : {
...         "_id" : "$country",
...         "totalRevenue" : {"$average" : "$revenue"},
...         "numSales" : {"$sum" : 1}
...     }
... })
```

Extreme operators. There are four operators to get the "edges" of a data set:

`"$max" : expr`
: Returns the greatest value of any of the inputs.

`"$min" : expr`
: Returns the smallest value of any of the inputs.

`"$first" : expr`
: This returns the first value seen by group, ignoring subsequent values. This is only sensible to use when you know the order that the data is being processed in: that is, after a sort.

`"$last" : expr`
: This is the opposite of the previous; it returns the last value seen by the group.

`"$max"` and `"$min"` look through each document and find the extreme values. Thus, these operators work well when you do not have sorted data and are a bit wasteful when data is sorted. For example, suppose that we had a set of student scores on a test. We could find the outliers in each grade as follows:

```
> db.scores.aggregate(
... {
...     "$group" : {
...         "_id" : "$grade",
...         "lowestScore" : {"$min" : "$score"},
...         "highestScore" : {"$max" : "$score"}
```

```
...     }
... })
```

Alternatively, "$first" and "$last" return useful results when your data is sorted by the fields you are looking for. For example, to get the same result as before we could do:

```
> db.scores.aggregate(
... {
...     "$sort" : {"score" : 1}
... },
... {
...     "$group" : {
...         "_id" : "$grade",
...         "lowestScore" : {"$first" : "$score"},
...         "highestScore" : {"$last" : "$score"}
...     }
... })
```

If your data is already sorted, `$first` and `$last` will be more efficient than `$min` and `$max`. If your data is not going to be sorted, `$min` and `$max` are more efficient than sorting your data and then running `$first` and `$last`.

Array operators. There are two operators available for array manipulation:

`"$addToSet" : expr`
: Keeps an array of values seen so far and, if *expr* is not present in the array, adds it. Each value appears at most once in the resulting array and ordering is not guaranteed.

`"$push" : expr`
: Indiscriminately adds each value seen to the array. Returns an array of all values.

Grouping behavior

"$group" is one of the two "roadblock" operators that cannot be handled in the streaming fashion described earlier. While most operators can continuously process documents as they arrive, "$group" must collect all documents, split them into groups, then send them to the next operator in the pipeline. This means that, with sharding, "$group" will first be run on each shard and then the individual shards' groups will be sent to the *mongos* to do the final grouping and the remainder of the pipeline will be run on the *mongos* (not the shards).

$unwind

Unwinding turns each field of an array into a separate document. For example, if we had a blog with comments, we could use unwind to turn each comment into its own "document":

```
> db.blog.findOne()
{
    "_id" : ObjectId("50eeffc4c82a5271290530be"),
    "author" : "k",
    "post" : "Hello, world!",
    "comments" : [
        {
            "author" : "mark",
            "date" : ISODate("2013-01-10T17:52:04.148Z"),
            "text" : "Nice post"
        },
        {
            "author" : "bill",
            "date" : ISODate("2013-01-10T17:52:04.148Z"),
            "text" : "I agree"
        }
    ]
}
> db.blog.aggregate({"$unwind" : "$comments"})
{
    "results" :
        {
            "_id" : ObjectId("50eeffc4c82a5271290530be"),
            "author" : "k",
            "post" : "Hello, world!",
            "comments" : {
                "author" : "mark",
                "date" : ISODate("2013-01-10T17:52:04.148Z"),
                "text" : "Nice post"
            }
        },
        {
            "_id" : ObjectId("50eeffc4c82a5271290530be"),
            "author" : "k",
            "post" : "Hello, world!",
            "comments" : {
                "author" : "bill",
                "date" : ISODate("2013-01-10T17:52:04.148Z"),
                "text" : "I agree"
            }
        }
    ],
    "ok" : 1
}
```

This is particularly useful if you want to return certain subdocuments from a query: `"$unwind"` the subdocuments and then `"$match"` the ones you want. For example, it is impossible in the normal query language to return all comments by a certain user and *only* those comments, not the posts they commented on. However, by projecting, unwinding, and matching, it becomes trivial:

```
> db.blog.aggregate({"$project" : {"comments" : "$comments"}},
... {"$unwind" : "$comments"},
... {"$match" : {"comments.author" : "Mark"}})
```

You might want to do a final projection to format the output more nicely, as all of the comments will still be in a `"comments"` subdocument.

$sort

You can sort by any field or fields, using the same syntax you would with the "normal" query language. If you are sorting a non-trivial number of documents, it is highly recommended that you do the sort at the beginning of the pipeline and have an index it can use. Otherwise, the sort may be slow and take a lot of memory.

You can use both existing fields and projected fields in a sort:

```
> db.employees.aggregate(
... {
...     "$project" : {
...         "compensation" : {
...             "$add" : ["$salary", "$bonus"]
...         },
...         "name" : 1
...     }
... },
... {
...     "$sort" : {"compensation" : -1, "name" : 1}
... })
```

This example would sort employees by compensation, from highest to lowest, and then name from A-Z.

Possible sorts are 1 (for ascending) and −1 (for descending).

`"$sort"` is another roadblock operation, like `"$group"` earlier. `"$sort"` must collect all documents to properly sort them and, with sharding, sends the individual shards' sorted results to the *mongos* for further processing.

$limit

`$limit` takes a number, *n*, and returns the first *n* resulting documents.

$skip

`$skip` takes a number, *n*, and discards the first *n* documents from the result set. As with "normal" querying, it isn't efficient for large skips, as it must find all of the matches that must be skipped and then discard them.

Using Pipelines

Attempt to filter out as many documents (and as many fields from the documents) as possible at the beginning of your pipeline before hitting any `"$project"`, `"$group"`, or `"$unwind"` operations. Once the pipeline isn't using the data directly from the collection, indexes can no longer be used to help filter and sort. The aggregation pipeline will attempt to reorder operations for you, if possible, to be able to use indexes.

MongoDB won't allow a single aggregation to use more than a fraction of the system's memory: if it calculates that an aggregation has used more than 20% of the memory, the aggregation will simply error out. Allowing output to be piped to a collection (which would minimize the amount of memory required) is planned for the future.

If you can quickly whittle down the result set size with a selective `"$match"`, you can use the pipeline for real-time aggregations. As pipelines need to include more documents and become more complex, it is less likely that you'll be able to get realtime results from them.

MapReduce

MapReduce is a powerful and flexible tool for aggregating data. It can solve some problems that are too complex to express using the aggregation framework's query language. MapReduce uses JavaScript as its "query language" so it can express arbitrarily complex logic. However, this power comes at a price: MapReduce tends to be fairly slow and should not be used for real-time data analysis.

MapReduce can be easily parallelized across multiple servers. It splits up a problem, sends chunks of it to different machines, and lets each machine solve its part of the problem. When all the machines are finished, they merge all the pieces of the solution back into a full solution.

MapReduce has a couple of steps. It starts with the map step, which *maps* an operation onto every document in a collection. That operation could be either "do nothing" or "emit these keys with *X* values." There is then an intermediary stage called the shuffle step: keys are grouped and lists of emitted values are created for each key. The reduce takes this list of values and *reduces* it to a single element. This element is returned to the shuffle step until each key has a list containing a single value: the result.

We'll go through a couple examples because MapReduce is an incredibly useful and powerful, but also somewhat complex, tool.

Example 1: Finding All Keys in a Collection

Using MapReduce for this problem might be overkill, but it is a good way to get familiar with how MapReduce works. If you already understand MapReduce, feel free to skip ahead to the last part of this section, where we cover MongoDB-specific MapReduce considerations.

MongoDB assumes that your schema is dynamic, so it does not keep track of the keys in each document. The best way, in general, to find all the keys across all the documents in a collection is to use MapReduce. In this example, we'll also get a count of how many times each key appears in the collection. This example doesn't include keys for embedded documents, but it would be a simple addition to the `map` function to do so.

For the mapping step, we want to get every key of every document in the collection. The `map` function uses a special function to "return" values that we want to process later: `emit`. `emit` gives MapReduce a key (like the one used by `group` earlier) and a value. In this case, we emit a count of how many times a given key appeared in the document (once: `{count : 1}`). We want a separate count for each key, so we'll call emit for every key in the document. `this` is a reference to the current document we are mapping:

```
> map = function() {
... for (var key in this) {
...     emit(key, {count : 1});
... }};
```

Now we have a ton of little `{count : 1}` documents floating around, each associated with a key from the collection. An array of one or more of these `{count : 1}` documents will be passed to the `reduce` function. The `reduce` function is passed two arguments: `key`, which is the first argument from `emit`, and an array of one or more `{count : 1}` documents that were emitted for that key:

```
> reduce = function(key, emits) {
... total = 0;
... for (var i in emits) {
...     total += emits[i].count;
... }
... return {"count" : total};
... }
```

`reduce` must be able to be called repeatedly on results from either the map phase or previous reduce phases. Therefore, `reduce` must return a document that can be re-sent to `reduce` as an element of its second argument. For example, say we have the key `x` mapped to three documents: `{count : 1, id : 1}`, `{count : 1, id : 2}`, and `{count : 1, id : 3}`. (The ID keys are just for identification purposes.) MongoDB might call `reduce` in the following pattern:

```
> r1 = reduce("x", [{count : 1, id : 1}, {count : 1, id : 2}])
{count : 2}
> r2 = reduce("x", [{count : 1, id : 3}])
{count : 1}
> reduce("x", [r1, r2])
{count : 3}
```

You cannot depend on the second argument always holding one of the initial documents (`{count : 1}` in this case) or being a certain length. `reduce` should be able to be run on any combination of `emit` documents and `reduce` return values.

Altogether, this MapReduce function would look like this:

```
> mr = db.runCommand({"mapreduce" : "foo", "map" : map, "reduce" : reduce})
{
    "result" : "tmp.mr.mapreduce_1266787811_1",
    "timeMillis" : 12,
    "counts" : {
        "input" : 6
        "emit" : 14
        "output" : 5
    },
    "ok" : true
}
```

The document MapReduce returns gives you a bunch of metainformation about the operation:

`"result" : "tmp.mr.mapreduce_1266787811_1"`
: This is the name of the collection the MapReduce results were stored in. This is a temporary collection that will be deleted when the connection that did the MapReduce is closed. We will go over how to specify a nicer name and make the collection permanent in a later part of this chapter.

`"timeMillis" : 12`
: How long the operation took, in milliseconds.

`"counts" : { ... }`
: This embedded document is mostly used for debugging and contains three keys:

  `"input" : 6`
  : The number of documents sent to the `map` function.

  `"emit" : 14`
  : The number of times `emit` was called in the `map` function.

  `"output" : 5`
  : The number of documents created in the result collection.

If we do a find on the resulting collection, we can see all the keys and their counts from our original collection:

```
> db[mr.result].find()
{ "_id" : "_id", "value" : { "count" : 6 } }
{ "_id" : "a", "value" : { "count" : 4 } }
{ "_id" : "b", "value" : { "count" : 2 } }
{ "_id" : "x", "value" : { "count" : 1 } }
{ "_id" : "y", "value" : { "count" : 1 } }
```

Each of the key values becomes an "_id", and the final result of the reduce step(s) becomes the "value".

Example 2: Categorizing Web Pages

Suppose we have a site where people can submit links to other pages, such as reddit. Submitters can tag a link as related to certain popular topics, e.g., "politics," "geek," or "icanhascheezburger." We can use MapReduce to figure out which topics are the most popular, as a combination of recent and most-voted-for.

First, we need a map function that emits tags with a value based on the popularity and recency of a document:

```
map = function() {
    for (var i in this.tags) {
        var recency = 1/(new Date() - this.date);
        var score = recency * this.score;

        emit(this.tags[i], {"urls" : [this.url], "score" : score});
    }
};
```

Now we need to reduce all of the emitted values for a tag into a single score for that tag:

```
reduce = function(key, emits) {
    var total = {urls : [], score : 0}
    for (var i in emits) {
        emits[i].urls.forEach(function(url) {
            total.urls.push(url);
        }
        total.score += emits[i].score;
    }
    return total;
};
```

The final collection will end up with a full list of URLs for each tag and a score showing how popular that particular tag is.

MongoDB and MapReduce

Both of the previous examples used only the `mapreduce`, `map`, and `reduce` keys. These three keys are required, but there are many optional keys that can be passed to the MapReduce command:

`"finalize" :` *`function`*
: A final step to send reduce's output to.

`"keeptemp" :` *`boolean`*
: If the temporary result collection should be saved when the connection is closed.

`"out" : string`
: Name for the output collection. Setting this option implies `keeptemp : true`.

`"query" : document`
: Query to filter documents by before sending to the `map` function.

`"sort" : document`
: Sort to use on documents before sending to the map (useful in conjunction with the `limit` option).

`"limit" : integer`
: Maximum number of documents to send to the `map` function.

`"scope" : document`
: Variables that can be used in any of the JavaScript code.

`"verbose" : boolean`
: Whether or not to use more verbose output in the server logs.

The finalize function

As with the previous `group` command, MapReduce can be passed a `finalize` function that will be run on the last `reduce`'s output before it is saved to a temporary collection.

Returning large result sets is less critical with MapReduce than `group` because the whole result doesn't have to fit in 4 MB. However, the information will be passed over the wire eventually, so `finalize` is a good chance to take averages, chomp arrays, and remove extra information in general.

Keeping output collections

By default, Mongo creates a temporary collection while it is processing the MapReduce with a name that you are unlikely to choose for a collection: a dot-separated string containing *mr*, the name of the collection you're MapReducing, a timestamp, and the job's ID with the database. It ends up looking something like *mr.stuff.18234210220.2*. MongoDB will automatically destroy this collection when the connection that did the MapReduce is closed. (You can also drop it manually when you're done with it.) If you want to persist this collection even after disconnecting, you can specify `keeptemp : true` as an option.

If you'll be using the temporary collection regularly, you may want to give it a better name. You can specify a more human-readable name with the `out` option, which takes a string. If you specify `out`, you need not specify `keeptemp : true`, since it is implied. Even if you specify a "pretty" name for the collection, MongoDB will use the autogenerated collection name for intermediate steps of the MapReduce. When it has finished, it will automatically and atomically rename the collection from the autogenerated name to your chosen name. This means that if you run MapReduce multiple times with the same target collection, you will never be using an incomplete collection for operations.

The output collection created by MapReduce is a normal collection, which means that there is no problem with doing a MapReduce on it or a MapReduce on the results from that MapReduce, ad infinitum!

MapReduce on a subset of documents

Sometimes you need to run MapReduce on only part of a collection. You can add a query to filter the documents before they are passed to the `map` function.

Every document passed to the `map` function needs to be deserialized from BSON into a JavaScript object, which is a fairly expensive operation. If you know that you will need to run MapReduce only on a subset of the documents in the collection, adding a filter can greatly speed up the command. The filter is specified by the `"query"`, `"limit"`, and `"sort"` keys.

The `"query"` key takes a query document as a value. Any documents that would ordinarily be returned by that query will be passed to the `map` function. For example, if we have an application tracking analytics and want a summary for the last week, we can use MapReduce on only the most recent week's documents with the following command:

```
> db.runCommand({"mapreduce" : "analytics", "map" : map, "reduce" : reduce,
                 "query" : {"date" : {"$gt" : week_ago}}})
```

The `sort` option is mostly useful in conjunction with `limit`. `limit` can be used on its own, as well, to simply provide a cutoff on the number of documents sent to the `map` function.

If, in the previous example, we wanted an analysis of the last 10,000 page views (instead of the last week), we could use `limit` and `sort`:

```
> db.runCommand({"mapreduce" : "analytics", "map" : map, "reduce" : reduce,
                 "limit" : 10000, "sort" : {"date" : -1}})
```

`query`, `limit`, and `sort` can be used in any combination, but `sort` isn't useful if `limit` isn't present.

Using a scope

MapReduce can take a code type for the `map`, `reduce`, and `finalize` functions, and, in most languages, you can specify a scope to be passed with code. However, MapReduce ignores this scope. It has its own scope key, `"scope"`, and you must use that if there are client-side values you want to use in your MapReduce. You can set them using a plain document of the form `variable_name : value`, and they will be available in your `map`, `reduce`, and `finalize` functions. The scope is immutable from within these functions.

For instance, in the example in the previous section, we calculated the recency of a page using `1/(new Date() - this.date)`. We could, instead, pass in the current date as part of the scope with the following code:

```
> db.runCommand({"mapreduce" : "webpages", "map" : map, "reduce" : reduce,
                 "scope" : {now : new Date()}})
```

Then, in the `map` function, we could say `1/(now - this.date)`.

Getting more output

There is also a verbose option for debugging. If you would like to see the progress of your MapReduce as it runs, you can specify `"verbose" : true`.

You can also use `print` to see what's happening in the `map`, `reduce`, and `finalize` functions. `print` will print to the server log.

Aggregation Commands

There are several commands that MongoDB provides for basic aggregation tasks over a collection. These commands were added before the aggregation framework and have been superceded by it, for the most part. However, complex groups may still require JavaScript and counts and distincts can be simpler to run as non-framework commands.

count

The simplest aggregation tool is `count`, which returns the number of documents in the collection:

```
> db.foo.count()
0
> db.foo.insert({"x" : 1})
> db.foo.count()
1
```

Counting the total number of documents in a collection is fast regardless of collection size.

You can also pass in a query and Mongo will count the number of results for that query:

```
> db.foo.insert({"x" : 2})
> db.foo.count()
2
> db.foo.count({"x" : 1})
1
```

This can be useful for getting a total for pagination: "displaying results 0–10 of 439." Adding criteria does make the count slower. Counts can use indexes, but indexes do not contain enough metadata to make counting any more efficient than actually doing a query for the criteria.

distinct

The `distinct` command finds all of the distinct values for a given key. You must specify a collection and key:

```
> db.runCommand({"distinct" : "people", "key" : "age"})
```

For example, suppose we had the following documents in our collection:

```
{"name" : "Ada", "age" : 20}
{"name" : "Fred", "age" : 35}
{"name" : "Susan", "age" : 60}
{"name" : "Andy", "age" : 35}
```

If you call distinct on the `"age"` key, you will get back all of the distinct ages:

```
> db.runCommand({"distinct" : "people", "key" : "age"})
{"values" : [20, 35, 60], "ok" : 1}
```

A common question at this point is if there's a way to get all of the distinct *keys* in a collection. There is no built-in way of doing this, although you can write something to do it yourself using MapReduce (described in "MapReduce" on page 140).

group

`group` allows you to perform more complex aggregation. You choose a key to group by, and MongoDB divides the collection into separate groups for each value of the chosen key. For each group, you can create a result document by aggregating the documents that are members of that group.

> If you are familiar with SQL, `group` is similar to SQL's `GROUP BY`.

Suppose we have a site that keeps track of stock prices. Every few minutes from 10 a.m. to 4 p.m., it gets the latest price for a stock, which it stores in MongoDB. Now, as part of a reporting application, we want to find the closing price for the past 30 days. This can be easily accomplished using `group`.

The collection of stock prices contains thousands of documents with the following form:

```
{"day" : "2010/10/03", "time" : "10/3/2010 03:57:01 GMT-400", "price" : 4.23}
{"day" : "2010/10/04", "time" : "10/4/2010 11:28:39 GMT-400", "price" : 4.27}
{"day" : "2010/10/03", "time" : "10/3/2010 05:00:23 GMT-400", "price" : 4.10}
{"day" : "2010/10/06", "time" : "10/6/2010 05:27:58 GMT-400", "price" : 4.30}
{"day" : "2010/10/04", "time" : "10/4/2010 08:34:50 GMT-400", "price" : 4.01}
```

> You should never store money amounts as floating-point numbers because of inexactness concerns, but for simplicity we'll do it in this example.

We want our results to be a list of the latest time and price for each day, something like this:

```
[
    {"time" : "10/3/2010 05:00:23 GMT-400", "price" : 4.10},
    {"time" : "10/4/2010 11:28:39 GMT-400", "price" : 4.27},
    {"time" : "10/6/2010 05:27:58 GMT-400", "price" : 4.30}
]
```

We can accomplish this by splitting the collection into sets of documents grouped by day then finding the document with the latest timestamp for each day and adding it to the result set. The whole function might look something like this:

```
> db.runCommand({"group" : {
... "ns" : "stocks",
... "key" : "day",
... "initial" : {"time" : 0},
... "$reduce" : function(doc, prev) {
...     if (doc.time > prev.time) {
...         prev.price = doc.price;
...         prev.time = doc.time;
...     }
... }}})
```

Let's break this command down into its component keys:

`"ns" : "stocks"`
: This determines which collection we'll be running the group on.

`"key" : "day"`
: This specifies the key on which to group the documents in the collection. In this case, that would be the `"day"` key. All the documents with a `"day"` key of a given value will be grouped together.

`"initial" : {"time" : 0}`
: The first time the `reduce` function is called for a given group, it will be passed the initialization document. This same accumulator will be used for each member of a given group, so any changes made to it can be persisted.

`"$reduce" : function(doc, prev) { ... }`
: This will be called once for each document in the collection. It is passed the current document and an accumulator document: the result so far for that group. In this example, we want the `reduce` function to compare the current document's time with the accumulator's time. If the current document has a later time, we'll set the accumulator's day and price to be the current document's values. Remember that there

is a separate accumulator for each group, so there is no need to worry about different days using the same accumulator.

In the initial statement of the problem, we said that we wanted only the last 30 days worth of prices. Our current solution is iterating over the entire collection, however. This is why you can include a "condition" that documents must satisfy in order to be processed by the group command at all:

```
> db.runCommand({"group" : {
... "ns" : "stocks",
... "key" : "day",
... "initial" : {"time" : 0},
... "$reduce" : function(doc, prev) {
...     if (doc.time > prev.time) {
...         prev.price = doc.price;
...         prev.time = doc.time;
...     }},
... "condition" : {"day" : {"$gt" : "2010/09/30"}}
... }})
```

> Some documentation refers to a "cond" or "q" key, both of which are identical to the "condition" key (just less descriptive).

Now the command will return an array of 30 documents, each of which is a group. Each group has the key on which the group was based (in this case, "day" : *string*) and the final value of prev for that group. If some of the documents do not contain the key, these will be grouped into a single group with a day : null element. You can eliminate this group by adding "day" : {"$exists" : true} to the "condition". The group command also returns the total number of documents used and the number of distinct values for "key":

```
> db.runCommand({"group" : {...}})
{
    "retval" :
        [
            {
                "day" : "2010/10/04",
                "time" : "Mon Oct 04 2010 11:28:39 GMT-0400 (EST)"
                "price" : 4.27
            },
            ...
        ],
    "count" : 734,
    "keys" : 30,
    "ok" : 1
}
```

We explicitly set the "price" for each group, and the "time" was set by the initializer and then updated. The "day" is included because the key being grouped by is included by default in each "retval" embedded document. If you don't want to return this key, you can use a finalizer to change the final accumulator document into anything, even a nondocument (e.g., a number or string).

Using a finalizer

Finalizers can be used to minimize the amount of data that needs to be transferred from the database to the user, which is important because the group command's output needs to fit in a single database response. To demonstrate this, we'll take the example of a blog where each post has tags. We want to find the most popular tag for each day. We can group by day (again) and keep a count for each tag. This might look something like this:

```
> db.posts.group({
... "key" : {"day" : true},
... "initial" : {"tags" : {}},
... "$reduce" : function(doc, prev) {
...     for (i in doc.tags) {
...         if (doc.tags[i] in prev.tags) {
...             prev.tags[doc.tags[i]]++;
...         } else {
...             prev.tags[doc.tags[i]] = 1;
...         }
...     }
... }})
```

This will return something like this:

```
[
    {"day" : "2010/01/12", "tags" : {"nosql" : 4, "winter" : 10, "sledding" : 2}},
    {"day" : "2010/01/13", "tags" : {"soda" : 5, "php" : 2}},
    {"day" : "2010/01/14", "tags" : {"python" : 6, "winter" : 4, "nosql": 15}}
]
```

Then we could find the largest value in the "tags" document on the client side. However, sending the entire tags document for every day is a lot of extra overhead to send to the client: an entire set of key/value pairs for each day, when all we want is a single string. This is why group takes an optional "finalize" key. "finalize" can contain a function that is run on each group once, right before the result is sent back to the client. We can use a "finalize" function to trim out all of the cruft from our results:

```
> db.runCommand({"group" : {
... "ns" : "posts",
... "key" : {"day" : true},
... "initial" : {"tags" : {}},
... "$reduce" : function(doc, prev) {
...     for (i in doc.tags) {
...         if (doc.tags[i] in prev.tags) {
...             prev.tags[doc.tags[i]]++;
```

```
...         } else {
...             prev.tags[doc.tags[i]] = 1;
...         }
...     },
... "finalize" : function(prev) {
...     var mostPopular = 0;
...     for (i in prev.tags) {
...         if (prev.tags[i] > mostPopular) {
...             prev.tag = i;
...             mostPopular = prev.tags[i];
...         }
...     }
...     delete prev.tags
... }}})
```

Now, we're only getting the information we want; the server will send back something like this:

```
[
    {"day" : "2010/01/12", "tag" : "winter"},
    {"day" : "2010/01/13", "tag" : "soda"},
    {"day" : "2010/01/14", "tag" : "nosql"}
]
```

`finalize` can either modify the argument passed in or return a new value.

Using a function as a key

Sometimes you may have more complicated criteria that you want to group by, not just a single key. Suppose you are using `group` to count how many blog posts are in each category. (Each blog post is in a single category.) Post authors were inconsistent, though, and categorized posts with haphazard capitalization. So, if you group by category name, you'll end up with separate groups for "MongoDB" and "mongodb." To make sure any variation of capitalization is treated as the same key, you can define a function to determine documents' grouping key.

To define a grouping function, you must use a `$keyf` key (instead of `"key"`). Using `"$keyf"` makes the `group` command look something like this:

```
> db.posts.group({"ns" : "posts",
... "$keyf" : function(x) { return x.category.toLowerCase(); },
... "initializer" : ... })
```

`"$keyf"` allows you can group by arbitrarily complex criteria.

CHAPTER 8

Application Design

This chapter covers designing applications to work effectively with MongoDB. It discusses:

- Trade-offs when deciding whether to embed data or to reference it
- Tips for optimizations
- Consistency considerations
- How to migrate schemas
- When MongoDB isn't a good choice of data store

Normalization versus Denormalization

There are many ways of representing data and one of the most important issues is how much you should normalize your data. *Normalization* is dividing up data into multiple collections with references between collections. Each piece of data lives in one collection although multiple documents may reference it. Thus, to change the data, only one document must be updated. However, MongoDB has no joining facilities, so gathering documents from multiple collections will require multiple queries.

Denormalization is the opposite of normalization: embedding all of the data in a single document. Instead of documents containing references to one definitive copy of the data, many documents may have copies of the data. This means that multiple documents need to be updated if the information changes but that all related data can be fetched with a single query.

Deciding when to normalize and when to denormalize can be difficult: typically, normalizing makes writes faster and denormalizing makes reads faster. Thus, you need to find what trade-offs make sense for your application.

Examples of Data Representations

Suppose we are storing information about students and the classes that they are taking. One way to represent this would be to have a *students* collection (each student is one document) and a *classes* collection (each class is one document). Then we could have a third collection (*studentClasses*) that contains references to the student and classes he is taking:

```
> db.studentClasses.findOne({"studentId" : id})
{
    "_id" : ObjectId("512512c1d86041c7dca81915"),
    "studentId" : ObjectId("512512a5d86041c7dca81914"),
    "classes" : [
        ObjectId("512512ced86041c7dca81916"),
        ObjectId("512512dcd86041c7dca81917"),
        ObjectId("512512e6d86041c7dca81918"),
        ObjectId("512512f0d86041c7dca81919")
    ]
}
```

If you are familiar with relational databases, you may have seen this type of join table before, although typically you'd have one student and one class per document (instead of a list of class `"_id"`s). It's a bit more MongoDB-ish to put the classes in an array, but you usually wouldn't want to store the data this way because it requires a lot of querying to get to the actual information.

Suppose we wanted to find the classes a student was taking. We'd query for the student in the *students* collection, query *studentClasses* for the course `"_id"`s, and then query the *classes* collection for the class information. Thus, finding this information would take three trips to the server. This is generally *not* the way you want to structure data in MongoDB, unless the classes and students are changing constantly and reading the data does not need to be done quickly.

We can remove one of the dereferencing queries by embedding class references in the student's document:

```
{
    "_id" : ObjectId("512512a5d86041c7dca81914"),
    "name" : "John Doe",
    "classes" : [
        ObjectId("512512ced86041c7dca81916"),
        ObjectId("512512dcd86041c7dca81917"),
        ObjectId("512512e6d86041c7dca81918"),
        ObjectId("512512f0d86041c7dca81919")
    ]
}
```

The `"classes"` field keeps an array of `"_id"`s of classes that John Doe is taking. When we want to find out information about those classes, we can query the classes collection with those "_id"s. This only takes two queries. This is fairly popular way to structure data that does not need to be instantly accessible and changes, but not constantly.

If we need to optimize reads further, we can get all of the information in a single query by fully denormalizing the data and storing each class as an embedded document in the "classes" field:

```
{
    "_id" : ObjectId("512512a5d86041c7dca81914"),
    "name" : "John Doe",
    "classes" : [
        {
            "class" : "Trigonometry",
            "credits" : 3,
            "room" : "204"
        },
        {
            "class" : "Physics",
            "credits" : 3,
            "room" : "159"
        },
        {
            "class" : "Women in Literature",
            "credits" : 3,
            "room" : "14b"
        },
        {
            "class" : "AP European History",
            "credits" : 4,
            "room" : "321"
        }
    ]
}
```

The upside of this is that it only takes one query to get the information. The downsides are that it takes up more space and is more difficult to keep in sync. For example, if it turns out that physics was supposed to be four credits (not three) every student in the physics class would need to have her document updated (instead of just updating a central "Physics" document).

Finally, you can use a hybrid of embedding and referencing: create an array of subdocuments with the frequently used information, but with a reference to the actual document for more information

```
{
    "_id" : ObjectId("512512a5d86041c7dca81914"),
    "name" : "John Doe",
    "classes" : [
        {
            "_id" : ObjectId("512512ced86041c7dca81916"),
            "class" : "Trigonometry"
```

```
            },
            {
                "_id" : ObjectId("512512dcd86041c7dca81917"),
                "class" : "Physics"
            },
            {
                "_id" : ObjectId("512512e6d86041c7dca81918"),
                "class" : "Women in Literature"
            },
            {
                "_id" : ObjectId("512512f0d86041c7dca81919"),
                "class" : "AP European History"
            }
        ]
    }
```

This approach is also a nice option because the amount of information embedded can change over time as your requirements changes: if you want to include more or less information on a page, you could embed more or less of it in the document.

Another important consideration is how often this information will change versus how often it's read. If it will be updated regularly, then normalizing it is a good idea. However, if it changes infrequently, then there is little benefit to optimize the update process at the expense of every read your application performs.

For example, a textbook normalization use case is to store a user and his address in separate collections. However, people almost never change their address, so you generally shouldn't penalize every read on the off chance that someone's moved. Your application should embed the address in the user document.

If you decide to use embedded documents and you need to update them, you should set up a cron job to ensure that any updates you do are successfully propagated to every document. For example, you might attempt to do a multiupdate but the server crashes before all of the documents have been updated. You need a way to detect this and retry the update.

To some extent, the more information you are generating the less of it you should embed. If the embedded fields or number of embedded fields is supposed to grow without bound then they should generally be referenced, not embedded. Things like comment trees or activity lists should be stored as their own documents, not embedded.

Finally, fields should be included that are integral to the data in the document. If a field is almost always excluded from your results when you query for this document, it's a good sign that it may belong in another collection. These guidelines are summarized in Table 8-1.

Table 8-1. Comparison of embedding versus references

Embedding is better for...	References are better for...
Small subdocuments	Large subdocuments
Data that does not change regularly	Volatile data
When eventual consistency is acceptable	When immediate consistency is necessary
Documents that grow by a small amount	Documents that grow a large amount
Data that you'll often need to perform a second query to fetch	Data that you'll often exclude from the results
Fast reads	Fast writes

Suppose we had a users collection. Here are some example fields we might have and whether or not they should be embedded:

Account preferences
: They are only relevant to this user document, and will probably be exposed with other user information in this document. Account preferences should generally be embedded.

Recent activity
: This one depends on how much recent activity grows and changes. If it is a fixed-size field (last 10 things), it might be useful to embed.

Friends
: Generally this should not be embedded, or at least not fully. See the section below on advice on social networking.

All of the content this user has produced
: No.

Cardinality

Cardinality is how many references a collection has to another collection. Common relationships are one-to-one, one-to-many, or many-to-many. For example, suppose we had a blog application. Each *post* has a *title*, so that's a one-to-one relationship. Each *author* has many *posts*, so that's a one-to-many relationship. And *posts* have many *tags* and *tags* refer to many *posts*, so that's a many-to-many relationship.

When using MongoDB, it can be conceptually useful to split "many" into subcategories: "many" and "few." For example, you might have a one-to-few cardinality between authors and posts: each author only writes a few posts. You might have many-to-few relation between blog posts and tags: your probably have many more blog posts than you have tags. However, you'd have a one-to-many relationship between blog posts and comments: each post has many comments.

When you've determined few versus many relations, it can help you decide what to embed versus what to reference. Generally, "few" relationships will work better with embedding, and "many" relationships will work better as references.

Friends, Followers, and Other Inconveniences

> Keep your friends close and your enemies embedded.

Many social applications need to link people, content, followers, friends, and so on. Figuring out how to balance embedding and referencing this highly connected information can be tricky. This section covers considerations for social graph data. But generally following, friending, or favoriting can be simplified to a publication-subscription system: one user is subscribing to notifications from another. Thus, there are two basic operations that need to be efficient: how to store subscribers and how to notify all interested parties of an event.

There are three ways people typically implement subscribing. The first option is that you can put the producer in the subscriber's document, which looks something like this:

```
{
    "_id" : ObjectId("51250a5cd86041c7dca8190f"),
    "username" : "batman",
    "email" : "batman@waynetech.com"
    "following" : [
        ObjectId("51250a72d86041c7dca81910"),
        ObjectId("51250a7ed86041c7dca81936")
    ]
}
```

Now, given a user's document, you can query for something like `db.activities.find({"user" : {"$in" : user["following"]}})` to find all of the activities that have been published that she'd be interested in. However, if you need to find everyone who is interested in a newly published activity, you'd have to query the `"following"` field across all users.

Alternatively, you could append the followers to the producer's document, like so:

```
{
    "_id" : ObjectId("51250a7ed86041c7dca81936"),
    "username" : "joker",
    "email" : "joker@mailinator.com"
    "followers" : [
        ObjectId("512510e8d86041c7dca81912"),
        ObjectId("51250a5cd86041c7dca8190f"),
        ObjectId("512510ffd86041c7dca81910")
    ]
}
```

Whenever this user does something, all the users we need to notify are right there. The downside is that now you need to query the whole users collection to find everyone a user follows (the opposite limitation as above).

Either of these options comes with an additional downside: they make your user document larger and more volatile. The `"following"` (or `"followers"`) field often won't even need to be returned: how often do you want to list every follower? If users are frequently followed or unfollowed, this can result in a lot of fragmentation, as well. Thus, the final option neutralizes these downsides by normalizing even further and storing subscriptions in another collection. Normalizing this far is often overkill, but it can be useful for an extremely volatile field that often isn't returned with the rest of the document. `"followers"` may be a sensible field to normalize this way.

Keep a collection that matches publishers to subscribers, with documents that look something like this:

```
{
    "_id" : ObjectId("51250a7ed86041c7dca81936"), // followee's "_id"
    "followers" : [
        ObjectId("512510e8d86041c7dca81912"),
        ObjectId("51250a5cd86041c7dca8190f"),
        ObjectId("512510ffd86041c7dca81910")
    ]
}
```

This keeps your user documents svelte but takes an extra query to get the followers. As `"followers"` arrays will generally change size a lot, this allows you to enable the `usePowerOf2Sizes` on this collection while keeping the *users* collection as small as possible. If you put this *followers* collection in another database, you can also compact it without affecting the *users* collection too much.

Dealing with the Wil Wheaton effect

Regardless of which strategy you use, embedding only works with a limited number of subdocuments or references. If you have celebrity users, they may overflow any document that you're storing followers in. The typical way of compensating this is to have a "continuation" document, if necessary. For example, you might have:

```
> db.users.find({"username" : "wil"})
{
    "_id" : ObjectId("51252871d86041c7dca8191a"),
    "username" : "wil",
    "email" : "wil@example.com",
    "tbc" : [
        ObjectId("512528ced86041c7dca8191e"),
        ObjectId("5126510dd86041c7dca81924")
    ]
    "followers" : [
        ObjectId("512528a0d86041c7dca8191b"),
```

```
            ObjectId("512528a2d86041c7dca8191c"),
            ObjectId("512528a3d86041c7dca8191d"),
            ...
        ]
    }
    {
        "_id" : ObjectId("512528ced86041c7dca8191e"),
        "followers" : [
            ObjectId("512528f1d86041c7dca8191f"),
            ObjectId("512528f6d86041c7dca81920"),
            ObjectId("512528f8d86041c7dca81921"),
            ...
        ]
    }
    {
        "_id" : ObjectId("5126510dd86041c7dca81924"),
        "followers" : [
            ObjectId("512673e1d86041c7dca81925"),
            ObjectId("512650efd86041c7dca81922"),
            ObjectId("512650fdd86041c7dca81923"),
            ...
        ]
    }
```

Then add application logic to support fetching the documents in the "to be continued" (`"tbc"`) array.

Optimizations for Data Manipulation

To optimize your application, you must first know what its bottleneck is by evaluating its read and write performance. Optimizing reads generally involves having the correct indexes and returning as much of the information as possible in a single document. Optimizing writes usually involves minimizing the number of indexes you have and making updates as efficient as possible.

There is often a trade-off between schemas that are optimized for writing quickly and those that are optimized for reading quickly, so you may have to decide which is a more important for your application. Factor in not only the importance of reads versus writes, but also their proportions: if writes are more important but you're doing a thousand reads to every write, you may still want to optimize reads first.

Optimizing for Document Growth

If you're going to need to update data, determine whether or not your documents are going to grow and by how much. If it is by a predictable amount, manually padding your documents will prevent moves, making writes faster. Check your padding factor: if it is about 1.2 or greater, consider using manual padding.

When you manually pad a document, you create the document with a large field that will later be removed. This preallocates the space that the document will eventually need. For example, suppose you had a collection of restaurant reviews and your documents looked like this:

```
{
    "_id" : ObjectId(),
    "restaurant" : "Le Cirque",
    "review" : "Hamburgers were overpriced."
    "userId" : ObjectId(),
    "tags" : []
}
```

The "tags" field will grow as users add tags, so the application will often have to perform an update like this:

```
> db.reviews.update({"_id" : id},
... {"$push" : {"tags" : {"$each" : ["French", "fine dining", "hamburgers"]}}}})
```

If "tags" generally doesn't grow to more than 100 bytes, you could manually pad the document to prevent any unwanted moves. If you leave the document without padding, moves will definitely occur as "tags" grows. To pad, add a final field to the document with whatever field name you'd like:

```
{
    "_id" : ObjectId(),
    "restaurant" : "Le Cirque",
    "review" : "Hamburgers were overpriced."
    "userId" : ObjectId(),
    "tags" : [],
    "garbage" : "..........................................................."+
        "..........................................................."+
        "..........................................................."
}
```

You can either do this on insert or, if the document is created with an upsert, use "$setOnInsert" to create the field when the document is first inserted.

When you update the document, always "$unset" the "garbage" field:

```
> db.reviews.update({"_id" : id},
... {"$push" : {"tags" : {"$each" : ["French", "fine dining", "hamburgers"]}}},
...  "$unset" : {"garbage" : true}})
```

The "$unset" will remove the "garbage" field if it exists and be a no-op if it does not.

If your document has one field that grows, try to keep is as the last field in the document (but before "garbage"). It is slightly more efficient for MongoDB not to have to rewrite fields after "tags" if it grows.

Removing Old Data

Some data is only important for a brief time: after a few weeks or months it is just wasting storage space. There are three popular options for removing old data: capped collections, TTL collections, and dropping collections per time period.

The easiest option is to use a capped collection: set it to a large size and let old data "fall off" the end. However, capped collections pose certain limitations on the operations you can do and are vulnerable to spikes in traffic, temporarily lowering the length of time that they can hold. See "Capped Collections" on page 109 for more information.

The second option is TTL collections: this gives you a finer-grain control over when documents are removed. However, it may not be fast enough for very high-write-volume collections: it removes documents by traversing the TTL index the same way a user-requested remove would. If TTL collections can keep up, though, they are probably the easiest solution. See "Time-To-Live Indexes" on page 114 for more information about TTL indexes.

The final option is to use multiple collections: for example, one collection per month. Every time the month changes, your application starts using this month's (empty) collection and searching for data in both the current and previous months' collections. Once a collection is older than, say, six months, you can drop it. This can keep up with nearly any volume of traffic, but it is more complex to build an application around, since it has to use dynamic collection (or database) names and possibly query multiple databases.

Planning Out Databases and Collections

Once you have sketched out what your documents look like, you must decide what collections or databases to put them in. This is often a fairly intuitive process, but there are some guidelines to keep in mind.

In general, documents with a similar schema should be kept in the same collection. MongoDB generally disallows combining data from multiple collections, so if there are documents that need to be queried or aggregated together, those are good candidates for putting in one big collection. For example, you might have documents that are fairly different "shapes," but if you're going to be aggregating them, they all need to live in the same collection.

For databases, the big issues to consider are locking (you get a read/write lock per database) and storage. Each database resides in its own files and often its own directory on disk, which means that you could mount different databases to different volumes. Thus, you may want all items within a database to be of similar "quality," similar access pattern, or similar traffic levels.

For example, suppose we have an application with several components: a logging component that creates a huge amount of not-very-valuable data, a user collection, and a couple of collections for user-generated data. The user collections are high-value: it is important that user data is safe. There is also a high-traffic collection for social activities, which is of lower importance but not quite as unimportant as the logs. This collection is mainly used for user notifications, so it is almost an append-only collection.

Splitting these up by importance, we might end up with three databases: *logs*, *activities*, and *users*. The nice thing about this strategy is that you may find that your highest-value data is also your smallest (for instance, users probably don't generate as much data as your logging does). You might not be able to afford an SSD for your entire data set, but you might be able to get one for your users. Or use RAID10 for users and RAID0 for logs and activities.

Be aware that there are some limitations when using multiple databases: MongoDB generally does not allow you to move data directly from one database to another. For example, you cannot store the results of a MapReduce in a different database than you ran the MapReduce on and you cannot move a collection from one database to another with the *renameCollection* command (e.g., you can rename *foo.bar* as *foo.baz*, but not *foo2.baz*).

Managing Consistency

You must figure out how consistent your application's reads need to be. MongoDB supports a huge variety in consistency levels, from always reading your own writes to reading data of unknown oldness. If you're reporting on the last year of activity, you might only need data that's correct to the last couple of days. Conversely, if you're doing real-time trading, you might need to immediately read the latest writes.

To understand how to achieve these varying levels of consistency, it is important to understand what MongoDB is doing under the hood. The server keeps a queue of requests for each connection. When the client sends a request, it will be placed at the end of its connection's queue. Any subsequent requests on the connection will occur after the enqueued operation is processed. Thus, a single connection has a consistent view of the database and can always read its own writes.

Note that this is a per-connection queue: if we open two shells, we will have two connections to the database. If we perform an insert in one shell, a subsequent query in the other shell might not return the inserted document. However, within a single shell, if we query for the document after inserting, the document will be returned. This behavior can be difficult to duplicate by hand, but on a busy server interleaved inserts and queries are likely to occur. Often developers run into this when they insert data in one thread and then check that it was successfully inserted in another. For a moment or two, it looks like the data was not inserted, and then it suddenly appears.

This behavior is especially worth keeping in mind when using the Ruby, Python, and Java drivers, because all three use connection pooling. For efficiency, these drivers open multiple connections (a *pool*) to the server and distribute requests across them. They all, however, have mechanisms to guarantee that a series of requests is processed by a single connection. There is detailed documentation on connection pooling in various languages on the MongoDB wiki.

When you send reads to a replica set secondary (see Chapter 11), this becomes an even larger issue. Secondaries may lag behind the primary, leading to reading data from seconds, minutes, or even hours ago. There are several ways of dealing with this, the easiest being to simply send all reads to the primary if you care about staleness. You could also set up an automatic script to detect lag on a secondary and put it into maintenance mode if it lags too far behind. If you have a small set, it might be worth using `"w" : setSize` as a write concern and sending subsequent reads to the primary if *getLastError* does not return successfully.

Migrating Schemas

As your application grows and your needs change, your schema may have to grow and change as well. There are a couple of ways of accomplishing this, and regardless of the method you chose, you should carefully document each schema that your application has used.

The simplest method is to simply have your schema evolve as your application requires, making sure that your application supports all old versions of the schema (e.g., accepting the existence or non-existence of fields or dealing with multiple possible field types gracefully). This technique can become messy, particularly if you have conflicting versions. For instance, one version might require a `"mobile"` field and one version might require *not* having a `"mobile"` field but does require another field, and yet another version thinks that the `"mobile"` field is optional. Keeping track of these requirements can gradually turn code into spaghetti.

To handle changing requirements in a slightly more structured way you can include a `"version"` field (or just `"v"`) in each document and use that to determine what your application will accept for document structure. This enforces your schema more rigorously: a document has to be valid for some version of the schema, if not the current one. However, it still requires supporting old versions.

The final option is to migrate all of your data when the schema changes. Generally this is not a good idea: MongoDB allows you to have a dynamic schema in order to avoid migrates because they put a lot of pressure on your system. However, if you do decide to change every document, you will need to ensure that all documents were successfully updated. MongoDB does not support atomic multiupdates (either they all happen or they all don't across multiple documents). If MongoDB crashes in the middle of a migrate, you could end up with some updated and some non-updated documents.

When Not to Use MongoDB

While MongoDB is a general-purpose database that works well for most applications, it isn't good at everything. Here are some tasks that MongoDB is not designed to do:

- MongoDB does not support transactions, so systems that require transactions should use another data store. There are a couple of ways to hack in simple transaction-like semantics, particularly on a single document, but there is no database enforcement. Thus, you can make all of your clients agree to obey whatever semantics you come up with (e.g., "Check the `"locks"` field before doing any operation") but there is nothing stopping an ignorant or malicious client from messing things up.
- Joining many different types of data across many different dimensions is something relational databases are fantastic at. MongoDB isn't supposed to do this well and most likely never will.
- Finally, one of the big (if hopefully temporary) reasons to use a relational database over MongoDB is if you're using tools that don't support MongoDB. From SQLAlchemy to Wordpress, there are thousands of tools that just weren't built to support MongoDB. The pool of tools that support MongoDB is growing but is hardly the size of relational databases' ecosystem, yet.

PART III
Replication

CHAPTER 9

Setting Up a Replica Set

This chapter introduces MongoDB's replication system: replica sets. It covers:

- What replica sets are
- How to set up a replica set
- What configuration options are available for replica set members

Introduction to Replication

Since the first chapter, we've been using a *standalone* server, a single *mongod* server. It's an easy way to get started but a dangerous way to run in production: what if your server crashes or becomes unavailable? Your database will at least be unavailable for a little while. If there are problems with the hardware, you may have to move your data to another machine. In the worst case, disk or network issues could leave you with corrupt or inaccessible data.

Replication is a way of keeping identical copies of your data on multiple servers and is recommended for all production deployments. Replication keeps your application running and your data safe, even if something happens to one or more of your servers.

With MongoDB, you set up replication by creating a *replica set*. A replica set is a group of servers with one *primary*, the server taking client requests, and multiple *secondaries*, servers that keep copies of the primary's data. If the primary crashes, the secondaries can elect a new primary from amongst themselves.

If you are using replication and a server goes down, you can still access your data from the other servers in the set. If the data on a server is damaged or inaccessible, you can make a new copy of the data from one the other members of the set.

This chapter introduces replica sets and covers how to set up replication on your system.

A One-Minute Test Setup

This section will get you started quickly by setting up a three-member replica set on your local machine. This setup is obviously not suitable for production, but it's a nice way to familiarize yourself with replication and play around with configuration.

> This quick-start method stores data in */data/db*, so make sure that directory exists and is writable by your user before running this code.

Start up a mongo shell with the `--nodb` option, which allows you to start a shell that is not connected to any *mongod*:

```
$ mongo --nodb
```

Create a replica set by running the following command:

```
> replicaSet = new ReplSetTest({"nodes" : 3})
```

This tells the shell to create a new replica set with three servers: one primary and two secondaries. However, it doesn't actually start the *mongod* servers until you run the following two commands:

```
> // starts three mongod processes
> replicaSet.startSet()
>
> // configures replication
> replicaSet.initiate()
```

You should now have three mongod processes running locally on ports 31000, 31001, and 31002. They will all be dumping their logs into the current shell, which is very noisy, so put this shell aside and open up a new one.

In the second shell, connect to the *mongod* running on port 31000:

```
> conn1 = new Mongo("localhost:31000")
connection to localhost:31000
testReplSet:PRIMARY>
testReplSet:PRIMARY> primaryDB = conn1.getDB("test")
test
```

Notice that, when you connect to a replica set member, the prompt changes to `testReplSet:PRIMARY>`. `"PRIMARY"` is the state of the member and `"testReplSet"` is an identifier for this set. You'll learn how to choose your own identifier later; `testReplSet` is the default name `ReplSetTest` uses.

Examples from now on will just use `>` for the prompt instead of `testReplSet:PRIMARY>` to keep things more readable.

Use your connection to the primary to run the *isMaster* command. This will show you the status of the set:

```
> primaryDB.isMaster()
{
    "setName" : "testReplSet",
    "ismaster" : true,
    "secondary" : false,
    "hosts" : [
        "wooster:31000",
        "wooster:31002",
        "wooster:31001"
    ],
    "primary" : "wooster:31000",
    "me" : "wooster:31000",
    "maxBsonObjectSize" : 16777216,
    "localTime" : ISODate("2012-09-28T15:48:11.025Z"),
    "ok" : 1
}
```

There are a bunch of fields in the output from *isMaster*, but the important ones indicate that you can see that this node is primary (the `"ismaster" : true` field) and that there is a list of hosts in the set.

> If this server says `"ismaster" : false`, that's fine. Look at the `"primary"` field to see which node is primary and then repeat the connection steps above for that host/port.

Now that you're connected to the primary, let's try doing some writes and see what happens. First, insert 1,000 documents:

```
> for (i=0; i<1000; i++) { primaryDB.coll.insert({count: i}) }
>
> // make sure the docs are there
> primaryDB.coll.count()
1000
```

Now check one of the secondaries and verify that they have a copy of all of these documents. Connect to either of the secondaries:

```
> conn2 = new Mongo("localhost:31001")
connection to localhost:31001
> secondaryDB = conn2.getDB("test")
test
```

Secondaries may fall behind the primary (or *lag*) and not have the most current writes, so secondaries will refuse read requests by default to prevent applications from accidentally reading stale data. Thus, if you attempt to query a secondary, you'll get an error that it's not primary:

```
> secondaryDB.coll.find()
error: { "$err" : "not master and slaveok=false", "code" : 13435 }
```

This is to protect your application from accidentally connecting to a secondary and reading stale data. To allow queries on the secondary, we set an "I'm okay with reading from secondaries" flag, like so:

```
> conn2.setSlaveOk()
```

Note that `slaveOk` is set on the *connection* (`conn2`), not the database (`secondaryDB`).

Now you're all set to read from this member. Query it normally:

```
> secondaryDB.coll.find()
{ "_id" : ObjectId("5037cac65f3257931833902b"), "count" : 0 }
{ "_id" : ObjectId("5037cac65f3257931833902c"), "count" : 1 }
{ "_id" : ObjectId("5037cac65f3257931833902d"), "count" : 2 }
...
{ "_id" : ObjectId("5037cac65f3257931833903c"), "count" : 17 }
{ "_id" : ObjectId("5037cac65f3257931833903d"), "count" : 18 }
{ "_id" : ObjectId("5037cac65f3257931833903e"), "count" : 19 }
Type "it" for more
>
> secondaryDB.coll.count()
1000
```

You can see that all of our documents are there.

Now, try to write to a secondary:

```
> secondaryDB.coll.insert({"count" : 1001})
> secondaryDB.runCommand({"getLastError" : 1})
{
    "err" : "not master",
    "code" : 10058,
    "n" : 0,
    "lastOp" : Timestamp(0, 0),
    "connectionId" : 5,
    "ok" : 1
}
```

You can see that the secondary does not accept the write. The secondary will only perform writes that it gets through replication, not from clients.

There is one other interesting feature that you should try out: automatic failover. If the primary goes down, one of the secondaries will automatically be elected primary. To try this out, stop the primary:

```
> primaryDB.adminCommand({"shutdown" : 1})
```

Run `isMaster` on the secondary to see who has become the new primary:

```
> secondaryDB.isMaster()
```

It should look something like this:

```
{
    "setName" : "testReplSet",
    "ismaster" : true,
    "secondary" : false,
    "hosts" : [
        "wooster:31001",
        "wooster:31000",
        "wooster:31002"
    ],
    "primary" : "wooster:31001",
    "me" : "wooster:31001",
    "maxBsonObjectSize" : 16777216,
    "localTime" : ISODate("2012-09-28T16:52:07.975Z"),
    "ok" : 1
}
```

Your primary may be the other server; whichever secondary noticed that the primary was down first will be elected. Now you can send writes to the new primary.

isMaster is a very old command, predating replica sets to when MongoDB only supported master-slave replication. Thus, it does not use the replica set terminology consistently: it still calls the primary a "master." You can generally think of "master" as equivalent to "primary" and "slave" as equivalent to "secondary."

When you're done working with the set, shut down the servers from your first shell. This shell will be full of log output from the members of the set, so hit Enter a few times to get back to a prompt. To shutdown the set, run:

```
> replicaSet.stopSet()
```

Congratulations! You just set up, used, and tore down replication.

There are a few key concepts to remember:

- Clients can send a primary all the same operations they could send a standalone server (reads, writes, commands, index builds, etc.).
- Clients cannot write to secondaries.
- Clients, by default, cannot read from secondaries. By explicitly setting an "I know I'm reading from a secondary" setting, clients can read from secondaries.

Now that you understand the basics, the rest of this chapter focuses on configuring a replica set under more realistic circumstances. Remember that you can always go back to `ReplSetTest` if you want to quickly try out a configuration or option.

Configuring a Replica Set

For actual deployments, you'll need to set up replication across multiple machines. This section takes you through setting up a real replica set that could be used by your application.

Let's say that you already have a standalone *mongod* on *server-1:27017* with some data on it. (If you do not have any pre-existing data, this will work the same way, just with an empty data directory.) The first thing you need to do is choose a name for your set. Any string whatsoever will do, so long as it's UTF-8.

Once you have a name for your replica set, restart *server-1* with the `--replSet` *`name`* option. For example:

```
$ mongod --replSet spock -f mongod.conf --fork
```

Now start up two more *mongod* servers with the `replSet` option and the same identifier (`spock`): these will be the other members of the set:

```
$ ssh server-2
server-2$ mongod --replSet spock -f mongod.conf --fork
server-2$ exit
$
$ ssh server-3
server-3$ mongod --replSet spock -f mongod.conf --fork
server-3$ exit
```

Each of the other members should have an empty data directory, even if the first member had data. They will automatically clone the first member's data to their machines once they have been added to the set.

For each member, add the `replSet` option to its *mongod.conf* file so that it will be used on startup from now on.

Once you've started the *mongod*s, you should have three *mongod*s running on three separate servers. However, each *mongod* does not yet know that the others exist. To tell them about one another, you have to create a configuration that lists each of the members and send this configuration to *server-1*. It will take care of propagating it to the other members.

First we'll create the configuration. In the shell, create a document that looks like this:

```
> config = {
    "_id" : "spock",
    "members" : [
        {"_id" : 0, "host" : "server-1:27017"},
        {"_id" : 1, "host" : "server-2:27017"},
        {"_id" : 2, "host" : "server-3:27017"}
    ]
}
```

There are several important parts of config. The config's "_id" is the name of the set that you passed in on the command line (in this example, "spock"). Make sure that this name matches exactly.

The next part of the document is an array of members of the set. Each of these needs two fields: a unique "_id" that is an integer and a hostname (replace the hostnames with whatever your servers are called).

This config object is your replica set configuration, so now you have to send it to a member of the set. To do so, connect to the server with data on it (*server-1:27017*) and initiate the set with this configuration:

```
> // connect to server-1
> db = (new Mongo("server-1:27017")).getDB("test")
>
> // initiate replica set
> rs.initiate(config)
{
    "info" : "Config now saved locally.  Should come online in about a minute.",
    "ok" : 1
}
```

server-1 will parse the configuration and send messages to the other members, alerting them of the new configuration. Once they have all loaded the configuration, they will elect a primary and start handling reads and writes.

> Unfortunately, you cannot convert a standalone server to a replica set without some downtime for restarting it and initializing the set. Thus, even if you only have one server to start out with, you may want to configure it as a one-member replica set. That way, if you want to add more members later, you can do so without downtime.

If you are starting a brand-new set, you can send the configuration to any member in the set. If you are starting with data on one of the members, you must send the configuration to the member with data. You cannot initiate a set with data on more than one member.

> You must use the *mongo* shell to configure replica sets. There is no way to do file-based replica set configuration.

rs Helper Functions

Note the rs in the rs.initiate() command above. rs is a global variable that contains replication helper functions (run rs.help() to see the helpers it exposes). These functions are almost always just wrappers around database commands. For example, the following database command is equivalent to `rs.initiate(config)`:

```
> db.adminCommand({"replSetInitiate" : config})
```

It is good to have a passing familiarity with both the helpers and the underlying commands, as it may sometimes be easier to use the command form instead of the helper.

Networking Considerations

Every member of a set must be able to make connections to every other member of the set (including itself). If you get errors about members not being able to reach other members that you know are running, you may have to change your network configuration to allow connections between them.

Also, replica sets configurations shouldn't use *localhost* as a hostname. There isn't much point to running a replica set on one machine and *localhost* won't resolve correctly from a foreign machine. MongoDB allows all-*localhost* replica sets for testing locally but will protest if you try to mix *localhost* and non-*localhost* servers in a config.

Changing Your Replica Set Configuration

Replica set configurations can be changed at any time: members can be added, removed, or modified. There are shell helpers for some common operations; for example, to add a new member to the set, you can use `rs.add`:

```
> rs.add("server-4:27017")
```

Similarly, you can remove members;

```
> rs.remove("server-1:27017")
Fri Sep 28 16:44:46 DBClientCursor::init call() failed
Fri Sep 28 16:44:46 query failed : admin.$cmd { replSetReconfig: {
    _id: "testReplSet", version: 2, members: [ { _id: 0, host: "ubuntu:31000" },
  { _id: 2, host: "ubuntu:31002" } ] } } to: localhost:31000
Fri Sep 28 16:44:46 Error: error doing query:
    failed src/mongo/shell/collection.js:155
Fri Sep 28 16:44:46 trying reconnect to localhost:31000
Fri Sep 28 16:44:46 reconnect localhost:31000 ok
```

Note that when you remove a member (or do almost any configuration change other than adding a member), you will get a big, ugly error about not being able to connect to the database in the shell. This is okay; it actually means the reconfiguration succeeded! When you reconfigure a set, the primary closes all connections as the last step in the reconfiguration process. Thus, the shell will briefly be disconnected but will automatically reconnect on your next operation.

The reason that the primary closes all connections is that it briefly steps down whenever you reconfigure the set. It should step up again immediately, but be aware that your set will not have a primary for a moment or two after reconfiguring.

You can check that a reconfiguration succeeded by run `rs.config()` in the shell. It will print the current configuration:

```
> rs.config()
{
    "_id" : "testReplSet",
    "version" : 2,
    "members" : [
        {
            "_id" : 1,
            "host" : "server-2:27017"
        },
        {
            "_id" : 2,
            "host" : "server-3:27017"
        },
        {
            "_id" : 3,
            "host" : "server-4:27017"
        }
    ]
}
```

Each time you change the configuration, the `"version"` field will increase. It starts at version 1.

You can also modify existing members, not just add and remove them. To make modifications, create the configuration document that you want in the shell and call `rs.reconfig`. For example, suppose we have a configuration such as the one shown here:

```
> rs.config()
{
    "_id" : "testReplSet",
    "version" : 2,
    "members" : [
        {
            "_id" : 0,
            "host" : "server-1:27017"
        },
        {
            "_id" : 1,
            "host" : "10.1.1.123:27017"
        },
        {
            "_id" : 2,
            "host" : "server-3:27017"
        }
```

```
    ]
}
```

Someone accidentally added member 1 by IP, instead of its hostname. To change that, first we load the current configuration in the shell and then we change the relevant fields:

```
> var config = rs.config()
> config.members[1].host = "server-2:27017"
```

Now that the config document is correct, we need to send it to the database using the `rs.reconfig` helper:

```
> rs.reconfig(config)
```

`rs.reconfig` is often more useful that `rs.add` and `rs.remove` for complex operations, such as modifying members' configuration or adding/removing multiple members at once. You can use it to make any legal configuration change you need: simply create the config document that represents your desired configuration and pass it to `rs.reconfig`.

How to Design a Set

To plan out your set, there are certain replica set concepts that you must be familiar with. The next chapter goes into more detail about these, but the most important is that replica sets are all about majorities: you need a majority of members to elect a primary, a primary can only stay primary so long as it can reach a majority, and a write is safe when it's been replicated to a majority. This *majority* is defined to be "more than half of all members in the set," as shown in Table 9-1.

Table 9-1. What is a majority?

Number of members in the set	Majority of the set
1	1
2	2
3	2
4	3
5	3
6	4
7	4

Note that it doesn't matter how many members are down or unavailable, as majority is based on the set's configuration.

For example, suppose that we have a five-member set and three members go down, as shown in Figure 9-1. There are still two members up. These two members cannot reach a majority of the set (at least three members), so they cannot elect a primary. If one of them were primary, it would step down as soon as it noticed that it could not reach a majority. After a few seconds, your set would consist of two secondaries and three unreachable members.

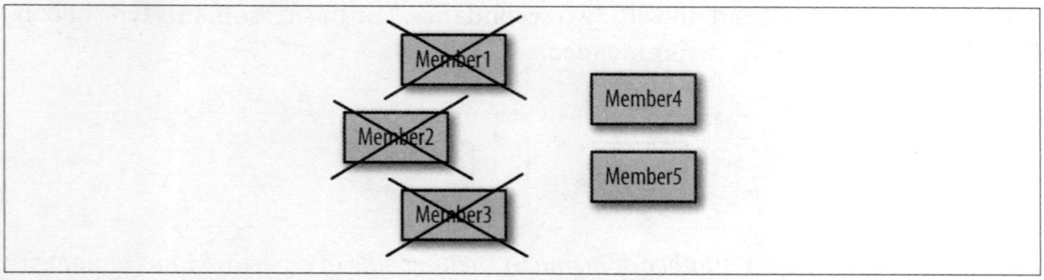

Figure 9-1. With a minority of the set available, all members will be secondaries

Many users find this frustrating: why can't the two remaining members elect a primary? The problem is that it's possible that the other three members didn't go down, and that it was the network that went down, as shown in Figure 9-2. In this case, the three members on the left will elect a primary, since they can reach a majority of the set (three members out of five).

In the case of a network partition, we do not want both sides of the partition to elect a primary: otherwise the set would have two primaries. Then both primaries would be writing to the data and the data sets would diverge. Requiring a majority to elect or stay primary is a neat way of avoiding ending up with more than one primary.

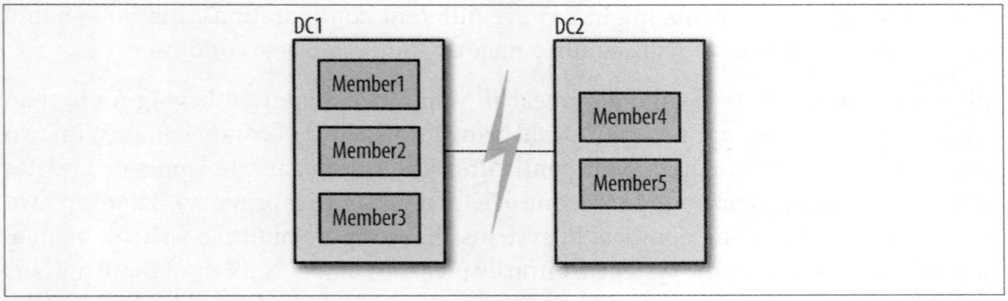

Figure 9-2. For the members, a network partition looks identical to servers on the other side of the partition going down

It is important to configure your set in such a way that you'll usually be able to have one primary. For example, in the five-member set described above, if members 1, 2, and 3 are in one data center and members 4 and 5 are in another, there should almost always be a majority available in the first data center (it's more likely to have a network break between data centers than within them).

One common setup that usually isn't what you want is a two member set: one primary and one secondary. Suppose one member becomes unavailable: the other member cannot see it, as shown in Figure 9-3. In this situation, neither side of the network partition has a majority so you'll end up with two secondaries. For this reason, this type of configuration is not generally recommended.

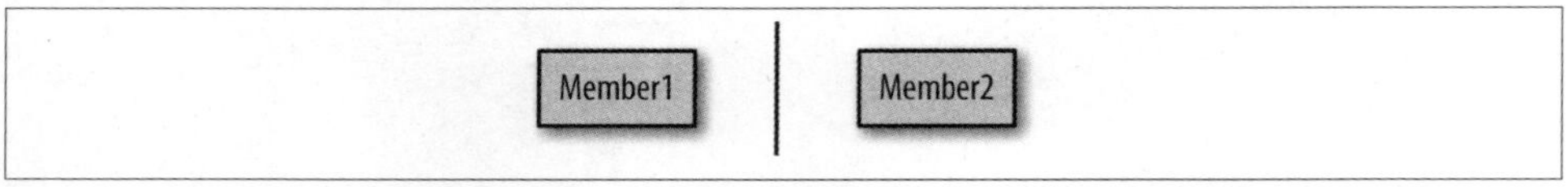

Figure 9-3. With an even number of members, neither side of a partition has a majority

There are a couple of configurations that *are* recommended:

- A majority of the set in one data center, as in Figure 9-2. This is a good design if you have a primary data center where you always want your replica set's primary to be located. So long as your primary data center is healthy, you will have a primary. However, if that data center becomes unavailable, your secondary data center will not be able to elect a new primary.
- An equal number of servers in each data center, plus a tie-breaking server in a third location. This is a good design if your data centers are "equal" in preference, since generally servers from either data center will be able to see a majority of the set. However, it involves having three separate locations for servers.

More complex requirements might require different configurations, but you should keep in mind how your set will acquire a majority under adverse conditions.

All of these complexities would disappear if MongoDB supported having more than one primary. However, multimaster would bring its own host of complexities. With two primaries, you would have to handle conflicting writes (for example, someone updates a document on one primary and someone deletes it on another primary). There are two popular ways of handling conflicts in systems that support multiple writers: manual reconciliation or having the system arbitrarily pick a "winner." Neither of these options is a very easy model for developers to code against, seeing that you can't be sure that the data you've written won't change out from under you. Thus, MongoDB chose to only support having a single primary. This makes development easier but can result in periods when the replica set is read-only.

How Elections Work

When a secondary cannot reach a primary, it will contact all the other members and request that it be elected primary. These other members do several sanity checks: Can they reach a primary that the member seeking election cannot? Is the member seeking election up to date with replication? Is there anyone with a higher priority available who should be elected instead?

If a member seeking election receives "ayes" from a majority of the set, it becomes primary. If even one server *vetoes* the election, the election is canceled. A member vetoes an election when it knows any reason that the member seeking election shouldn't become primary.

You may see a very large negative number in the logs, since a veto is registered as 10,000 votes. Often you'll see messages about election results being 9,999 or similar if one member voted for a member and another member vetoed the election:

```
Wed Jun 20 17:44:02 [rsMgr] replSet info electSelf 1
Wed Jun 20 17:44:02 [rsMgr] replSet couldn't elect self, only received -9999 votes
```

If two members vetoed and one voted for, the election results would be 19,999, and so on. These messages are normal and nothing to worry about.

The member seeking election (the *candidate*) must be up to date with replication, as far as the members it can reach know. All replicated operations are strictly ordered by ascending timestamp, so the candidate must have operations later than or equal to any member it can reach.

For example, suppose that the latest operation that the candidate has replicated is op 123. It contacts the other members of the set and one of them has replicated up to operation 124. That member will veto the candidate's election. The candidate will continue syncing and once it has synced operation 124, it will call for an election again (if no one else has become primary in that time). This time around, assuming nothing else is wrong with candidate, the member that previously vetoed the election will vote for the candidate.

Assuming that the candidate receives "ayes" from a majority of voters, it will transition into primary state.

A common point of confusion is that members always seek election for themselves. For simplicity's sake, neighbors cannot "nominate" another server to be primary, they can only vote for it if it is seeking election.

Member Configuration Options

The replica sets we have set up so far have been fairly uniform in that every member has the same configuration as every other member. However, there are many situations when you don't want members to be identical: you might want one member to preferentially be primary or make a member invisible to clients so that no read requests can be routed to it. These and many other configuration options can be specified in the member subdocuments of the replica set configuration. This section outlines the member options that you can set.

Creating Election Arbiters

The example above shows the disadvantages two-member sets have for majority requirements. However, many people with small deployments do not want to keep three copies of their data, feeling that two is enough and keeping a third copy is not worth the administrative, operational, and financial costs.

For these deployments, MongoDB supports a special type of member called an *arbiter*, whose only purpose is to participate in elections. Arbiters hold no data and aren't used by clients: they just provide a majority for two-member sets.

As arbiters don't have any of the traditional responsibilities of a *mongod* server, you can run an arbiter as a lightweight process on a wimpier server than you'd generally use for MongoDB. It's often a good idea, if possible, to run an arbiter in a separate failure domain from the other members, so that it has an "outside perspective" on the set, as described in the recommended deployments listed in "How to Design a Set" on page 178.

You start up an arbiter in the same way that you start a normal *mongod*, using the `--replSet name` option and an empty data directory. You can add it to the set using the `rs.addArb()` helper:

```
> rs.addArb("server-5:27017")
```

Equivalently, you can specify the `arbiterOnly` option in the member configuration:

```
> rs.add({"_id" : 4, "host" : "server-5:27017", "arbiterOnly" : true})
```

An arbiter, once added to the set, is an arbiter forever: you cannot reconfigure an arbiter to become a nonarbiter, or vice versa.

One other thing that arbiters are good for is breaking ties in larger clusters. If you have an even number of nodes, you may have half the nodes vote for one member and half for another. Adding an arbiter can add a deciding vote.

Use at most one arbiter

Note that, in both of the use cases above, you need *at most* one arbiter. You do not need an arbiter if you have an odd number of nodes. A common misconception seems to be that you should add extra arbiters "just in case." However, it doesn't help elections go any faster or provide any data safety to add extra arbiters.

Suppose you have a three members set. Two members are required to elect a primary. If you add an arbiter, you'll have a four member set, so three members will be required to choose a primary. Thus, your set is potentially less stable: instead of requiring 67% of your set to be up, you're now requiring 75%.

Having extra members can also make elections take longer. If you have an even number of nodes because you added an arbiter, your arbiters can cause ties, not prevent them.

The downside to using an arbiter

If you have a choice between a data node and an arbiter, choose a data node. Using an arbiter instead of a data node in a small set can make some operational tasks more difficult. For example, suppose you are running a replica set with two "normal" members and one arbiter, and one of the data-holding members goes down. If that member is well and truly dead (the data is unrecoverable), you will have to get a copy of the data from the current primary to the new server you'll be using as a secondary. Copying data can put a lot of stress on a server and, thus, slow down your application. (Generally, copying a few gigabytes to a new server is trivial but more than a hundred starts becoming impractical.)

Conversely, if you have three data-holding members, there's more "breathing room" if a server completely dies. You can use the remaining secondary to bootstrap a new server instead of depending on your primary.

In the two-member-plus-arbiter scenario, the primary is the last remaining good copy of your data *and* the one trying to handle load from your application while you're trying to get another copy of your data online.

Thus, if possible, use an odd number of "normal" members instead of an arbiter.

Priority

Priority is how strongly this member "wants" to become primary. Priority can range from 0 to 100 and the default is 1. Setting priority to 0 has a special meaning: members with 0 priority can never become primary. These members are called *passive* members.

The highest-priority member will always be elected primary (so long as they can reach a majority of the set and have the most up-to-date data). For example, suppose you add a member with priority of 1.5 to the set, like so:

```
> rs.add({"_id" : 4, "host" : "server-4:27017", "priority" : 1.5})
```

Assuming the other members of the set have priority 1, once *server-4* caught up with the rest of the set, the current primary would automatically step down and *server-4* would elect itself. If *server-4* was, for some reason, unable to catch up, the current primary would stay primary. Setting priorities will never cause your set to go primary-less. It will also never cause a member who is behind to become primary (until it has caught up).

One interesting wrinkle with priority is that reconfigurations must always be sent to a member that could be primary with the new configuration. Therefore, you cannot set the current primary's priority to 0 with a single reconfig (and you cannot configure a set where all of the priorities are 0).

The absolute value of a priority only matters in relation to whether it is greater or less than the other priorities in the set: members with priorities of 500, 1, and 1 will behave the same way as another set with priorities 2, 1, and 1.

Hidden

Clients do not route requests to hidden members and hidden members are not preferred as replication sources (although they will be used if more desirable sources are not available). Thus, many people will hide less powerful or backup servers.

For example, suppose you had a set that looked like this:

```
> rs.isMaster()
{
    ...
    "hosts" : [
        "server-1:27107",
        "server-2:27017",
        "server-3:27017"
    ],
    ...
}
```

To hide *server-3*, add the `hidden: true` field to its configuration. A member must have a priority of 0 to be hidden (you can't have a hidden primary):

```
> var config = rs.config()
> config.members[2].hidden = 0
0
> config.members[2].priority = 0
0
> rs.reconfig(config)
```

Now running `isMaster()` will show:

```
> rs.isMaster()
{
    ...
    "hosts" : [
        "server-1:27107",
        "server-2:27017"
    ],
    ...
}
```

`rs.status()` and `rs.config()` will still show the member; it only disappears from `isMaster()`. When clients connect to a replica set, they call `isMaster()` to determine the members of the set. Thus, hidden members will never be used for read requests.

To unhide a member, change the `hidden` option to false or remove the option entirely.

Slave Delay

It's always possible for your data to be nuked by human error: someone might accidentally drop your main database or a newly deployed version of your application might have a bug that replaces all of your data with garbage. To defend against that type of problem, you can set up a delayed secondary using the *slaveDelay* setting.

A delayed secondary purposely lags by the specified number of seconds. This way, if someone fat-fingers away your main collection, you can restore it from an identical copy of the data from earlier. This is covered in "Restoring from a Delayed Secondary" on page 221.

`slaveDelay` requires the member's priority to be 0. If your application is routing reads to secondaries, you should make slave delayed members hidden so that reads are not routed to them.

Building Indexes

Sometimes a secondary does not need to have the same (or any) indexes that exist on the primary. If you are using a secondary only for backup data or offline batch jobs, you might want to specify `"buildIndexes" : false` in the member's configuration. This option prevents the secondary from building any indexes.

This is a permanent setting: members that have `"buildIndexes" : false` specified can never be reconfigured to be "normal" index-building members again. If you want to change a non-index-building member to an index-building one, you must remove it from the set, delete all of its data, re-add it to the set, and allow it to resync from scratch.

Again, this option requires the member's priority to be 0.

CHAPTER 10

Components of a Replica Set

This chapter covers how the pieces of a replica set fit together, including:

- How replica set members replicate new data
- How bringing up new members works
- How elections work
- Possible server and network failure scenarios

Syncing

Replication is concerned with keeping an identical copy of data on multiple servers. The way MongoDB accomplishes this is by keeping a log of operations, or *oplog*, containing every write that a primary performs. This is a capped collection that lives in the *local* database on the primary. The secondaries query this collection for operations to replicate.

Each secondary maintains its own oplog, recording each operation it replicates from the primary. This allows any member to be used as a sync source for any other member, as shown in Figure 10-1. Secondaries fetch operations from the member they are syncing from, apply the operations to their data set, and then write the operations to the oplog. If applying an operation fails (which should only happen if the underlying data has been corrupted or in some way differs from the primary), the secondary will exit.

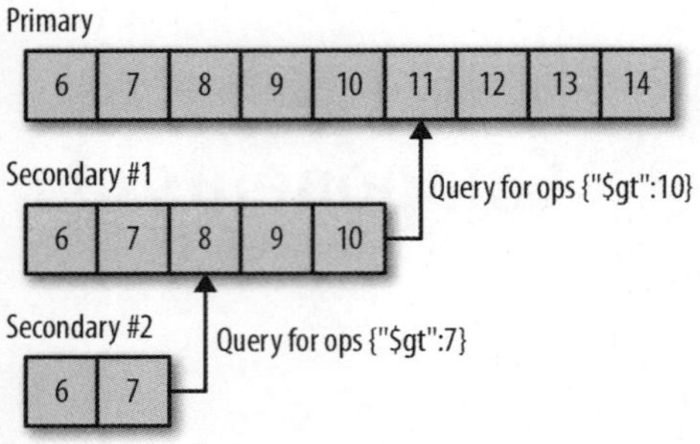

Figure 10-1. Oplog keep an ordered list of write operations that have occurred. Each member has its own copy of the oplog, which should be identical to the primary's (modulo some lag).

If a secondary goes down for any reason, when it restarts it will start syncing from the last operation in its oplog. As operations are applied to data and then written to the oplog, the secondary may replay operations that it has already applied to its data. MongoDB is designed for it to handle this correctly: replaying oplog ops multiple times yields the same result as replaying them once.

As the oplog is a fixed size, it can only hold a certain number of operations. In general, the oplog will use space at approximately the same rate as writes come into the system: if you're writing 1 KB/minute on the primary, your oplog is probably going to fill up at about 1 KB/minute. However, there are a few exceptions: operations that effect multiple documents, such as removes or a multi-updates, that will be exploded into many oplog entries. The single operation on the primary will be split into one oplog op per document affected. Thus, if you remove 1,000,000 documents from a collection with `db.coll.remove()`, it will become 1,000,000 oplog entries removing one document at a time. If you are doing lots of bulk operations, this can fill up your oplog more quickly than you might expect.

Initial Sync

When a member of the set starts up, it will check if it is in a valid state to begin syncing from someone. If not, it will attempt to make a full copy of data from another member of the set. This is called *initial syncing* and there are several steps to the process, which you can follow in the *mongod*'s log:

1. First, the member does some preliminary bookkeeping: it chooses a member to sync from, creates an identifier for itself in *local.me*, and drops all existing databases to start with a clean slate:

   ```
   Mon Jan 30 11:09:18 [rsSync] replSet initial sync pending
   Mon Jan 30 11:09:18 [rsSync] replSet syncing to: server-1:27017
   ```

```
Mon Jan 30 11:09:18 [rsSync] build index local.me { _id: 1 }
Mon Jan 30 11:09:18 [rsSync] build index done 0 records 0 secs
Mon Jan 30 11:09:18 [rsSync] replSet initial sync drop all databases
Mon Jan 30 11:09:18 [rsSync] dropAllDatabasesExceptLocal 1
```

Note that any existing data will be dropped at this point. Only do an initial sync if you do not want the data in your data directory or have moved it elsewhere, as *mongod*'s first action is to delete it all.

2. Cloning is the initial data copy of all records from the sync source. This is usually the most time-consuming part of the process:

```
Mon Jan 30 11:09:18 [rsSync] replSet initial sync clone all databases
Mon Jan 30 11:09:18 [rsSync] replSet initial sync cloning db: db1
Mon Jan 30 11:09:18 [FileAllocator] allocating new datafile /data/db/db1.ns,
    filling with zeroes...
```

3. Then the first oplog application occurs, which applies any operations that happened during the clone. This may have to reclone certain documents that were moved and, therefore, missed by the cloner:

```
Mon Jan 30 15:38:36 [rsSync] oplog sync 1 of 3
Mon Jan 30 15:38:36 [rsBackgroundSync] replSet syncing to: server-1:27017
Mon Jan 30 15:38:37 [rsSyncNotifier] replset setting oplog notifier to
    server-1:27017
Mon Jan 30 15:38:37 [repl writer worker 2] replication update of non-mod
    failed:
    { ts: Timestamp 1352215827000|17, h: -5618036261007523082, v: 2, op: "u",
      ns: "db1.someColl", o2: { _id: ObjectId('50992a2a7852201e750012b7') },
      o: { $set: { count.0: 2, count.1: 0 } } }
Mon Jan 30 15:38:37 [repl writer worker 2] replication info
    adding missing object
Mon Jan 30 15:38:37 [repl writer worker 2] replication missing object
    not found on source. presumably deleted later in oplog
```

This is roughly what the logs will look like if some documents had to be recloned. Depending on the level of traffic and the types of operations that where happening on the sync source, you may or may not have missing objects.

4. Then the second oplog application occurs, which applies operations that happened during the first oplog application:

```
Mon Jan 30 15:39:41 [rsSync] oplog sync 2 of 3
```

This one generally passes without much fanfare. It is only distinct from the first application in that there should no longer be anything to reclone.

5. At this point, the data should exactly match the data set as it existed at some point on the primary so that the secondary can start building indexes. This can be quite time-consuming if you have large collections or lots of indexes:

```
Mon Jan 30 15:39:43 [rsSync] replSet initial sync building indexes
Mon Jan 30 15:39:43 [rsSync] replSet initial sync cloning indexes for : db1
Mon Jan 30 15:39:43 [rsSync] build index db.allObjects { someColl: 1 }
```

```
Mon Jan 30 15:39:44 [rsSync] build index done.  scanned 209844 total records.
    1.96 secs
```

6. Then the final oplog application occurs; this final step is merely to prevent the member from becoming a secondary while it is still far behind the sync source. It applies all of the operations that happened while indexes were building:

   ```
   Tue Nov  6 16:05:59 [rsSync] oplog sync 3 of 3
   ```

7. At this point, the member finishes the initial sync process and transitions to normal syncing, which allows it to become a secondary:

   ```
   Mon Jan 30 16:07:52 [rsSync] replSet initial sync done
   Mon Jan 30 16:07:52 [rsSync] replSet syncing to: server-1:27017
   Mon Jan 30 16:07:52 [rsSync] replSet SECONDARY
   ```

The best way to track an initial sync's progress is by watching the server's log.

Doing an initial sync is very easy from an operator perspective: start up a *mongod* with a clean data directory. However, it is often preferable to restore from backup instead, as covered in Chapter 22. Restoring from backup is often faster than copying all of your data through *mongod*.

Also, cloning can ruin the sync source's *working set*. Many deployments end up with a subset of their data that's frequently accessed and always in memory (because the OS is accessing it frequently). Performing an initial sync forces the member to page all of its data into memory, evicting the frequently-used data. This can slow down a member dramatically as requests that were being handled by data in RAM are suddenly forced to go to disk. However, for small data sets and servers with some breathing room, initial syncing is a good, easy option.

One of the most common issues people run into with initial sync is when step 2 (cloning) or step 5 (building indexes) takes too long. In these cases, the new member can "fall off" the end of sync source's oplog: the new member gets so far behind the sync source that it can no longer catch up because the sync source's oplog has overwritten the data the member would need to use to continue replicating.

There is no way to fix this other than attempting the initial sync at a less-busy time or restoring from a backup. The initial sync cannot proceed if the member has fallen off of the sync source's oplog. The next section covers this in more depth.

Handling Staleness

If a secondary falls too far behind the actual operations being performed on the sync source, the secondary will go *stale*. A stale secondary is unable to continue catch up because every operation in the sync source's oplog is too far ahead: it would be skipping operations if it continued to sync. This could happen if the slave has had downtime, has more writes than it can handle, or is too busy handling reads.

When a secondary goes stale, it will attempt to replicate from each member of the set in turn to see if there's anyone with a longer oplog that it can bootstrap from. If there is no one with a long-enough oplog, replication on that member will halt and it will need to be fully resynced (or restored from a more recent backup).

To avoid out-of-sync secondaries, it's important to have a large oplog so that the primary can store a long history of operations. A larger oplog will obviously use more disk space. But in general this is a good trade-off to make because the disk space tends to be cheap and little of the oplog is usually in use, and therefore it doesn't take up much RAM. For more information on sizing the oplog, see "Resizing the Oplog" on page 220.

Heartbeats

Members need to know about the other members' states: who's primary, who they can sync from, and who's down. To keep an up-to-date view of the set a member sends out a *heartbeat request* to every other member of the set every two seconds. A heartbeat request is a short message that checks everyone's state.

One of the most important functions of heartbeats is to let the primary know if it can reach a majority of the set. If a primary can no longer reach a majority of the servers, it will demote itself and become a secondary.

Member States

Members also communicate what state they are in via heartbeats. We've already discussed two states: primary and secondary. There are several other normal states that you'll often see members be in:

STARTUP
: This is the state MongoDB goes into when you first start a member. It's the state when MongoDB is attempting to load a member's replica set configuration. Once the configuration has been loaded, it transitions to STARTUP2.

STARTUP2
: This state will last throughout the initial sync process but on a normal member, it should only ever last a few seconds. It just forks off a couple of threads to handle replication and elections and then transitions into the next state: RECOVERING.

RECOVERING
: This state means that the member is operating correctly but is not available for reads. This state is a bit overloaded: you may see it in a variety of situations.

On startup, a member has to make a couple checks to make sure it's in a valid state before accepting reads; therefore, all members will go through recovering state briefly on startup before becoming secondaries. A member can also go into RECOVERING state during long-running operations such as compact or in response to the *replSetMaintenance* command (see "Using Maintenance Mode" on page 213).

A member will also go into RECOVERING state if it has fallen too far behind the other members to catch up. This is, generally, a failure state that requires resyncing the member. The member does not go into an error state at this point because it lives in hope that someone will come online with a long-enough oplog that it can bootstrap itself back to non-staleness.

ARBITER
: Arbiters have a special state and should always be in state ARBITER during normal operation.

There are also a few states that indicate a problem with the system. These include:

DOWN
: If a member was up but then becomes unreachable. Note that a member reported as "down" might, in fact, still be up, just unreachable due to network issues.

UNKNOWN
: If a member has never been able to reach another member, it will not know what state it's in, so it will report it as unknown. This generally indicates that the unknown member is down or that there are network problems between the two members.

REMOVED
: This is the state of a member that has been removed from the set. If a removed member is added back into the set, it will transition back into its "normal" state.

ROLLBACK
: This state is used when a member is rolling back data, as described in "Rollbacks" on page 193. At the end of the rollback process, a server will transition back into the recovering state and then become a secondary.

FATAL
: Something uncorrectable has gone wrong and this member has given up trying to function normally. You should take a look at the log to figure out what has caused it to go into this state (grep for `"replSet FATAL"` to find the point where it went into the FATAL state). You generally will have to shut down the server and resync it or restore from backup once it's in this state.

Elections

A member will seek election if it cannot reach a primary (and is itself eligible to become primary). A member seeking election will send out a notice to all of the members it can reach. These members may know of reasons that this member is an unsuitable primary: it may be behind in replication or there may already be a primary that the member seeking election cannot reach. In these cases, the other members will not allow the election to proceed.

Assuming that there is no reason to object, the other members will vote for the member seeking election. If the member seeking election receives votes from a majority of the set, the election was successful and will transition into primary state. If it did not receive a majority if votes, it will remain a secondary and may try to become a primary again later. A primary will remain primary until it cannot reach a majority of members, goes down, is stepped down, or the set is reconfigured.

Assuming that the network is healthy and a majority of the servers are up, elections should be fast. It will take a member up to two seconds to notice that a primary has gone down (due to the heartbeats mentioned earlier) and it will immediately start an election, which should only take a few milliseconds. However, the situation is often non-optimal: an election may be triggered due to networking issues or overloaded servers responding too slowly. In these cases, heartbeats will take up to 20 seconds to timeout. If, at that point, the election results in a tie, everyone will have to wait 30 seconds to attempt another election. Thus, if everything goes wrong, an election may take a few minutes.

Rollbacks

The election process described in the previous section means that if a primary does a write and goes down before the secondaries have a chance to replicate it, the next primary elected may not have the write. For example, suppose we have two data centers, one with the primary and a secondary, and the other with three secondaries, as shown in Figure 10-2.

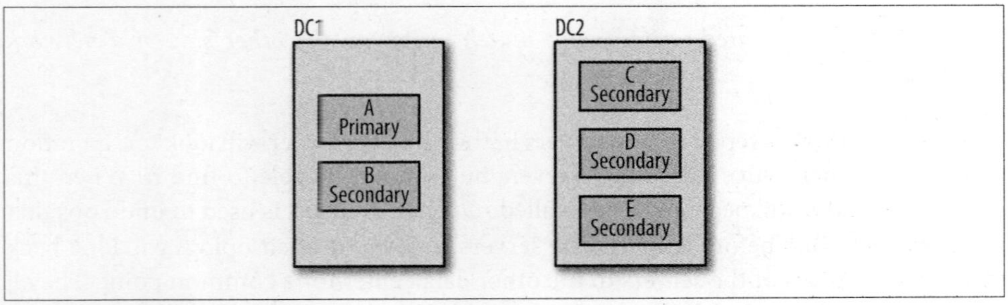

Figure 10-2. A possible two-data-center configuration

Suppose that there is a network partition between the two data centers, as shown in Figure 10-3. The servers in the first data center are up to operation 126, but that data center hasn't yet replicated to the servers in the other data center.

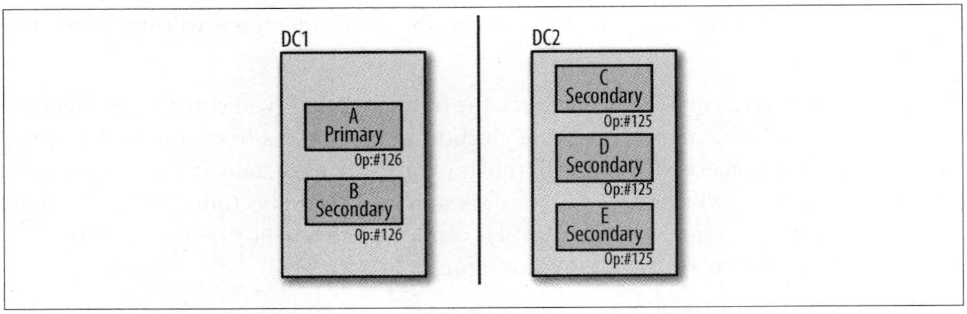

Figure 10-3. Replication across data centers can be slower than within a single data center

The servers in the other data center can still reach a majority of the set (three out of five servers). Thus, one of them may be elected primary. This new primary begins taking its own writes, as shown in Figure 10-4.

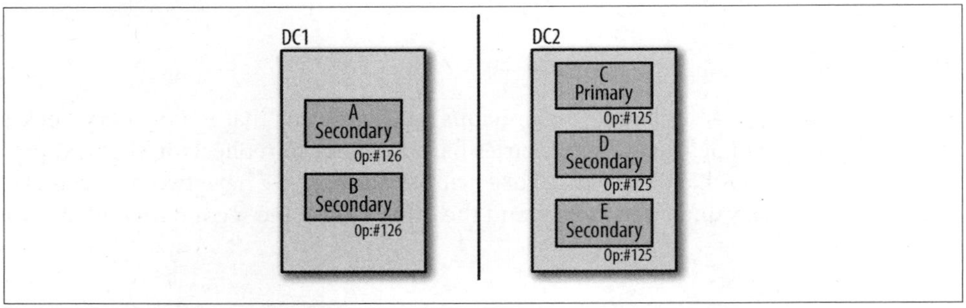

Figure 10-4. Unreplicated writes won't match writes on the other side of a network partition

When the network is repaired, the servers in the first data center will look for operation 126 to start syncing from the other servers but will not be able to find it. When this happens, *A* and *B* will begin a process called *rollback*. Rollback is used to undo ops that were not replicated before failover. The servers with 126 in their oplogs will look back through the oplogs of the servers in the other data center for a common point. They'll find that operation 125 is the latest operation that matches. Figure 10-5 shows what the oplogs would look like.

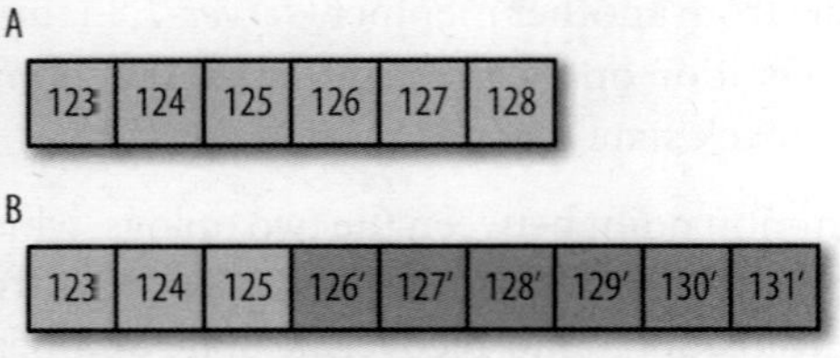

Figure 10-5. Two members with conflicting oplogs: A apparently crashed before replicating ops 126–128, so these operations are not present on B, which has more recent operations. A will have to rollback these three operations before resuming syncing.

At this point, the server will go through the ops it has and write its version of each document affected by those ops to a *.bson* file in a *rollback* directory of your data directory. Thus, if (for example) operation 126 was an update, it will write the document updated by 126 to *collectionName.bson*. Then it will copy the version of that document from the current primary.

The following is a paste of the log entries generated from a typical rollback:

```
Fri Oct  7 06:30:35 [rsSync] replSet syncing to: server-1
Fri Oct  7 06:30:35 [rsSync] replSet our last op time written: Oct  7
    06:30:05:3
Fri Oct  7 06:30:35 [rsSync] replset source's GTE: Oct  7 06:30:31:1
Fri Oct  7 06:30:35 [rsSync] replSet rollback 0
Fri Oct  7 06:30:35 [rsSync] replSet ROLLBACK
Fri Oct  7 06:30:35 [rsSync] replSet rollback 1
Fri Oct  7 06:30:35 [rsSync] replSet rollback 2 FindCommonPoint
Fri Oct  7 06:30:35 [rsSync] replSet info rollback our last optime:   Oct  7
    06:30:05:3
Fri Oct  7 06:30:35 [rsSync] replSet info rollback their last optime: Oct  7
    06:30:31:2
Fri Oct  7 06:30:35 [rsSync] replSet info rollback diff in end of log times:
    -26 seconds
Fri Oct  7 06:30:35 [rsSync] replSet rollback found matching events at Oct  7
   06:30:03:4118
Fri Oct  7 06:30:35 [rsSync] replSet rollback findcommonpoint scanned : 6
Fri Oct  7 06:30:35 [rsSync] replSet replSet rollback 3 fixup
Fri Oct  7 06:30:35 [rsSync] replSet rollback 3.5
Fri Oct  7 06:30:35 [rsSync] replSet rollback 4 n:3
Fri Oct  7 06:30:35 [rsSync] replSet minvalid=Oct  7 06:30:31 4e8ed4c7:2
Fri Oct  7 06:30:35 [rsSync] replSet rollback 4.6
Fri Oct  7 06:30:35 [rsSync] replSet rollback 4.7
Fri Oct  7 06:30:35 [rsSync] replSet rollback 5 d:6 u:0
Fri Oct  7 06:30:35 [rsSync] replSet rollback 6
Fri Oct  7 06:30:35 [rsSync] replSet rollback 7
Fri Oct  7 06:30:35 [rsSync] replSet rollback done
Fri Oct  7 06:30:35 [rsSync] replSet RECOVERING
Fri Oct  7 06:30:36 [rsSync] replSet syncing to: server-1
Fri Oct  7 06:30:36 [rsSync] replSet SECONDARY
```

The server begins syncing from another member (*server-1*, in this case) and realizes that it cannot find its latest operation on the sync source. At that point, it starts the rollback process by going into rollback state ("`replSet ROLLBACK`").

At step 2, it finds the common point between the two oplogs, which was 26 seconds ago. It then begins undoing the operations from the last 26 seconds from its oplog. Once the rollback is complete, it transitions into recovering state and begins syncing normally again.

To apply operations that have been rolled back to the current primary, first use *mongorestore* to load them into a temporary collection:

```
$ mongorestore --db stage --collection stuff \
> /data/db/rollback/important.stuff.2012-12-19T18-27-14.0.bson
```

Now you should examine the documents (using the shell) and compare them to the current contents of the collection from whence they came. For example, if someone had created a "normal" index on the rollback member and a unique index on current primary, you'd want to make sure that there weren't any duplicates in the rolled-back data and resolve them if there were.

Once you have a version of the documents that you like in your staging collection, load it into your main collection:

```
> staging.stuff.find().forEach(function(doc) {
...     prod.stuff.insert(doc);
... })
```

If you have any insert-only collections, you can directly load the rollback documents into the collection. However, if you are doing updates on the collection you will need to be more careful about how you merge rollback data.

One often-misused member configuration option is the number of votes each member has. Manipulating the number of votes is almost always not what you want and causes a lot of rollbacks (which is why it was not included in the list of member properties in the last chapter). Do not change the number of votes unless you are prepared to deal with regular rollbacks.

For more information on preventing rollbacks, see Chapter 11.

When Rollbacks Fail

In some cases, MongoDB decides that the rollback is too large to undertake. Rollback can fail if there are more than 300 MB of data or about 30 minutes of operations to roll back. In these cases, you must resync the node that is stuck in rollback.

The most common cause of this is when secondaries are lagging and the primary goes down. If one of the secondaries becomes primary, it will be missing a lot of operations from the old primary. The best way to make sure you don't get a member stuck in rollback is to keep your secondaries as up to date as possible.

CHAPTER 11

Connecting to a Replica Set from Your Application

This chapter covers how applications interact with replica sets, including:

- How connections and failovers work
- Waiting for replication on writes
- Routing reads to the correct member

Client-to-Replica-Set Connection Behavior

From an application's point of view, a replica set behaves much like a standalone server. By default, client libraries will connect to the primary and route all traffic to it. Your application can perform reads and writes as though it were talking to a standalone server while your replica set quietly keeps hot standbys ready in the background.

Connections to a replica set are similar to connections to a single server. Use the `MongoClient`-equivalent in your driver and provide a list of *seeds* for the driver to connect to. Seeds are members of the replica set. You do not have to list all members (although you can): when the driver connects to the seeds, it will discover the other members from them. A connection string usually looks something like this:

```
"mongodb://server-1:27017,server-2:27017"
```

See your driver's documentation for details.

When a primary goes down, the driver will automatically find the new primary (once one is elected) and will route requests to it as soon as possible. However, while there is no reachable primary your application will be unable to perform writes.

There may be no primary available for a brief time (during an election) or for an extended period of time (if no reachable member can become primary). By default, the driver will not service any requests—read or write—during this period. However, you can optionally use secondaries for read requests.

A common desire is to have the driver hide the entire election process (the primary going away and a new primary being elected) from the user. However, this is not possible or desirable in many cases, so no driver handles failover this way. First, a driver can only hide a lack of primary for so long: a set could exist forever with no primary. Second, a driver often finds out that the primary went down because an operation failed, which means that the driver doesn't know whether or not the primary processed the operation before going down. Thus, the driver leaves it to the user: Do you want to retry the operation on the new primary, if one is elected quickly? Assume it got through on the old primary? Check and see if the new primary has the operation? The strategy that makes sense will depend on your application.

There isn't a general way to discover whether an operation succeeded or not before a server crashed, although depending on your application you might be able to craft a custom solution. For example, if the driver just inserted the document `{"_id" : 1}` and received an error that the primary crashed, when it reconnects to the newly elected primary it could check if `{"_id" : 1}` exists or not.

Waiting for Replication on Writes

To ensure that writes will be persisted no matter what happens to the set, you must ensure that the write propagates to a majority of the members of the set, as mentioned in the previous chapter.

Earlier, we used the *getLastError* command to check that writes were successful. We can use that same command to ensure that a write has been replicated to secondaries. The *"w"* parameter forces *getLastError* to wait until the given number of members has the last write. MongoDB has a special keyword that you can pass to `"w"` for this: `"majority"`. In the shell, this looks like:

```
> db.runCommand({"getLastError" : 1, "w" : "majority"})
{
    "n" : 0,
    "lastOp" : Timestamp(1346790783000, 1),
    "connectionId" : 2,
    "writtenTo" : [
        { "_id" : 0 , "host" : "server-0" },
        { "_id" : 1 , "host" : "server-1" },
        { "_id" : 3 , "host" : "server-3" }
    ],
    "wtime" : 76,
    "err" : null,
```

```
    "ok" : 1
}
```

Notice the new field in *getLastError*'s output, `"writtenTo"`. It is only present if you use the `"w"` option and it is a list of servers that the last operation was replicated to.

Suppose that we run the command above, but only the primary and an arbiter are up: the primary cannot replicate the write to any other member of the set. *getLastError* doesn't know how long to wait for replication, so it will wait forever. Thus, you should always set *wtimeout* to a reasonable value. `"wtimeout"` is another option to *getLastError* and specifies in milliseconds how long the command should wait before returning failure: MongoDB was unable to replicate to `"w"` members in the time specified.

The code below will wait for one second before giving up:

```
> db.runCommand({"getLastError" : 1, "w" : "majority", "wtimeout" : 1000})
```

This may fail for a variety of reasons: the other members may be down or lagging or unavailable due to network issues. If *getLastError* times out, your application has to decide what to do next. Note that *getLastError* timing out doesn't mean that the write failed. It merely means that it failed to replicate far enough in the time specified. The write is still present on any servers it made it to and will continue to propagate to the other members of the set as quickly as possible.

A common use for `"w"` is to throttle writes. MongoDB lets you write "too fast." It will let you write to the primary so quickly that the secondaries cannot keep up. A common way of preventing this is to periodically call *getLastError* with `"w"` set to something higher than 1. This forces writes on that particular connection to wait for replication. Note that it only blocks writes on that connection: writes can still occur on any other connection.

If you wish to make your application behave sensibly and robustly, regularly call *getLastError* with `"majority"` and a reasonable timeout. If this begins timing out, look into what's wrong with your set.

What Can Go Wrong?

Suppose your application sends a write to the primary. It calls *getLastError* (without the `"majority"` option) and receives confirmation that the write was written, but the primary crashes before any secondaries have had a chance to replicate that write.

Now your application thinks that it'll be able to access that write (*getLastError* confirmed that the write succeeded) and the current members of the replica set don't have a copy of it.

At some point, a secondary may be elected primary and start taking new writes. When the former primary comes back up, it will discover that it has writes that the current primary does not. To correct this, it will undo any writes that do not match the sequence of operations on the current primary. These operations are not lost, but they are written to special *rollback* files that have to be manually applied to the current primary. MongoDB cannot automatically apply these writes, since they may conflict with other writes that have happened since the crash. Thus, the write essentially disappears until an admin gets a chance to apply the rollback files to the current primary.

Writing to a majority prevents this situation: if the application initially used `"w" : "majority"` and gets a confirmation that the write succeeded, then the new primary would have to have a copy of the write to be elected (a member must be up to date to be elected primary). If *getLastError* failed, then the application would know to try again, given that the write had not been propagated to a majority of the set before the primary crashed.

See Chapter 10 for more details on rollbacks.

Other Options for "w"

`"majority"` is not the only option that you can pass to *getLastError*, MongoDB also lets you specify an arbitrary number of servers to replicate to by passing `"w"` a number, as below:

```
> db.runCommand({"getLastError" : 1, "w" : 2, "wtimeout" : 500})
```

This would wait until two members (the primary and one secondary) had the write.

Note that the *"w"* value includes the primary. If you want the write propagated to `n` secondaries, you should set `"w"` to `n+1` (to include the primary). Setting `"w" : 1` is the same as not passing the `"w"` option at all because it just checks that the write was successful on the primary, which is what *getLastError* does anyway.

The downside to using a literal number is that you have to change your application if your replica set configuration changes.

Custom Replication Guarantees

Writing to a majority of a set is considered "safe." However, some sets may have more complex requirements: you may want to make sure that a write makes it to at least one server in each data center or a majority of the nonhidden nodes. Replica sets allows you to create custom rules that you can pass to *getLastError* to guarantee replication to whatever combination of servers you need.

Guaranteeing One Server per Data Center

Network issues between data centers are much more common than within data centers and it is more likely for an entire data center to go dark than an equivalent smattering of servers across multiple data centers. Thus, you might want some data-center-specific logic for writes. Guaranteeing a write to every data center before confirming success means that, in the case of a write followed by the data center going offline, every other data center will have at least one local copy.

To set this up, first classify the members by data center. You do this by adding a `"tags"` field to their replica set configuration:

```
> var config = rs.config()
> config.members[0].tags = {"dc" : "us-east"}
> config.members[1].tags = {"dc" : "us-east"}
> config.members[2].tags = {"dc" : "us-east"}
> config.members[3].tags = {"dc" : "us-east"}
> config.members[4].tags = {"dc" : "us-west"}
> config.members[5].tags = {"dc" : "us-west"}
> config.members[6].tags = {"dc" : "us-west"}
```

The `"tags"` field is an object, as each member can have multiple tags. It might be a `"high quality"` server in the *"us-east"* data center, for example, in which case we'd want a tags field such as `{"dc": "us-east", "quality" : "high"}`.

The second step is to add a rule by creating a `"getLastErrorMode"` field in our replica set config. Each rule is of the form `"`*`name`*`" : {"`*`key`*`" : `*`number`*`}}`. `"`*`name`*`"` is the name for the rule, which should describe what the rule does in a way that clients can understand, as they'll be using this name when they call *getLastError*. In this example, we might call this rule `"eachDC"` or something more abstract such as `"user-level safe"`.

The `"`*`key`*`"` field is the key field from the tags, so in this example it will be `"dc"`. The *`number`* is the number groups that are needed to fulfil this rule. In this case, *`number`* is 2 (because we want at least one server from `"us-east"` and one from `"us-west"`). *`num ber`* always means "at least one server from each of *`number`* groups."

We add `"getLastErrorModes"` to the replica set config and reconfigure to create the rule:

```
> config.settings = {}
> config.settings.getLastErrorModes = [{"eachDC" : {"dc" : 2}}]
> rs.reconfig(config)
```

`"getLastErrorModes"` lives in the `"settings"` subobject of a replica set config, which contains a few set-level optional settings.

Now we can use this rule for writes:

```
> db.foo.insert({"x" : 1})
> db.runCommand({"getLastError" : 1, "w" : "eachDC", "wtimeout" : 1000})
```

Note that rules are somewhat abstracted away from the application developer: they don't have to know which servers are in "eachDC" to use the rule, and the rule can change without their application having to change. We could add a datacenter or change set members and the application would not have to know.

Guaranteeing a Majority of Nonhidden Members

Often, hidden members are somewhat second-class citizens: you're never going to fail over to them and they certainly aren't taking any reads. Thus, you may only care that nonhidden members received a write and let the hidden members sort it out for themselves.

Suppose we have five members, *host0* through *host4*, *host4* being a hidden member. We want to make sure that a majority of the nonhidden members have a write, that is, at least three of *host0*, *host1*, *host2*, and *host3*. To create a rule for this, first we tag each of the nonhidden members with its own tag:

```
> var config = rs.config()
> config.members[0].tags = [{"normal" : "A"}]
> config.members[1].tags = [{"normal" : "B"}]
> config.members[2].tags = [{"normal" : "C"}]
> config.members[3].tags = [{"normal" : "D"}]
```

The hidden member, *host4*, is not given a tag.

Now we add a rule for the majority of these servers:

```
> config.settings.getLastErrorModes = [{"visibleMajority" : {"normal" : 3}}]
> rs.reconfig(config)
```

Finally, you can use this rule in your application:

```
> db.foo.insert({"x" : 1})
> db.runCommand({"getLastError" : 1, "w" : "visibleMajority", "wtimeout": 1000})
```

This will wait until at least three of the nonhidden member have the write.

Creating Other Guarantees

The rules you can create are limitless. Remember that there are two steps to creating a custom replication rule:

1. Tag members by assigning them key-value pairs. The keys describe classifications; for example, you might have keys such as `"data_center"` or `"region"` or `"serverQuality"`. Values determine which group a server belongs to within a classification. For example, for the key `"data_center"`, you might have some servers tagged `"us-east"`, some `"us-west"`, and others `"aust"`.
2. Create a *rule* based on the classifications you create. Rules are always of the form `{"`*`name`*`" : {"`*`key`*`" : `*`number`*`}}`, where at least one server from *`number`* groups must have a write before it has succeeded. For example, you could create a rule `{"twoDCs" : {"data_center" : 2}}`, which would mean that at least one server in two of the data centers tagged must confirm a write before it is successful.

Then you can use this rule in *getLastError*.

Rules are immensely powerful ways to configure replication, although they are complex to understand and set up. Unless you have fairly involved replication requirements, you should be perfectly safe sticking with `"w" : "majority"`.

Sending Reads to Secondaries

By default, drivers will route all requests to the primary. This is generally what you want, but you can configure other options by setting *read preferences* in your driver. Read preferences let you specify the types of servers queries should be sent to.

Sending read requests to secondaries is generally a bad idea. There are some specific situations in which it makes sense, but you should generally send all traffic to the primary. If you are considering sending reads to secondaries, make sure to weigh the pros and cons very carefully before allowing it. This section covers why it's a bad idea and the specific conditions when it makes sense to do so.

Consistency Considerations

Applications that require strongly consistent reads should not read from secondaries.

Secondaries should usually be within a few milliseconds of the primary. However, there is no guarantee of this. Sometimes secondaries can fall behind by minutes, hours, or even days due to load, misconfiguration, network errors, or other issues. Client libraries cannot tell how up to date a secondary is, so clients will cheerfully send queries to secondaries that are far behind. Hiding a secondary from client reads can be done but is a manual process. Thus, if your application needs data that is predictably up to date, it should not read from secondaries.

If your application needs to read its own writes (e.g., insert a document and then query for it and find it) you should not send the read to a secondary (unless the write waits for replication to all secondaries using `"w"` as shown earlier). Otherwise, an application may perform a successful write, attempt to read the value, and not be able to find it (because it sent the read to a secondary, which hadn't replicated yet). Clients can issue requests faster than replication can copy operations.

To always send read requests to the primary, set your read preference to `Primary` (or leave it alone, since `Primary` is the default). If there is no primary, queries will error out. This means that your application cannot perform queries if the primary goes down. However, it is certainly an acceptable option if your application can deal with downtime during failovers or network partitions or if getting stale data is unacceptable.

Load Considerations

Many users send reads to secondaries to distribute load. For example, if your servers can only handle 10,000 queries a second and you need to handle 30,000, you might set up a couple of secondaries and have them take some of the load. However, this is a dangerous way to scale because it's easy to accidentally overload your system and difficult to recover from once you do.

For example, suppose that you have the situation above: 30,000 reads per second. You decide to create a replica set with four members to handle this: each secondary is well below it's maximum load and the system works perfectly.

Until one of the secondaries crashes.

Now each of the remaining members are handling 100% of their possible load. If you need to rebuild the member that crashed, it may need to copy data from one of the other servers, overwhelming the remaining servers. Overloading a server often makes it perform slower, lowering the set's capacity even further and forcing other members to take more load, causing them to slow down in a death spiral.

Overloading can also cause replication to slow down, making the remaining secondaries fall behind. Suddenly you have a member down, a member lagging, and everything is too overloaded to have any wiggle room.

If you have a good idea of how much load a server can take, you might feel like you can plan this out better: use five servers instead of four and the set won't be overloaded if one goes down. However, even if you plan it out perfectly (and only lose the number of servers you expected), you still have to fix the situation with the other servers under more stress than they would be otherwise.

A better choice is to use sharding to distribute load. We'll cover how to set sharding up in Chapter 13.

Reasons to Read from Secondaries

There are a few cases in which it's reasonable to send application reads to secondaries. For instance, you may want your application to still be able to perform reads if the primary goes down (and you do not care if those reads are somewhat stale). The is the most common case for distributing reads to secondaries: you'd like a temporary read-only mode when your set loses a primary. This read preference is called `Primary preferred`.

One common argument for reading from secondaries is to get low-latency reads. You can specify `Nearest` as your read preference to route requests to the lowest-latency member based on average ping time from the driver to the replica set member. If your application needs to access the same document with low latency in multiple data centers, this is the only way to do it. If, however, your documents are more location-based (application servers in this data center need low-latency access to some of your data, or application servers in another data center need low-latency access to other data), this should be done with sharding. Note that you must use sharding if your application requires low-latency reads *and* low-latency writes: replica sets only allow writes to one location (wherever the primary is).

You must be willing to sacrifice consistency if you are reading from members that may not have replicated all the writes yet. Alternatively, you could sacrifice write speed if you wanted to wait until writes had been replicated to all members.

If your application can truly function acceptably with arbitrarily stale data, you can use `Secondary` or `Secondary preferred` read preferences. `Secondary` will always send read requests to a secondary. If there are no secondaries available, this will error out rather than send reads to the primary. It can be used for applications that do not care about stale data and want to use the primary for writes only. If you have any concerns about staleness of data, this is not recommended.

`Secondary preferred` will send read requests to a secondary, if one is available. If no secondaries are available, requests will be sent to the primary.

Sometimes, read load is drastically different than write load: you're reading entirely different data than you're writing. You might want dozens of indexes for offline processing that you don't want to have on the primary. In this case, you might want to set up a secondary with different indexes than the primary. If you'd like to use a secondary for this purpose, you'd probably create a connection directly to it from the driver, instead of using a replica set connection.

Consider which of the options makes sense for your application. You can also combine options: if some read requests must be from the primary, use `Primary` for those. If you are OK with other reads not having the most up-to-date data, use `Primary preferred` for those. And if certain requests require low latency over consistency, use `Nearest` for those.

CHAPTER 12
Administration

This chapter covers replica set administration, including:

- Techniques for performing maintenance on individual members
- Configuring sets under a variety of circumstances
- Getting information about and resizing your oplog
- Doing some more exotic set configurations
- Converting from master-slave to a replica set

Starting Members in Standalone Mode

A lot of maintenance tasks cannot be performed on secondaries (because they involve writes) and shouldn't be performed on primaries. Thus, the following sections frequently mention starting up a server in *standalone mode*. This means restarting the member so that it is a standalone server, not a member of a replica set (temporarily).

To start up a member in standalone mode, first look at the command line argument. Suppose it looks something like this:

```
> db.serverCmdLineOpts()
{
    "argv" : [ "mongod", "-f", "/var/lib/mongod.conf" ],
    "parsed" : {
        "replSet": "mySet",
        "port": "27017",
        "dbpath": "/var/lib/db"
    },
    "ok" : 1
}
```

To perform maintenance on this server we can restart it without the `replSet` option. This will allow us to read and write to it as a normal standalone *mongod*. We don't want the other servers in the set to be able to contact it, so we'll make it listen on a different port (so that the other members won't be able to find it). Finally, we want to keep the `dbpath` the same, as we are presumably starting it up this way to manipulate the server's data somehow. Thus, we start up this server with the following arguments:

```
$ mongod --port 30000 --dbpath /var/lib/db
```

It will now be a running as a standalone server, listening on port 30000 for connections. The other members of the set will attempt to connect to it on port 27017 and assume that it is down.

When we have finished performing maintenance on the server, we can shut it down and restart it with its original options. It will automatically sync up with the rest of the set, replicating any operations that it missed while it was "away."

Replica Set Configuration

Replica set configuration is always kept in a document in the *local.system.replset* collection. This document is the same on all members of the set. Never update this document using *update*. Always use an `rs` helper or the *replSetReconfig* command.

Creating a Replica Set

You create a replica set by starting up the *mongods* that you want to be members and then passing one of them a configuration through `rs.initiate`:

```
> var config = {
... "_id" : setName,
... "members" : [
...     {"_id" : 0, "host" : host1},
...     {"_id" : 1, "host" : host2},
...     {"_id" : 2, "host" : host3}
... ]}
> rs.initiate(config)
```

You should always pass a config object to `rs.initiate`. If you do not, MongoDB will attempt to automatically generate a config for a one-member replica set. It may not use the hostname that you want or correctly configure the set.

You only call `rs.initiate` on one member of the set. The member that receives the initiate will pass the configuration on to the other members.

Changing Set Members

When you add a new set member, it should either have nothing in its data directory (in which case it will initial sync) or have a copy of the data from another member. See Chapter 22 for more information about backing up and restoring replica set members.

Connect to the primary and add the new member:

```
> rs.add("spock:27017")
```

Alternatively, you can specify a more complex member config as a document:

```
> rs.add({"_id" : 5, "host" : "spock:27017", "priority" : 0, "hidden" : true})
```

You can also remove members by their `"host"` field:

```
> rs.remove("spock:27017")
```

You can change a member's settings by reconfiguring. There are a few restrictions in changing a member's settings:

- You cannot change a member's `"_id"`.
- You cannot make the member you're sending the reconfig to (generally the primary) priority 0.
- You cannot turn an arbiter into a nonarbiter and visa versa.
- You cannot change a member with `"buildIndexes" : false` to `"buildIndexes" : true`.

Notably, you *can* change a member's `"host"` field. Thus, if you incorrectly specify a host (say, use a public IP instead of a private one) you can later go back and simply change the config to use the correct IP.

To change a hostname, you could do something like this:

```
> var config = rs.config()
> config.members[0].host = "spock:27017"
spock:27017
> rs.reconfig(config)
```

This same strategy applies to change any other option: fetch the config with `rs.config()`, modify any parts of it that you wish, and reconfigure the set by passing `rs.reconfig()` the new configuration.

Creating Larger Sets

Replica sets are limited to 12 members and only 7 voting members. This is to reduce the amount of network traffic required for everyone to heartbeat everyone else and to limit the amount of time elections take. However, it can be too restrictive: see "Master-Slave" on page 225 if you require more that 11 secondaries.

If you are creating a replica set that has more than 7 members, every additional member must be given 0 votes. You can do this by specifying it in the member's config:

```
> rs.add({"_id" : 7, "host" : "server-7:27017", "votes" : 0})
```

This prevents these members from casting positive votes in elections, although they can still veto.

Please do not alter votes if you can possibly avoid it. Votes have weird, non-intuitive implications for elections and consistency guarantees. Only use votes if you are creating a set with more than seven members or you want to prevent automatic failover, as described in "Mimicking Master-Slave Behavior with Replica Sets" on page 226. Often, developers mistakenly think that a member having more votes will make it more likely to be primary (which it won't). If you wish a member to be preferentially chosen as primary, use priorities (see "Priority" on page 183).

Forcing Reconfiguration

When you permanently lose a majority of the set, you may want to reconfigure the set while it doesn't have a primary. This is a little tricky: usually you'd send the reconfig to the primary. In this case, you can *force reconfigure* the set by sending a reconfig command to a secondary. Connect to a secondary in the shell and pass it a reconfig with the `"force"` option:

```
> rs.reconfig(config, {"force" : true})
```

Forced reconfigurations follow the same rules as a normal reconfiguration: you must send a valid, well-formed configuration with the correct options. The `"force"` option doesn't allow invalid configs; it just allows a secondary to accept a reconfig.

Forced reconfigurations bump the replica set `"version"` number by a large amount. You may see it jump by thousands. This is normal: it is to prevent version number collisions (just in case there's a reconfig on either side of a network partition).

When the secondary receives the reconfig, it will update its configuration and pass the new config along to the other members. The other members of the set will only pick up on a change of config if they recognize the sending server as a member of their current config. Thus, if some of your members have changed hostnames, you should force reconfig from a member that kept its old hostname. If everyone has a new hostname, you should shut down each member of the set, start it up in standalone mode, change its *local.system.replset* document manually, and then restart the member.

Manipulating Member State

There are several ways to manually change member state for maintenance or in response to load. Note that there is no way to force a member to become primary other than configuring the set appropriately.

Turning Primaries into Secondaries

You can demote a primary to a secondary using the `stepDown` function:

```
> rs.stepDown()
```

This makes the primary step down into secondary state for 60 seconds. If no other primary has been elected in that time period, it will be able to attempt a reelection. If you would like it to remain a secondary for a longer or shorter amount of time, you can specify your own number of seconds for it to stay in SECONDARY state:

```
> rs.stepDown(600) // 10 minutes
```

Preventing Elections

If you need to do some maintenance on the primary but don't want any of the other eligible members to become primary in the interim, you can force them to stay secondaries by running *freeze* on each of them:

```
> rs.freeze(10000)
```

Again, this takes a number of seconds to remain secondary.

When you have finished whatever maintenance you are doing and want to "unfreeze" the other members you can run the command again, giving a timeout of 0 seconds:

```
> rs.freeze(0)
```

This will allow the member to hold an election, if it chooses.

You can also unfreeze primaries that have been stepped down by running `rs.freeze(0)`.

Using Maintenance Mode

Maintenance mode occurs when you perform a long-running op on a replica set member: it forces the member into RECOVERING state. Sometimes, a member will go into maintenance mode automatically, for example, if you run a compact on it. When the compact begins, the member will go into RECOVERING state so that reads will no longer go to that member. Clients will stop using it for reads (if they were) and it should no longer be used as a replication source.

You can force a member to go into maintenance mode by running the *replSetMaintenanceMode* command on it. You might want to do this if a member begins to fall behind and you don't want any read load on it. For example, you could have a script like this, which detects if a member is behind and then puts it in maintenance mode:

```
function maybeMaintenanceMode() {
    var local = db.getSisterDB("local");

    // Return if this member isn't a secondary (it might be a primary
    // or already in recovering)
    if (!local.isMaster().secondary) {
        return;
    }

    // Find the last optime written on this member
    var last = local.oplog.rs.find().sort({"$natural" : -1}).next();
    var lastTime = last['ts']['t'];

    // If more than 30 seconds behind
    if (lastTime < (new Date()).getTime()-30) {
        db.adminCommand({"replSetMaintenanceMode" : true});
    }
};
```

To get out of maintenance mode, pass the command `false`:

```
> db.adminCommand({"replSetMaintenanceMode" : false});
```

Monitoring Replication

It is important to be able to monitor the status of a set: not only that everyone is up, but what states they are in and how up-to-date the replication is. There are several commands you can use to see replica set information. MMS (see Chapter 21) also keeps some useful stats on replication.

Often issues with replication are transient: a server could not reach another server but now it can. The easiest way to see issues like this is to look at the logs. Make sure you know where the logs are being stored (and that they *are* being stored) and that you can access them.

Getting the Status

One of the most useful commands you can run is *replSetGetStatus*, which gets the current information about every member of the set (from the of view of the member you're running it on). There is a helper for this command in the shell:

```
> rs.status()
{
    "set" : "spock",
    "date" : ISODate("2012-10-17T18:17:52Z"),
    "myState" : 2,
    "syncingTo" : "server-1:27017",
```

```
    "members" : [
        {
            "_id" : 0,
            "name" : "server-1:27017",
            "health" : 1,
            "state" : 1,
            "stateStr" : "PRIMARY",
            "uptime" : 74824,
            "optime" : { "t" : 1350496621000, "i" : 1 },
            "optimeDate" : ISODate("2012-10-17T17:57:01Z"),
            "lastHeartbeat" : ISODate("2012-10-17T17:57:00Z"),
            "pingMs" : 3,
        },
        {
            "_id" : 1,
            "name" : "server-2:27017",
            "health" : 1,
            "state" : 2,
            "stateStr" : "SECONDARY",
            "uptime" : 161989,
            "optime" : { "t" : 1350377549000, "i" : 500 },
            "optimeDate" : ISODate("2012-10-17T17:57:00Z"),
            "self" : true
        },
        {
            "_id" : 2,
            "name" : "server-3:27017",
            "health" : 1,
            "state" : 3,
            "stateStr" : "RECOVERING",
            "uptime" : 24300,
            "optime" : { "t" : 1350411407000, "i" : 739 },
            "optimeDate" : ISODate("2012-10-16T18:16:47Z"),
            "lastHeartbeat" : ISODate("2012-10-17T17:57:01Z"),
            "pingMs" : 12,
            "errmsg" : "still syncing, not yet to minValid optime 507e9a30:851"
        }
    ],
    "ok" : 1
}
```

These are some of the most useful fields:

`self`
: This field is only present in the member `rs.status()` was run on, in this case, *server-2*.

`stateStr`
: A string describing the state of the server. See "Member States" on page 191 to see descriptions of the various states.

`uptime`
: The number of seconds a member has been reachable (or the time since this server was started for the `"self"` member). Thus, *server-2* has been up for 161989 seconds, or about 45 hours. *server-1* has been available for the last 21 hours and *server-3* has been available for the last 7 hours.

`optimeDate`
: The last optime in each member's oplog (where that member is synced to). Note that this is the state of each member as reported by the heartbeat, so the optime reported here may be off by a couple of seconds.

`lastHeartbeat`
: The time this server last received a heartbeat from the member. If there have been network issues or the server has been busy, this may be longer than two seconds ago.

`pingMs`
: The running average of how long heartbeats to this server have taken. This is used in determining which member to sync from.

`errmsg`
: Any status message that the member chose to return in the heartbeat request. These are often merely informational, not error messages. For example, the `"errmsg"` field in *server-3* indicates that this server is in the process of initial syncing. The hexadecimal number 507e9a30:851 is the timestamp of the operation this member needs to get to to complete the initial sync.

There are a several fields that give overlapping information: `"state"` is the same as `"stateStr"`, it's simply the internal id for the state. `"health"` merely reflects whether a given server is reachable (1) or unreachable (0), which is also shown by `"state"` and `"stateStr"` (they'll be UNKNOWN or DOWN if the server is unreachable). Similarly, `"optime"` and `"optimeDate"` are the same value represented in two ways: one represents milliseconds since the epoch (`"t" : 135...`) and the other is a more human-readable date.

Note that this is report is from the point of view of whichever member of the set you run it on: it may be incorrect or out of date due to network issues.

Visualizing the Replication Graph

If you run `rs.status()` on a secondary, there will be a top-level field called `"syncingTo"`. This gives the host that this member is replicating from. By running the *replSetGetStatus* command on each member of the set, you can figure out the replication graph. For example, assuming `server1` was a connection to *server1*, `server2` was a connection to *server2*, and so on, you might have something like:

```
> server1.adminCommand({replSetGetStatus: 1})['syncingTo']
server0:27017
> server2.adminCommand({replSetGetStatus: 1})['syncingTo']
server1:27017
> server3.adminCommand({replSetGetStatus: 1})['syncingTo']
server1:27017
> server4.adminCommand({replSetGetStatus: 1})['syncingTo']
server2:27017
```

Thus, *server0* is the source for *server1*, *server1* is the replication source for *server2* and *server3*, and *server2* is the replication source for *server4*.

MongoDB determines who to sync to based on ping time. When one member heartbeats another, it times how long that request took. MongoDB keeps a running average of these times. When it has to choose a member to sync from, it looks for the member that is closest to it and ahead of it in replication (thus, you cannot end up with a replication cycle: members will only replicate from the primary or secondaries that are strictly further ahead).

Thus, if you bring up a new member in a secondary data center, it is more likely to sync from the other members in that data center than a member in your primary data center (thus minimizing WAN traffic), as show in Figure 12-1.

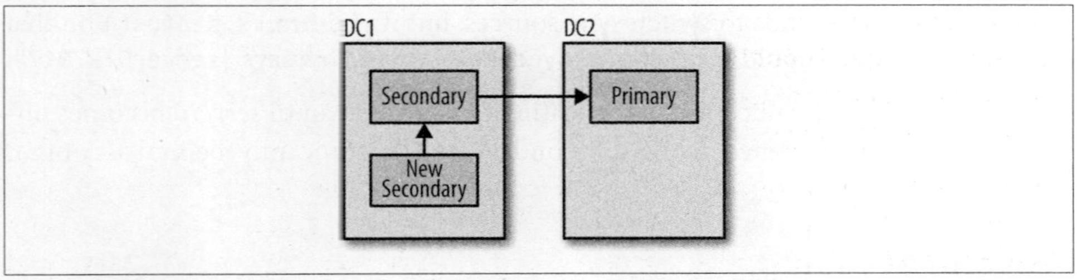

Figure 12-1. New secondaries will generally choose to sync from a member in the same data center

However, there are some downsides to automatic replication chaining: more replication hops mean that it takes a bit longer to replicate writes to all servers. For example, let's say that everything is in one data center but, due to the vagaries of network speeds when you added members, MongoDB ends up replicating in a line, as shown in Figure 12-2.

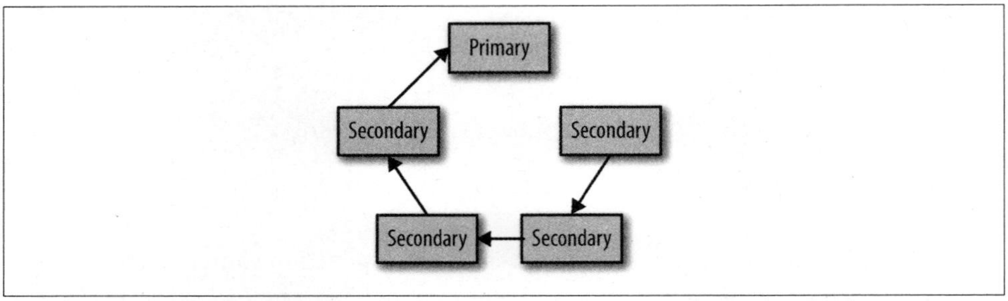

Figure 12-2. As replication chains get longer, it takes longer for all members to get a copy of the data

This is highly unlikely, but not impossible. It is, however, probably undesirable: each secondary in the chain will have to be a bit further behind than the secondary "in front" of it. You can fix this by modifying the replication source for a member using the *replSetSyncFrom* command (or the `rs.syncFrom()` helper).

Connect to the secondary whose replication source you want to change and run this command, passing it the server you'd prefer this member to sync from:

```
> secondary.adminCommand({"replSetSyncFrom" : "server0:27017"})
```

It may take a few seconds to switch sync sources, but if you run `rs.status()` on that member again, you should see that the `"syncingTo"` field now says `"server0:27017"`.

At this point, *server4* will continue replicating from *server0* until *server0* becomes unavailable or, if it happened to be a secondary, falls significantly behind the other members.

Replication Loops

A replication loop is when members end up replicating from one another, for example, *A* is syncing from *B* who is syncing from *C* who is syncing from *A*. As none of the members in a replication loop can be a primary, the members will not receive any new operations to replicate and fall behind. On the plus side, replication loops should be impossible when members choose who to sync from automatically.

However, you can force replication loops using the *replSetSyncFrom* command. Inspect the `rs.status()` output careful before manually changing sync targets and be careful not to create loops. The *replSetSyncFrom* command will warn you if you do not choose to sync from a member who is strictly ahead, but it will allow it.

Disabling Chaining

Chaining is when a secondary syncs from another secondary (instead of the primary). As mentioned earlier, members may decide to sync from other members automatically.

You can disable chaining, forcing everyone to sync from the primary, by changing the "allowChaining" setting to false (if not specified, it defaults to true):

```
> var config = rs.config()
> // create the settings subobject, if it does not already exist
> config.settings = config.settings || {}
> config.settings.allowChaining = false
> rs.reconfig(config)
```

With allowChaining set to false, all members will sync from the primary. If the primary becomes unavailable, they will fall back to syncing from secondaries.

Calculating Lag

One of the most important metrics to track for replication is how well the secondaries are keeping up with the primary. *Lag* is how far behind a secondary is, which means the difference in timestamp between the last operation the primary has performed and the timestamp of the last operation the secondary has applied.

You can use rs.status() to see a member's replication state, but you can also get a quick summary (along with oplog size) by running db.printReplicationInfo() (on a primary) and db.printSlaveReplicationInfo() on a secondary. Note that these are both functions of db, not rs.

db.printReplicationInfo gives a summary of the primary's oplog:

```
> db.printReplicationInfo();
    configured oplog size:   10.48576MB
    log length start to end: 34secs (0.01hrs)
    oplog first event time:  Tue Mar 30 2010 16:42:57 GMT-0400 (EDT)
    oplog last event time:   Tue Mar 30 2010 16:43:31 GMT-0400 (EDT)
    now:                     Tue Mar 30 2010 16:43:37 GMT-0400 (EDT)
```

This gives information about the size of the oplog and the date ranges of operations contained in the oplog. In this example, the oplog is about 10 MB and is only able to fit about 30 seconds of operations.

If this were a real deployment, the oplog should be much larger (see "Resizing the Oplog" on page 220 for instructions on changing oplog size). We want the log length to be *at least* as long as the time it takes to do a full resync. That way, we don't run into a case where a secondary falls off the end of the oplog before finishing its initial sync.

The log length is computed by taking the time difference between the first and last operation in the oplog once the oplog has filled up. If the server has just started with nothing in the oplog, then the earliest operation will be relatively recent. In that case, the log length will be small, even though the oplog probably still has free space available. The length is a more useful metric for servers that have been operating long enough to write through their entire oplog at least once.

You can also use the `db.printSlaveReplicationInfo()` function on a secondary to get information about who it is syncing from and how far behind it is:

```
> db.printSlaveReplicationInfo();
    source:   server-0:27017
    syncedTo: Tue Mar 30 2012 16:44:01 GMT-0400 (EDT)
    = 12secs ago (0hrs)
```

This will show who the slave is syncing from. In this case, the secondary is 12 seconds behind the primary.

Remember that a replica set member's lag is calculated relative to the primary, not against "wall time." This usually is irrelevant, but on very low-write systems, this can cause phantom replication lag "spikes." For example, suppose you do a write once an hour. Right after that write, before it's replicated, the secondary will look like it's an hour behind the primary. However, it'll be able to catch up with that "hour" of operations in a few milliseconds. This can sometimes cause confusion when monitoring a low-throughput system.

Resizing the Oplog

Your primary's oplog should be thought of as your maintenance window. If your primary has an oplog that is an hour long, then you only have one hour to fix anything that goes wrong before your secondaries fall too far behind and must be resynced from scratch. Thus, you generally want to have an oplog that can hold a couple days to a week's worth of data, to give yourself some breathing room if something goes wrong.

Unfortunately, there's no easy way to tell how long your oplog is going to be before it fills up and there's no way to resize it while your server is running. However, it is possible to cycle through you servers, taking each one offline, making its oplog larger, and then adding it back into the set. Remember that each server that could become a primary should have a large enough oplog to give you a sane maintenance window.

To increase the size of your oplog, perform the following steps:

1. If this is currently the primary, step it down and wait for the other servers to catch up.

2. Shut down the server.
3. Start it up as a standalone server.
4. Temporarily store the last insert in the oplog in another collection:

```
> use local
> // op: "i" finds the last insert
> var cursor = db.oplog.rs.find({"op" : "i"})
> var lastInsert = cursor.sort({"$natural" : -1}).limit(1).next()
> db.tempLastOp.save(lastInsert)
>
> // make sure it was saved! It's very important that you don't lose this op
> db.tempLastOp.findOne()
```

   We could use the last update or delete, but $-operators cannot be inserted into a collection.

5. Drop the current oplog

```
> db.oplog.rs.drop()
```

6. Create a new oplog:

```
> db.createCollection("oplog.rs", {"capped" : true, "size" : 10000})
```

7. Put the last op back in the oplog:

```
> var temp = db.tempLastOp.findOne()
> db.oplog.rs.insert(temp)
>
> // make sure that this was actually inserted
> db.oplog.rs.findOne()
```

   Make sure that the last op was inserted into the oplog. If it was not, the server will drop all of its data and resync when you add it back into the set.

8. Finally, restart the server as a member of the replica set. Remember that it only has one op in the oplog to start out with, so you won't be able to see its true oplog length (how long it is in time) for a while. Also, it won't be a very good sync source if other members are behind.

You generally should not decrease the size of your oplog: although it may be months long, there is usually ample disk space for it and it does not use up any valuable resources like RAM or CPU.

Restoring from a Delayed Secondary

Suppose someone accidentally drops a database but, luckily, you had a delayed secondary. Now you need to get rid of the data on the other members and use the delayed slave as your definitive source of data. There are a couple of ways to do this.

This is the simplest way:

1. Shut down all the other members.
2. Delete all the data in their data directories. Make sure every member (other than the delayed secondary) has an empty data directory.
3. Restart all the members. They will begin making a copy of the delayed secondary's data.

This is certainly easy, but your replica set will essentially be one rather overloaded secondary for however long it takes the other members to initial sync.

The other option may or may not work better, depending on your amount of data:

1. Shut down all the members, including the delayed secondary.
2. Delete the data files from the non-delayed servers.
3. Copy the delayed secondary's data files to the other servers.
4. Start up everyone.

Note that this will mean all the servers will have the same oplog size as the delayed secondary, which may not be what you want.

Building Indexes

If you send an index build to the primary, the primary will build the index normally and then the secondaries will build the index when they replicate the "build index" operation. Although this is the easiest way to build an index, index builds are resource-intensive operations that can make members unavailable. If all of your secondaries start building an index at the same time, almost every member of your set will be offline until the index build completes.

Therefore, you may want to build an index on one member at a time to minimize impact on your application. To accomplish this, do the following:

1. Shut down a secondary.
2. Restart it as a standalone server.
3. Build the index on the standalone server.
4. When the index build is complete, restart the server as a member of the replica set.
5. Repeat steps 1 through 4 for each secondary in the replica set.

You should now have a set where every member other than the primary has the index built. Now there are two options, and you should choose the one that will impact your production system the least:

1. Build the index on the primary. If you have an "off" time when you have less traffic, that would probably be a good time to build it. You also might want to modify read preferences to temporarily shunt more load onto secondaries while the build is in progress.

   The primary will replicate the index build to the secondaries, but they will already have the index so it will be a no-op for them.

2. Step down the primary, then follow steps 1 through 4 as outlined earlier. This requires a failover, but you will have a normally-functioning primary while the old primary is building its index. After its index build is complete, you can reintroduce it to the set.

Note that you could also use this technique to build different indexes on a secondary than you have on the rest of the set. This could be useful for offline processing, but make sure a member with different indexes can never become primary: its priority should always be 0.

If you are building a unique index, make sure that the primary is not inserting duplicates or that you build the index on the primary first. Otherwise, the primary could be inserting duplicates that would then cause replication errors on secondaries. If this occurs, the secondary will shut itself down. You will have to restart it as a stand alone, remove the unique index, and restart it.

Replication on a Budget

If it is difficult get more than one high-quality server, consider getting a secondary server that is strictly for disaster recovery, with less RAM, CPU, slower disk IO, etc. The good server will always be your primary and the cheaper server will never handle any client traffic (configure your clients to send all reads to the primary). Here are all the options to set for the cheaper box:

`"priority" : 0`
: You do not want this server to ever become primary.

`"hidden" : true`
: You do not want clients ever sending reads to this secondary.

`"buildIndexes" : false`
: This is optional, but it can decrease the load this server has to handle considerably. If you ever need to restore from this server, you'll need to rebuild indexes.

`"votes" : 0`
: If you only have two machines, set the votes on this secondary to 0 so that the primary can stay primary if this machine goes down. If you have a third server (even just your application server), run an arbiter on that instead of setting votes to 0.

This will give you the safety and security of having a secondary without having to invest in two high-performance servers.

How the Primary Tracks Lag

Each member that has ever been a sync source keeps a collection called *local.slaves*, which holds information about which servers are syncing from it and how up to date they are. When you run a query using `w`, MongoDB looks through this information to decide if enough secondaries are up to date enough to proceed.

The *local.slaves* collection is actually an "echo" of an in-memory data structure, so it may be a few seconds out of date:

```
> db.slaves.find()
{ "_id" : ObjectId("4c1287178e00e93d1858567c"), "host" : "10.4.1.100",
  "ns" : "local.oplog.rs", "syncedTo" : { "t" : 1276282710000, "i" : 1 } }
{ "_id" : ObjectId("4c128730e6e5c3096f40e0de"), "host" : "10.4.1.101",
  "ns" : "local.oplog.rs", "syncedTo" : { "t" : 1276282710000, "i" : 1 } }
```

The `"_id"` of each server is important: it is an identifier for the syncing member. You can see what a member's `"_id"` is by connecting to it and looking at the *local.me* collection:

```
> db.me.findOne()
{ "_id" : ObjectId("50e6edb517c789e46695212f"), "host" : "server-1" }
```

Occasionally, due to configuration issues, you may end up with multiple servers with the same `"_id"`. If this happens, only one will be able to report how far it has replicated to the primary. This, in turn, can cause issues with your application (if you're depending on a certain number of servers reporting that they got a write) and sharding (migrates cannot proceed until a majority of secondaries have replicated the migration). If multiple machines have the same `"_id"`, you can fix it by logging into each machine, dropping the *local.me* collection, and restarting the *mongod*. On startup, *mongod* will repopulate *local.me* with a new `"_id"`.

If a server's address changes, you may get errors in the logs about duplicate key exceptions in the local database, given that the slave's `"_id"` will be the same but its hostname will have changed. If this occurs, you can drop the *local.slaves* collection and the errors will stop (this is simpler than the previous case because you just need to clear the old data, not resolve conflicting data).

The *local.slaves* collection is never cleaned up by *mongod*, so it may list servers that haven't used the member as a sync source in months or members that aren't even part of the set anymore. As the collection is merely a dumping ground for MongoDB to report on replication status, there's no harm in leaving old entries in there. However, if you find the old entries confusing or cluttered, you can drop the whole collection. It will be repopulated after a few seconds with updated entries from the servers that are currently syncing from it.

If you have secondaries that are chained, you may notice that the primary has several *local.slaves* documents for a certain server. This is because each secondary will "forward" any replication requests it gets to its sync target so that the primary knows where each secondary has synced to. These are called "ghost syncs" because the requests don't actually request any ops back; they just inform the primary of where the secondaries have synced to.

> The *local* database is used for replication information because it is not replicated. Thus, if you have data that you want to be local to a certain machine, you can load it into collections in the local database.

Master-Slave

MongoDB originally supported a more traditional master-slave setup (no automatic failover and you declare who the master and slaves are). There are exactly two reasons to consider using master-slave instead of replica sets: you need more than 11 secondaries or you need to replicate individual databases. Unless your application unavoidably requires it, *use replica sets*. They are much better maintained and fully featured. Master-slave will be deprecated at some point, probably once replica sets support unlimited members.

However, there are still times when you may need more than 11 slaves or need to replicate a single database. In these cases, you still do need master-slave.

To set up a master, start your server with `--master`. To start a slave, use two options: `--slave` and `--source` *`master`*. `--source` specifies the sync source: the host and port of the master. Note that you do not use the `--replSet` option: you're not setting up a replica set.

For example, if you have two servers, *server-0* and *server-1*, you can do:

```
$ # server-0
$ mongod --master
$
$ # server-1
$ mongod --slave --source server-0:27017
```

At that point, master-slave is set up, and there is no further configuration necessary. You can begin writing to the master and the slave will replicate the changes.

Master-slave can also be used to replicate a single database. You can use `--only` option to select a database to replicate:

```
$ mongod --slave --source server-1:27017 --only super-important-db
```

Drivers will not automatically distribute reads to slaves if you set a read preference. You must make an explicit connection to a slave to read from it.

Converting Master-Slave to a Replica Set

Converting from a master-slave setup to replica sets requires some downtime. Here are the steps:

1. Stop all writes on your system. This is very important, as your former slave will briefly not have an oplog, so it won't be able to catch up with any writes it misses during the upgrade.
2. Shut down all *mongod* servers.
3. Restart the master with the `--replSet` option instead of `--master`.
4. Initialize the set with one member: the former master. It will become primary.
5. Start up the slaves with the `--replSet` option and the `--fastsync` option. Ordinarily, if you added a member to the set without an oplog, it would go through the full initial sync process. The `fastsync` option tells the member to not worry that it doesn't have an oplog, just start syncing from the latest time on the master.
6. Add the former slave to the set with `rs.add()`.
7. Repeat steps 4 and 5 for each slave.
8. Once all slaves have been converted into secondaries, you can turn on writes to the system.
9. Remove `fastsync` from your config file, command line alias, and long-term memory. It is an extremely dangerous option to use because it makes the member skip operations on restart. Its *only* use is to convert from master-slave to replica sets. Now that you've converted, you no longer need it.

Your master-slave setup should now be a replica set.

Mimicking Master-Slave Behavior with Replica Sets

You usually want a primary to be available as often as possible, thus you should allow automatic failover if the primary becomes unavailable. However, for some sets you may want to require an operator to manually promote a new primary and never allow an automatic failover. This makes replica sets behave the same way as master-slave does (and is preferable to using master-slave to get this behavior).

To achieve this, reconfigure the set so that every member except the primary has a `priority` of 0 and `votes` of 0. This way, no member will seek election if the primary goes down. Also, the current primary can remain primary (as it has the only vote in the system) even if all of the other members go down.

For example, this configuration would create a 5-member set where *server-0* was always primary and the other four members were always secondaries:

```
{
    "_id" : "spock",
    "members" : [
        {"_id" : 0, "host" : "server-0:27017"},
        {"_id" : 1, "host" : "server-1:27017", "priority" : 0, "votes" : 0},
        {"_id" : 2, "host" : "server-2:27017", "priority" : 0, "votes" : 0},
        {"_id" : 3, "host" : "server-3:27017", "priority" : 0, "votes" : 0},
        {"_id" : 4, "host" : "server-4:27017", "priority" : 0, "votes" : 0}
    ]
}
```

If the primary goes down, an operator must manually intervene to select a new primary.

To manually promote a new primary, connect to the secondary that you would like to become primary and run a forced reconfig, changing its `priority` and `votes` to 1 and the former primary's to 0.

For example, if *server-0* went down, connect to the server that you would like to be the new primary, say, *server-1*. Then change the config as follows:

```
> var config = rs.config()
> config.members[1].priority = 1
> config.members[1].votes = 1
> config.members[0].priority = 0
> config.members[0].votes = 0
> rs.reconfig(config, {"force" : true})
```

Now, if you run `rs.config()`, it should look like this:

```
> rs.config()
{
    "_id" : "spock",
    "version" : 3
    "members" : [
        {"_id" : 0, "host" : "server-0:27017", "priority" : 0, "votes" : 0},
        {"_id" : 1, "host" : "server-1:27017"},
        {"_id" : 2, "host" : "server-2:27017", "priority" : 0, "votes" : 0},
        {"_id" : 3, "host" : "server-3:27017", "priority" : 0, "votes" : 0},
        {"_id" : 4, "host" : "server-4:27017", "priority" : 0, "votes" : 0}
    ]
}
```

If the new primary fails, repeat the process.

PART IV
Sharding

CHAPTER 13

Introduction to Sharding

This chapter covers how to scale with MongoDB:

- What sharding is and the components of a cluster
- How to configure sharding
- The basics of how sharding interacts with your application

Introduction to Sharding

Sharding refers to the process of splitting data up across machines; the term *partitioning* is also sometimes used to describe this concept. By putting a subset of data on each machine, it becomes possible to store more data and handle more load without requiring larger or more powerful machines, just a larger quantity of less-powerful machines.

Manual sharding can be done with almost any database software. Manual sharding is when an application maintains connections to several different database servers, each of which are completely independent. The application manages storing different data on different servers and querying against the appropriate server to get data back. This approach can work well but becomes difficult to maintain when adding or removing nodes from the cluster or in the face of changing data distributions or load patterns.

MongoDB supports *autosharding*, which tries to both abstract the architecture away from the application and simplify the administration of such a system. MongoDB allows your application to ignore the fact that it isn't talking to a standalone MongoDB server, to some extent. On the operations side, MongoDB automates balancing data across shards and makes it easier to add and remove capacity.

Sharding is the most difficult and complex way of configuring MongoDB, both from a development and operational point of view. There are many components to configure and monitor and data moves around the cluster automatically. You should be comfortable with standalone servers and replica sets before attempting to deploy or use a sharded cluster.

Understanding the Components of a Cluster

MongoDB's sharding allows you to create a cluster of many machines (*shards*) and break up your collection across them, putting a subset of data on each shard. This allows your application to grow beyond the resource limits of a standalone server or replica set.

> Many people are confused about the difference between replication and sharding. Remember that replication creates an exact copy of your data on multiple servers, so every server is a mirror-image of every other server. Conversely, every shard contains a different subset of data.

One of the goals of sharding is to make a cluster of 5, 10, or 1,000 machines look like a single machine to your application. To hide these details from the application, we run a routing process called `mongos` in front of the shards. This router keeps a "table of contents" that tells it which shard contains which data. Applications can connect to this router and issue requests normally, as shown in Figure 13-1. The router, knowing what data is on which shard, is able to forward the requests to the appropriate shard(s). If there are responses to the request, the router collects them, merges them, and sends them back to the application. As far as the application knows, it's connected to a standalone `mongod`, as in Figure 13-2.

A One-Minute Test Setup

As in the replication section, we will start by setting up a quick cluster on a single machine. First, start a mongo shell with the `--nodb` option:

```
$ mongo --nodb
```

To create a cluster, use the `ShardingTest` class:

```
> cluster = new ShardingTest({"shards" : 3, "chunksize" : 1})
```

The `chunksize` option is covered in Chapter 16. For now, simply set it to 1.

Running this command creates a new cluster with three shards (*mongod* processes) running on ports 30000, 30001, and 30002. By default, `ShardingTest` starts a *mongos* on port 30999. We will to connect to this *mongos* to play around with the cluster.

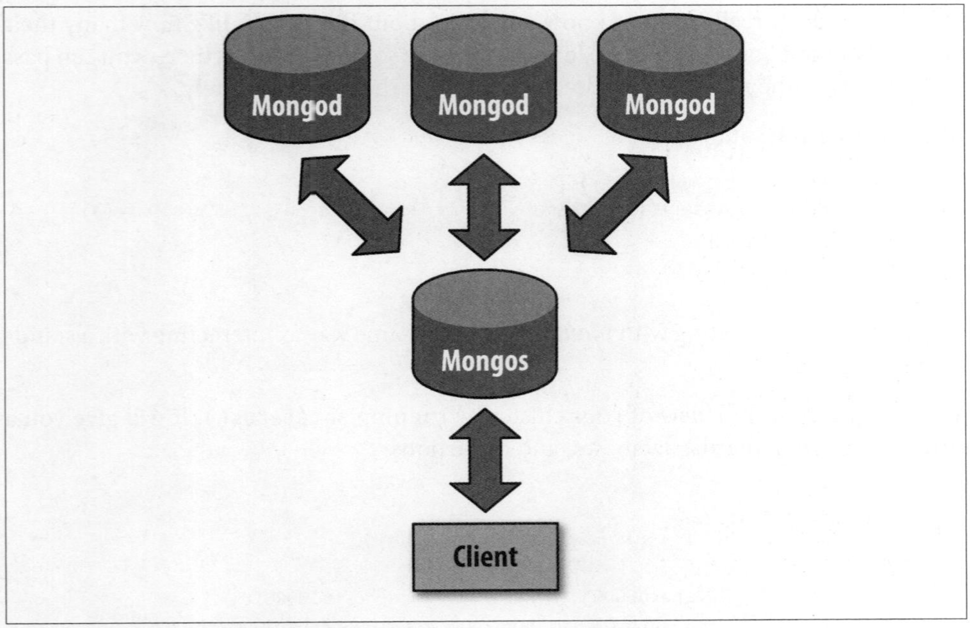

Figure 13-1. Sharded client connection

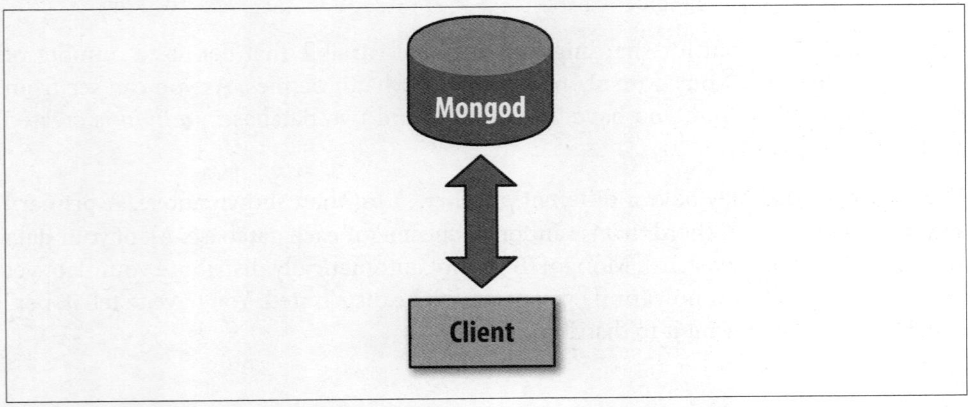

Figure 13-2. Nonsharded client connection

Your entire cluster will be dumping its logs to your current shell, so open up a second shell and use that to connect to your cluster's *mongos*:

```
> db = (new Mongo("localhost:30999")).getDB("test")
```

Now you are in the situation show in Figure 13-1: the shell is the client and is connected to a *mongos*. You can start passing requests to the *mongos* and it'll route them to the shards. You don't really have to know anything about the shards, like how many their are or what their addresses are. So long as there are some shards out there, you can pass the requests to the *mongos* and allow it to forward them appropriately.

Start by inserting some data:

```
> for (var i=0; i<100000; i++) {
...     db.users.insert({"username" : "user"+i, "created_at" : new Date()});
... }
> db.users.count()
100000
```

As you can see, interacting with *mongos* works the same way as interacting with a standalone server does.

You can get an overall view of your cluster by running `sh.status()`. It will give you a summary of your shards, databases, and collections:

```
> sh.status()
--- Sharding Status ---
  sharding version: { "_id" : 1, "version" : 3 }
  shards:
        {  "_id" : "shard0000",  "host" : "localhost:30000" }
        {  "_id" : "shard0001",  "host" : "localhost:30001" }
        {  "_id" : "shard0002",  "host" : "localhost:30002" }
  databases:
        {  "_id" : "admin",  "partitioned" : false,  "primary" : "config" }
        {  "_id" : "test",  "partitioned" : false,  "primary" : "shard0001" }
```

`sh` is similar to `rs`, but for sharding: it is a global variable that defines a number of sharding helper functions. Run `sh.help()` to see what it defines. As you can see from the `sh.status()` output, you have three shards and two databases (*admin* is created automatically).

Your *test* database may have a different *primary shard* than shown above. A primary shard is a "home base" shard that is randomly chosen for each database. All of your data will be on this primary shard. MongoDB cannot automatically distribute your data yet because it doesn't know how (or if) you want it to be distributed. You have to tell it, per-collection, how you want it to distribute data.

> A primary shard is different than a replica set primary. A primary shard refers to the entire replica set composing a shard. A primary in a replica set is the single server in the set that can take writes.

To shard a particular collection, first enable sharding on the collection's database. To do so, run the `enableSharding` command:

```
> sh.enableSharding("test")
```

Now sharding is enabled on the *test* database, which allows you to shard collections within the database.

When you shard a collection, you choose a *shard key*. This is a field or two that MongoDB uses to break up data. For example, if you choose to shard on "username", MongoDB would break up the data into ranges of usernames: "a1-steak-sauce" through "defcon", "defcon1" through "howie1998", and so on. Choosing a shard key can be thought of as choosing an ordering for the data in the collection. This is a similar concept to indexing, and for good reason: the shard key becomes the most important index on your collection as it gets bigger. To even create a shard key, the field(s) must be indexed.

Before enabling sharding, we have to create an index on the key we want to shard by:

```
> db.users.ensureIndex({"username" : 1})
```

Now we'll shard the collection by "username":

```
> sh.shardCollection("test.users", {"username" : 1})
```

Although we are choosing a shard key without much thought here, it is an important decision that should be carefully considered in a real system. See Chapter 15 for more advice on choosing a shard key.

If you wait a few minutes and run sh.status() again, you'll see that there's a lot more information displayed than there was before:

```
--- Sharding Status ---
  sharding version: { "_id" : 1, "version" : 3 }
  shards:
    {  "_id" : "shard0000",  "host" : "localhost:30000" }
    {  "_id" : "shard0001",  "host" : "localhost:30001" }
    {  "_id" : "shard0002",  "host" : "localhost:30002" }
  databases:
    {  "_id" : "admin",  "partitioned" : false,  "primary" : "config" }
    {  "_id" : "test",  "partitioned" : true,  "primary" : "shard0000" }
        test.users chunks:
            shard0001    4
            shard0002    4
            shard0000    5
        { "username" : { $minKey : 1 } } -->> { "username" : "user1704" }
            on : shard0001
        { "username" : "user1704" } -->> { "username" : "user24083" }
            on : shard0002
        { "username" : "user24083" } -->> { "username" : "user31126" }
            on : shard0001
        { "username" : "user31126" } -->> { "username" : "user38170" }
            on : shard0002
        { "username" : "user38170" } -->> { "username" : "user45213" }
            on : shard0001
        { "username" : "user45213" } -->> { "username" : "user52257" }
            on : shard0002
        { "username" : "user52257" } -->> { "username" : "user59300" }
```

```
        on : shard0001
    { "username" : "user59300" } -->> { "username" : "user66344" }
        on : shard0002
    { "username" : "user66344" } -->> { "username" : "user73388" }
        on : shard0000
    { "username" : "user73388" } -->> { "username" : "user80430" }
        on : shard0000
    { "username" : "user80430" } -->> { "username" : "user87475" }
        on : shard0000
    { "username" : "user87475" } -->> { "username" : "user94518" }
        on : shard0000
    { "username" : "user94518" } -->> { "username" : { $maxKey : 1 } }
        on : shard0000
```

The collection has been split up into a dozen chunks, where each chunk is a subset of your data. These are listed by shard key range (the `{"username" : minValue} -->> {"username" : maxValue}` denotes the range of each chunk). Looking at the `"on" : shard` part of the output, you can see that these chunks have been evenly distributed between the shards.

This process of a collection being split into chunks is shown in Figure 13-3 through Figure 13-5. Before sharding, the collection is essentially a single chunk. Sharding splits this into smaller chunks based on the shard key, as shown in Figure 13-4. These chunks can then be distributed across the cluster, as Figure 13-5 shows.

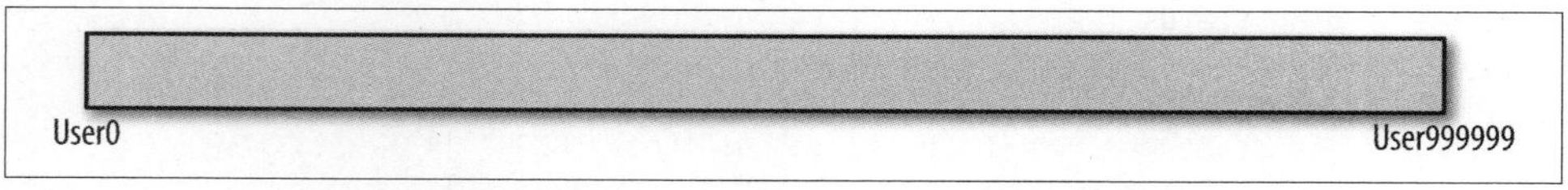

Figure 13-3. Before a collection is sharded, it can be thought of as a single chunk from the smallest value of the shard key to the largest

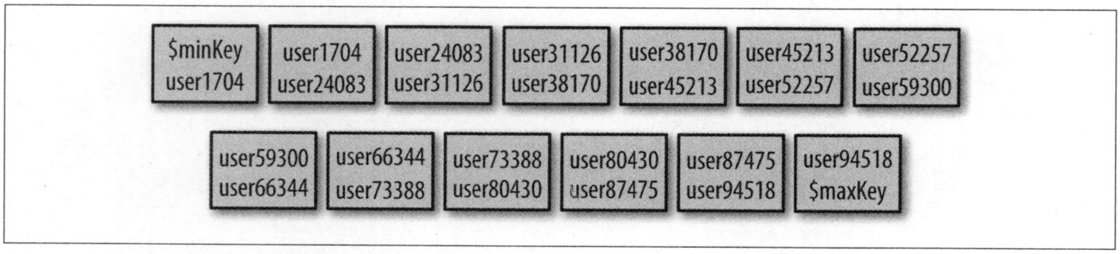

Figure 13-4. Sharding splits the collection into many chunks based on shard key ranges

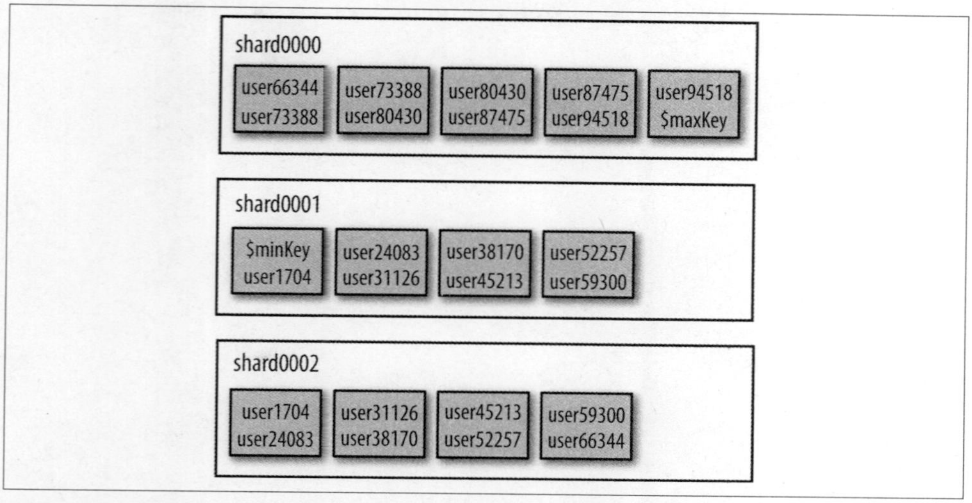

Figure 13-5. Chunks are evenly distributed across the available shards

Notice the keys at the beginning and end of the chunk list: `$minKey` and `$maxKey`. `$minKey` can be thought of as "negative infinity." It is smaller than any other value in MongoDB. Similarly, `$maxKey` is like "positive infinity." It is greater than any other value. Thus, you'll always see these as the "caps" on your chunk ranges. The values for your shard key will always be between `$minKey` and `$maxKey`. These values are actually BSON types and should not be used in your application; they are mainly for internal use. If you wish to refer to them in the shell, use the `MinKey` and `MaxKey` constants.

Now that the data is distributed across multiple shards, let's try doing some queries. First, try a query on a specific username:

```
> db.users.find({username: "user12345"})
{
    "_id" : ObjectId("50b0451951d30ac5782499e6"),
    "username" : "user12345",
    "created_at" : ISODate("2012-11-24T03:55:05.636Z")
}
```

As you can see, querying works normally. However, let's run an `explain` to see what MongoDB is doing under the covers:

```
> db.users.find({username: "user12345"}}).explain()
{
  "clusteredType" : "ParallelSort",
  "shards" : {
    "localhost:30001" : [
      {
        "cursor" : "BtreeCursor username_1",
        "nscanned" : 1,
        "nscannedObjects" : 1,
```

```
          "n" : 1,
          "millis" : 0,
          "nYields" : 0,
          "nChunkSkips" : 0,
          "isMultiKey" : false,
          "indexOnly" : false,
          "indexBounds" : {
            "username" : [
              [
                "user12345",
                "user12345"
              ]
            ]
          }
        }
      ]
    },
    "n" : 1,
    "nChunkSkips" : 0,
    "nYields" : 0,
    "nscanned" : 1,
    "nscannedObjects" : 1,
    "millisTotal" : 0,
    "millisAvg" : 0,
    "numQueries" : 1,
    "numShards" : 1
}
```

There are two parts to this `explain`: a somewhat usual-looking `explain` output nested inside of another `explain`'s output. The way to read this is that the outer explain is from the *mongos*: this describes what the *mongos* had to do to process this query. The inner `explain` is from any shards that were used in the query, in this case, *localhost:30001*.

As "`username`" is the shard key, *mongos* could send the query directly to the correct shard. Contrast that with the results for querying for all of the data:

```
> db.users.find().explain()
{
  "clusteredType" : "ParallelSort",
  "shards" : {
    "localhost:30000" : [
      {
        "cursor" : "BasicCursor",
        "nscanned" : 37393,
        "nscannedObjects" : 37393,
        "n" : 37393,
        "millis" : 38,
        "nYields" : 0,
        "nChunkSkips" : 0,
        "isMultiKey" : false,
        "indexOnly" : false,
        "indexBounds" : {
```

```
            }
        }
    ],
    "localhost:30001" : [
        {
            "cursor" : "BasicCursor",
            "nscanned" : 31303,
            "nscannedObjects" : 31303,
            "n" : 31303,
            "millis" : 37,
            "nYields" : 0,
            "nChunkSkips" : 0,
            "isMultiKey" : false,
            "indexOnly" : false,
            "indexBounds" : {

            }
        }
    ],
    "localhost:30002" : [
        {
            "cursor" : "BasicCursor",
            "nscanned" : 31304,
            "nscannedObjects" : 31304,
            "n" : 31304,
            "millis" : 36,
            "nYields" : 0,
            "nChunkSkips" : 0,
            "isMultiKey" : false,
            "indexOnly" : false,
            "indexBounds" : {

            }
        }
    ]
},
"n" : 100000,
"nChunkSkips" : 0,
"nYields" : 0,
"nscanned" : 100000,
"nscannedObjects" : 100000,
"millisTotal" : 111,
"millisAvg" : 37,
"numQueries" : 3,
"numShards" : 3
}
```

As you can see from this `explain`, this query has to visit all three shards to find all the data. In general, if we are not using the shard key in the query, *mongos* will have to send the query to every shard.

Queries that contain the shard key and can be sent to a single shard or subset of shards are called *targeted* queries. Queries that must be sent to all shards are called *scatter-gather* queries: *mongos* scatters the query to all the shards and then gathers up the results.

Once you are finished experimenting, shut down the set. Switch back to your original shell and hit Enter a few times to get back to the command line. Then run `cluster.stop()` to cleanly shut down all of the servers:

```
> cluster.stop()
```

If you are ever unsure of what an operation will do, it can be helpful to use `ShardingTest` to spin up a quick local cluster and try it out.

CHAPTER 14

Configuring Sharding

In the previous chapter, you set up a "cluster" on one machine. This chapter covers how to set up a more realistic cluster and how each piece fits, in particular:

- How to set up config servers, shards, and *mongos* processes
- How to add capacity to a cluster
- How data is stored and distributed

When to Shard

Deciding when to shard is a balancing act. You generally do not want to shard too early because it adds operational complexity to your deployment and forces you to make design decisions that are difficult to change later. On the other hand, you do not want to wait too long to shard because it is difficult to shard an overloaded system without downtime.

In general, sharding is used to:

- Increase available RAM
- Increase available disk space
- Reduce load on a server
- Read or write data with greater throughput than a single `mongod` can handle

Thus, good monitoring is important to decide when sharding will be necessary. Carefully measure each of these metrics. Generally people speed toward one of these bottlenecks much faster than the others, so figure out which one your deployment will need to provision for first and make plans well in advance about when and how you plan to convert your replica set.

As you add shards, performance should increase roughly linearly per shard up to hundreds of shards. However, you will usually experience a performance drop if you move from a non-sharded system to just a few shards. Due to the overhead of moving data, maintaining metadata, and routing, small numbers of shards will generally have higher latency and may even have lower throughput than a non-sharded system. Thus, you may want to jump directly to three or more shards.

Starting the Servers

The first step in creating a cluster is to start up all of the processes required. As mentioned in the previous chapter, we need to set up the *mongos* and the shards. There's also a third component, the config servers, which are an important piece. They are normal *mongod* servers that store the cluster configuration: who the shards are, what collections are sharded by, and the chunks.

Config Servers

Config servers are the brains of your cluster: they hold all of the metadata about which servers hold what data. Thus, they must be set up first and the data they hold is *extremely* important: make sure that they are running with journaling enabled and that their data is stored on non-ephemeral drives. Each config server should be on a separate physical machine, preferable geographically distributed.

The config servers must be started before any of the *mongos* processes, as *mongos* pulls its configuration from them. Config servers are standalone *mongod* processes, so you can start them up the same way you would a "normal" *mongod*:

```
$ # server-config-1
$ mongod --configsvr --dbpath /var/lib/mongodb -f /var/lib/config/mongod.conf
$
$ # server-config-2
$ mongod --configsvr --dbpath /var/lib/mongodb -f /var/lib/config/mongod.conf
$
$ # server-config-3
$ mongod --configsvr --dbpath /var/lib/mongodb -f /var/lib/config/mongod.conf
```

When you start up config servers, do *not* use the `--replSet` option: config servers are not members of a replica set. *mongos* writes to all three config servers and does a two-phase-commit-type operation to ensure that all three servers have the same data, so all three must be writable (in a replica set, only the primary is writable by clients).

> A common question is why *three* config servers? The reasoning behind the choice is that one config server is not enough: you need redundancy. Conversely, you don't want too many config servers, since confirming actions with all of them would be prohibitively time consuming. Also, if any of them goes down, you cluster's metadata becomes read-only. Thus, three was chosen as enough to give redundancy but not have the downsides of having too many servers. It will probably be made more flexible in the future.

The `--configsvr` option indicates to the *mongod* that you are planning to use it as a config server. It is not strictly required, as all it does is change the default port *mongod* listens on to 27019 and the default data directory to */data/configdb* (you can override either or both of these settings with `--port` and `--dbpath`).

It is recommended that you use this option because it makes it easier to tell, operationally, what these servers are doing. If you start up your config servers without the `--configsvr` option, though, it's not a problem.

In terms of provisioning, config servers do not need much space or many resources. A generous estimate is 1 KB of config server space per 200 MB of actual data: they really are just tables of contents. As they don't use many resources, you can deploy config servers on machines running other things, like app servers, shard *mongod*s, or *mongos* processes.

If all of your config servers are lost, you must dig through the data on your shards to figure out which data is where. This is possible, but slow and unpleasant. Take frequent backups of config server data. Always take a backup of your config servers before performing any cluster maintenance.

The mongos Processes

Once you have three config servers running, start a `mongos` process for your application to connect to. *mongos* processes need to know where the config servers are, so you must always start *mongos* with the `--configdb` option:

```
$ mongos --configdb config-1:27019,config-2:27019,config-3:27019 \
> -f /var/lib/mongos.conf
```

By default, *mongos* runs on port 27017. Note that it does not need a data directory (*mongos* holds no data itself, it loads the cluster configuration from the config servers on startup). Make sure that you set `logpath` to save the *mongos* log somewhere safe.

You can start as many *mongos* processes as you'd like. A common setup is one *mongos* process per application server (running on the same machine as the application server).

Each *mongos* must use the exact same list of config servers, down to the order in which they are listed.

Adding a Shard from a Replica Set

Finally, you're ready to add a shard. There are two possibilities: you may have an existing replica set or you may be starting from scratch. We will cover starting from an existing set below. If you are starting from scratch, initialize an empty set and follow the steps below.

If you already have a replica set serving your application, that will become your first shard. To convert it into a shard, you are going to tell the *mongos* the replica set name and give it a seed list of replica set members.

For example, if you have a replica set named `spock` on *server-1*, *server-2*, *server-3*, *server-4*, and *server-5*, you would connect to the *mongos* and run:

```
> sh.addShard("spock/server-1:27017,server-2:27017,server-4:27017")
{
    "added" : "spock/server-1:27017,server-2:27017,server-4:27017",
    "ok" : true
}
```

You can specify all the members of the set, but you do not have to. *mongos* will automatically detect any members that were not included in the seed list. If you run `sh.status()`, you'll see that MongoDB soon lists the shard as `"spock/server-1:27017,server-2:27017,server-4:27017,server-3:27017,server-5:27017"`.

The set name, "spock", is taken on as an identifier for this shard. If we ever want to remove this shard or migrate data to it, we'll use "spock" to describe it. This works better than using a specific server (e.g., *server-1*), as replica set membership and status can change over time.

Once you've added the replica set as a shard you can convert your application from connecting to the replica set to connecting to the *mongos*. When you add the shard, *mongos* registers that all the databases in the replica set are "owned" by that shard, so it will pass through all queries to your new shard. *mongos* will also automatically handle failover for your application as your client library would: it will pass the errors through to you.

Test failing over a shard's primary in a development environment to ensure that your application handles the errors received from *mongos* correctly (they should be identical to the errors that you receive from talking to the primary directly).

> Once you have added a shard, you *must* set up all clients to send requests to the *mongos* instead of contacting the replica set. Sharding will not function correctly if some clients are still making requests to the replica set directly (not through the *mongos*). Switch all clients to contacting the *mongos* immediately after adding the shard and set up a firewall rule to ensure that they are unable to connect directly to the shard.

There is a `--shardsvr` option, analogous to the `--configsvr` option mentioned previously. As before, `--shardsvr` has little practical effect (it changes the default port to 27018) but can be nice to include operationally.

You can also create stand-alone-*mongod* shards (instead of replica set shards), but this is not recommend for production (`ShardingTest` in the previous chapter did this). To add a single *mongod* as a shard simply specify the hostname of the standalone server in the call to `addShard`:

```
> sh.addShard("some-server:27017")
```

Stand-alone-server shards default to being named shard0000, shard0001, and so on. If you plan to switch to replica sets later, start with one-member replica sets instead of standalone servers. Switching from a stand-alone-server shard to a replica set requires downtime (see "Server Administration" on page 285).

Adding Capacity

When you want to add more capacity, you'll need to add more shards. To add a new, empty shard, create a replica set. Make sure it has a distinct name from any of your other shards. Once it is initialized and has a primary, add it to your cluster by running the `addShard` command through *mongos*, specifying the new replica set's name and its hosts as seeds.

If you have several existing replica sets that are not shards, you can add all of them as new shards in your cluster so long as they do not have any database names in common. For example, if you had one replica set with a "blog" database, one with a "calendar" database, and one with the "mail", "tel", and "music" databases, you could add each replica set as a shard and end up with a cluster with three shards and five databases. However, if you had a fourth replica set that also had a database named "tel", *mongos* would refuse to add it to the cluster.

Sharding Data

MongoDB won't distribute your data automatically until you tell it how to do so. You must explicitly tell both the database and collection that you want them to be distributed.

For example, suppose we want to shard the *artists* collection in the *music* database on the "name" key. First, we enable sharding for the database, *music*:

```
> db.enableSharding("music")
```

Sharding a database is always prerequisite to sharding one of its collections.

Once you've enabled sharding on the database level, you can shard a collection by running `sh.shardCollection`:

```
> sh.shardCollection("music.artists", {"name" : 1})
```

Now the collection will be sharded by the "name" key. If you are sharding an existing collection there must be an index on the "name" field; otherwise the `shardCollection` call will return an error. If you get an error, create the index (*mongos* will return the index it suggests as part of the error message) and retry the `shardCollection` command.

If the collection you are sharding does not yet exist, *mongos* will automatically create the shard key index for you.

The *shardCollection* command splits the collection into *chunks*, which are the unit MongoDB uses to move data around. Once the command returns successfully, MongoDB will begin balancing the collection across the shards in your cluster. This process is not instantaneous. For large collections it may take hours to finish this initial balancing.

How MongoDB Tracks Cluster Data

Each *mongos* must always know where to find a document, given its shard key. Theoretically, MongoDB could track where each and every document lived, but this becomes unwieldy for collections with millions or billions of documents. Thus, MongoDB groups documents into *chunks*, which are documents in a given range of the shard key. A chunk always lives on a single shard, so MongoDB can keep a small table of chunks mapped to shards.

For example, if a user collection's shard key is `{"age" : 1}`, one chunk might be all documents with an "age" field between 3 and 17. If *mongos* gets a query for `{"age" : 5}`, it can route the query to the shard where the 3–17 chunk lives.

As writes occur, the number and size of the documents in a chunk might change. Inserts can make a chunk contain more documents, removes fewer. If we were making a game for children and preteens, our chunk for ages 3–17 might get larger and larger (one would hope). Almost all of our users would be in that chunk, and so on a single shard, somewhat defeating the point of distributing our data. Thus, once a chunk grows to a certain size, MongoDB automatically splits it into two smaller chunks. In this example, the chunk might be split into one chunk containing documents with ages 3 through 11 and the another containing 12 through 17. Note that these two chunks still cover the entire age range that the original chunk covered: 3–17. As these new chunks grow, they can be split into still smaller chunks until there is a chunk for each age.

You cannot have chunks with overlapping ranges, like 3–15 and 12–17. If you could, MongoDB would need to check both chunks when attempting to find an age in the overlap, like 14. It is more efficient to only have to look in one place, particularly once chunks begin moving around the cluster.

A document always belongs to one and only one chunk. One consequence to this rule is that you cannot use an array field as your shard key, since MongoDB creates multiple index entries for arrays. For example, if a document had [5, 26, 83] in its `"age"` field, it would belong in up to three chunks.

> A common misconception is that the data in a chunk is physically grouped on disk. This is incorrect: chunks have no effect on how *mongod* stores collection data.

Chunk Ranges

Each chunk is described by the range it contains. A newly sharded collection starts off with a single chunk and every document lives in this chunk. This chunk's bounds are negative infinity to infinity, shown as `$minKey` and `$maxKey` in the shell.

As this chunk grows, MongoDB will automatically split it into two chunks, with the range negative infinity to `<some value>` and `<some value>` to infinity. `<some value>` is the same for both chunks: the lower chunk contains everything up to (but not including) `<some value>` and the upper chunk actually contains `<some value>`.

This may be more intuitive with an example: suppose we were sharding by `"age"` as described earlier. All documents with `"age"` between 3 and 17 are contained on one chunk: `3 ≤ age < 17`. When this is split, we end up with two ranges: `3 ≤ age < 12` on one chunk and `12 ≤ age < 17` on the other. 12 is called the *split point*.

Chunk information is stored in the *config.chunks* collection. If you looked at the contents of that collection, you'd see documents that looked something like this (some fields have been omitted for clarity):

```
> db.chunks.find(criteria, {"min" : 1, "max" : 1})
{
    "_id" : "test.users-age_-100.0",
    "min" : {"age" : -100},
    "max" : {"age" : 23}
}
{
    "_id" : "test.users-age_23.0",
```

```
        "min" : {"age" : 23},
        "max" : {"age" : 100}
    }
    {
        "_id" : "test.users-age_100.0",
        "min" : {"age" : 100},
        "max" : {"age" : 1000}
    }
```

Based on the *config.chunks* documents shown, here are a few examples of where various documents would live:

`{"_id" : 123, "age" : 50}`
: This document would live in the second chunk, as that chunk contains all documents with `"age"` between 23 and 100.

`{"_id" : 456, "age" : 100}`
: This document would live on the third chunk, as lower bounds are inclusive. The second chunk contains all documents up to `"age" : 100`, but not any documents where `"age"` equals 100.

`{"_id" : 789, "age" : -101}`
: This document would not be in any of these chunks. It would be in some chunk with a range lower than the first chunk's.

With a compound shard key, shard ranges work the same way that sorting by the two keys would work. For example, suppose that we had a shard key on `{"username" : 1, "age" : 1}`. Then we might have chunk ranges such as:

```
{
    "_id" : "test.users-username_MinKeyage_MinKey",
    "min" : {
        "username" : { "$minKey" : 1 },
        "age" : { "$minKey" : 1 }
    },
    "max" : {
        "username" : "user107487",
        "age" : 73
    }
}
{
    "_id" : "test.users-username_\"user107487\"age_73.0",
    "min" : {
        "username" : "user107487",
        "age" : 73
    },
    "max" : {
        "username" : "user114978",
        "age" : 119
    }
}
```

```
{
    "_id" : "test.users-username_\"user114978\"age_119.0",
    "min" : {
        "username" : "user114978",
        "age" : 119
    },
    "max" : {
        "username" : "user122468",
        "age" : 68
    }
}
```

Thus, *mongos* can easily find on which chunk someone with a given username (or a given username and age) lives. However, given just an age, *mongos* would have to check all, or almost all, chunks. If we wanted to be able to target queries on age to the right chunk, we'd have to use the "opposite" shard key: `{"age" : 1, "username" : 1}`. This is often a point of confusion: a range over the second half of a shard key will cut across multiple chunks.

Splitting Chunks

mongos tracks how much data it inserts per chunk and, once that reaches a certain threshold, checks if the chunk needs to be split, as shown in Figure 14-1 and Figure 14-2. If the chunk does need to be split, *mongos* will update the chunk's metadata on the config servers. Chunk splits are just a metadata change (no data is moved). New chunk documents are created on the config servers and the old chunk's range (`"max"`) is modified. Once that process is complete, the *mongos* resets its tracking for the original chunk and creates new trackers for the new chunks.

When *mongos* asks a shard if a chunk needs to be split, the shard makes a rough calculation of the chunk size. If it finds that the chunk is getting large, it finds split points and sends those to the *mongos* (as shown in Figure 14-3).

A shard may not be able to find any split points though, even for a large chunk, as there are a limited number of ways to legally split a chunk. Any two documents with the same shard key must live in the same chunk so chunks can only be split between documents where the shard key's value changes. For example, if the shard key was `"age"`, the following chunk could be split at the points where the shard key changed, as indicated:

```
{"age" : 13, "username" : "ian"}
{"age" : 13, "username" : "randolph"}
------------ // split point
{"age" : 14, "username" : "randolph"}
{"age" : 14, "username" : "eric"}
{"age" : 14, "username" : "hari"}
{"age" : 14, "username" : "mathias"}
------------ // split point
```

```
{"age" : 15, "username" : "greg"}
{"age" : 15, "username" : "andrew"}
```

mongos will not necessarily split a chunk at every split point available, but those are the possibilities it has to choose from.

For example, if the chunk contained the following documents, it could not be split (unless the application started inserting fractional ages):

```
{"age" : 12, "username" : "kevin"}
{"age" : 12, "username" : "spencer"}
{"age" : 12, "username" : "alberto"}
{"age" : 12, "username" : "tad"}
```

Thus, having a variety of values for your shard key is important. Other important properties will be covered in the next chapter.

If one of the config servers is down when a *mongos* tries to do a split, the *mongos* won't be able to update the metadata (as shown in Figure 14-4). All config servers must be up and reachable for splits to happen. If the *mongos* continues to receive write requests for the chunk, it will keep trying to split the chunk and fail. As long as the config servers are not healthy, splits will continue not to work and all the split attempts can slow down the *mongos* and shard involved (which repeats the process shown in Figure 14-1 through Figure 14-4 for each incoming write). This process of *mongos* repeatedly attempting to split a chunk and being unable to is called a *split storm*. The only way to prevent split storms is to ensure that your config servers are up and healthy as much of the time as possible. You can also restart a *mongos* to reset its write counter (so that it is no longer at the split threshold).

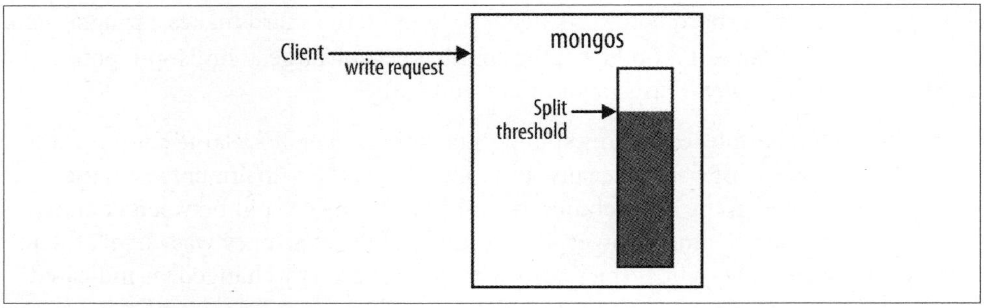

Figure 14-1. When a client writes to a chunk, mongos will check its split threshold for the chunk

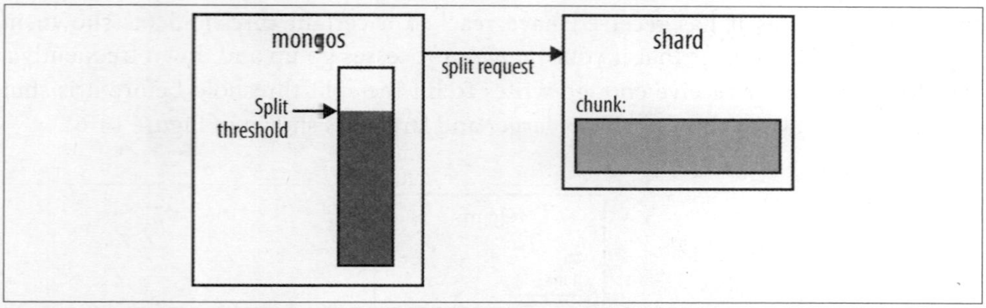

Figure 14-2. If the split threshold has been reached, mongos will send a request for split points to the shard

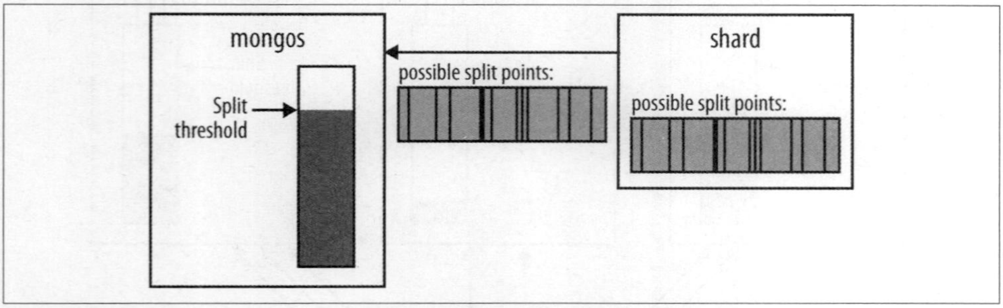

Figure 14-3. The shard calculates split points for the chunk and sends them to the mongos

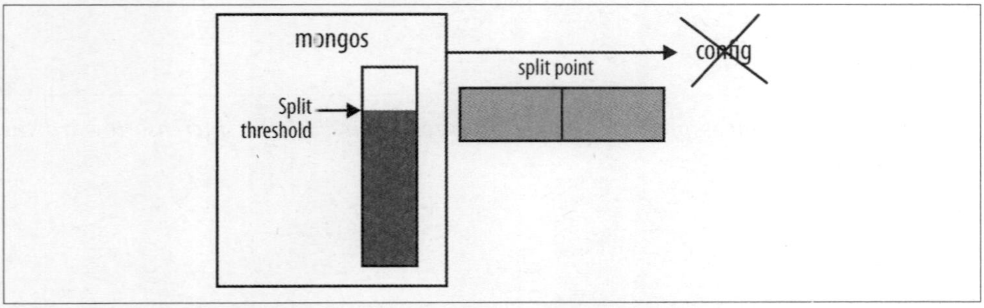

Figure 14-4. The mongos chooses a split point and attempts to inform the config server but cannot reach it. Thus, it is still over its split threshold for the chunk and any subsequent writes will trigger this process again.

Another issue is that *mongos* might never realize that it needs to split a large chunk. There is no global counter of how big each chunk is. Each *mongos* simply calculates whether the writes it has received have reached a certain threshold (as shown in Figure 14-5). This means that if your *mongos* processes go up and down frequently a *mongos* might never receive enough writes to hit the split threshold before it is shut down again and your chunks will get larger and larger (as shown in Figure 14-6).

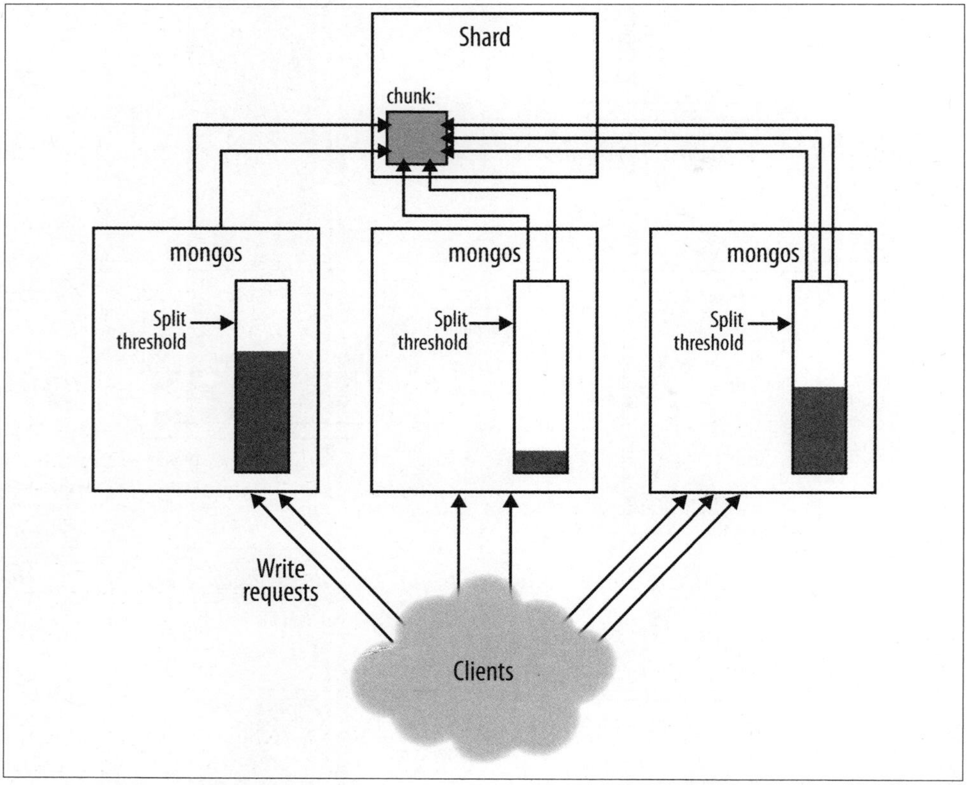

Figure 14-5. As mongos processes perform writes, their counters increase toward the split threshold

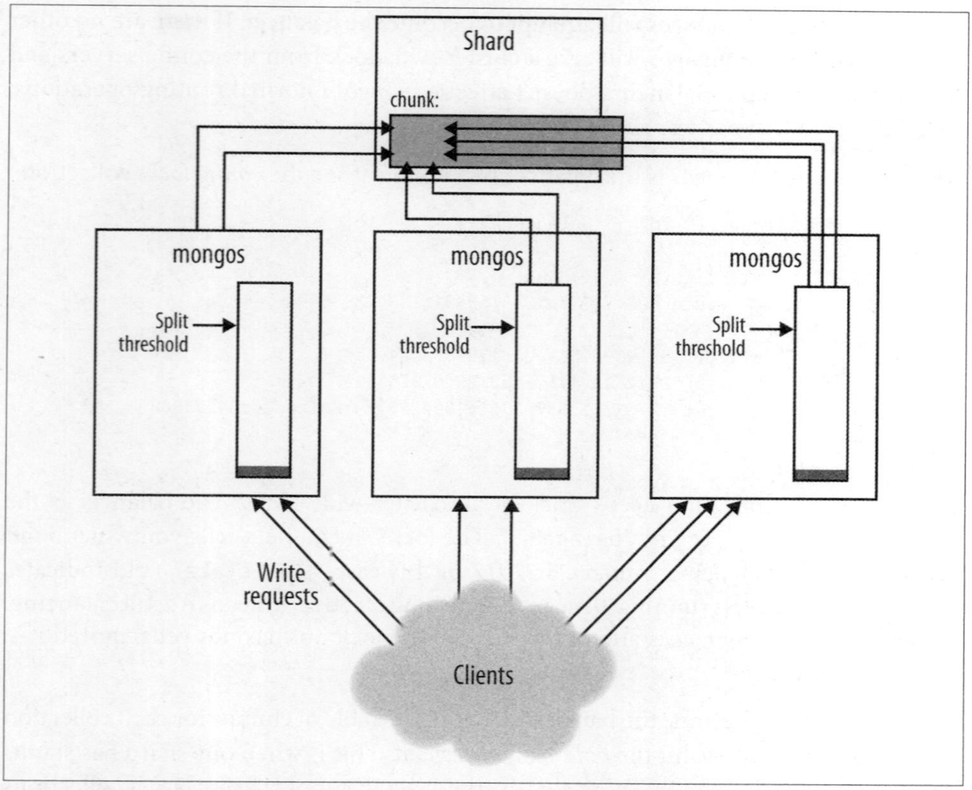

Figure 14-6. If mongos processes are regularly restarted their counters may never hit the threshold, making chunks grow without bound

The first way to prevent this is to have fewer *mongos* churn. Leave *mongos* processes up, when possible, instead of spinning them up when they are needed and then turning them off when they are not. However, some deployments may find it too expensive to run *mongos* processes that aren't being used. If you are in this situation, another way of getting more splits is to make the chunk size smaller than you actually want it to be. This will prompt splits to happen at a lower threshold.

You can turn off chunk splitting by starting every *mongos* with `--nosplit`.

The Balancer

The *balancer* is responsible for migrating data. It regularly checks for imbalances between shards and, if it finds an imbalance, will begin migrating chunks. Although the balancer is often referred to as a single entity, each *mongos* plays the part of "the balancer" occasionally.

Every few seconds, a *mongos* will attempt to become the balancer. If there are no other balancers active, the *mongos* will take a cluster-wide lock from the config servers and do a balancing round. Balancing doesn't affect a *mongos*'s normal routing operations, so clients using that *mongos* should be unaffected.

You can see which *mongos* is the balancer by looking at the the *config.locks* collection:

```
> db.locks.findOne({"_id" : "balancer"})
{
    "_id" : "balancer",
    "process" : "router-23:27017:1355763351:1804289383",
    "state" : 0,
    "ts" : ObjectId("50cf939c051fcdb8139fc72c"),
    "when" : ISODate("2012-12-17T21:50:20.023Z"),
    "who" : "router-23:27017:1355763351:1804289383:Balancer:846930886",
    "why" : "doing balance round"
}
```

The *config.locks* collection keeps track of all cluster-wide locks. The balancer is the document with the `"_id"` of `"balancer"`. The lock's `"who"` field tells you which *mongos* is—or was—balancing: *router-23:27017* in this case. The `"state"` field indicates whether the balancer is running; 0 means it is no longer active, 2 means it's still balancing. (1 means that the *mongos* is attempting to take the lock but has not yet acquired it—you won't usually see 1.)

Once a *mongos* has become the balancer, it checks its table of chunks for each collection to see if any shards have hit the *balancing threshold*. This is when one shard has significantly more chunks than the other shards (the exact threshold varies: larger collections tolerate larger imbalances than smaller ones). If an imbalance is detected, the balancer will redistribute chunks until all shards are within one chunk of one another. If no collections have hit the balancing threshold. The *mongos* stops being the balancer.

Assuming that some collections have hit the threshold, the balancer will begin migrating chunks. It chooses a chunk from the overloaded shard and asks the shard if it should split the chunk before migrating. Once it does any necessary splits, it migrates the chunk to a machine with fewer chunks.

An application using the cluster does not need be aware that the data is moving: all reads and writes are routed to the old chunk until the move is complete. Once the metadata is updated, all *mongos* processes attempting to access the data in the old location will get an error. These errors should not be visible to the client: the *mongos* will silently handle the error and retry the operation on the new shard.

This is a common cause of errors you might see in *mongos* logs that are about being "unable to `setShardVersion`." When *mongos* gets this type of error, it looks up the new location of the data from the config servers, updates its chunk table, and attempts the request again. If it successfully retrieves the data from the new location, it will return it to the client as though nothing went wrong (but it will print a message in the log that the error occurred).

If the *mongos* is unable to retrieve the new chunk location because the config servers are unavailable, it will return an error to the client. This is another reason why it is important to always have config servers up and healthy.

CHAPTER 15

Choosing a Shard Key

The most important and difficult task when using sharding is choosing how your data will be distributed. To make intelligent choices about this, you have to understand how MongoDB distributes data. This chapter helps you make a good choice of shard key by covering:

- How to decide among multiple possible shard keys
- Shard keys for several use cases
- What you can't use as a shard key
- Some alternative strategies if you want to customize how data is distributed
- How to manually shard your data

This chapter assumes that you understand the basic components of sharding as covered in the previous chapters.

Taking Stock of Your Usage

When you shard a collection you choose a field or two to use to split up the data. This key (or keys) is called a *shard key*. Once you have more than a few shards, it's almost impossible to change your shard key, so it is important to choose correctly (or at least notice any issues quickly).

To choose a good shard key, you need to understand your workload and how your shard key is going to distribute your application's requests. This can be difficult to picture, so try to work out some examples or, even better, try it out on a backup data set with sample traffic. This section has lots of diagrams and explanations, but there is no substitute for trying it on your own data set.

For each collection that you're planning to shard, start by answering the following questions:

- How many shards are you planning to grow to? A three-shard cluster has a great deal more flexibility than a thousand-shard cluster. As a cluster gets larger, you should not plan to fire off queries that can hit all shards, so almost all queries must include the shard key.
- Are you sharding to decrease read or write latency? (*Latency* refers to how long something takes, e.g., a write takes 20 ms, but we need it to take 10 ms.) Decreasing write latency usually involves sending requests to geographically closer or more powerful machines.
- Are you sharding to increase read or write throughput? (*Throughput* refers to how many requests the cluster can handle at the same time: the cluster can do 1,000 writes in 20 ms, but we need it to do 5,000 writes in 20 ms.) Increasing throughput usually involves adding more parallelization and making sure that requests are distributed evenly across the cluster.
- Are you sharding to increase system resources (e.g., give MongoDB more RAM per GB of data)? If so, you want to keep working set size as small possible.

Use these answers to evaluate the following shard key descriptions and decide whether the shard key you choose would work well in your situation. Does it give you the targeted queries that you need? Does it change the throughput or latency of your system in the ways you need? If you need a compact working set, does it provide that?

Picturing Distributions

There are three basic distributions that are the most common ways people choose to split their data: ascending key, random, and location-based. There are other types of keys that could be used, but most use cases fall into one of these categories. Each is discussed in the following sections.

Ascending Shard Keys

Ascending shard keys are generally something like a `"date"` field or `ObjectId`—anything that steadily increases over time. An autoincrementing primary key is another example of an ascending field, albeit one that doesn't show up in MongoDB much (unless you're importing from another database).

Suppose that we shard on an ascending field, like `"_id"` on a collection using ObjectIds. If we shard on `"_id"`, then this will be split into chunks of `"_id"` ranges, as in Figure 15-1. These chunks will be distributed across our sharded cluster of, let's say, three shards, as shown in Figure 15-2.

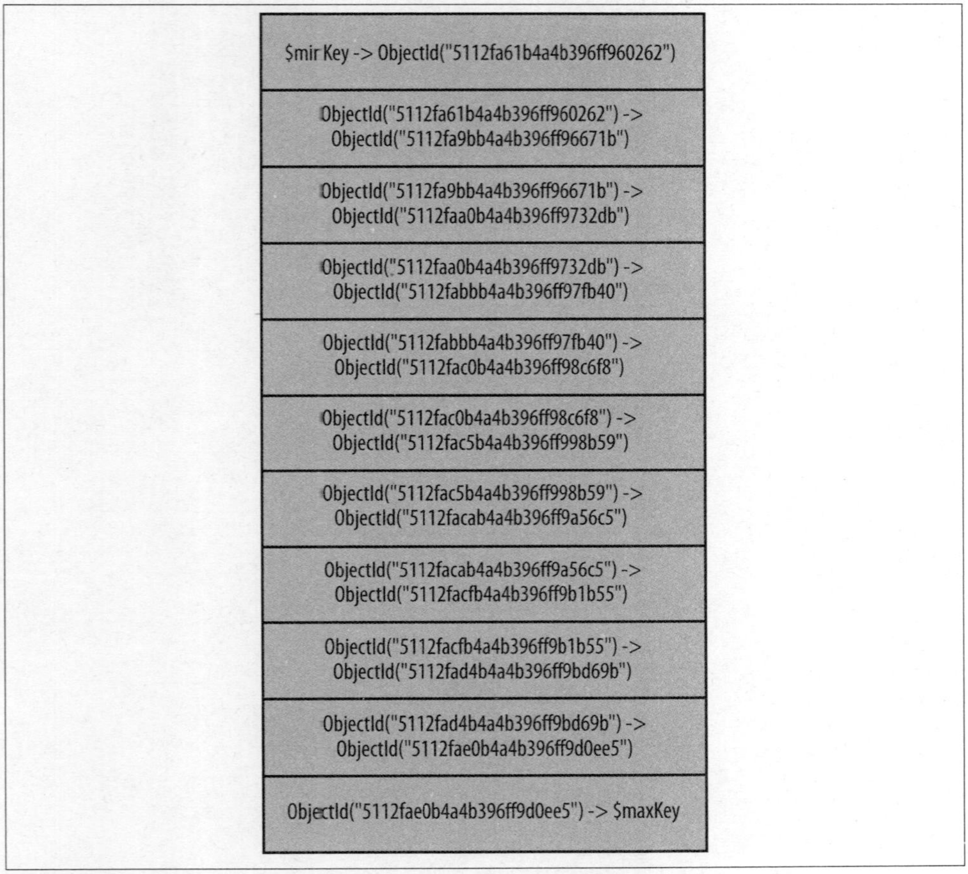

Figure 15-1. The collection is split into ranges of ObjectIds. Each range is a chunk.

Suppose we create a new document. Which chunk will it be in? The answer is the chunk with the range `ObjectId("5112fae0b4a4b396ff9d0ee5")` through `$maxKey`. This is called the *max chunk*, as it is the chunk containing `$maxKey`.

If we insert another document, it will also be in the max chunk. In fact, every subsequent insert will be into the max chunk! Every insert's `"_id"` field will be closer to infinity than the previous (because `ObjectId`s are always ascending), so they will all go to into the max chunk.

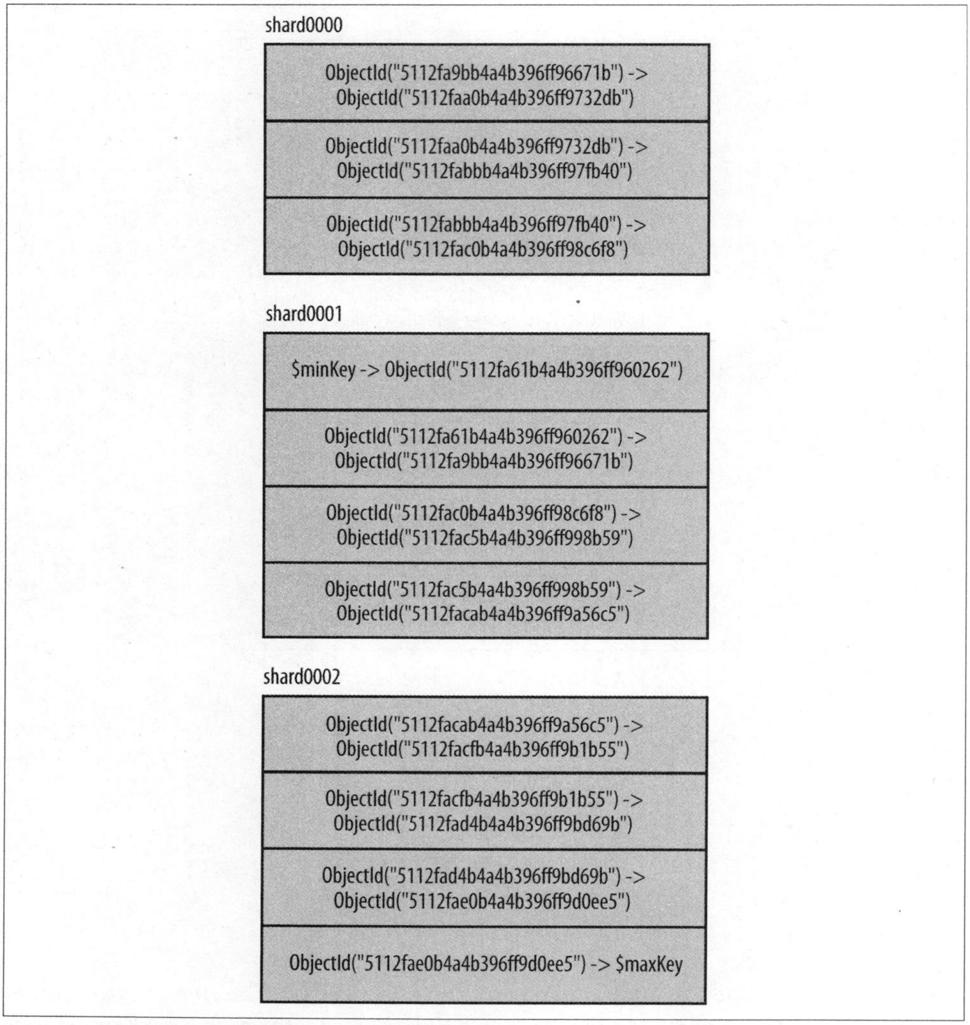

Figure 15-2. Chunks are distributed across shards in a random order

This has a couple of interesting (and often undesirable) properties. First, all of your writes will be routed to one shard (shard0002, in this case). This chunk will be the only one growing and splitting, as it is the only one that receives inserts. As you insert data, new chunks will "fall off" of this chunk's butt, as shown in Figure 15-3.

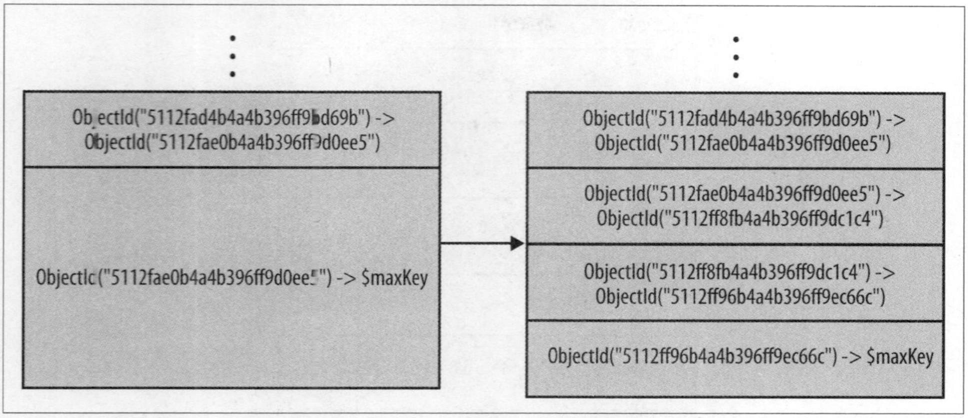

Figure 15-3. The max chunk continues growing and being split into multiple chunks

This pattern often makes it more difficult for MongoDB to keep chunks evenly balanced because all the chunks are being created by one shard. Therefore, MongoDB must constantly move chunks to other shards instead of correcting small imbalances that might occur in a more evenly distributed systems.

Randomly Distributed Shard Keys

On the other end of the spectrum are randomly distributed shard keys. Randomly distributed keys could be usernames, email addresses, UUIDs, MD5 hashes, or any other key that has no identifiable pattern in your dataset.

Suppose the shard key is a random number between 0 and 1. We'll end up with a random distribution of chunks on the various shards, as shown in Figure 15-4.

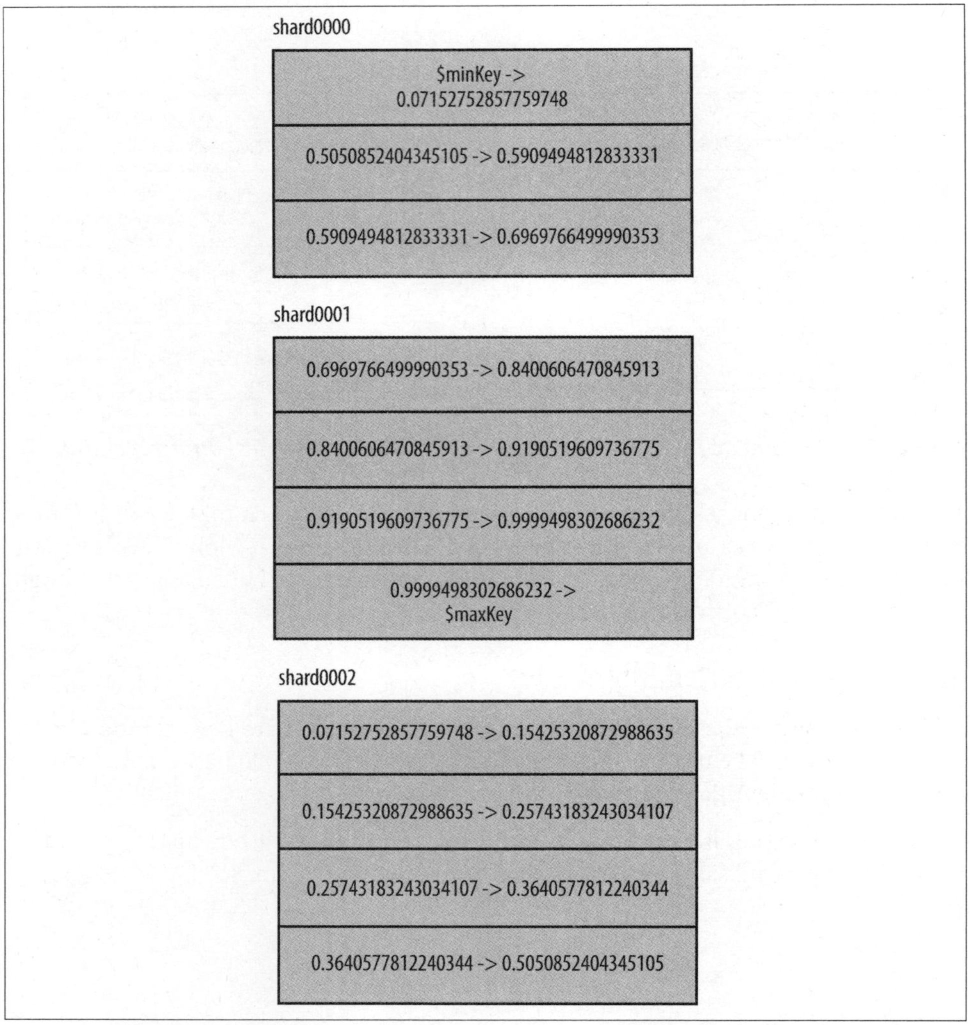

Figure 15-4. As in the previous section, chunks are distributed randomly around the cluster

As more data is inserted, the data's random nature means that inserts should hit every chunk fairly evenly. You can prove this to yourself by inserting 10,000 documents and seeing where they end up:

```
> var servers = {}
> var findShard = function (id) {
...     var explain = db.random.find({_id:id}).explain();
...     for (var i in explain.shards) {
...         var server = explain.shards[i][0];
```

```
...         if (server.n == 1) {
...             if (server.server in servers) {
...                 servers[server.server]++;
...             } else {
...                 servers[server.server] = 1;
...             }
...         }
...     }
... }
> for (var i = 0; i < 10000; i++) {
...     var id = ObjectId();
...     db.random.insert({"_id" : id, "x" : Math.random()});
...     findShard(id);
... }
> servers
{
    "spock:30001" : 2942,
    "spock:30002" : 4332,
    "spock:30000" : 2726
}
```

As writes are randomly distributed, shards should grow at roughly the same rate, limiting the number of migrates that need to occur.

The only downside to randomly distributed shard keys is that MongoDB isn't efficient at randomly accessing data beyond the size of RAM. However, if you have the capacity or don't mind the performance hit, random keys nicely distribute load across your cluster.

Location-Based Shard Keys

Location-based shard keys may be things like a user's IP, latitude and longitude, or address. Location shard keys are not necessarily related to a physical location field: the "location" might be a more abstract way that data should be grouped together. In any case, it is a key where documents with some similarity fall into a range based on this field. This can be handy for both putting data close to its users and keeping related data together on disk.

For example, suppose we have a collection of documents that are sharded on an IP address. Documents will be organized into chunks based on their addresses and randomly spread across the cluster, as shown in Figure 15-5.

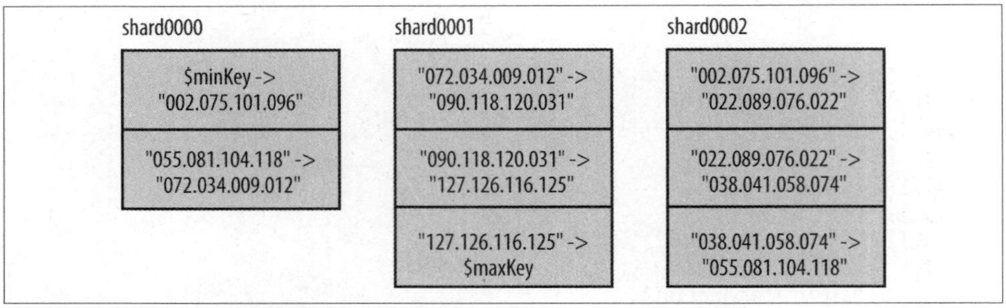

Figure 15-5. A sample distribution of chunks in the IP address collection

If we wanted certain chunk ranges to be attached to certain shards, we could *tag* these shards and then assign chunk ranges to tags. In this example, suppose that we wanted to keep certain IP blocks on certain shards: say, "56.*.*.*" (the United States Postal Service's IP block) on shard0000 and "17.*.*.*" (Apple's IP block) on either shard0000 or shard0002. We do not care where the other IPs live. We could request that the balancer do this by setting up tag ranges:

```
> sh.addShardTag("shard0000", "USPS")
> sh.addShardTag("shard0000", "Apple")
> sh.addShardTag("shard0002", "Apple")
```

Next, we create the rules:

```
> sh.addTagRange("test.ips", {"ip" : "056.000.000.000"},
... {"ip" : "057.000.000.000"}, "USPS")
```

This attaches all IPs greater than or equal to 56.0.0.0 and less than 57.0.0.0 to the shard tagged "USPS". Next, we add a rule for Apple:

```
> sh.addTagRange("test.ips", {"ip" : "017.000.000.000"},
... {"ip" : "018.000.000.000"}, "Apple")
```

When the balancer moves chunks, it will attempt to move chunks with those ranges to those shards. Note that this process is not immediate. Chunks that were not covered by a tag range will be moved around normally. The balancer will continue attempting to distribute chunks evenly among shards.

Shard Key Strategies

This section presents a number of shard key options for various types of applications.

Hashed Shard Key

For loading data as fast as possible, hashed shard keys are the best option. A hashed shard key can make any field randomly distributed, so it is a good choice if you're going to be using an ascending key a in a lot of queries but want writes to be random distributed.

The trade-off is that you can never do a targeted range query with a hashed shard key. If you will not be doing range queries, though, hashed shard keys are a good option.

To create a hashed shard key, first create a hashed index:

```
> db.users.ensureIndex({"username" : "hashed"})
```

Next, shard the collection with:

```
> sh.shardCollection("app.users", {"username" : "hashed"})
{ "collectionsharded" : "app.users", "ok" : 1 }
```

If you create a hashed shard key on a nonexistent collection, *shardCollection* behaves interestingly: it assumes that you want evenly distributed chunks, so it immediately creates a bunch of empty chunks and distributes them around your cluster. For example, suppose our cluster looked like this before creating the hashed shard key:

```
> sh.status()
--- Sharding Status ---
  sharding version: { "_id" : 1, "version" : 3 }
  shards:
        {  "_id" : "shard0000",  "host" : "localhost:30000" }
        {  "_id" : "shard0001",  "host" : "localhost:30001" }
        {  "_id" : "shard0002",  "host" : "localhost:30002" }
  databases:
        {  "_id" : "admin",  "partitioned" : false,  "primary" : "config" }
        {  "_id" : "test",  "partitioned" : true,  "primary" : "shard0001" }
```

Immediately after *shardCollection* returns there are two chunks on each shard, evenly distributing the key space across the cluster:

```
> sh.status()
--- Sharding Status ---
  sharding version: { "_id" : 1, "version" : 3 }
  shards:
    {  "_id" : "shard0000",  "host" : "localhost:30000" }
    {  "_id" : "shard0001",  "host" : "localhost:30001" }
    {  "_id" : "shard0002",  "host" : "localhost:30002" }
  databases:
    {  "_id" : "admin",  "partitioned" : false,  "primary" : "config" }
    {  "_id" : "test",  "partitioned" : true,  "primary" : "shard0001" }
        test.foo
            shard key: { "username" : "hashed" }
            chunks:
                shard0000       2
                shard0001       2
                shard0002       2
            { "username" : { "$MinKey" : true } }
                -->> { "username" : NumberLong("-6148914691236517204") }
                on : shard0000 { "t" : 3000, "i" : 2 }
```

```
{ "username" : NumberLong("-6148914691236517204") }
    -->> { "username" : NumberLong("-3074457345618258602") }
    on : shard0000 { "t" : 3000, "i" : 3 }
{ "username" : NumberLong("-3074457345618258602") }
    -->> { "username" : NumberLong(0) }
    on : shard0001 { "t" : 3000, "i" : 4 }
{ "username" : NumberLong(0) }
    -->> { "username" : NumberLong("3074457345618258602") }
    on : shard0001 { "t" : 3000, "i" : 5 }
{ "username" : NumberLong("3074457345618258602") }
    -->> { "username" : NumberLong("6148914691236517204") }
    on : shard0002 { "t" : 3000, "i" : 6 }
{ "username" : NumberLong("6148914691236517204") }
    -->> { "username" : { "$MaxKey" : true } }
    on : shard0002 { "t" : 3000, "i" : 7 }
```

Note that there are no documents in the collection yet, but when you start inserting them, writes should be evenly distributed across the shards from the get-go. Ordinarily, you would have to wait for chunks to grow, split, and move to start writing to other shards. With this automatic priming, you'll immediately have chunk ranges on all shards.

There are some limitations on what your shard key can be if you're using a hashed shard key. First, you cannot use the `unique` option. As with other shard keys, you cannot use array fields. Finally, be aware of is that floating point values will be rounded to whole numbers before hashing, so 1 and 1.999999 will both be hashed to the same value.

Hashed Shard Keys for GridFS

Before attempting to shard GridFS collections, make sure that you understand how GridFS stores data (see Chapter 6 for an explanation).

In the following explanation, the term "chunks" is overloaded since GridFS splits files into chunks and sharding splits collections into chunks. Thus, the two types of chunks are referred to as "GridFS chunks" and "sharding chunks" later in the chapter.

GridFS collections are generally excellent candidates for sharding, as they contain massive amounts of file data. However, neither of the indexes that are automatically created on *fs.chunks* are particularly good shard keys: `{"_id" : 1}` is an ascending key and `{"files_id" : 1, "n" : 1}` picks up *fs.files*' `"_id"` field, so it is also an ascending key.

However, if you create a hashed index on the `"files_id"` field, each file will be randomly distributed across the cluster. But a file will always be contained in a single chunk. This is the best of both worlds: writes will go to all shards evenly and reading a file's data will only ever have to hit a single shard.

To set this up, you must create a new index on {"files_id" : "hashed"} (as of this writing, *mongos* cannot use a subset of the compound index as a shard key). Then shard the collection on this field:

```
> db.fs.chunks.ensureIndex({"files_id" : "hashed"})
> sh.shardCollection("test.fs.chunks", {"files_id" : "hashed"})
{ "collectionsharded" : "test.fs.chunks", "ok" : 1 }
```

As a side note, the *fs.files* collection may or may not need to be sharded, as it will be much smaller than *fs.chunks*. You can shard it if you would like, but it less likely to be necessary.

The Firehose Strategy

If you have some servers that are more powerful than others, you might want to let them handle proportionally more load than your less-powerful servers. For example, suppose you have one shard that is composed of SSDs that can handle 10 times the load of your other machines (backed by spinning disks). Luckily, you have 10 other shards. You could force all inserts to go to the SSD, and then allow the balancer to move older chunks to the other shards. This would give lower-latency writes than the spinning disks would.

To use this strategy, we have to pin the highest chunk to the SSD. First, tag the SSD:

```
> sh.addShardTag("shard-name", "ssd")
```

Now, pin the current value of the ascending key through infinity to that shard, so all new writes go to it:

```
> sh.addTagRange("dbName.collName", {"_id" : ObjectId()},
... {"_id" : MaxKey}, "ssd")
```

Now all inserts will be routed to this last chunk, which will always live on the shard tagged "ssd".

However, ranges from now through infinity will be trapped on this shard unless we modify the tag range. We could set up a cron job to update the tag range once a day, like this:

```
> use config
> var tag = db.tags.findOne({"ns" : "dbName.collName",
... "max" : {"shardKey" : MaxKey}})
> tag.min.shardKey = ObjectId()
> db.tags.save(tag)
```

Then all of the previous day's chunks would be able to move to other shards.

Another downside of this strategy is that it requires some changes to scale. If your SSD can no longer handle the number of writes coming in, there is no trivial way to split the load between this server and another.

If you do not have a high-performance server to firehose into or you are not using tagging, do not use an ascending key as the shard key. If you do, all writes will go to a single shard.

Multi-Hotspot

Standalone *mongod* servers are most efficient when doing ascending writes. This conflicts with sharding, in that sharding is most efficient when writes are spread over the cluster. This technique basically creates multiple hotspots—optimally several on each shard—so that writes are evenly balanced across the cluster but, within a shard, ascending.

To accomplish this, we use a compound shard key. The first value in the compound key is a rough, random value with low-ish cardinality. You can picture each value in the first part of the shard key as a chunk, as shown in Figure 15-6. This will eventually work itself out as you insert more data, although it will probably never be divided up this neatly (right on the `$minKey` lines). However, if you insert enough data, you should eventually have approximately one chunk per random value. As you continue to insert data, you'll end up with multiple chunks with the same random value, which brings us to the second part of the shard key.

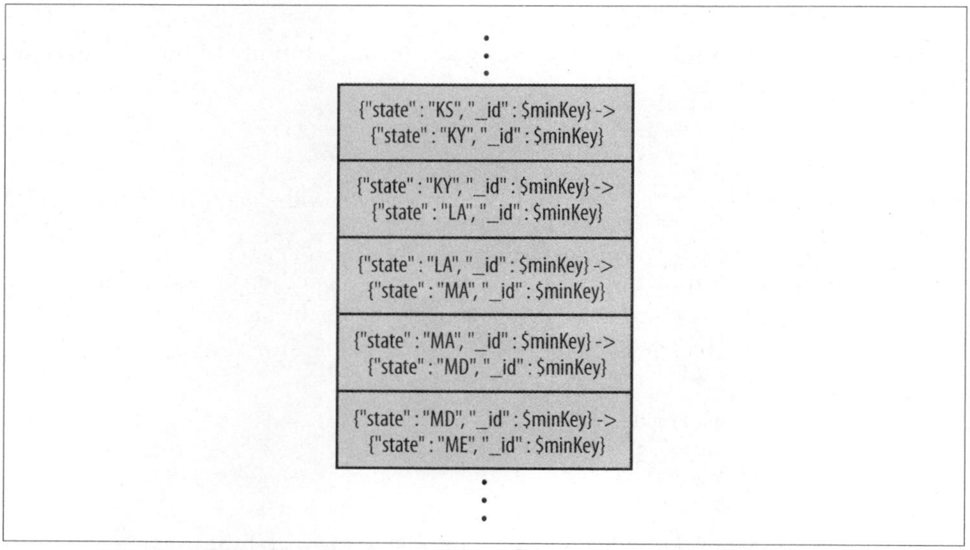

Figure 15-6. A subset of the chunks. Each chunk contains a single state and a range of _ids

The second part of the shard key is an ascending key. This means that, within a chunk, values are always increasing, as shown in the sample documents in Figure 15-7. Thus, if you had one chunk per shard, you'd have the perfect setup: ascending writes on every shard, as shown in Figure 15-8. Of course having *n* chunks with *n* hotspots spread across *n* shards isn't very extensible: add a new shard and it won't get any writes because there's no hot chunk to put on it. Thus, you want a few hotspot chunks per shard (to give you room to grow). However, you don't want too many. A few hotspot chunks will keep the effectiveness of ascending writes. But having, say, a thousand "hotspots" on a shard will end up being equivalent to random writes.

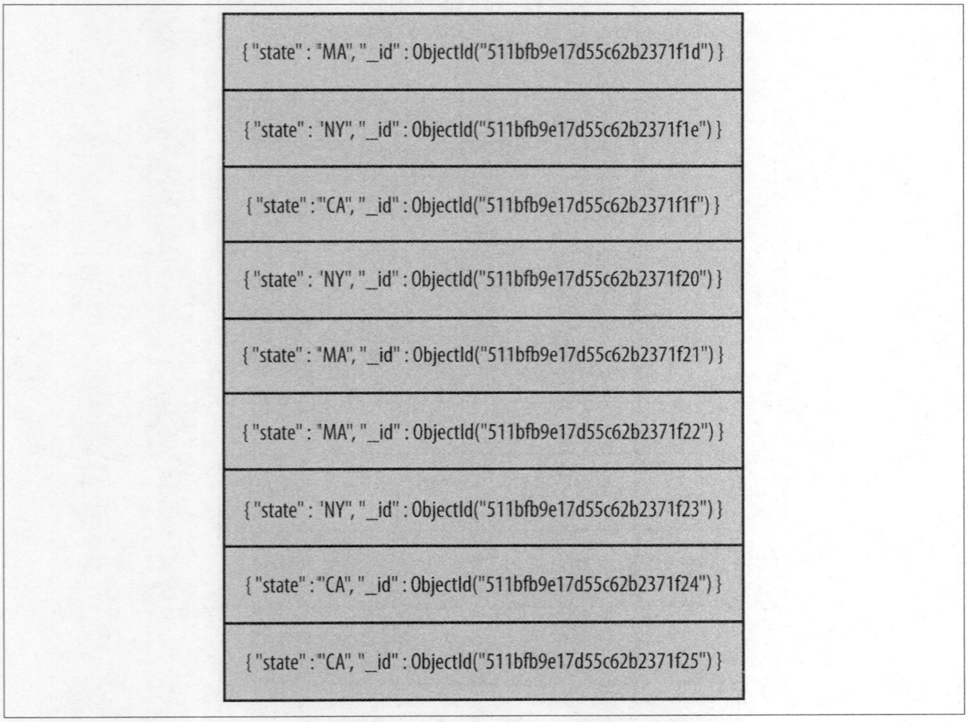

Figure 15-7. A sample list of inserted documents. Note that all _ids are increasing.

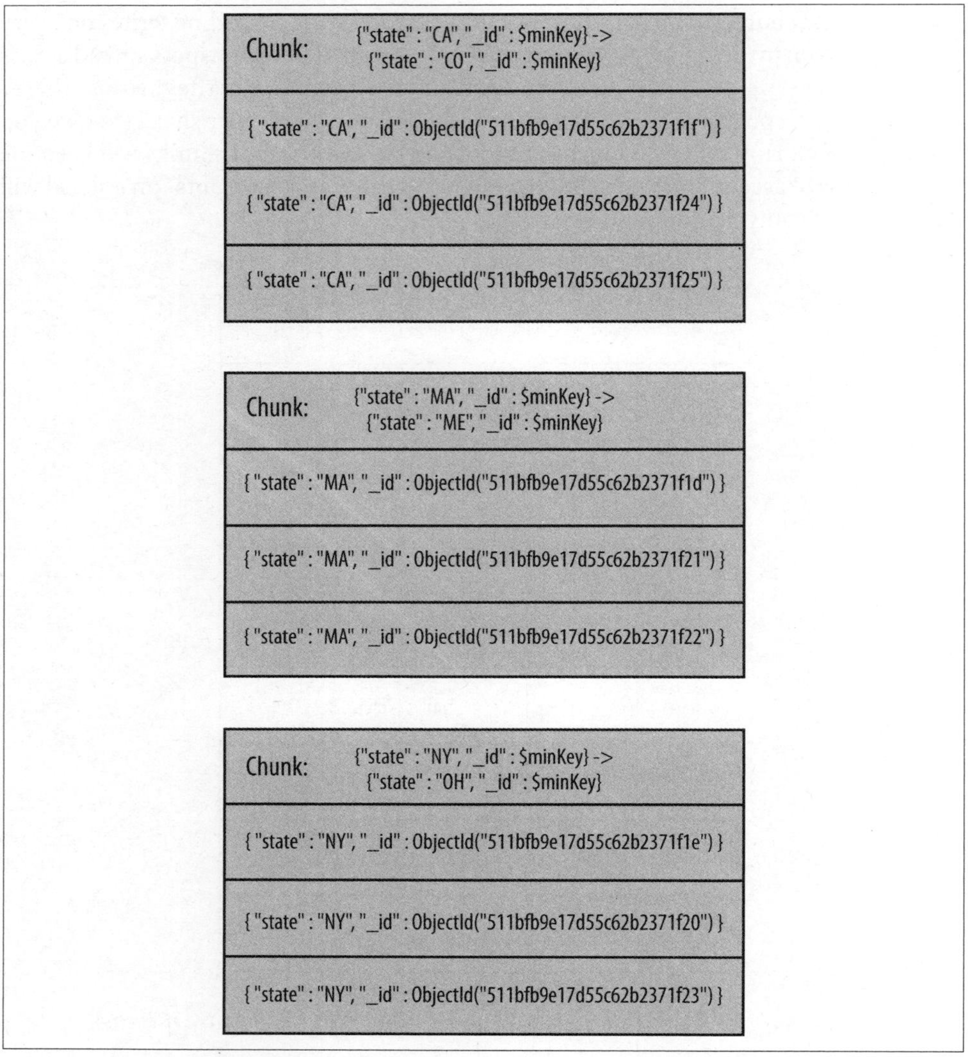

Figure 15-8. The inserted documents, split into chunks. Note that, within each chunk, the _ids are increasing.

You can picture this setup as each chunk being a stack of ascending documents. There are multiple stacks on each shard, each ascending until the chunk is split. Once a chunk is split, only one of the new chunks will be a hotspot chunk: the other chunk will essentially be "dead" and never grow again. If the stacks are evenly distributed across the shards, writes will be evenly distributed.

Shard Key Rules and Guidelines

There are several practical restrictions to be aware of before choosing a shard key.

Determining which key to shard on and creating shard keys should be reminiscent of indexing because the two concepts are similar. In fact, often your shard key may just be the index you use most often (or some variation on it).

Shard Key Limitations

Shard keys cannot be arrays. `sh.shardCollection()` will fail if any key has an array value and inserting an array into that field is not allowed.

Once inserted, a document's shard key value cannot be modified. To change a document's shard key, you must remove the document, change the key, and reinsert it. Thus, you should choose a field that is unchangeable or changes infrequently.

Most special types of index cannot be used for shard keys. In particular, you cannot shard on a geospatial index. Using a hashed index for a shard key is allowed, as covered previously.

Shard Key Cardinality

Whether your shard key jumps around or increases steadily, it is important to choose a key with values that will vary. As with indexes, sharding performs better on high cardinality fields. If, for example, we had a `"logLevel"` key that had only values `"DEBUG"`, `"WARN"`, or `"ERROR"`, MongoDB wouldn't be able to break up your data into more than three chunks (because there would be only three different values for the shard key). If you have a key with little variation and want to use it as a shard key anyway, you can do so by creating a compound shard key on that key and a key that varies more, like `"logLevel"` and `"timestamp"`. It is important that the combination of keys has high cardinality.

Controlling Data Distribution

Sometimes, automatic data distribution will not fit your requirements. This section gives you some options beyond choosing a shard key and allowing MongoDB to do everything automatically.

As your cluster gets larger or busier, these solutions become less practical. However, for small clusters, you may want more control.

Using a Cluster for Multiple Databases and Collections

MongoDB evenly distributes collections across every shard your cluster, which works well if you're storing homogeneous data. However, if you have a log collection that is "lower-value" than your other data, you might not want it taking up space on your more expensive servers. Or, if you have one powerful shard, you might want to use it for only a realtime collection and not allow other collections to use it. You can set up separate clusters, but you can also give MongoDB specific directions about where you want it to put certain data.

To set this up, use the `sh.addShardTag()` helper in the shell:

```
> sh.addShardTag("shard0000", "high")
> // shard0001 - no tag
> // shard0002 - no tag
> // shard0003 - no tag
> sh.addShardTag("shard0004", "low")
> sh.addShardTag("shard0005", "low")
```

Then we can assign different collections to different shards. For instance, our realtime collection:

```
> sh.addTagRange("super.important", {"shardKey" : MinKey},
... {"shardKey" : MaxKey}, "high")
```

This says, "for negative infinity to infinity for this collection, store it on shards tagged 'high.'" This means that no data from the important collection will be stored on any other server. Note that this does not effect how other collections are distributed: other collections will still be evenly distributed between this shard and the others.

We can perform a similar operation to keep the log collection on a low-quality server:

```
> sh.addTagRange("some.logs", {"shardKey" : MinKey},
... {"shardKey" : MaxKey}, "low")
```

The log collections will now be split evenly between shard0004 and shard0005.

Assigning a tag range to a collection does not affect it instantly. It is an instruction to the balancer that, when it runs, these are the viable targets to move the collection to. Thus, if the entire log collection is on shard0002 or evenly distributed among the shards, it will take a little while for all of the chunks to be migrated to shard0004 and shard0005.

As another example, perhaps we have a collection where we don't want it on the shard tagged "high" but do want it on any other one. We can add a new tag to all of the non-high-performance shards to create a new grouping. Shards can have as many tags as you need:

```
> sh.addShardTag("shard0001", "whatever")
> sh.addShardTag("shard0002", "whatever")
> sh.addShardTag("shard0003", "whatever")
```

```
> sh.addShardTag("shard0004", "whatever")
> sh.addShardTag("shard0005", "whatever")
```

Now we can specify that we want this collection (call it *"normal.coll"*) distributed across these five shards:

```
> sh.addTagRange("normal.coll", {"shardKey" : MinKey},
... {"shardKey" : MaxKey}, "whatever")
```

You cannot assign collections dynamically, i.e., "when a collection is created, randomly home it to a shard." However, you could have a cron job that went through and did it for you.

If you make a mistake or change your mind, you can remove shard tags with *sh.removeShardTag()*:

```
> sh.removeShardTag("shard0005", "whatever")
```

If you remove all tags described by a tag range (for example, if untagging the shard marked `"high"`) the balancer won't distribute the data anywhere because there aren't any valid locations listed. All the data will still be readable and writable; it just won't be able to migrate until you modify your tags or tag ranges.

There is no helper for removing tag ranges, but you can do so manually. To deal with tag ranges manually, access the *config.tags* namespace through the *mongos*. Similarly, shard tag information is kept in the *config.shards* namespace in the `"tags"` field of each shard document. If a shard has no `"tags"` field, then it has no tags.

Manual Sharding

Sometimes, for complex requirements or special situations, you may prefer to have complete control over which data is distributed where. You can turn off the balancer if you don't want data to be automatically distributed and use the *moveChunk* command to manually distribute data.

To turn off the balancer, connect to a *mongos* (any *mongos* is fine) and update the *config.settings* namespace with the following:

```
> db.settings.update({"_id" : "balancer"}, {"enabled" : false}, true)
```

Note that this is an upsert: it creates the balancer setting if one does not exist.

If there is currently a migrate in progress, this setting will not take effect until the migrate has completed. However, once any in-flight migrations have finished, the balancer will stop moving data around.

Once the balancer is off, you can move data around manually (if necessary). First, find out which chunks are where by looking at *config.chunks*:

```
> db.chunks.find()
```

Now, use the `moveChunk` command to migrate chunks to other shards. Specify the lower bound of the chunk-to-be-migrated and give the name of the shard that you want to move the chunk to:

```
> sh.moveChunk("test.manual.stuff",
... {user_id: NumberLong("-1844674407370955160")}, "test-rs1")
{ "millis" : 4079, "ok" : 1 }
```

However, unless you are in an exceptional situation, you should use MongoDB's automatic sharding instead of doing it manually. If you end up with a hotspot on a shard that you weren't expecting, you might end up with most of your data on that shard.

In particular, do not combine setting up unusual distributions manually with running the balancer. If the balancer detects an uneven number of chunks it will simply reshuffle all of your work to get the collection evenly balanced again. If you want uneven distribution of chunks, use the shard tagging technique discussed in "Using a Cluster for Multiple Databases and Collections" on page 272.

CHAPTER 16
Sharding Administration

A sharded cluster is the most difficult type of deployment to administer. This chapter gives advice on performing administrative tasks on all parts of a cluster, including:

- Inspecting what the cluster's state is: who its members are, where data is held, and what connections are open
- How to add, remove, and change members of a cluster
- Administering data movement and manually moving data

Seeing the Current State

There are several helpers available to find out what data is where, what the shards are, and what the cluster is doing.

Getting a Summary with sh.status

`sh.status()` gives you an overview of your shards, databases, and sharded collections. If you have a small number of chunks, it will print a breakdown of which chunks are where as well. Otherwise it will simply give the collection's shard key and how many chunks each shard has:

```
> sh.status()
--- Sharding Status ---
  sharding version: { "_id" : 1, "version" : 3 }
  shards:
    { "_id" : "shard0000", "host" : "localhost:30000",
      "tags" : [ "USPS" , "Apple" ] }
    {  "_id" : "shard0001",  "host" : "localhost:30001" }
    {  "_id" : "shard0002",  "host" : "localhost:30002",  "tags" : [ "Apple" ] }
  databases:
    {  "_id" : "admin",  "partitioned" : false,  "primary" : "config" }
```

```
{  "_id" : "test",  "partitioned" : true,  "primary" : "shard0001" }
  test.foo
    shard key: { "x" : 1, "y" : 1 }
    chunks:
      shard0000    4
      shard0002    4
      shard0001    4
    { "x" : { $minKey : 1 }, "y" : { $minKey : 1 } } -->>
        { "x" : 0, "y" : 10000 } on : shard0000
    { "x" : 0, "y" : 10000 } -->> { "x" : 12208, "y" : -2208 }
        on : shard0002
    { "x" : 12208, "y" : -2208 } -->> { "x" : 24123, "y" : -14123 }
        on : shard0000
    { "x" : 24123, "y" : -14123 } -->> { "x" : 39467, "y" : -29467 }
        on : shard0002
    { "x" : 39467, "y" : -29467 } -->> { "x" : 51382, "y" : -41382 }
        on : shard0000
    { "x" : 51382, "y" : -41382 } -->> { "x" : 64897, "y" : -54897 }
        on : shard0002
    { "x" : 64897, "y" : -54897 } -->> { "x" : 76812, "y" : -66812 }
        on : shard0000
    { "x" : 76812, "y" : -66812 } -->> { "x" : 92793, "y" : -82793 }
        on : shard0002
    { "x" : 92793, "y" : -82793 } -->> { "x" : 119599, "y" : -109599 }
        on : shard0001
    { "x" : 119599, "y" : -109599 } -->> { "x" : 147099, "y" : -137099 }
        on : shard0001
    { "x" : 147099, "y" : -137099 } -->> { "x" : 173932, "y" : -163932 }
        on : shard0001
    { "x" : 173932, "y" : -163932 } -->>
        { "x" : { $maxKey : 1 }, "y" : { $maxKey : 1 } } on : shard0001
  test.ips
    shard key: { "ip" : 1 }
    chunks:
      shard0000    2
      shard0002    3
      shard0001    3
    { "ip" : { $minKey : 1 } } -->> { "ip" : "002.075.101.096" }
      on : shard0000
    { "ip" : "002.075.101.096" } -->> { "ip" : "022.089.076.022" }
      on : shard0002
    { "ip" : "022.089.076.022" } -->> { "ip" : "038.041.058.074" }
      on : shard0002
    { "ip" : "038.041.058.074" } -->> { "ip" : "055.081.104.118" }
      on : shard0002
    { "ip" : "055.081.104.118" } -->> { "ip" : "072.034.009.012" }
      on : shard0000
    { "ip" : "072.034.009.012" } -->> { "ip" : "090.118.120.031" }
      on : shard0001
    { "ip" : "090.118.120.031" } -->> { "ip" : "127.126.116.125" }
      on : shard0001
    { "ip" : "127.126.116.125" } -->> { "ip" : { $maxKey : 1 } }
```

```
        on : shard0001
        tag: Apple { "ip" : "017.000.000.000" } -->> { "ip" : "018.000.000.000" }
        tag: USPS { "ip" : "056.000.000.000" } -->> { "ip" : "057.000.000.000" }
  { "_id" : "test2", "partitioned" : false, "primary" : "shard0002" }
```

Once there are more than a few chunks, `sh.status()` will summarize the chunk stats instead of pinting each chunk. To see all chunks, run `sh.status(true)` (the `true` tells `sh.status()` to be verbose)

All the information `sh.status()` shows is gathered from your *config* database.

`sh.status()` runs a MapReduce to collect this data, so you cannot run `sh.status()` when using the `--noscripting` option.

Seeing Configuration Information

All of the configuration information about your cluster is kept in collections in the *config* database on the config servers. You can access it directly, but the shell has several helpers for exposing this information in a more readable way. However, you can always directly query the *config* database for metadata about your cluster.

> Never connect directly to your config servers, as you do not want to take the chance of accidentally changing or removing config server data. Instead, connect to the *mongos* and use the *config* database to see its data, as you would for any other database:
>
> ```
> mongos> use config
> ```
>
> If you manipulate config data through *mongos* (instead of connecting directly to the config servers), *mongos* will ensure that all of your config servers stay in sync and prevent various dangerous actions like accidentally dropping the *config* database.

In general, you should not directly change any data in the *config* database (exceptions are noted below). If you do change anything, you will generally have to restart all of your *mongos* servers to see its effect.

There are several collections in the *config* database. This section covers what each one contains and how it can be used.

config.shards

The *shards* collection keeps track of all the shards in the cluster. A typical document in the *shards* collection might looks something like this:

```
> db.shards.findOne()
{
    "_id" : "spock",
    "host" : "spock/server-1:27017,server-2:27017,server-3:27017",
```

```
        "tags" : [
            "us-east",
            "64gb mem",
            "cpu3"
        ]
    }
```

The shard's "_id" is picked up from the replica set name, so each replica set in your cluster must have a unique name.

When you update your replica set configuration (e.g., adding or removing members), the "host" field will be updated automatically.

config.databases

The *databases* collection keeps track of all of the databases, sharded and non, that the cluster knows about:

```
> db.databases.find()
{ "_id" : "admin", "partitioned" : false, "primary" : "config" }
{ "_id" : "test1", "partitioned" : true, "primary" : "spock" }
{ "_id" : "test2", "partitioned" : false, "primary" : "bones" }
```

If *enableSharding* has been run on a database, "partitioned" will be true. The "primary" is the database's "home base." By default, all new collections in that database will be created on the database's primary shard.

config.collections

The *collections* collection keeps track of all sharded collections (non-sharded collections are not shown). A typical document looks something like this:

```
> db.collections.findOne()
{
    "_id" : "test.foo",
    "lastmod" : ISODate("1970-01-16T17:53:52.934Z"),
    "dropped" : false,
    "key" : { "x" : 1, "y" : 1 },
    "unique" : true
}
```

The important fields are:

"_id"
: The namespace of the collection.

"key"
: The shard key. In this case, it is a compound key on "x" and "y".

"unique"
: Indicates that the shard key is a unique index. This field is not displayed unless it is true (the shard key is unique). By default, the shard key is not unique.

config.chunks

The *chunks* collection keeps a record of each chunk in all the collections. A typical document in the *chunks* collection might look something like this:

```
{
    "_id" : "test.hashy-user_id_-1034308116544453153",
    "lastmod" : { "t" : 5000, "i" : 50 },
    "lastmodEpoch" : ObjectId("50f5c648866900ccb6ed7c88"),
    "ns" : "test.hashy",
    "min" : { "user_id" : NumberLong("-1034308116544453153") },
    "max" : { "user_id" : NumberLong("-732765964052501510") },
    "shard" : "test-rs2"
}
```

The most useful fields are:

`"_id"`
: The unique identifier for the chunk. Generally this is the namespace, shard key, and lower chunk boundary.

`"ns"`
: The collection that this chunk is from.

`"in"`
: The smallest value in the chunk's range (inclusive).

`"max"`
: All values in the chunk are smaller than this value.

`"shard"`
: Which shard the chunk resides on.

The `"lastmod"` and `"lastmodEpoch"` fields are used to track chunk versioning. For example, if a chunk `"foo.bar-_id-1"` split into two chunks, we'd want a way of distinguishing the new, smaller `"foo.bar-_id-1"` chunk from its previous incarnation. Thus, the `"t"` and `"i"` fields are the *major* and *minor* chunk versions: major versions change when a chunk is migrated to a new shard and minor versions change when a chunk is split.

`sh.status()` uses the *config.chunks* collection to gather most of its information.

config.changelog

The *changelog* collection is useful for keeping track of what a cluster is doing, since it records all of the splits and migrates that have occurred.

Splits are recorded in a document that looks like this:

```
{
    "_id" : "router1-2013-02-09T18:08:12-5116908cab10a03b0cd748c3",
    "server" : "spock-01",
```

```
        "clientAddr" : "10.3.1.71:62813",
        "time" : ISODate("2013-02-09T18:08:12.574Z"),
        "what" : "split",
        "ns" : "test.foo",
        "details" : {
            "before" : {
                "min" : { "x" : { $minKey : 1 }, "y" : { $minKey : 1 } },
                "max" : { "x" : { $maxKey : 1 }, "y" : { $maxKey : 1 } },
                "lastmod" : Timestamp(1000, 0),
                "lastmodEpoch" : ObjectId("000000000000000000000000")
            },
            "left" : {
                "min" : { "x" : { $minKey : 1 }, "y" : { $minKey : 1 } },
                "max" : { "x" : 0, "y" : 10000 },
                "lastmod" : Timestamp(1000, 1),
                "lastmodEpoch" : ObjectId("000000000000000000000000")
            },
            "right" : {
                "min" : { "x" : 0, "y" : 10000 },
                "max" : { "x" : { $maxKey : 1 }, "y" : { $maxKey : 1 } },
                "lastmod" : Timestamp(1000, 2),
                "lastmodEpoch" : ObjectId("000000000000000000000000")
            }
        }
    }
```

The "details" give information about what the original document looked like and what it split into.

This output is what the first chunk split of a collection looks like. Note that each new chunk has its minor version increment: "lastmod" is Timestamp(1000, 1) and Timestamp(1000, 2), respectively.

Migrates are a bit more complicated and actually create four separate changelog documents: one noting the start of the migrate, one for the "from" shard, one for the "to" shard, and one for the migrate's commit (when the migration is finalized). The middle two documents are of interest because these give a breakdown of how long each step in the process took. This can give you an idea whether it's the disk, network, or something else that is causing a bottleneck on migrates.

For example, the document created by the "from" shard looks like this:

```
{
    "_id" : "router1-2013-02-09T18:15:14-5116923271b903e42184211c",
    "server" : "spock-01",
    "clientAddr" : "10.3.1.71:27017",
    "time" : ISODate("2013-02-09T18:15:14.388Z"),
    "what" : "moveChunk.to",
    "ns" : "test.foo",
    "details" : {
        "min" : { "x" : 24123, "y" : -14123 },
        "max" : { "x" : 39467, "y" : -29467 },
```

```
        "step1 of 5" : 0,
        "step2 of 5" : 0,
        "step3 of 5" : 900,
        "step4 of 5" : 0,
        "step5 of 5" : 142
    }
};
```

Each of the steps listed in "details" is timed and the "stepN of 5" messages show how long the step took, in milliseconds. When the "from" shard receives a *moveChunk* command from the *mongos*, it:

1. Checks the command parameters.
2. Confirms with the config servers that it can acquire a distributed lock for the migrate.
3. Tries to contact the "to" shard.
4. The data is copied. This is referred to and logged as "the critical section."
5. Coordinates with the "to" shard and config servers to confirm the migrate.

Note that the "to" and "from" shards must be in close communication starting at "step4 of 5": the shards directly talk to one another and the config server to perform the migration. If the "from" server has flaky network connectivity during the final steps, it may end up in a state where it cannot undo the migrate and cannot move forward with it. In this case, the *mongod* will shut down.

The "to" shard's changelog document is similar to the "from" shard's, but the steps are a bit different. It looks like:

```
{
    "_id" : "router1-2013-02-09T18:15:14-51169232ab10a03b0cd748e5",
    "server" : "spock-01",
    "clientAddr" : "10.3.1.71:62813",
    "time" : ISODate("2013-02-09T18:15:14.391Z"),
    "what" : "moveChunk.from",
    "ns" : "test.foo",
    "details" : {
        "min" : { "x" : 24123, "y" : -14123 },
        "max" : { "x" : 39467, "y" : -29467 },
        "step1 of 6" : 0,
        "step2 of 6" : 2,
        "step3 of 6" : 33,
        "step4 of 6" : 1032,
        "step5 of 6" : 12,
        "step6 of 6" : 0
    }
}
```

When the "to" shard receives a command from the "from" shard, it:

1. Migrates indexes. If this shard has never held chunks from the migrated collection before, it needs to know what fields are indexed. If this isn't the first time a chunk from this collection is being moved to this shard, then this should be a no-op.
2. Deletes any existing data in the chunk range. There might be data left over from a failed migration or restore procedure which we wouldn't want to interfere with the current data.
3. Copy all documents in the chunk to the "to" shard.
4. Replay any operations that happened to these document during the copy (on the "to" shard).
5. Wait for the "to" shard to have replicated the newly migrated data to a majority of servers.
6. Commit the migrate by changing the chunk's metadata to say that it lives on the "to" shard.

config.tags

This collection is created if you configure shard tags for your system. Each tag is associated with a chunk range:

```
> db.tags.find()
{
    "_id" : {
        "ns" : "test.ips",
        "min" : {"ip" : "056.000.000.000"}
    },
    "ns" : "test.ips",
    "min" : {"ip" : "056.000.000.000"},
    "max" : {"ip" : "057.000.000.000"},
    "tag" : "USPS"
}
{
    "_id" : {
        "ns" : "test.ips",
        "min" : {"ip" : "017.000.000.000"}
    },
    "ns" : "test.ips",
    "min" : {"ip" : "017.000.000.000"},
    "max" : {"ip" : "018.000.000.000"},
    "tag" : "Apple"
}
```

config.settings

This collection contains documents representing the current balancer settings and chunk size. By changing the documents in this collection, you can turn the balancer on or off or change the chunk size. Note that you should always connect to *mongos*, not the config servers directly, to change values in this collection.

Tracking Network Connections

There are a lot of connections between the components of a cluster. This section covers some sharding-specific information. See Chapter 23 for more information on networking.

Getting Connection Statistics

There is a command, *connPoolStats*, for finding out connection information about *mongoses* and *mongods*. This gives you information about how many connections a server has open, and to what:

```
> db.adminCommand({"connPoolStats" : 1})
{
    "createdByType": {
        "sync": 857,
        "set": 4
    },
    "numDBClientConnection": 35,
    "numAScopedConnection": 0,
    "hosts": {
        "config-01:10005,config-02:10005,config-03:10005": {
            "created": 857,
            "available": 2
        },
        "spock/spock-01:10005,spock-02:10005,spock-03:10005": {
            "created": 4,
            "available": 1
        }
    },
    "totalAvailable": 3,
    "totalCreated": 861,
    "ok": 1
}
```

Hosts of the form `"host1,host2,host3"` are config server connections, also known as "sync" connections. Hosts that look like `"name/host1,host2,...,hostN"` are connections to shards. The `"available"` counts are how many connections are currently available in the connection pools on this instance.

Note that this command only works on *mongos* processes and *mongod*s that are members of a shard.

You may see connections to other shards in the output of *connPoolStats* from a shard, as shards connect to other shards to migrate data. The primary of one shard will connect directly to the primary of another shard and "suck" its data.

When a migrate occurs, a shard sets up a `ReplicaSetMonitor` (a process that monitors replica set health) to track the health of the shard on the other side of the migrate. *mongod* never destroys this monitor, so you may see messages in one replica set's log about the members of another replica set. This is totally normal and should have no effect on your application.

Limiting the Number of Connections

When a client connects to a *mongos*, *mongos* creates a connection to at least one shard to pass along the client's request. Thus, every client connection into a *mongos* yields at least one outgoing connection from *mongos* to the shards.

If you have many *mongos* processes, they may create more connections than your shards can handle: a *mongos* allows up to 20,000 connections (same as *mongod*), so if you have 5 *mongos* processes with 10,000 client connections each, they may be attempting to create 50,000 connections to a shard!

To prevent this, you can use the `maxConns` option to your command line configuration for *mongos* to limit the number of connections it can create. The following formula can be used to calculate the maximum number of connections a shard can handle from a single *mongos*:

$$\text{maxConns} = 20{,}000 - (\text{numMongosProcesses} \times 3) - (\text{numMembersPerReplicaSet} \times 3) - (\text{other} / \text{numMongosProcesses})$$

Breaking down the pieces of this formula:

(numMongosProcesses × 3)
: Each *mongos* creates three connections per *mongod*: a connection to forward client requests, an error-tracking connection (the *writeback listener*), and a connection to monitor the replica set's status.

(numMembersPerReplicaSet × 3)
: The primary creates a connection to each secondary and each secondary creates two connections to the primary, for a total of three connections.

(other / numMongosProcesses)
: `other` is the number of miscellaneous processes that may connect to your *mongods*, such as MMS agents, direct shell connections (for administration), or connections to other shards for migrations.

Note that `maxConns` only prevents *mongos* from creating more than this many connections. It doesn't mean that it does anything particularly helpful when it runs out of connections: it will block requests, waiting for connections to be "freed." Thus, you must prevent your application from using this many connections, especially as your number of *mongos* processes grows.

When a MongoDB instance exits cleanly it closes all connections before stopping. The members who were connected to it will immediately get socket errors on those connections and be able to refresh them. However, if a MongoDB instance suddenly goes offline due to a power loss, crash, or network problems, it probably won't cleanly close all of its sockets. In this case, other servers in the cluster may be under the impression that their connection is healthy until they try to perform an operation on it. At that point, they will get an error and refresh the connection (if the member is up again at that point).

This is a quick process when there are only a few connections. However, when there are thousands of connections that must be refreshed one by one you can get a lot of errors because each connection to the downed member must be tried, determined to be bad, and re-established. There isn't a particularly good way of preventing this aside from restarting processes that get bogged down in a reconnection storm.

Server Administration

As your cluster grows, you'll need to add capacity or change configurations. This section covers how to add and remove servers from your cluster.

Adding Servers

You can add new *mongos* processes at any time. Make sure their `--configdb` option specifies the correct set of config servers and they should be immediately available for clients to connect to.

To add new shards, use the '`addShard`" command as show in Chapter 14.

Changing Servers in a Shard

As you use your sharded cluster, you may want to change the servers in individual shards. To change a shard's membership, connect directly to the shard's primary (not through the *mongos*) and issue a replica set reconfig. The cluster configuration will pick up the change and update *config.shards* automatically. Do not modify *config.shards* by hand.

The only exception to this is if you started your cluster with standalone servers as shards, not replica sets.

Changing a shard from a standalone server to replica set

The easiest way to do this is to add a new, empty replica set shard and then remove the standalone server shard (see "Removing a Shard" on page 286).

If you wish to turn the standalone server into a replica set the process is fairly complex and involves downtime:

1. Stop requests to the system.
2. Shut down the standalone server (call it *server-1*) and all *mongos* processes.
3. Restart the *server-1* in replica set mode (with the `--replSet` option).
4. Connect to *server-1* and initiate the set as a one-member replica set.
5. Connect to each config server and replace this shard's entry in *config.shards* to have a `setName/server-1:27017` form for the shard name. Make sure all three config servers have identical information. It is risky to manually edit config servers!

   A good way of ensuring that they are identical is to run the *dbhash* command on each config server:

   ```
   > db.runCommand({"dbhash" : 1})
   ```

   This comes up with an MD5 sum for each collection. Some collections in the *config* database will be different on different config servers, but *config.shards* should not be.
6. Restart all *mongos* processes. They will read the shard data off of the config servers at start up and treat the replica set as a shard.
7. Restart all shards' primaries to refresh their config data.
8. Send requests to the system again.
9. Add other members to *server-1*'s set.

This process is complex, error prone, and not recommended. If at all possible, just add a new shard that's an empty replica set and let migrations take care of moving your data to it.

Removing a Shard

In general, shards should not be removed from a cluster. If you are regularly adding and removing shards, you are putting a lot more stress on the system than necessary. If you add too many shards it is better to let your system grow into it, not remove them and add them back later. However, if necessary, you can remove shards.

First make sure that the balancer is on. The balancer will be tasked with moving all the data on this shard to other shards in a process called *draining*. To start draining, run the removeShard command. removeShard takes the shard's name and drains all the chunks on a given shard to the other shards:

```
> db.adminCommand({"removeShard" : "test-rs3"})
{
    "msg" : "draining started successfully",
    "state" : "started",
    "shard" : "test-rs3",
    "note" : "you need to drop or movePrimary these databases",
    "dbsToMove" : [
        "blog",
        "music",
        "prod"
    ],
    "ok" : 1
}
```

Draining can take a long time if there are a lot of chunks or large chunks to move. If you have jumbo chunks (see "Jumbo Chunks" on page 292), you may have to temporarily raise the chunk size to allow draining to move them.

If you want to keep tabs on how much has been moved, run *removeShard* again to give you the current status:

```
> db.adminCommand({"removeShard" : "test-rs3"})
{
    "msg" : "draining ongoing",
    "state" : "ongoing",
    "remaining" : {
        "chunks" : NumberLong(5),
        "dbs" : NumberLong(0)
    },
    "ok" : 1
}
```

You can run *removeShard* as many times as you want.

Chunks may have to split to be moved, so you may see the number of chunks increase in the system during the drain. For example, suppose we have a 5-shard cluster with the following chunk distributions:

```
test-rs0    10
test-rs1    10
test-rs2    10
test-rs3    11
test-rs4    11
```

This cluster has a total of 52 chunks. If we remove *test-rs3*, we might end up with:

```
test-rs0    15
test-rs1    15
test-rs2    15
test-rs4    15
```

The cluster now has 60 chunks, 18 of which came from shard *test-rs3* (11 were there to start and 7 were created from draining splits).

Once all the chunks have been moved, if there are still databases "homed" on the shard, you'll need to remove them before the shard can be removed. The output of *removeShard* will be something like:

```
> db.adminCommand({"removeShard" : "test-rs3"})
{
    "msg" : "draining ongoing",
    "state" : "ongoing",
    "remaining" : {
        "chunks" : NumberLong(0),
        "dbs" : NumberLong(3)
    },
    "note" : "you need to drop or movePrimary these databases",
    "dbsToMove" : [
        "blog",
        "music",
        "prod"
    ],
    "ok" : 1
}
```

To finish the remove, move the homed databases with the *movePrimary* command:

```
> db.adminCommand({"movePrimary" : "blog", "to" : "test-rs4"})
{
    "primary " : "test-rs4:test-rs4/ubuntu:31500,ubuntu:31501,ubuntu:31502",
    "ok" : 1
}
```

Once you have moved any databases, run *removeShard* one more time:

```
> db.adminCommand({"removeShard" : "test-rs3"})
{
    "msg" : "removeshard completed successfully",
    "state" : "completed",
    "shard" : "test-rs3",
    "ok" : 1
}
```

This is not strictly necessary, but it confirms that you have completed the process. If there are no databases homed on this shard, you will get this response as soon as all chunks have been migrated off.

Once you have started a shard draining, there is no built-in way to stop it.

Changing Config Servers

Changing anything about your config servers is difficult, dangerous, and generally involves downtime. *Before doing any maintenance on config servers, take a backup.*

All *mongos* processes need to have the same value for `--configdb` whenever they are running. Thus, to change the config servers, you must shut down all your *mongos* processes, make sure they are all down (no *mongos* process can still be running with the old `--configdb` argument), and then restart them with the new `--configdb` argument.

For example, one of the most common tasks is to move from one config server to three. To accomplish this, shut down your *mongos* processes, your config server, and all your shards. Copy the data directory of your config servers to the two new config servers (so that there is an identical data directory on all three servers). Now, start up all three config servers and the shards. Then start each of the *mongos* processes with `--configdb` pointing to all three config servers.

Balancing Data

In general, MongoDB automatically takes care of balancing data. This section covers how to enable and disable this automatic balancing as well as how to intervene in the balancing process.

The Balancer

Turning off the balancer is a prerequisite to nearly any administrative activity. There is a shell helper to make this easier:

```
> sh.setBalancerState(false)
```

With the balancer off a new balancing round will not begin, but it will not force an ongoing balancing round to stop immediately: migrations generally cannot stop on a dime. Thus, you should check the *config.locks* collection to see whether or not a balancing round is still in progress:

```
> db.locks.find({"_id" : "balancer"})["state"]
0
```

`0` means the balancer is off. See "The Balancer" on page 253 for an explanation of the balancer states.

Balancing puts load on your system: the destination shard must query the source shard for all the documents in a chunk, insert them, and then the source shard must delete them. There are two circumstances in particular where migrations can cause performance problems:

1. Using a hotspot shard key will force constant migrations (as all new chunks will be created on the hotspot). Your system must have the capacity to handle the flow of data coming off of your hotspot shard.

2. Adding a new shard will trigger a stream of migrations as the balancer attempts to populate it.

If you find that migrations are affecting your application's performance, you can schedule a window for balancing in the *config.settings* collection. Run the following update to only allow balancing between 1 p.m. and 4 p.m.:

```
> db.settings.update({"_id" : "balancer"},
... {"$set" : {"activeWindow" : {"start" : "13:00", "stop" : "16:00"}}},
... true )
```

If you set a balancing window, monitor it closely to ensure that *mongos* can actually keep your cluster balanced in the time that you have allotted it.

You must be careful if you plan to combine manual balancing with the automatic balancer, since the automatic balancer always determines what to move based on the current state of the set and does not take into account the set's history. For example, suppose you have `shardA` and `shardB`, each holding 500 chunks. `shardA` is getting a lot of writes, so you turn off the balancer and move 30 of the most active chunks to `shardB`. If you turn the balancer back on at this point, it will immediately swoop in and move 30 chunks (possibly a different 30) back from `shardB` to `shardA` to balance the chunk counts.

To prevent this, move 30 quiescent chunks from `shardB` to `shardA` before starting the balancer. That way there will be no imbalance between the shards and the balancer will be happy to leave things as they are. Alternatively, you could perform 30 splits on `shardA`'s chunks to even out the chunk counts.

Note that the balancer only uses number of chunks as a metric, not size of data. Thus, a shard with a few large chunks may end up as the target of a migration from a shard with many small chunks (but a smaller data size).

Changing Chunk Size

There can be anywhere from zero to millions of documents in a chunk. Generally, the larger a chunk is, the longer it takes to migrate to another shard. In Chapter 13, we used a chunk size of 1 MB, so that we could see chunk movement easily and quickly. This is generally impractical in a live system. MongoDB would be doing a lot of unnecessary work to keep shards within a few megabytes of each other in size. By default, chunks are 64 MB, which is generally a good balance between ease of migration and migratory churn.

Sometimes you may find that migrations are taking too long with 64 MB chunks. To speed them up, you can decrease your chunk size. To do this, connect to *mongos* through the shell and update the *config.settings* collection:

```
> db.settings.findOne()
{
```

```
    "_id" : "chunksize",
    "value" : 64
}
> db.settings.save({"_id" : "chunksize", "value" : 32})
```

The previous update would change your chunk size to 32 MB. Existing chunks would not be changed immediately, but as splits occurred chunks would trend toward that size. *mongos* processes will automatically load the new chunk size value.

Note that this is a cluster-wide setting: it affects all collections and databases. Thus, if you need a small chunk size for one collection and a large chunk size for another, you may have to compromise with a chunk size in between the two ideals (or put the collections in different clusters).

If MongoDB is doing too many migrations or your documents are large, you may want to increase your chunk size.

Moving Chunks

As mentioned earlier, all the data in a chunk lives on a certain shard. If that shard ends up with more chunks than the other shards, MongoDB will move some chunks off it. Moving a chunk is called a *migration* and is how MongoDB balances data across your cluster.

You can manually move chunks using the *moveChunk* shell helper:

```
> sh.moveChunk("test.users", {"user_id" : NumberLong("1844674407370955160")},
... "spock")
{ "millis" : 4079, "ok" : 1 }
```

This would move the chunk containing the document with "`user_id`" of 1844674407370955160 to the shard named "`spock`". You must use the shard key to find which chunk to move ("`user_id`", in this case). Generally, the easiest way to specify a chunk is by its lower bound, although any value in the chunk will work (the upper bound will not, as it is not actually in the chunk). This command will move the chunk before returning, so it may take a while to run. The logs are the best place to see what it is doing if it takes a long time.

If a chunk is larger than the max chunk size, *mongos* will refuse to move it:

```
> sh.moveChunk("test.users", {"user_id" : NumberLong("1844674407370955160")},
... "spock")
{
    "cause" : {
        "chunkTooBig" : true,
        "estimatedChunkSize" : 2214960,
        "ok" : 0,
        "errmsg" : "chunk too big to move"
    },
    "ok" : 0,
```

```
        "errmsg" : "move failed"
    }
```

In this case, you must manually split the chunk before moving it, using the *splitAt* command:

```
    > db.chunks.find({"ns" : "test.users",
    ... "min.user_id" : NumberLong("1844674407370955160")})
    {
        "_id" : "test.users-user_id_NumberLong(\"1844674407370955160\")",
        "ns" : "test.users",
        "min" : { "user_id" : NumberLong("1844674407370955160") },
        "max" : { "user_id" : NumberLong("2103288923412120952") },
        "shard" : "test-rs2"
    }
    > sh.splitAt("test.ips", {"user_id" : NumberLong("2000000000000000000")})
    { "ok" : 1 }
    > db.chunks.find({"ns" : "test.users",
    ... "min.user_id" : {"$gt" : NumberLong("1844674407370955160")},
    ... "max.user_id" : {"$lt" : NumberLong("2103288923412120952")}})
    {
        "_id" : "test.users-user_id_NumberLong(\"1844674407370955160\")",
        "ns" : "test.users",
        "min" : { "user_id" : NumberLong("1844674407370955160") },
        "max" : { "user_id" : NumberLong("2000000000000000000") },
        "shard" : "test-rs2"
    }
    {
        "_id" : "test.users-user_id_NumberLong(\"2000000000000000000\")",
        "ns" : "test.users",
        "min" : { "user_id" : NumberLong("2000000000000000000") },
        "max" : { "user_id" : NumberLong("2103288923412120952") },
        "shard" : "test-rs2"
    }
```

Once the chunk has been split into smaller pieces, it should be movable. Alternatively, you can raise the max chunk size and then move it, but you should break up large chunks whenever possible. Sometimes, though, they cannot be broken up: these are called *jumbo chunks*.

Jumbo Chunks

Suppose you choose the `"date"` field as your shard key. The `"date"` field in this collection is a string that looks like `"`*`year/month/day`*`"`, which means that *mongos* can create at most one chunk per day. This works fine for a while, until your application suddenly goes viral and gets a thousand times its typical traffic for one day.

This day's chunk is going to be much larger than any other day's, but it is also completely unsplittable because every document has the same value for the shard key.

Once a chunk is larger than the max chunk size set in *config.settings*, the balancer will not be allowed to move the chunk. These unsplittable, unmovable chunks are called *jumbo chunks* and they are inconvenient to deal with.

Let's take an example. Suppose there are three shards, *shard1*, *shard2*, and *shard3*. If you use the hotspot shard key pattern described in "Ascending Shard Keys" on page 258, all your writes will be going to one shard, say *shard1*. *mongos* will try to balance the number of chunks evenly between the shards. But the only chunks that the balancer can move are the non-jumbo chunks, so it will migrate all the small chunks off the hotspot shard.

Now all the shards will have roughly the same number of chunks, but all of *shard2* and *shard3*'s chunks will be less than 64 MB in size. And if jumbo chunks are being created, more and more of *shard1*'s chunks will be more than 64 MB in size. Thus, *shard1* will fill up a lot faster than the other two shards, even though the number of chunks is perfectly balanced between the three.

Thus, one of the indicators that you have jumbo chunk problems is that one shard's size is growing much faster than the others. You can also look at `sh.status()` to see if you have jumbo chunks: they will be marked with a `"jumbo"` attribute:

```
> sh.status()
...
    { "x" : -7 } -->> { "x" : 5 } on : shard0001
    { "x" : 5 } -->> { "x" : 6 } on : shard0001 jumbo
    { "x" : 6 } -->> { "x" : 7 } on : shard0001 jumbo
    { "x" : 7 } -->> { "x" : 339 } on : shard0001
...
```

You can use the `dataSize` command to check chunk sizes.

First, we use the *config.chunks* collection to find the chunk ranges:

```
> use config
> var chunks = db.chunks.find({"ns" : "acme.analytics"}).toArray()
```

Use these chunk ranges to find possible jumbo chunks:

```
> use dbName
> db.runCommand({"dataSize" : "dbName.collName",
... "keyPattern" : {"date" : 1}, // shard key
... "min" : chunks[0].min,
... "max" : chunks[0].max})
{ "size" : 11270888, "numObjects" : 128081, "millis" : 100, "ok" : 1 }
```

Be careful—the *dataSize* command does have to scan the chunk's data to figure out how big it is. If you can, narrow down your search by using your knowledge of your data: were jumbo chunks created on certain date? For example, if there was a really busy day on November 1, look for chunks with that day in their shard key range. If you're using GridFS and sharding by `"files_id"`, you can look at the *fs.files* collection to find a file's size.

Distributing jumbo chunks

To fix a cluster thrown off-balance by jumbo chunks, you must evenly distribute them among the shards.

This is a complex manual process, but should not cause any downtime (it may cause slowness, as you'll be migrating a lot of data). In the description below, the shard with the jumbo chunks is referred to as the "from" shard. The shards that the jumbo chunks are migrated to are called the "to" shards. Note that you may have multiple "from" shards that you wish to move chunks off of. Repeat these steps for each:

1. Turn off the balancer. You don't want to the balancer trying to "help" during this process:

   ```
   > sh.setBalancerState(false)
   ```

2. MongoDB will not allow you to move chunks larger than the max chunk size, so temporarily raise the chunk size. Make a note of what your original chunk size is and then change it to something large, like 10,000. Chunk size is specified in megabytes:

   ```
   > use config
   > db.settings.findOne({"_id" : "chunksize"})
   {
       "_id" : "chunksize",
       "value" : 64
   }
   > db.settings.save({"_id" : "chunksize", "value" : 10000})
   ```

3. Use the `moveChunk` command to move jumbo chunks off the "from" shard. If you are concerned about the impact migrations will have on your application's performance, use the `secondaryThrottle` option to prevent them from happening too quickly:

   ```
   > db.adminCommand({"moveChunk" : "acme.analytics",
   ... "find" : {"date" : new Date("10/23/2012")},
   ... "to" : "shard0002",
   ... "secondaryThrottle" : true})
   ```

   `secondaryThrottle` forces migrations to periodically wait until a majority of secondaries have replicated the migration. It only works if you are running with shards that are replica sets (not standalone servers).

4. Run *splitChunk* on the remaining chunks on the donor shard until it has a roughly even number of chunks as the other shards.

5. Set chunk size back to its original value:

   ```
   > db.settings.save({"_id" : "chunksize", "value" : 64})
   ```

6. Turn on the balancer:

```
> sh.setBalancerState(true)
```

When the balancer is turned on again it cannot move the jumbo chunks again, as they are essentially held in place by their size.

Preventing jumbo chunks

As the amount of data you are storing grows, the manual process described in the previous section becomes unsustainable. Thus, if you're having problems with jumbo chunks, you should make it a priority to prevent them from forming.

To prevent jumbo chunks, modify your shard key to have more granularity. You want almost every document to have a unique value for the shard key, or at least never have more than *chunksize*-worth of data with a single shard key value.

For example, if you were using the year/month/day key described earlier it can quickly be made finer-grained by adding hours, minutes, and seconds. Similarly, if you're sharding on something coarsely-grained key like log level, add a second field to your shard key with a lot of granularity, such as an MD5 hash or UUID. Then you can always split a chunk, even if the first field is the same for many documents.

Refreshing Configurations

As a final tip, sometimes *mongos* will not update its configuration correctly from the config servers. If you ever get a configuration that you don't expect or a *mongos* seems to be out of date or cannot find data that you know is there, use the *flushRouterConfig* command to manually clear all caches:

```
> db.adminCommand({"flushRouterConfig" : 1})
```

If *flushRouterConfig* does not work, restarting all your *mongos* or *mongod* processes clears any possible cache.

PART V

Application Administration

CHAPTER 17

Seeing What Your Application Is Doing

Once you have an application up and running, how do you know what it's doing? This chapter covers how to figure out what kind of queries MongoDB is running, how much data is being written, and how to investigate what MongoDB is actually doing. You'll learn:

- How to find slow operations and kill them
- Getting and interpreting statistics about your collections and databases
- Using command-line tools to give you a picture of what MongoDB is doing

Seeing the Current Operations

An easy way to find slow operations is to see what is running. Anything slow is more likely to show up and have been running for longer. It's not guaranteed, but it's a good first step to see what might be slowing down an application.

To see the operations that are running, use the `db.currentOp()` function:

```
> db.currentOp()
{
    "inprog" : [
        {
            "opid" : 34820,
            "active" : true,
            "secs_running" : 0,
            "op" : "query",
            "ns" : "test.users",
            "query" : {
                "count" : "users",
                "query" : {
                    "username" : "user12345"
                },
```

```
                "fields" : {

                }
            },
            "client" : "127.0.0.1:39931",
            "desc" : "conn3",
            "threadId" : "0x7f12d61c7700",
            "connectionId" : 3,
            "locks" : {
                "^" : "r",
                "^test" : "R"
            },
            "waitingForLock" : false,
            "numYields" : 0,
            "lockStats" : {
                "timeLockedMicros" : {

                },
                "timeAcquiringMicros" : {
                    "r" : NumberLong(9),
                    "w" : NumberLong(0)
                }
            }
        },
        ...
    ]
}
```

This displays a list of operations that the database is performing. Here are some of the more important fields in the output:

`"opid"`
: This is the operation's unique identifier. You can use this number to kill an operation (see "Killing Operations" on page 301).

`"active"`
: If this operation is running. If this field is `false`, it means the operation has yielded or is waiting for a lock.

`"secs_running"`
: How long this operation has been running. You can use this to find queries that are taking too long or sucking up database resources.

`"op"`
: The type of operation. This is generally a query, insert, update, or remove. Note that database commands are processed as queries.

`"desc"`
: This can be correlated with messages in the logs. Every log message related to this connection will be prefixed with `[conn3]`, so you can use this to grep the logs for relevant information.

`"locks"`
: This describes the types of locks taken by this operation. `"^"` indicates the global lock.

`"waitingForLock"`
: Whether this operation is currently blocking, waiting to acquire a lock.

`"numYields"`
: The number of times this operation has *yielded*, releasing its lock to allow other operations to go. Generally, any operation that searches for documents (queries, updates, and removes) can yield. An operation will only yield if there are other operations enqueued and waiting to take its lock. Basically, if there are no operations in `"waitingForLock"` state, the current operations will not yield.

`"lockstats.timeAcquiringMicros"`
: This shows how long it took this operation to acquire the locks it needed.

You can filter `currentOp()` to only look for operations fulfilling certain criteria, such as operations on a certain namespace or ones that have been running for a certain length of time. Filter the results by passing in a query argument:

```
> db.currentOp({"ns" : "prod.users"})
```

You can query on any field in `currentOp`, using all the normal query operators.

Finding Problematic Operations

The most common use for `db.currentOp()` is looking for slow operations. You can use the filtering technique described in the previous section to find all queries that take longer than a certain amount of time, which may suggest a missing index or improper field filtering.

Sometimes people will find that unexpected queries are running, generally because there's an app server running an old or buggy version of software. The `"client"` field can help track down where unexpected operations are coming from.

Killing Operations

If you find an operation that you want to stop, you can kill it by passing `db.killOp()` its `"opid"`:

```
> db.killOp(123)
```

Not all operations can be killed. In general, operations can only be killed when they yield, so updates, finds, and removes can all be killed. Operations holding or waiting for a lock usually cannot be killed.

Once you have sent a "kill" message to an operation, it will have a `"killed"` field in the `db.currentOp` output. However, it won't actually be dead until it disappears from list of current opertations.

False Positives

If you look for slow operations, you may see some long-running internal operations listed. There are several long-running requests MongoDB may have running, depending on your setup. The most common are the replication thread (which will continue fetching more operations from the sync source for as long as possible) and the writeback listener for sharding. Any long-running query on *local.oplog.rs* can be ignored as well as any *writebacklistener* commands.

If you kill either of these operations, MongoDB will just restart them. However, you generally should not do that. Killing the replication thread will briefly halt replication and killing the writeback listener may cause *mongos* to miss legitimate write errors.

Preventing Phantom Operations

There is an odd, MongoDB-specific issue that you may run into, particularly if you're bulk-loading data into a collection. Suppose you have a job that is firing thousands of update operations at MongoDB and MongoDB is grinding to a halt. You quickly stop the job and kill off all the updates that are currently occurring. However, you continue to see new updates appearing as soon as you kill the old ones, even though the job is no longer running!

If you are loading data using unacknowledged writes, your application will fire writes at MongoDB, potentially faster than MongoDB can process them. If MongoDB gets backed up, these writes will pile up in the operating system's socket buffer. When you kill the writes MongoDB is working on, this allows MongoDB to start processing the writes in the buffer. Even if you stop the client sending the writes, any writes that made it into the buffer will get processed by MongoDB, since they've already been "received" (just not processed).

The best way to prevent these phantom writes is to do acknowledged writes: make each write wait until the previous write is complete, not just until the previous write is sitting in a buffer on the database server.

Using the System Profiler

To find slow operations you can use the *system profiler*, which records operations in a special *system.profile* collection. The profiler can give you tons of information about operations that are taking a long time, but at a cost: it slows down *mongod*'s overall performance. Thus, you may only want to turn on the profiler periodically to capture a slice of traffic. If your system is already heavily loaded, you may wish to use another technique described in this chapter to diagnose issues.

By default, the profiler is off and does not record anything. You can turn it on by running `db.setProfilingLevel()` in the shell:

```
> db.setProfilingLevel(2)
{ "was" : 0, "slowms" : 100, "ok" : 1 }
```

Level 2 means "profile everything." Every read and write request received by the database will be recorded in the *system.profile* collection of the current database. Profiling is enabled per-database and incurs a heavy performance penalty: every write has to be written an extra time and every read has to take a write lock (because it must write an entry to the *system.profile* collection). However, it will give you an exhaustive listing of what your system is doing:

```
> db.foo.insert({x:1})
> db.foo.update({},{$set:{x:2}})
> db.foo.remove()
> db.system.profile.find().pretty()
{
    "ts" : ISODate("2012-11-07T18:32:35.219Z"),
    "op" : "insert",
    "ns" : "test.foo",
    "millis" : 37,
    "client" : "127.0.0.1",
    "user" : ""
}
{
    "ts" : ISODate("2012-11-07T18:32:47.334Z"),
    "op" : "update",
    "ns" : "test.foo",
    "query" : {

    },
    "updateobj" : {
        "$set" : {
            "x" : 2
        }
    },
    "nscanned" : 1,
    "fastmod" : true,
    "millis" : 3,
    "client" : "127.0.0.1",
    "user" : ""
}
{
    "ts" : ISODate("2012-11-07T18:32:50.058Z"),
    "op" : "remove",
    "ns" : "test.foo",
    "query" : {
```

```
        },
        "millis" : 0,
        "client" : "127.0.0.1",
        "user" : ""
}
```

You can use the "client" field to see which users are sending which operations to the database. If we were using authentication, we could see which user was doing each operation, too.

Often, you do not care about most of the operations that your database is doing, just the slow ones. For this, you can set the profiling level to 1: profile only slow operations. By default, level 1 profiles operations that take longer that 100 ms. You can also specify a second argument, which defines what "slow" means to you. This would record all operations that took longer than 500 ms:

```
> db.setProfilingLevel(1, 500)
{ "was" : 2, "slowms" : 100, "ok" : 1 }
```

To turn profiling off, set the profiling level to 0:

```
> db.setProfilingLevel(0)
{ "was" : 1, "slowms" : 500, "ok" : 1 }
```

Generally do not set `slowms` to a low value. Even with profiling off, `slowms` has an effect on *mongod*: it sets the threshold printing slow operation in the log. Thus, if you set `slowms` to 2, every operation that takes longer than 2 ms will show up in the log, even with profiling off. Thus, if you lower `slowms` to profile something, you might want to raise it again before turning off profiling.

You can see the current profiling level with `db.getProfilingLevel()`. The profiling level is not persistent: restarting the database clears the level.

There are command-line options for configuring the profiling level, `--profile` *`level`* and `--slowms` *`time`*, but bumping the profiling level is generally a temporary debugging measure, not something you want to add to your configuration long-term.

If you turn on profiling and the *system.profile* collection does not already exist, MongoDB creates a small capped collection for it (a few megabytes in size). If you want to run the profiler for an extended period of time, this may not be enough space for the number of operations you need to record. You can make a larger *system.profile* collection by turning off profiling, dropping the *system.profile* collection, and creating a new *system.profile* capped collection that is the size you desire. Then enable profiling on the database.

Calculating Sizes

In order to provision the correct amount of disk and RAM, it is useful to know how much space documents, indexes, collections, and databases are taking up. See "Calculating the Working Set" on page 348 for information on calculating your working set.

Documents

The easiest way to get the size of a document is to use the shell's `Object.bsonsize()` function. Pass in any document to get the size it would be when stored in MongoDB.

For example, you can see that storing `_id`s as `ObjectId`s is more efficient than storing them as strings:

```
> Object.bsonsize({_id:ObjectId()})
22
> // ""+ObjectId() converts the ObjectId to a string
> Object.bsonsize({_id:""+ObjectId()})
39
```

More practically, you can pass in documents directly from your collections:

```
> Object.bsonsize(db.users.findOne())
```

This shows you exactly how many bytes a document is taking up on disk. However, this does not count padding or indexes, which can often be significant factors in the size of a collection.

Collections

For seeing information about a whole collection, there is a `stats` function:

```
> db.boards.stats()
{
    "ns" : "brains.boards",
    "count" : 12,
    "size" : 32292,
    "avgObjSize" : 2691,
    "storageSize" : 270336,
    "numExtents" : 3,
    "nindexes" : 2,
    "lastExtentSize" : 212992,
    "paddingFactor" : 1.0099999999999825,
    "flags" : 1,
    "totalIndexSize" : 16352,
    "indexSizes" : {
        "_id_" : 8176,
        "username_1_slug_1" : 8176
    },
    "ok" : 1
}
```

stats starts with the namespace ("brains.boards") and then the count of all documents in the collection. The next couple of fields have to do with the size of the collection. "size" is what you'd get if you called Object.bsonsize() on each element in the collection and added up all the sizes: it's the actual number of bytes the document in the collection are taking up. Equivalently, if you take the "avgObjSize" and multiply it by "count", you'll get "size".

As mentioned above, a total count of the documents' bytes leaves out some important space a collection uses: the padding around each document and the indexes. "storage Size" not only includes those, but also empty space that has been set aside for the collection but not yet used. Collections always have empty space at the "end" so that new documents can be added quickly.

"nindexes" is the number of indexes on the collection. An index is not counted in "nindexes" until it finishes being built and cannot be used until it appears in this list. Each index is currently one "bucket" (8 KB), since the collection is so small. In general, indexes will be a lot larger than the amount of data they store, as there is a lot of free space to optimize adding new entries. You can minimize this free space by having right-balanced indexes (as described in "Introduction to Compound Indexes" on page 84). Indexes that are randomly distributed will generally be approximately 50% free space, whereas ascending-order indexes will be 10% free space.

As your collections get bigger, it may become difficult to read stats() output with sizes in the billions of bytes or beyond. Thus, you can pass in a scaling factor: 1024 for kilobytes, 1024*1024 for megabytes, and so on. For example, this would get the collection stats in terabytes:

```
> db.big.stats(1024*1024*1024*1024)
```

Databases

Databases have a stats function that's similar to collections':

```
> db.stats()
{
    "db" : "brains",
    "collections" : 11,
    "objects" : 1109,
    "avgObjSize" : 299.79440937781783,
    "dataSize" : 332472,
    "storageSize" : 1654784,
    "numExtents" : 15,
    "indexes" : 11,
    "indexSize" : 114464,
    "fileSize" : 201326592,
    "nsSizeMB" : 16,
    "ok" : 1
}
```

First, we have the name of the database and the number of collections it contains. `"objects"` is the total count of documents across all collections in this database.

The bulk of the document contains information about the size of your data. `"fileSize"` should always be the largest: that is the total amount allocated to the database files. This number should be equivalent to adding the sizes of all of the *brains.** files in your data directory.

The next largest field is generally going to be `"storageSize"`, which is the total amount of space the database is using. This doesn't match `"fileSize"` because `"fileSize"` includes preallocated files. For example, if you have *brains.0*, *brains.1*, and *brains.2* in your data directory, *brains.2* will be filled with zeros. As soon as anything is written to *brains.2*, *brains.3* will be allocated. You should always have an empty (full of zeros) file for each database: as soon as it's written to, the next file will be preallocated. Thus, this empty file (plus anything not being used yet in the previous files) is the difference between `"fileSize"` and `"storageSize"`.

`"dataSize"` is the amount of space the data in this database is taking up. Note that this does not include space on the free list, but it does include documents' padding. Thus, the difference between this and the `"storageSize"` should be the size of documents deleted.

`db.stats()` can take a scale argument the same way that the collections' `stats()` function can.

If you call `db.stats()` on a nonexistent database, the `"nsSizeMB"` will be 0. This is the size of the *.ns* file, which is essentially a database's table of contents. Any database that exists needs a *.ns* file

Keep in mind that listing databases on a system with a high lock percent can be very slow and block other operations. Avoid doing it, if possible.

Using mongotop and mongostat

MongoDB comes with a few command-line tools that can help you determine what MongoDB is doing by printing stats every few seconds.

mongotop is similar to the top UNIX utility: it gives you an overview of which collections are busiest. You can also run *mongotop --locks* to give you locking statistics for each database.

mongostat gives server-wide information. By default, *mongostat* prints out a list of statistics once per second, although this is configurable by passing a different number of seconds on the command line. Each of the fields gives a count of how many times the activity has happened since the field was last printed.

insert/query/update/delete/getmore/command
: These are simple counts of how many of each of these operations there have been.

flushes
: How many times *mongod* has flushed data to disk.

mapped
: The amount of memory *mongod* has mapped. This is generally roughly the size of your data directory.

vsize
: The amount of virtual memory *mongod* is using. This is generally twice the size of your data directory (once for the mapped files, once again for journaling).

res
: This is the amount of memory *mongod* is using. This should generally be as close as possible to all the memory on the machine.

locked db
: This shows the database that spent the most time locked in the last timeslice. It reports the percent of time the database was locked combined with how long the global lock was held, meaning that this value might be over 100%.

idx miss %
: This is the most confusingly-named field in the output. It is how many index accesses had to page fault: the index entry (or section of index being searched) was not in memory, so *mongod* had to go to disk.

qr|qw
: This is the queue size for reads and writes: how many reads and writes are blocking, waiting to be processed.

ar|aw
: How many active clients there are: clients currently performing reads and writes.

netIn
: Number of network bytes in, as counted by MongoDB (not necessarily the same as what the OS would measure).

netOut
: Number of network bytes out, as counted by MongoDB.

conn
: The number of connections this server has open, both incoming and outgoing.

time
: The time at which these statistics were taken.

You can run *mongostat* on a replica set or sharded cluster. If you use the `--discover` option, *mongostat* will try to find all the members of the set or cluster from the member it initially connects to and will print one line per server per second for each. For a large cluster, this can get unmanageable fast, but it can be useful for small clusters and tools that can consume the data and present it in a more readable form.

mongostat is a great way to get a quick snapshot of what your database is doing, but for long-term monitoring a tool like MMS is preferred (see Chapter 21).

CHAPTER 18
Data Administration

This chapter covers how to administrate your collections and databases. Generally the things covered in this section are not daily tasks but can be critically important for your application's performance, for instance:

- Setting up authentication and user accounts
- Creating indexes on a running system
- "Preheating" a new server to allow it to come online quickly
- Defragmenting data files
- Preallocating new data files manually

Setting Up Authentication

One of the first priorities for systems administrators is to ensure their system is secure. The best way to handle security with MongoDB is to run it in a trusted environment, ensuring that only trusted machines are able to connect to the server. That said, MongoDB supports per-connection authentication, albeit with a fairly coarse-grained permissions scheme.

> There are more sophisticated security features in MongoDB Enterprise. See *http://docs.mongodb.org/manual/security* for the most up-to-date information about authentication and authorization.

Authentication Basics

Each database in a MongoDB instance can have any number of users. When security is enabled, only authenticated users of a database are able to perform read or write operations.

There are two special databases: users in the *admin* and *local* databases can perform operations on any database. A user that belongs to either one of these databases can be thought of as a superuser. After authenticating, admin users are able to read or write from *any* database and are able to perform certain admin-only commands, such as `listDatabases` or `shutdown`.

Before starting the database with security turned on, it's important that at least one admin user has been added. Let's run through a quick example, starting from a shell connected to a server without authentication turned on:

```
> use admin
switched to db admin
> db.addUser("root", "abcd");
{
    "user" : "root",
    "readOnly" : false,
    "pwd" : "1a0f1c3c3aa1d592f490a2addc559383"
}
> use test
switched to db test
> db.addUser("test_user", "efgh");
{
    "user" : "test_user",
    "readOnly" : false,
    "pwd" : "6076b96fc3fe6002c810268702646eec"
}
> db.addUser("read_user", "ijkl", true);
{
    "user" : "read_user",
    "readOnly" : true,
    "pwd" : "f497e180c9dc0655292fee5893c162f1"
}
```

Here we've added an admin user, `root`, and two users on the *test* database. One of those users, `"read_only"`, has read permissions only and cannot write to the database. From the shell, a read-only user is created by passing `true` as the third argument to `addUser`. To call `addUser`, you must have write permissions for the database in question; in this case we can call `addUser` on any database because we have not enabled security yet.

> The addUser method is useful for more than just adding new users: it can be used to change a user's password or read-only status. Just call addUser with the username and a new password or read-only setting for the user.

Now let's restart the server, this time adding the `--auth` command-line option to enable security. After enabling security, we can reconnect from the shell and try it:

```
> use test
switched to db test
> db.test.find();
error: { "$err" : "unauthorized for db [test] lock type: -1 " }
> db.auth("read_user", "ijkl");
1
> db.test.find();
{ "_id" : ObjectId("4bb007f53e8424663ea6848a"), "x" : 1 }
> db.test.insert({"x" : 2});
unauthorized
> db.auth("test_user", "efgh");
1
> db.test.insert({"x": 2});
> db.test.find();
{ "_id" : ObjectId("4bb007f53e8424663ea6848a"), "x" : 1 }
{ "_id" : ObjectId("4bb0088cbe17157d7b9cac07"), "x" : 2 }
> show dbs
assert: assert failed : listDatabases failed:{
    "assertion" : "unauthorized for db [admin] lock type: 1
",
    "errmsg" : "db assertion failure",
    "ok" : 0
}
> use admin
switched to db admin
> db.auth("root", "abcd");
1
> show dbs
admin
local
test
```

When we first connect, we are unable to perform any operations (read or write) on the *test* database. After authenticating as the `read_user` user, however, we are able to perform a simple `find`. When we try to insert data, we are again met with a failure because of the lack of authorization. `test_user`, which was not created as read-only, is able to insert data normally. As a non-admin user, though, `test_user` is not able to list all the available databases using the `show dbs` helper. The final step is to authenticate as an admin user, `root`, who is able to perform operations on any database.

Setting Up Authentication

If authentication is enabled, clients must be logged in to perform any reads or writes. However, there is one oddity in MongoDB's authentication scheme: before you create a user in the *admin* database, clients that are "local" to the server can perform reads and writes on the database.

Generally, this is not an issue: create your admin user and use authentication normally. The only exception is sharding. With sharding, the *admin* database is kept on the config servers, so shard *mongods* have no idea it even exists. Therefore, as far as they know, they are running with authentication enabled but no admin user. Thus, shards will allow a local client to read and write from them without authentication.

Hopefully this wouldn't be an issue: optimally your network will be configured so that only *mongos* processes are accessible to clients. However, if you are worried about clients running locally on shards and connecting directly to them instead of going through the *mongos*, you may wish to add admin users to your shards.

Note that you do not want the sharded cluster to know about these admin users: it already has an *admin* database. The *admin* databases you're creating on the shards are for your use only. To do this, connect to the primary of each shard and run the `addUser()` function:

```
> db.addUser("someUser", "theirPassword")
```

Make sure that the replica sets you create users on are already shards in the cluster. If you create an admin user and then try to add the *mongods* as a shard the *addShard* command will not work (because the cluster already contains an *admin* database).

How Authentication Works

Users of a given database are stored as documents in its *system.users* collection. The structure of a user document is `{"user" : username, "readOnly" : true, "pwd" : password hash}`. The `password hash` is a hash based on the `username` and password chosen.

Knowing where and how user information is stored makes performing some common administration tasks trivial. For example, to remove a user, simply remove the user document from the *system.users* collection:

```
> db.auth("test_user", "efgh");
1
> db.system.users.remove({"user" : "test_user"});
> db.auth("test_user", "efgh");
0
```

When a user authenticates, the server keeps track of that authentication by tying it to the connection used for the `authenticate` command. This means that if a driver or tool is employing connection pooling or fails over to another node, authenticated users will need to reauthenticate on new connections. This should be handled invisibly by the driver.

Creating and Deleting Indexes

Chapter 5 covered what commands to run to create an index, but it didn't go into the operational aspects of doing so. Creating an index is one of the most resource-intensive operations you can do on a database, so schedule index creations carefully.

Building an index requires MongoDB to find the indexed field (or lack thereof) in every document in the collection, then sort all the values found. As you might imagine, this becomes a very expensive task as your collection gets bigger. Thus, indexing should be done in a way that affects your production server as little as possible.

Creating an Index on a Standalone Server

On a standalone server, build the index in the background during an off-time. There isn't much else you can do to minimize impact. To build an index in the background, run ensureIndex with the `"background" : true` option:

```
> db.foo.ensureIndex({"someField" : 1}, {"background" : true})
```

Any type of index can be built in the background.

A foreground index build takes less time than a background index build but locks the database for the duration of the process. Thus, no other operations can read or write to the database while a foreground index is building. Background indexes yield the write lock regularly to allow other operations to go. This means that they can take longer—much longer on write-heavy servers—but the server can serve other clients while building an index.

Creating an Index on a Replica Set

The easiest way to create an index on a replica set is to create it on the primary and wait for it to be replicated to the secondaries. On small collections, this should have minimal impact.

If you have a large collection, this can lead to the situation where all of your secondaries start building the index at the same time. Suddenly all of your secondaries will be unavailable for client reads and may fall behind in replication. Thus, for larger collections, this is the preferred technique:

1. Shut down a secondary.
2. Start it up as a standalone node, as described in Chapter 6.

3. Build the index on that server.
4. Reintroduce the member into the replica set.
5. Repeat for each secondary.

When you have finished this process, only the primary should be left without an index. Now there are two options: you can either build the index on the primary in the background (which will put more strain on the primary) or you can step down the primary and then follow steps 1 through 4 to build the index on it as you did with the other members of the set. This involves a failover, which may be more or less preferable than adding load to the primary.

You can also use this isolate-and-build technique to build an index on a member of the set that isn't configured to build indexes (one that has the `"buildIndexes" : false` option set): start it as a standalone member, build the index, and add it back into the set.

If you cannot use the rotation method for whatever reason, plan to build new indexes during an off time (at night, a holiday, a weekend, etc.).

Creating an Index on a Sharded Cluster

To create indexes on a sharded cluster, we want to follow the same procedure as described for replica sets and build the index on one shard at a time.

First, turn off the balancer. Then follow the procedure outlined in the previous section for each shard, treating it as a individual replica set. Finally, run *ensureIndex* through the *mongos* and turn the balancer back on again.

This procedure is only required for adding an index to existing shards: new shards will pick up on the index when they start receiving chunks from a collection.

Removing Indexes

If an index is no longer necessary, you can remove it with the `dropIndexes` command and the index name. Query the *system.indexes* collection to figure out what the index name is, as even the autogenerated names vary somewhat from driver to driver:

```
> db.runCommand({"dropIndexes" : "foo", "index" : "alphabet"})
```

You can drop all indexes on a collection by passing in `"*"` as the value for the `"index"` key:

```
> db.runCommand({"dropIndexes" : "foo", "index" : "*"})
```

This leaves the `"_id"` index. The only way to get rid of that one is to drop the whole collection. Removing all the documents in a collection (with `remove`) does not affect the indexes; they will be repopulated when new documents are inserted.

Beware of the OOM Killer

The Linux out-of-memory killer will kill processes that are using a lot of memory. Because of the way MongoDB uses memory, it is not usually an issue, but index creations are the one time it can be. If you are building an index and your *mongod* suddenly disappears, check */var/log/messages* for notices from the OOM killer. Running a background index build or adding some swap space can prevent this. If you have administrative permissions on the machine, you may want to make MongoDB unkillable.

See "The OOM Killer" on page 383 for more information.

Preheating Data

When you restart a machine or bring up a new server, it can take a while for MongoDB to get all the right data from disk into memory. If your performance constraints require that data be in RAM, it can be disastrous to bring a new server online and then let your application hammer it while it gradually pages in the data it needs.

There are a couple of ways to get your data into RAM before officially bringing the server online, to prevent it from messing up your application.

> Restarting MongoDB does change what's in RAM. RAM is managed by the OS and the OS won't evict data from memory until the space is needed for something else. Thus, if the *mongod* process needs to be restarted it should not affect what data is in memory. (However, *mongod* will report low resident memory until it has a chance to ask the OS for the data it needs.)

Moving Databases into RAM

If you need a database in RAM, you can use the UNIX *dd* tool to load it before starting the *mongod*:

```
$ for file in /data/db/brains.*
> do
> dd if=$file of=/dev/null
> done
```

Replace *brains* with the name of the database you want to load.

Replacing */data/db/brains.** with */data/db/** will load the whole data directory (all databases) into RAM (assuming there's enough room for all of them). If you load a database or set of databases into memory and it takes up more memory than you have, some of its data will fall back out of memory immediately. In this situation, you may want to use one of the techniques outlined in the next section to move more specific parts of your data into memory.

When you start the *mongod*, it will ask the operating system for the data files and the operating system, knowing that the data files are in memory, will be able to quickly access it.

However, this technique is only helpful if your entire database fits in memory. If it does not, you can do more fine-grained preheating using the following techniques.

Moving Collections into RAM

MongoDB has a command for preheating data called *touch*. Start *mongod* (perhaps on a different port or firewalled off from your application) and *touch* a collection to load it into memory:

```
> db.runCommand({"touch" : "logs", "data" : true, "index" : true})
```

This will load all the documents and indexes into memory for the *logs* collection. You can specify to only load documents or only load indexes. Once `touch` completes, you can allow your application to access MongoDB.

However, an entire collection (even just the indexes) can still be too much data. For example, your application might only require one index to be in memory, or only a small fraction of the documents. In that case, you'll have to custom preheat the data.

Custom-Preheating

When you have more complex preheating needs, you may have to roll your own preheating scripts. Here are some common preheating requirements and how to deal with them:

Load a specific index

Let's say we have an index such as `{"friends" : 1, "date" : 1}` that must be in RAM. We can load this index into memory by doing a covered query (see "Using covered indexes" on page 90):

```
> db.users.find({}, {"_id" : 0, "friends" : 1, "date" : 1}).
... hint({"friends" : 1, "date" : 1}).explain()
```

The `explain` forces mongod to iterate through all of the results for you. You must specify that you only want to return the indexed fields (the second argument to `find`) or the query will end up loading all the *documents* into memory, too (which you may want, but it's good to be aware of). Note that this will always load the index and documents into memory for indexes that cannot be covered, such as multikey indexes.

Load recently updated documents

If you have an index on a date field that you update when you update the document, you can query on recent dates to load recent documents.

If you don't have an index on the date field, this query will end up loading all documents in the collection into memory, so don't bother. If you don't have a date field, you might be able to use the "_id" field if you're mostly concerned with recent inserts (see below).

Load recently created documents

If you are using `ObjectId`s for your `"_id"` field, you can use the fact that recently created documents contain a timestamp to query for them. For example, suppose we wanted to find all documents created in the last week. We could create an `"_id"` that was less than every `ObjectId` created in the last week:

```
> lastWeek = (new Date(year, month, day)).getTime()/1000
1348113600
```

Replace year, month, and date appropriately and this gives you the date, in seconds. Now we need to get an `ObjectId` from this time. First, convert it into a hex string, then append 16 zeros to it:

```
> hexSecs = lastWeek.toString(16)
505a94c0
> minId = ObjectId(hexSecs+"0000000000000000")
ObjectId("505a94c00000000000000000")
```

Now we just have to query for it:

```
> db.logs.find({"_id" : {"$gt" : minId}}).explain()
```

This will load all the docs (and some right-hand branches of the `"_id"` index) from the last week.

Replay application usage

MongoDB has a facility for recording and replaying traffic called the *diaglog*. Enabling the diaglog incurs a performance penalty, so it is best to use it temporarily to gather a "representative" slice of traffic. To gather traffic, run the following command in the *mongo* shell:

```
> db.adminCommand({"diagLogging" : 2})
```

The 2 option means "capture reads." The 1 option will capture writes and the 3 option captures both (0 is the default: off). You probably don't want to capture writes because you don't want extra writes applied to your new member when you replay the diaglog.

Now let the diaglog record operations by letting *mongod* run for however long you want while sending it traffic. Reads will be stored in the *diaglog* file in the data directory. Reset `diagLogging` to 0 when you're done:

```
> db.adminCommand({"diagLogging" : 0})
```

To use your diaglog files, start up your new server and, from the server where the diaglog files live, run:

```
$ nc hostname 27017 < /data/db/diaglog* | hexdump -c
```

Replace the IP, port, and data directory, if necessary. This sends the recorded operations to *hostname:27017* as a series of normal queries.

Note that the diaglog will capture the command turning on the diaglog, so you'll have to log into the server and turn it off when you're done replaying the diaglog (you also might want to delete the diaglog files it generates from the replay).

These techniques can be combined: you could load a couple of indexes while replaying the diaglog, for example. You can also run them all at the same time if you aren't bottlenecked on disk IO, either through multiple shells or the `startParallelShell` command (if the shell is local to the *mongod*):

```
> p1 = startParallelShell("db.find({}, {x:1}).hint({x:1}).explain()", port)
> p2 = startParallelShell("db.find({}, {y:1}).hint({y:1}).explain()", port)
> p3 = startParallelShell("db.find({}, {z:1}).hint({z:1}).explain()", port)
```

Replace *port* with the port on which *mongod* is running.

Compacting Data

MongoDB uses a lot of disk space. Sometimes, if you have deleted or updated a lot of data, you'll end up with collection fragmention. Fragmentation occurs when your data files have a lot of empty space that MongoDB can't reuse because the individual chunks of free space are too small. In this case, you'll see messages like this in the log:

```
Fri Oct  7 06:15:03 [conn2] info DFM::findAll(): extent 0:3000 was empty,
    skipping ahead. ns:bar.foo
```

This message is, in and of itself, harmless. However, it means that an entire extent had no documents in it. To get rid of empty extents and repack collections efficiently, use the *compact* command:

```
> db.runCommand({"compact" : "collName"})
```

Compaction is very resource-intensive: you should not plan to do a compaction on a *mongod* that's serving clients. Thus, the recommended procedure is similar to that of building indexes: compact data on each of the secondaries, then step down the primary and run the final compaction on it.

When you run a *compact* on a secondary it will drop into recovering state, which means that it will return errors if sent read requests and it cannot be used as a sync source. When the compaction is finished, it will return to secondary state.

Compaction fits documents as closely as it can, as though the padding factor was 1. If you need a higher padding factor for the collection, you can specify it as an argument to compact:

```
> db.runCommand({"compact" : "collName", "paddingFactor" : 1.5})
```

You can specify a padding factor between 1 and 4. This does not permanently affect the padding factor, just how MongoDB rearranges documents. Once the compaction is finished, the padding factor will go back to whatever it was originally.

Compacting does not decrease the amount of disk space a collection uses: it just puts all of the documents at the "beginning" of a collection, on the assumption that the collection will expand again to use the available space. Thus, compaction is only a brief reprieve if you are running out of disk space: it will not decrease the amount of disk space MongoDB is using, although it may make MongoDB not need to allocate new space for longer.

You can reclaim disk space by running a *repair*. Repair makes a full copy of the data so you must have free space equal to the size of your current data files. This is often annoying, as the most common reason to do a repair is that their machine is running low on disk space. However, if you can mount another disk, you can specify a *repair path*, which is the directory (your newly-mounted drive) that repair should use for the new copy of the data.

Since it makes a totally clean copy of your data you can interrupt a repair at any time with no effect on your original data set. If you run into the problem in the middle of a repair, you can delete the temporary repair files without affecting your actual data files.

To repair, start *mongod* with the `--repair` option (and `--repairpath`, if desired).

You can run repair on a single database in the shell by calling `db.repairDatabase()`.

Moving Collections

You can rename a collection using the *renameCollection* command. This cannot move collections between databases, but it can change the collection's name. This operation is almost instantaneous, regardless of the size of the collection being renamed. On busy systems, it can take a few nerve-wracking seconds, but it can be performed in production with no performance penalty:

```
> db.sourceColl.renameCollection("newName")
```

You can optionally pass a second argument: what to do with the *newName* collection if it already exists. The options are `true` (drop it) or `false` (the default: error out if it exists).

To move a collection to another database, you must either dump/restore it or manually copy the documents (do a *find* and iterate over the results, inserting them into the new database).

You can move a collection to a different *mongod* using the *cloneCollection* command:

```
> db.runCommand({"cloneCollection" : "collName", "from" : "hostname:27017"})
```

You cannot use *cloneCollection* move a collection within a *mongod*: it can only move collections between servers.

Preallocating Data Files

If you know that your *mongod* will need certain data files, you can run the following script to preallocate them before your application goes online. This can be especially helpful for the oplog (which you know will be a certain size) and any databases that you know will be a given size, at least for a while:

```
#!/bin/bash

# Make sure db name was passed in
if test $# -lt 2 || test $# -gt 3
then
    echo "$0 <db> <number-of-files>"
fi

db=$1
num=$2

for i in {0..$num}
do
      echo "Preallocating $db.$i"
      head -c 2146435072 /dev/zero > $db.$i
done
```

Store this in a file (say, *preallocate*), and make the file executable. Go to your data directory and allocate the files that you need:

```
$ # create test.0-test.100
$ preallocate test 100
$
$ # create local.0-local.4
$ preallocate local 4
```

Once you start the database and it accesses the datafiles for the first time, you cannot delete any of the data files. For example, if you allocated data files *test.0* through *test.100* and then start the database and realize that you only need *test.0* through *test.20*, you should not delete *test.21-test.100*. Once MongoDB is aware of them, it will be unhappy if they go away.

CHAPTER 19

Durability

Durability is the guarantee that an operation that is committed will survive permanently. MongoDB has highly configurable durability settings, from absolutely no guarantees to completely durable. This section covers:

- How MongoDB guarantees durability
- How to configure your application and server to give you the level of durability you need
- The implications of running without journaling enabled
- What MongoDB does not guarantee

MongoDB can ensure data integrity after crashes and hard shutdowns, assuming disk and software are behaving correctly.

Note that relational databases usually use durability to describe transaction persistence. As MongoDB does not support transactions, it is used a bit differently here.

What Journaling Does

As you perform writes, MongoDB creates a *journal* that contains the exact disk location and bytes changed for that write. Thus, if the server suddenly stops, on startup the journal can be used to replay any writes that were not flushed to disk before the shutdown.

The data files are flushed to disk every 60 seconds (by default), so the journal only needs to hold around 60 seconds of write data. Journaling preallocates a couple of empty files for this purpose that it puts in */data/db/journal*, with the names *_j.0*, *_j.1*, and so on.

After you've been running MongoDB for a long time, you may look in your journal directory and see something like *_j.6217*, *_j.6218*, and *_j.6219*. These are the current journal files. The numbers will continue to increase the longer MongoDB is running. On clean shutdown, the journal files will be removed (as there is no need for them after a clean shutdown).

If there is a crash (or `kill -9`), *mongod* will replay its journal files on startup, spitting out a lot of lines of checksumming. These lines are verbose and indecipherable, but they are an indication that everything is working as it should. You may want to try running `kill -9` on *mongod* in development so you know what to expect on restart if it happens in production.

Planning Commit Batches

By default, MongoDB writes to the journal every 100 ms once a few megabytes of data have been written, whichever comes sooner. This means that MongoDB commits changes in batches: every write isn't flushed to disk immediately, but with the default settings you are unlikely to lose more than 100 ms of writes in the event of a crash.

However, this guarantee is not strong enough for some applications, so there are several ways to get stronger durability guarantees. You can ensure a write has been durably written by passing the `j` option to *getLastError*. *getLastError* will wait for the previous write to be written to the journal and journaling will only wait 30 ms (instead of 100 ms) to journal the next batch of writes:

```
> db.foo.insert({"x" : 1})
> db.runCommand({"getLastError" : 1, "j" : true})
> // The {"x" : 1} document is now safely on disk
```

Note that this means that, if you use `"j" : true` as an option on every write, your write speed will essentially be throttled to 33 writes/sec:

$$(1 \text{ write/30ms}) \times (1000\text{ms/second}) = 33.3 \text{ writes/second}$$

It generally doesn't take this long to flush writes to disk, so you'll find your write performance improves if you allow MongoDB to batch most writes instead of committing after every one. However, the option is always there for important writes.

Committing a write commits all previous writes, as well. Thus, if you have 50 important writes, you could use "normal" *getLastError* (without the `j` option) and then call it with the `j` option after the final write. If that succeeds, you know that all 50 writes are flushed safely to disk.

If you have many connections with incoming writes, you can mitigate the speed penalty of using `j` by having many writes happen in parallel. This can increase throughput, even though latency is high.

Setting Commit Intervals

Another option for making journaling less intrusive is that you can shorten (or lengthen) the amount of time between journal commits. Run the *setParameter* command to set the `journalCommitInterval` to a value between 2 ms and 500 ms. This would commit to the journal every 10 ms:

```
> db.adminCommand({"setParameter" : 1, "journalCommitInterval" : 10})
```

This can also be set as a command line option: `--journalCommitInterval`.

Regardless of the interval set, calling getLastError with `"j" : true` will cut the time to a third of the time set.

If clients try to write faster than the journal can flush, *mongod* will block writes until the journal finishes writing to disk. This is the only time that *mongod* will throttle writes.

Turning Off Journaling

Journaling is recommended for all production deployments, but in some cases you may wish to turn it off. Journaling impacts the speed with which MongoDB can write, even without the `j` option. If value of the data is not worth the speed penalty, you may wish to disable journaling.

The downside to disabling journaling is that MongoDB has no way of ensuring data integrity after a crash. After a crash without journaling, you should assume that your data is corrupt and must either be repaired or replaced. *You should not use data after a crash without journaling unless you don't care if your database suddenly stops working.*

Assuming that you would prefer your database to continue to work after a crash, there are a few options.

Replacing Data Files

This is your best option. Delete all of the files in the data directory and get new ones: restore from a backup, take a snapshot of a known-clean member, or initial sync the server if it's a member of a replica set. If you have a replica set with a small amount of data, resyncing is probably your best option: stop the member (if it's not already down), delete everything in its data directory, and start it back up again.

Repairing Data Files

If you have no backups, no copies, and no other members of the set, you'll need to make due with whatever data can be salvaged. You need to use a "repair" tool on the database, but repairs are really corruption-ectomies: they'll remove any corruption, but you may not have much clean data left.

There are two repair tools that come with *mongod*: the *repair* built into *mongod* itself and a more hardcore *repair* built into *mongodump*. The *mongodump* repair may find more of your data, but it takes a long time to do it (and the built-in repair is not exactly speedy). Additionally, if you use *mongodump*'s repair, you'll still need to restore the data before you're ready to start up again.

Thus, you should judge how much time you're willing to devote to data recovery and choose accordingly.

To use the *repair* built into *mongod*, run mongod with the `--repair` option:

```
$ mongod --dbpath /path/to/corrupt/data --repair
```

MongoDB will not start listening on 27017 when running a repair, but you can watch the log to see what it is doing. Note that *repair* makes a complete copy of your existing data, so if you have 80 GB of data, so you need 80 GB of *free* disk space. To help with this (a bit), repair supports a `--repairpath` option. This lets you mount an "emergency drive" and repair your data onto that if you don't have enough space left on your primary disk. Running with `--repairpath` looks like:

```
$ mongod --dbpath /path/to/corrupt/data \
>     --repair --repairpath /media/external-hd/data/db
```

If *repair* gets killed or errors out (say, runs out of disk space), you won't be in any worse of a situation. Repair writes all of its output to new files, not changing your original files until the very end, so your original data files will be in no worse shape than when you started the repair.

The other option is using the `--repair` option on *mongodump*. This looks like:

```
$ mongodump --repair
```

Neither of these are particularly great options, but they should let you get *mongod* running with a clean dataset again.

The mongod.lock File

There is a special file called *mongod.lock* in your data directory that is important when you're running without journaling (if you are running with journaling, it should never come up).

When *mongod* exits it clears *mongod.lock* so that *mongod* knows on startup that it shut down cleanly. Conversely, if the lock file was not cleaned out, *mongod* knows that it existed uncleanly.

If *mongod* detects that it previously exited uncleanly, it will not allow you to start up again so that you know you have to get a clean copy of your data. However, some people have realized that you can get around this check by deleting the lock file before starting *mongod*. Please don't do this. Routinely deleting the lock file on startup means that you don't know and don't care whether your data is corrupt. Unless this is the case, respect the lock file. If it prevents *mongod* from starting, fix your data, and don't delete *mongod.lock*.

Sneaky Unclean Shutdowns

One important reason to not delete the lock file is that you may not even notice a hard crash. Suppose that you reboot a machine for some routine maintenance. The init scripts should take care of shutting down *mongod* before the server shuts down. However, init systems will generally try shutting down a process gently and, if it doesn't shut down after a couple of seconds, hard-kill it. On a busy system, MongoDB can easily take 30 seconds to shut down: it is the unusual init script that will wait for it. Thus, you may have more hard shutdowns than you're aware of.

What MongoDB Does Not Guarantee

There are a couple of situations where MongoDB cannot guarantee durability, such as if there are hardware issues or filesystem bugs. In particular, if a hard disk is corrupt, there is nothing MongoDB can do to protect your data.

Also, different varieties of hardware and software may have different durability guarantees. For example, some cheaper or older hard disks report a write's success while the write is queued up to be written, not when it has actually been written. MongoDB cannot defend against misreporting at this level: if the system crashes, data may be lost.

Basically, MongoDB is only as safe as the underlying system: if the hardware or filesystem destroys the data, MongoDB cannot prevent it. Use replication to defend against system issues. If one machine fails, hopefully another will still be functioning correctly.

Checking for Corruption

The validate command can be used to check a collection for corruption. To run validate on the *foo* collection, do:

```
> db.foo.validate()
{
    "ns" : "test.foo",
    "firstExtent" : "0:2000 ns:test.foo",
    "lastExtent" : "1:3eae000 ns:test.foo",
    "extentCount" : 11,
    "datasize" : 75960008,
    "nrecords" : 1000000,
    "lastExtentSize" : 37625856,
    "padding" : 1,
    "firstExtentDetails" : {
        "loc" : "0:2000",
```

```
            "xnext" : "0:f000",
            "xprev" : "null",
            "nsdiag" : "test.foo",
            "size" : 8192,
            "firstRecord" : "0:20b0",
            "lastRecord" : "0:3fa0"
        },
        "deletedCount" : 9,
        "deletedSize" : 31974824,
        "nIndexes" : 2,
        "keysPerIndex" : {
            "test.foo.$_id_" : 1000000,
            "test.foo.$str_1" : 1000000
        },
        "valid" : true,
        "errors" : [ ],
        "warning" : "Some checks omitted for speed. use {full:true}
            option to do more thorough scan.",
        "ok" : 1
    }
```

The main field you're looking for is `"valid"`, near the end, which will hopefully be true. If it is not, validate will give some details about the corruption it found.

Most of the output from validate describes internal structures of the collection, which are not particularly useful for debugging. See Appendix B for more information on collection internals.

`firstExtent`
: The disk offset of first extent in this collection. It is located in the file *test.0* at byte offset 0x2000.

`lastExtent`
: The offset of the last extent in this collection. It is in *test.1* at byte offset 0x3eae000.

`extentCount`
: The number of extents in the collection.

`lastExtentSize`
: The size in bytes of the most-recently-allocated extent. Extents get larger as a collection expands, growing up to 2 GB in size.

`firstExtentDetails`
: A subobject describing the first extent in the collection. It contains pointers to the previous and next extents (`"xnext"` and `"xprev"`), the extent's size (note how much smaller it is than the last extent in the collection: the first extent will generally be quite small), and pointers to the first and last record in the extent. The records are the structures that actually hold documents.

deletedCount
: The number of documents that have been removed from this collection during its lifetime.

deletedSize
: The size of the free list (all of the free space available) for this collection. This is not just documents that have been deleted but all the space that has been preallocated, as well.

You can only run validate on collections, not indexes, so you generally cannot tell if an index is corrupt unless you *walk* it. Walk an index by running a query for every document in the collection hinting the desired index. Then traverse all results.

If you get an assertion about invalid BSONObj, this is usually corruption. The worst errors are those that mention *pdfile*. *pdfile* is basically the core of MongoDB's data storage: an assertion originating from *pdfile* almost guarantees that your data files are corrupt.

If you are hitting corruption, you may see something like this in your logs:

```
Tue Dec 20 01:12:09 [initandlisten] Assertion: 10334:
    Invalid BSONObj size: 285213831 (0x87040011)
    first element: _id: ObjectId('4e5efa454b4ae20fa6000013')
```

If the first element shown is garbage, there isn't much you can do. If the first element is viewable (as the `ObjectId` in this example is), you may be able to remove the corrupt document. You can try by running:

```
> db.remove({_id: ObjectId('4e5efa454b4ae20fa6000013')})
```

Replace the `"_id"` with the `"_id"` from your log's assertion. Note that this technique may not work if the corruption is not limited to that document: you may still have to repair.

Durability with Replication

Due to the majority issues discussed in Chapter 10, a write to a replica set may be rolled back until it has been written to a majority of the set. To put together the options here with the journaling ones above, you can say:

```
> db.runCommand({"getLastError" : 1, "j" : true, "w" : "majority"})
```

As of this writing, this only guarantees that the write has been written durably to the primary and has been written (not necessarily durably) to the secondaries. Theoretically, it is possible for a majority of the servers to crash in the 100 ms between the write being written and it being journaled, in which case it would be rolled back on the current primary. This is an edge case but is obviously sub-optimal. Unfortunately it is not trivial to fix, but there are a few open bugs to change this behavior.

PART VI

Server Administration

CHAPTER 20

Starting and Stopping MongoDB

In Chapter 2, we covered the basics of starting MongoDB. This chapter will go into more detail about which options are important for setting up MongoDB in production, including:

- Commonly used options
- Starting up and shutting down MongoDB
- Security-related options
- Logging considerations

Starting from the Command Line

The MongoDB server is started with the `mongod` executable. `mongod` has many configurable startup options; to view all of them, run `mongod --help` from the command line. A couple of the options are widely used and important to be aware of:

`--dbpath`
: Specify an alternate directory to use as the data directory; the default is */data/db/* (or, on Windows, *\data\db* on the MongoDB binary's volume). Each `mongod` process on a machine needs its own data directory, so if you are running three instances of `mongod` on one machine, you'll need three separate data directories. When `mongod` starts up, it creates a *mongod.lock* file in its data directory, which prevents any other `mongod` process from using that directory. If you attempt to start another MongoDB server using the same data directory, it will give an error:

```
"Unable to acquire lock for lockfilepath: /data/db/mongod.lock."
```

`--port`
: Specify the port number for the server to listen on. By default, `mongod` uses port 27017, which is unlikely to be used by another process (besides other `mongod` processes). If you would like to run more than one `mongod` process on a single machine, you'll need to specify different ports for each one. If you try to start `mongod` on a port that is already being used, it will give an error:

```
"Address already in use for socket: 0.0.0.0:27017"
```

`--fork`
: Fork the server process, running MongoDB as a daemon.

If you are starting up *mongod* for the first time (with an empty data directory), it can take the filesystem a few minutes to allocate database files. The parent process will not return from forking until the preallocation is done and mongod is ready to start accepting connections. Thus, *fork* may appear to hang. You can tail the log to see what it is doing. You must use `--logpath` if you specify `--fork`.

`--logpath`
: This option sends all output to the specified file rather than outputting on the command line. This will create the file if it does not exist, assuming you have write permissions to the directory. It will also overwrite the log file if it already exists, erasing any older log entries. If you'd like to keep old logs around, use the `--logappend` option in addition to `--logpath` (highly recommended).

`--directoryperdb`
: This puts each database in its own directory. This allows you to mount different databases on different disks, if necessary or desired. Common uses for this are putting a local database (replication) on its own disk or moving a database to a different disk if the original one fills up. You could also put databases that handle more load on faster disks and lower on slower. It basically gives you more flexibility to move things around later.

`--config`
: Use a configuration file for additional options not specified on the command line. This is typically used to make sure options are the same between restarts. See "File-Based Configuration" on page 336 for details.

For example, to start the server as a daemon listening on port 5586 and sending all output to *mongodb.log*, we could run this:

```
$ ./mongod --port 5586 --fork --logpath mongodb.log --logappend
forked process: 45082
all output going to: mongodb.log
```

Note that *mongod* may decide to preallocate journal files before it considers itself "started." If it does, *fork* will not return to the command prompt until the preallocation has finished. You can tail *mongodb.log* (or wherever you redirected the log file) to watch its progress.

When you first install and start MongoDB, it is a good idea to look at the log. This might be an easy thing to miss, especially if MongoDB is being started from an init script, but the log often contains important warnings that prevent later errors from occurring. If you don't see any warnings in the MongoDB log on startup, then you are all set. (Startup warnings will also appear on shell startup.)

If there are any warnings in the startup banner, take note of them. MongoDB will warn you about a variety of issues: that you're running on a 32-bit machine (which MongoDB is not designed for), that you have NUMA enabled (which can slow your application to a crawl), or that your system does not allow enough open file descriptors (MongoDB uses a lot of file descriptors).

The log preamble won't change when you restart the database, so feel free to run MongoDB from an init script and ignore the logs, once you know what they say. However, its a good idea to check again each time you do an install, upgrade, or recover from a crash, just to make sure MongoDB and your system are on the same page.

When you start the database, MongoDB will write a document to the *local.startup_log* collection that describes the version of MongoDB, underlying system, and flags used:

```
> db.startup_log.findOne()
{
    "_id" : "spock-1360621972547",
    "hostname" : "spock",
    "startTime" : ISODate("2013-02-11T22:32:52Z"),
    "startTimeLocal" : "Mon Feb 11 17:32:52.547",
    "cmdLine" : {

    },
    "pid" : 28243,
    "buildinfo" : {
        "version" : "2.4.0-rc1-pre-",
        ...
        "versionArray" : [
            2,
            4,
            0,
            -9
        ],
        "javascriptEngine" : "V8",
        "bits" : 64,
        "debug" : false,
        "maxBsonObjectSize" : 16777216
    }
}
```

This collection can be useful for tracking upgrades and changes in behavior.

File-Based Configuration

MongoDB supports reading configuration information from a file. This can be useful if you have a large set of options you want to use or are automating the task of starting up MongoDB. To tell the server to get options from a configuration file, use the `-f` or `--config` flags. For example, run `mongod --config ~/.mongodb.conf` to use *~/.mongodb.conf* as a configuration file.

The options supported in a configuration file are exactly the same as those accepted at the command line. Here's an example configuration file:

```
# Start MongoDB as a daemon on port 5586

port = 5586
fork = true # daemonize it!
logpath = /var/log/mongodb.log
logappend = true
```

This configuration file specifies the same options we used earlier when starting with regular command-line arguments. It also highlights most of the interesting aspects of MongoDB configuration files:

- Any text on a line that follows the # character is ignored as a comment
- The syntax for specifying options is *`option = value`*, where *`option`* is case-sensitive
- For command-line switches like `--fork`, the value `true` should be used

Stopping MongoDB

Being able to safely stop a running MongoDB server is at least as important as being able to start one. There are a couple of different options for doing this effectively.

The cleanest way to shut down a running server is to use the `shutdown` command, `{"shutdown" : 1}`. This is an admin command and must be run on the *admin* database. The shell features a helper function to make this easier:

```
> use admin
switched to db admin
> db.shutdownServer()
server should be down...
```

The *shutdown* command, when run on a primary, steps down the primary and waits for a secondary to catch up before shutting down the server. This minimizes the chance of rollback, but the shutdown isn't guaranteed to succeed. If there is no secondary available that can catch up within a few seconds, the *shutdown* command will fail and the (former) primary will not shut down:

```
> db.shutdownServer()
{
    "closest" : NumberLong(1349465327),
    "difference" : NumberLong(20),
    "errmsg" : "no secondaries within 10 seconds of my optime",
    "ok" : 0
}
```

You can force the *shutdown* command to shutdown a primary by using the force option:

```
db.adminCommand({"shutdown" : 1, "force" : true})
```

This is equivalent to sending a SIGINT or SIGTERM signal (all three of these options result in a clean shutdown, but there may be unreplicated data). If the server is running as the foreground process in a terminal, a SIGINT can be sent by pressing Ctrl-C. Otherwise, a command like `kill` can be used to send the signal. If `mongod` has 10014 as its PID, the command would be `kill -2 10014` (SIGINT) or `kill 10014` (SIGTERM).

When `mongod` receives a SIGINT or SIGTERM, it will do a clean shutdown. This means it will wait for any running operations or file preallocations to finish (this could take a moment), close all open connections, flush all data to disk, and halt.

Security

Do not set up publicly addressable MongoDB servers. You should restrict access as tightly as possible between the outside world and MongoDB. The best way to do this is to set up firewalls and only allow MongoDB to be reachable on internal network addresses. Chapter 23 covers what connections are necessary to allow between MongoDB servers and clients.

Beyond firewalls, there are a few options you can add to your config file to make it more secure:

`--bind_ip`
: Specify the interfaces that you want MongoDB to listen on. Generally you want this to be an internal IP: something application servers and other members of your cluster can access but is inaccessible to the outside world. *localhost* is fine for *mongos* processes if you're running the application server on the same machine. For config servers and shards, they'll need to be addressable from other machines, so stick with non-*localhost* addresses.

`--nohttpinterface`
: By default, MongoDB starts a tiny HTTP server on a port 1000 above wherever you started MongoDB. This gives you some information about your system, but nothing you can't get elsewhere and is somewhat useless on a machine you probably only access via SSH and exposes information that should be inaccessable to the outside world.

Unless you're in development, this should be turned off.

`--nounixsocket`
: If you're not planning to connect via file system socket, you might as well disable this option. You would only connect via file system socket on a machine that is also running an application server: you must be local to use a file system socket.

`--noscripting`
: This entirely disallows server-side JavaScript execution. Most security issues that have been reported with MongoDB have been JavaScript-related and it is generally safer to disallow it, if your application allows.

  Several shell helpers assume that JavaScript is available on the server, notably `sh.status()`. You will see errors if you attempt to run any of these helpers with JavaScript disabled.

Do not enable the REST interface. It is disabled by default and allows running many commands on the server. It is not intended for production use.

Data Encryption

As of this writing, MongoDB provides no built-in mechanism for encrypting data stored. If you require data to be encrypted, use filesystem encryption. Another possibility is manually encrypting certain fields (although MongoDB has no special ability to query for encrypted values).

SSL Connections

By default, connections to MongoDB transfer data unencrypted. However, SSL connection support is available. Due to licensing issues the default builds do not have SSL, but you can download a subscriber build at *http://www.10gen.com*, which supports SSL. You can also compile MongoDB from source to enable SSL support. Consult your driver's documentation on how to create SSL connections using your language.

Logging

By default, *mongod* sends its logs to stdout. Most init scripts use the `--logpath` option to send logs to a file. If you have multiple MongoDB instances on a single machine (say, a *mongod* and a *mongos*), make sure that their logs are stored in separate files. Make sure that you know where the logs are and have read access to the files.

MongoDB spits out a lot of log messages, but please do not run with the `--quiet` option (which suppresses some of them). Leaving the log level at the default is usually perfect: there is enough info for basic debugging (why is this slow, why isn't this starting up, etc.), but the log does not take up too much space. If you are debugging a specific issue with your application, there are a couple options for getting more info from the logs.

First, you can change the log level, either by restarting MongoDB with more v's or running the *setParameter* command:

```
> db.adminCommand({"setParameter" : 1, "logLevel" : 3})
```

Remember to turn log level back down to 0, or your logs may be needlessly noisy. You can turn log level up to 5, at which point mongod will print out almost every action it takes, including the contents of every request handled. This can cause a lot of IO as *mongod* writes everything to the log file, which can slow down a busy system. Turning on profiling is a better option if you need to see every operation as it's happening.

By default, MongoDB logs information about queries that take longer than 100 ms to run. If 100 ms it too short or too long for your application, you can change the threshold with *setProfilingLevel*:

```
> // Only log queries that take longer than 500ms
> db.setProfilingLevel(1, 500)
{ "was" : 0, "slowms" : 100, "ok" : 1 }
> db.setProfilingLevel(0)
{ "was" : 1, "slowms" : 500, "ok" : 1 }
```

The second line will turn off profiling, but the value in milliseconds given in the first line will continue to be used as a threshold for the log (across all databases). You can also set this parameter by restarting MongoDB with the `--slowms` option.

Finally, set up a cron job that rotates your log every day or week. If MongoDB was started with `--logpath`, sending the process a SIGUSR1 signal will make it rotate the log. There is also a *logRotate* command that does the same thing:

```
> db.adminCommand({"logRotate" : 1})
```

You cannot rotate logs if MongoDB was not started with `--logpath`.

CHAPTER 21
Monitoring MongoDB

Before you deploy, it is important to set up some type of monitoring. Monitoring should allow you to track what your server is doing and alert you if something goes wrong. This chapter will cover:

- How to track MongoDB's memory usage
- How to track application performance metrics
- How to diagnose replication issues

Examples use chapters from the *Mongo Monitoring Service* (MMS) to demonstrate what to look for when monitoring. There are installation instructions for MMS at *https://mms.10gen.com*. If you do not want to use MMS, please use some type of monitoring. It will help you detect potential issues before they cause problems and let you diagnose issues when they occur.

Monitoring Memory Usage

Accessing data in memory is fast and accessing data on disk is slow. Unfortunately, memory is expensive (and disk is cheap) and typically MongoDB uses up memory before any other resource. This section covers how to monitor MongoDB's interactions with disk and memory, and what to watch for.

Introduction to Computer Memory

Computers tend to have a small amount of fast-to-access memory and a large amount of slow-to-access disk. When you request a page of data that is stored on disk (and not yet in memory), your system *page faults* and copies the page from disk into memory. It can then access the page in memory extremely quickly. If your program stops regularly using the page and your memory fills up with other pages, the old page will be *evicted* from memory and only live on disk again.

Copying a page from disk into memory takes a lot longer than reading a page from memory. Thus, the less MongoDB has to copy data from disk, the better. If MongoDB can operate almost entirely in memory, it will be able to access data much faster. Thus, MongoDB's memory usage is one of the most important stats to track.

Tracking Memory Usage

There are several "types" of memory MongoDB reports using. First is *resident memory*: this is the memory that MongoDB explicitly owns in RAM. For example, if we query for a document and it is paged into memory, that page is added to MongoDB's resident memory.

MongoDB is given an address for that page. This address isn't the literal address of the page in RAM. It's a *virtual address*. MongoDB can pass it to the kernel and the kernel will look up where the page really lives. This way, if the kernel needs to evict the page from memory, MongoDB can still use the address to access it. MongoDB will request the memory from the kernel, the kernel will look at its page cache, see that the page is not there, page fault to copy the page into memory, and return it to MongoDB. The pages of data MongoDB has addresses for is how MongoDB's *mapped memory* is calculated: it includes all of the data MongoDB has ever accessed. It will usually be about the size of your data set.

MongoDB keeps an extra virtual address for each page of mapped memory for journaling to use (see Chapter 19). This doesn't mean that there are two copies of the data in memory, just two addresses. Thus, the total *virtual memory* MongoDB uses will be approximately twice your mapped memory size (or twice your data size). If journaling is disabled, mapped and virtual memory sizes will be approximately equal.

Note that both virtual memory and mapped memory are not "real" memory allocations: they do not tell you anything about how much RAM is being used. They are just mappings that MongoDB is keeping. Theoretically, MongoDB could have a petabyte of memory mapped and only a couple of gigabytes in RAM. Thus, you do not have to worry if mapped or virtual memory sizes exceed RAM.

Figure 21-1 shows the MMS graph for memory information, which describes how much resident, virtual, and mapped memory MongoDB is using. On a box dedicated to MongoDB, resident should be a little less than the total memory size (assuming your working set is as large or larger than memory). Resident memory is that only statistic that actually tracks how much data is in physical RAM, but by itself this stat does not tell you much about how MongoDB is using memory.

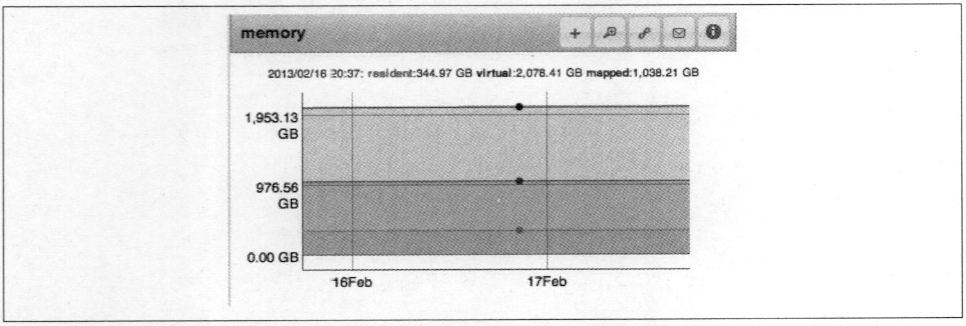

Figure 21-1. From the top line to the bottom: virtual, mapped, and resident memory

If your data fits entirely in memory, resident should be approximately the size of your data. When we talk about data being "in memory," we're always talking about the data being in RAM.

Tracking Page Faults

As you can see from Figure 21-1, memory metrics tend to be fairly steady, but as your data set grows virtual and mapped will grow with it. Resident will grow to the size of your available RAM and then hold steady.

You can use other statistics to find out how MongoDB is using memory, not just how much of each type it has. One useful stat is number of page faults, which tells you how often the data MongoDB is looking for is not in RAM. Figure 21-2 and Figure 21-3 are graphs page faults over time. Figure 21-3 is page faulting less than Figure 21-2, but by itself this information is not very useful. If the disk in Figure 21-2 can handle that many faults and the application can handle the delay of the disk seeks, there is no particular problem with having so many faults (or more). On the other hand, if your application cannot handle the increased latency of reading data from disk, you have no choice but to store all of your data in memory (or use SSDs).

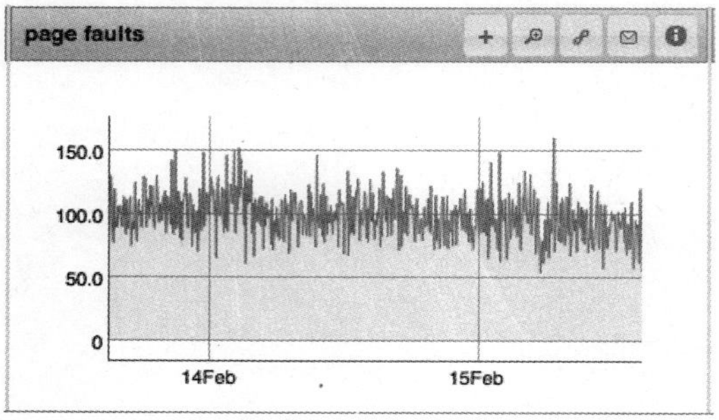

Figure 21-2. A system that is page faulting hundreds of times a minute

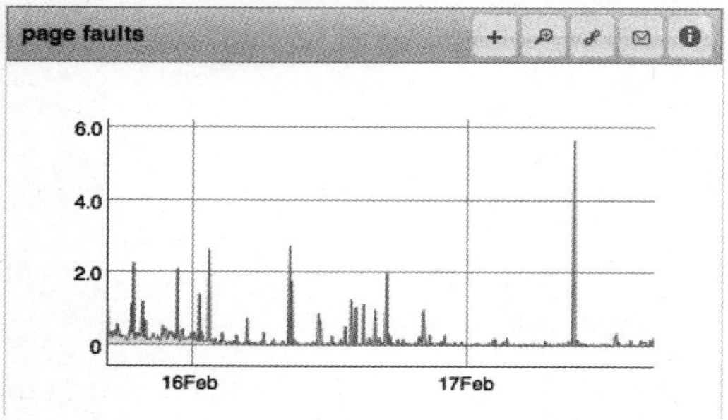

Figure 21-3. A system that is page faulting a few times a minute

Regardless of how forgiving the application is, page faults become a problem when the disk is overloaded. The amount of load a disk can handle isn't linear: once a disk begins getting overloaded, each operation must queue for a longer and longer period of time, creating a chain reaction. There is usually a tipping point where disk performance begins degrading quickly. Thus, it is a good idea to stay away from the maximum load that your disk can handle.

Track your page fault numbers over time. If your application is behaving well with a certain number of page faults, you have a baseline for how many page faults the system can handle. If page faults begin to creep up and performance deteriorates, you have a threshold to alert on.

You can see page fault stats per-database by looking at "`recordStats`" field of *serverStatus*'s output:

```
> db.adminCommand({"serverStatus" : 1})["recordStats"]
{
    "accessesNotInMemory": 200632,
    "test": {
```

```
            "accessesNotInMemory": 1,
            "pageFaultExceptionsThrown": 0
        },
        "pageFaultExceptionsThrown": 6633,
        "admin": {
            "accessesNotInMemory": 1247,
            "pageFaultExceptionsThrown": 1
        },
        "bat": {
            "accessesNotInMemory": 199373,
            "pageFaultExceptionsThrown": 6632
        },
        "config": {
            "accessesNotInMemory": 0,
            "pageFaultExceptionsThrown": 0
        },
        "local": {
            "accessesNotInMemory": 2,
            "pageFaultExceptionsThrown": 0
        }
    },
```

`"accessesNotInMemory"` gives you a count of how many times MongoDB has had to go to disk (since startup).

Minimizing Btree Misses

Accessing index entries that are not in memory is particularly inefficient, as it often causes two page faults. There is one fault to load the index entry into memory and then another to load the document into memory. When an index lookup causes a page fault it's called a *btree miss*. MongoDB also tracks *btree hits*: when an index access does not have to go to disk. Both are shown in Figure 21-4.

Indexes are so frequently used that they are generally in memory, but if there is too little memory, a lot of indexes, or an unusual access pattern (e.g., a lot of table scans), btree misses may be higher. They should generally be low so if you're seeing a lot of them, track down the cause.

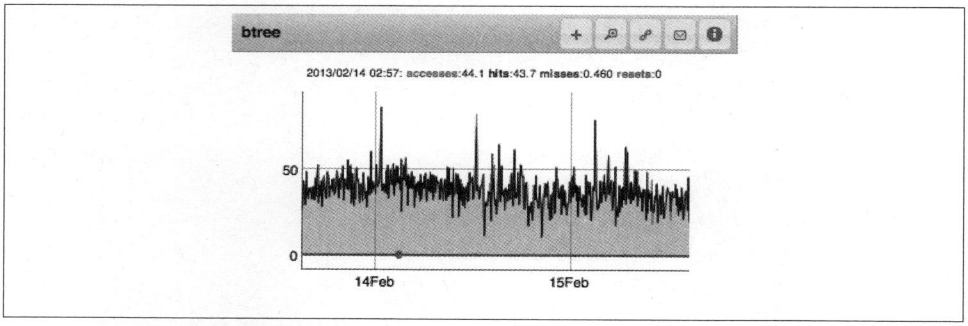

Figure 21-4. A chart showing btree stats

IO Wait

Page faults in general are closely tied to how long the CPU is idling waiting for the disk, called *IO wait*. Some IO wait is normal (MongoDB has to go to disk sometimes and, although it tries not to block anything when it does, cannot completely avoid it). The important thing is that IO wait is not increasing or near 100%, as shown in Figure 21-5. This indicates that the disk is getting overloaded.

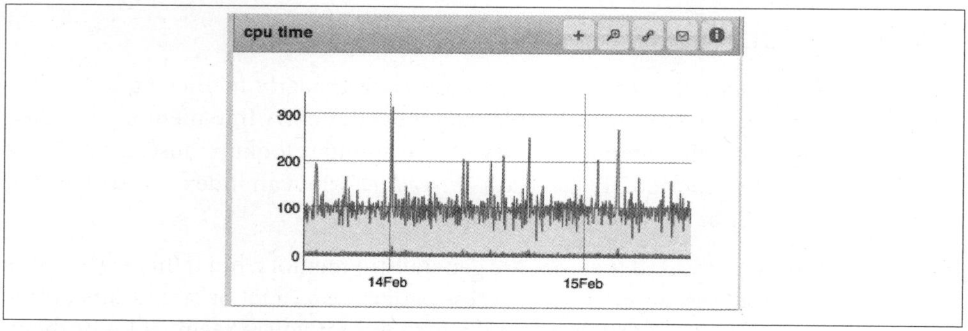

Figure 21-5. IO wait hovering around 100%

MMS can track CPU information if you install the munin plug-in. See their website for installation instructions.

Tracking Background Flush Averages

One other disk metric to watch is how long it takes MongoDB to write its dirty pages to disk, also known as the *background flush average*. This is a good canary-in-the-coal-mine stat. If the background flush average starts creeping up, you know that your disk is having trouble keeping up with requests.

At least once a minute (by default), MongoDB will flush all writes that have happened to disk. (Depending on the operating system, MongoDB may flush writes more frequently if there are a lot of dirty pages.) You can also configure the interval by passing a number of seconds to the `--syncdelay` option when starting *mongod*. More frequent syncs will make the amount of data to be synced smaller, but can also be less efficient.

> A common misconception is that `syncdelay` has something to do with data durability. It has absolutely no effect on durability. To ensure durability, use journaling. `syncdelay` is only for tuning disk performance.

Generally, you want to see background flush averages of less than a second. On a slow disk or a busy system, this can creep up, taking longer and longer as the disk gets overloaded. At some point, the disk will be so overloaded that flushes will take longer than 60 seconds, meaning MongoDB will be trying to flush constantly (which puts even more load on the disk). Occasional spikes in disk flush times are expected. What you don't want to see is a trend towards tens of seconds.

Figure 21-6 shows a graph of background flush averages over time. This system's hard drive is working hard: it always takes it more than 5 seconds to write the preceding minute's data to disk. This is a bit slow, especially with the regular spikes of nearly 20 seconds, so it might be worth turning `syncdelay` down a bit, say to 40 seconds, and seeing if writing less data per flush helped.

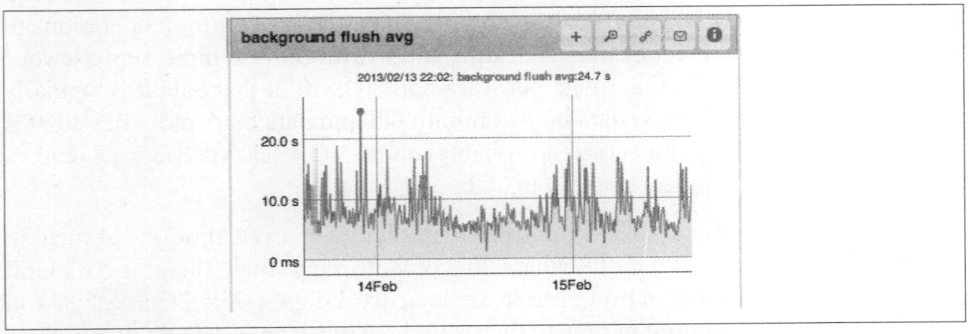

Figure 21-6. Background flush averages on a somewhat overloaded system

If background flush average creeps up beyond what is reasonable for your disks (probably a few seconds) over a broad time period, start thinking about how you're going to lighten the load on your disks.

MongoDB only has to flush dirty data (that is, data that's changed) so background flush average will generally reflect write load. Thus, if you have a low write load, background flush average may not show that your disk is straining. You should always track IO wait and page faults in addition to background flush average.

Calculating the Working Set

In general, the more of your data that is in memory, the faster MongoDB will perform. Thus, in order from fastest to slowest, an application could have:

1. The entire data set in memory. This is nice to have but is often too expensive or infeasible. It may be necessary for applications that depend on fast response times.
2. The *working set* in memory. This is the most common choice.

   Your working set is the data and indexes that your application uses. This may be everything, but generally there's a core data set (for example, the users collection and the last month of activity) that covers 90% of requests. If this working set fits in RAM, MongoDB will generally be fast: it only has to go to disk for a few "unusual" requests.
3. The indexes in memory.
4. The working set of indexes in memory. This generally requires right-balanced indexes (see Chapter 5).
5. No useful subset of data in memory. If possible, avoid this. It will be slow.

You must know what your working set is (and how large it is) to know if you can keep it in memory. The best way to calculate working set is to track common operations to find out how much your application is reading and writing. For example, suppose your application creates 2 GB of new data per week and 800 MB of that data it is regularly accessed. Users tend to access data up to a month old and data that's older than that is mostly unused. Your working set size is probably about 3.2 GB (800 MB/week × 4 weeks), plus a fudge factor for indexes, so call it 5 GB.

One way to think about this is to track data accessed over time, as shown in Figure 21-7. If you choose a cutoff where 90% of your request fall, then the data (and indexes) generated in that period of time are your working set, like Figure 21-8. You can measure for that amount of time to figure out how much your data set grows. Note that this example uses time, but it's possible that there's another access pattern that makes more sense for your application (time being the most common one).

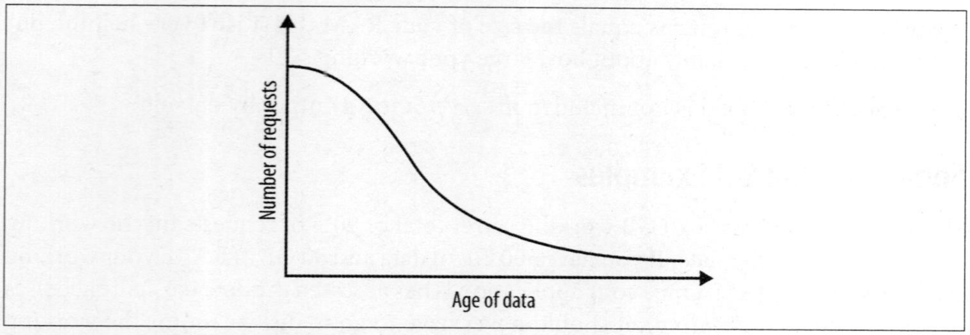

Figure 21-7. A plot of data accesses by age of data

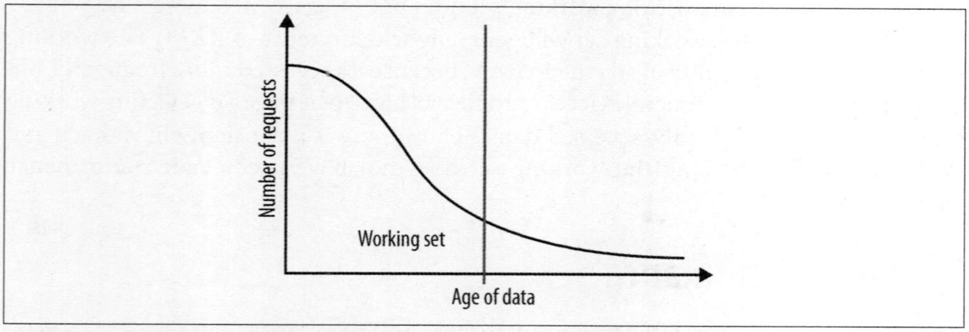

Figure 21-8. The working set is data used in the requests before the cutoff of "frequent requests"

You can also use MongoDB's stats to estimate the working set. MongoDB keeps a map of what it thinks is its memory, which you can see by passing in the `"workingSet" : 1` option to *serverStatus*:

```
> db.adminCommand({"serverStatus" : 1, "workingSet" : 1})
{
...
    "workingSet" : {
        "note" : "thisIsAnEstimate",
        "pagesInMemory" : 18,
        "computationTimeMicros" : 3685,
        "overSeconds" : 2363
    },
...
}
```

`"pagesInMemory"` is how many pages MongoDB thinks are currently in memory. MongoDB does not actually know how many pages are in memory, but it should be close. If the number of pages returns equals the size of your RAM this it isn't very helpful; but if it is smaller it is probably about how large your working set is.

The "workingSet" field is not included in *serverStatus*'s output by default.

Some Working Set Examples

Suppose that you have a 40 GB working set. A total of 90% of requests hit the working set, and 10% hit other data. If you have 500 GB of data and 50 GB of RAM, your working set fits entirely in RAM. Once your application is has accessed the data it usually accesses (a process called *preheating*), it should never have to go to disk again for the working set. It had 10 GB of space for the 460 GB of less-frequently-accessed data. Obviously, MongoDB will almost always have to go to disk for the nonworking set data.

On the other hand, suppose our working set does not fit in RAM. Say we have only 35 GB of RAM. Then the working set will generally take up most of RAM. The working set has a higher probability of staying in RAM because it's accessed more frequently, but at some point the less-frequently-accessed data will have to be paged in, evicting working set (or other less-frequently-accessed data). Thus, there is a constant churn back and forth from disk: accessing the working set does not have predictable performance anymore.

Tracking Performance

Performance of queries is often important to track and keep consistent. There are several ways to track if MongoDB is having trouble with the current request load.

CPU is generally IO bound with MongoDB (IO wait is high, and the other metrics are negligible). However, if user or system time is approaching 100% (or 100% multiplied by the number of CPUs you have) the most common cause is that you're missing an index on a frequently-used query. The other possibility is that you are running a lot of MapReduces or other server-side JavaScript. It is a good idea to track CPU (particularly after deploying a new version of your application) to ensure that all your queries are behaving as they should.

Note that the graph shown in Figure 21-9 is fine: if there is a low number of page faults, IO wait may be dwarfed by other CPU activities. It is only when the other activities creep up that bad indexes may be a culprit.

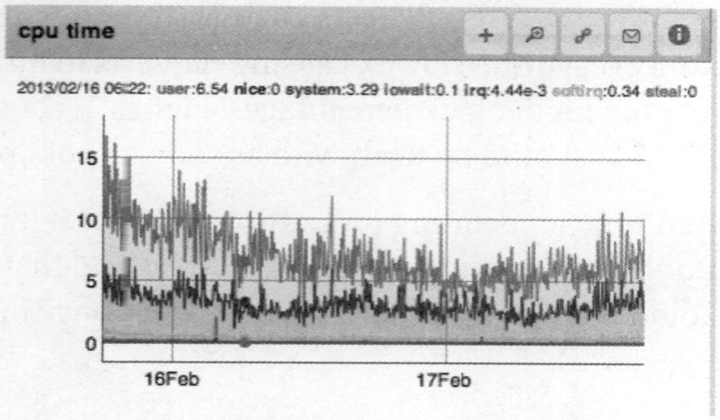

Figure 21-9. A CPU with minimal IO wait. The top line is user and the lower line is system. The other stats are very close to 0%.

A similar metric is queuing: how many request are waiting to be processed by MongoDB. A request is considered queued when it is waiting for the lock it needs to do a read or a write. Figure 21-10 shows a graph of read and write queues over time. No queues are preferred (basically an empty graph), but this graph is nothing to be alarmed about. In a busy system, it isn't unusual for an operation to have to wait a bit for the correct lock to be available.

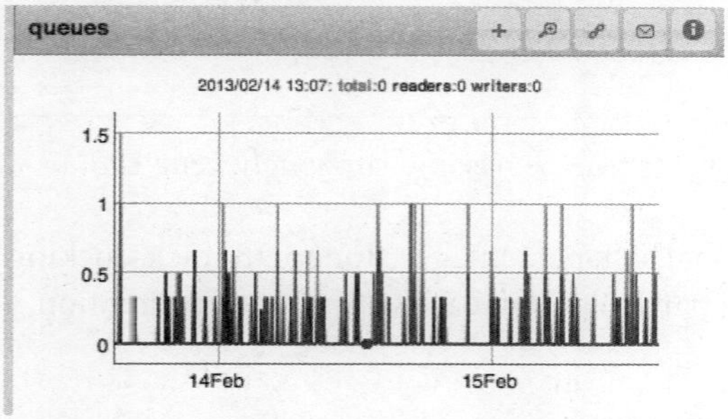

Figure 21-10. Read and write queues over time

You can see if requests are piling up by looking at the number of requests enqueued. Generally, queue size should be low. A large and ever-present queue is an indication that *mongod* cannot keep up with its load. You should decrease the load on that server as fast as possible.

You can correlate statistics about queuing with lock percentage: the amount of time MongoDB spends locked. Often disk IO will throttle writes more than locking but locking is still important to track, especially for systems with fast disks or many sequential writes. Again, one of the most common causes of high lock percentage is that you are missing an index. As lock percentage increases, operations on average have to wait longer and longer for a lock. Thus, there is an unfortunate cascading nature to high lock percentages making everything slower, causing requests to build up, causing more load on the system and even higher lock percentages. Figure 21-11 shows an alarmingly high lock percentage, which should be dealt with as soon as possible.

Lock percentage is often spiky depending on traffic levels; but if it trends upwards over time it's a good indication that your system is under stress and that something needs to change. Thus, you should alert on lock percentage over a long time (so that a sudden spike in traffic won't trigger it).

On the other hand, you may want to also trigger an alert if lock percentage suddenly spikes, say 25% over its normal value. This might be an indication that your system cannot handle load spikes and that you may have to add capacity.

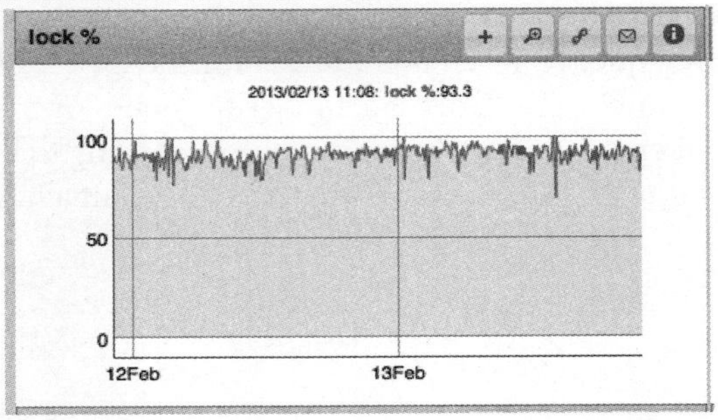

Figure 21-11. A lock percentage hovering worryingly near 100%

In addition to the global lock percentage, MongoDB tracks locking per database, so you can see if you have a particular database with a lot of contention.

Tracking Free Space

One other metric that is basic but important to monitor is disk usage: track free disk space. Sometimes users wait until their disk runs out of space before they think about how they want to handle it. By monitoring your disk usage, you can predict how long your current drive will be sufficient and plan in advance what to do when it is not.

As you run out of space, there are several options:

- If you are using sharding, add another shard.
- Shut down each member of a replica set (one at a time) and copy its data to a larger disk, which can then be mounted. Restart the member and proceed to the next.

- Replace members of your replica set with members with a larger drive: remove an old member and add a new member, and allow that one to catch up with the rest of the set. Repeat for each member of the set.
- If you are using the `directoryperdb` option and you have a particularly fast-growing database, move it to its own drive. Then mount the volume as a directory in your data directory. This way the rest of your data doesn't have to be moved.

Regardless of the technique you choose, plan ahead to minimize the impact on your application. You need time to take backups, modify each member of your set in turn, and copy your data from place to place.

Monitoring Replication

Replication lag and oplog length are important to track.

Lag is when the secondaries cannot keep up with the primary. Lag is calculated by subtracting the time of the last op applied on a secondary from the time of the last op on the primary. For example, if a secondary just applied an op with the timestamp 3:26:00 p.m. and the primary just applied an op with the timestamp 3:29:45 p.m., the secondary is lagging by 3 minutes and 45 seconds. You want lag to be as close to 0 as possible, and it is generally on the order of milliseconds. If a secondary is keeping up with the primary, the replication lag should look something like the graph shown in Figure 21-12: basically 0 all the time.

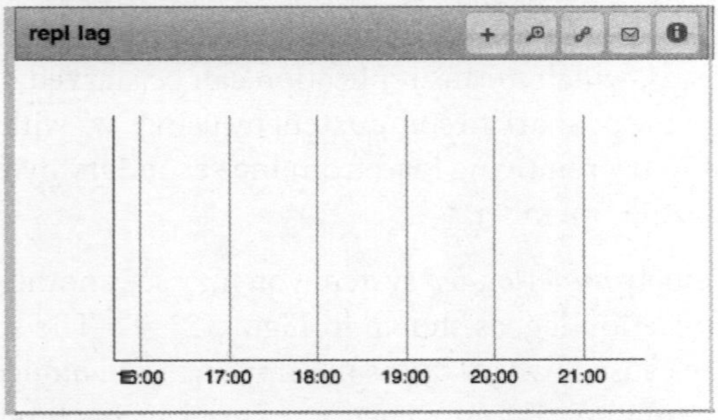

Figure 21-12. A replica set with no lag. This is what you want to see.

If a secondary cannot replicate writes as fast as the primary can write, you'll start seeing nonzero lag. The most extreme case of this is when replication is *stuck*: it cannot apply any more operations for some reason. At this point, lag will grow by one second per second, creating the steep slope shown in Figure 21-13. This could be caused by network issues or a missing "`_id`" index, which is required on every collection for replication to function properly.

If a collection is missing an "_id" index, take the server out of the replica set, start it as a standalone server, and build the "_id" index. Make sure you create the "_id" index as a *unique* index. Once created, the "_id" index cannot be dropped or changed (other than by dropping the whole collection).

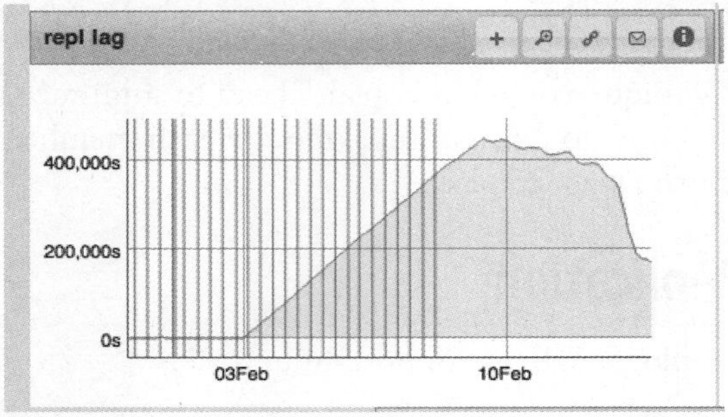

Figure 21-13. Replication getting stuck and, just before February 10, beginning to recover. The red lines are server restarts.

If a system is overloaded, a secondary may gradually fall behind. But you generally won't see the characteristic "one second per second" slope in the graph, but some replication will still be happening. Still, it is important to be aware if the secondaries cannot keep up with peak traffic or are gradually falling further behind.

Primaries do not throttle writes to "help" secondaries catch up, so it common for secondaries to fall behind on overloaded systems (particularly as MongoDB tends to prioritize writes over reads, which means replication can be starved on the primary). You can force throttling of the primary to some extent by using "w" with your write concern. You also might want to try removing load from the secondary by routing any requests it was handling to another member.

If you are on an extremely *underloaded* system you may see another interesting pattern: sudden spikes in replication lag, as shown in Figure 21-14. The spikes shown are not actually lag—they are caused by variations in sampling. The *mongod* is processing one write every couple of minutes. Because lag is measured as the difference between timestamps on the primary and secondary, measuring the timestamp of the secondary right before a write on the primary makes it look minutes behind. If you increase the write rate, these spikes should disappear.

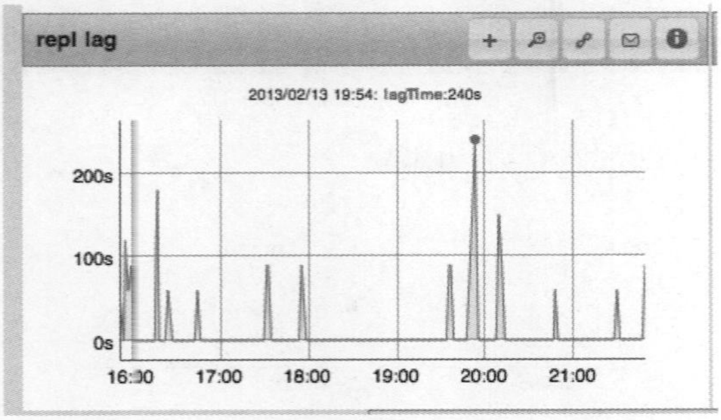

Figure 21-14. A low-write system can cause "phantom" lag

The other important metric to track is the length of each member's oplog. Every member that might become primary should have an oplog longer than a day. If a member may be a sync source for another member, it should have an oplog longer than the time an initial sync takes to complete. Figure 21-15 shows what a standard oplog-length graph looks like. This oplog has an excellent length: 1,111 hours is over a month of data! In general, oplogs should be as long as you can afford the disk space to make them. Given the way they're used, they take up basically no memory and a long oplog can mean the difference between a painful ops experience and an easy one.

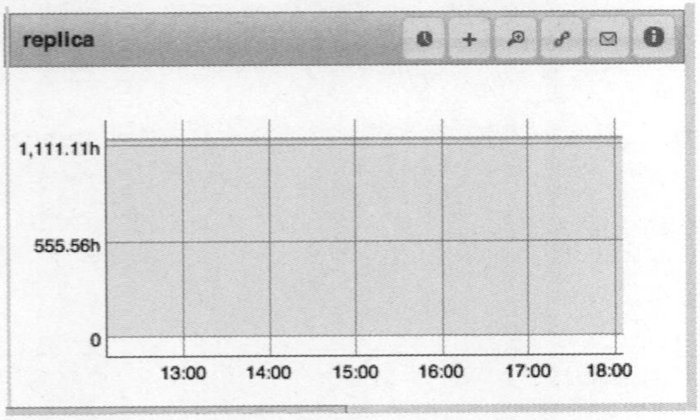

Figure 21-15. A typical oplog-length graph

Figure 21-16 shows a slightly unusual variation caused by a fairly short oplog and variable traffic. This is still healthy, but the oplog on that machine is probably too short (between 6 and 11 hours of maintenance window). The administrator may want to make the oplog longer when she gets a chance.

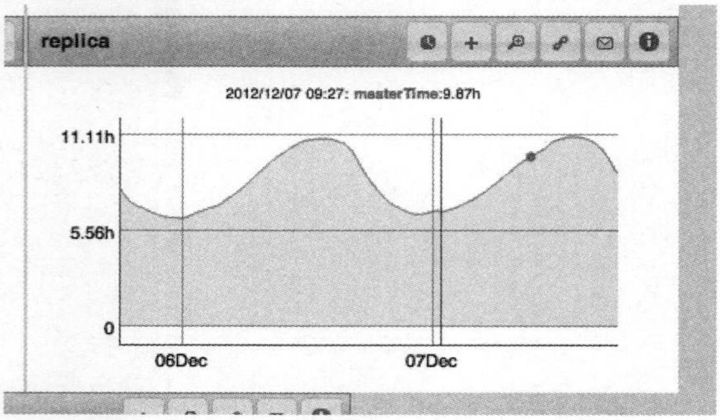

Figure 21-16. An oplog length of an application with daily traffic peaks

CHAPTER 22
Making Backups

It is important to take regular backups of your system. Backups are good protection against most types of failure, and very little can't be solved by restoring from a clean backup. This chapter covers the common options for taking backups:

- Single-server backups
- Special considerations for backing up replica sets
- How to back up a sharded cluster

Backups are only useful if you are confident about deploying them in an emergency. Thus, for any backup technique you choose, be sure to practice both taking backups and restoring from backups until you are comfortable with the restore procedure.

Backing Up a Server

There are a variety of ways of taking backups. Regardless of method, taking a backup can cause strain on a system: it generally requires reading all your data into memory. Thus, backups should generally be done on replica set secondaries (as opposed to the primary) or, for standalone servers, at an off time.

The techniques in this section apply to any *mongod*, whether a standalone or a member of a replica set, unless otherwise noted.

Filesystem Snapshot

The simplest way to make a backup is to take a filesystem snapshot. However, this requires your filesystem to support snapshotting and you must be running *mongod* with journaling enabled. If your system fulfills these two prerequisites, this method requires no preparation: simply take a snapshot at any time.

To restore, ensure that *mongod* is not running. The exact command for restoring from a snapshot varies by filesystem, but basically you restore the snapshot and then start *mongod*. As you took a snapshot on a live system, the snapshot is essentially what the data files would look like if *mongod* had been *kill -9*-ed at the time the snapshot was taken. Thus, on startup, *mongod* will replay the journal files and then begin running normally.

Copying Data Files

Another way of creating backups is to make a copy of everything in the data directory. Because you cannot copy all of the files at the same moment without filesystem support, you must prevent the data files from changing while you are making the copy. This can be accomplished with a command called `fsynclock`:

```
> db.fsyncLock()
```

This command *locks* the database against any further writes and then flushes all dirty data to disk (*fsync*), ensuring that the files in the data directory have the latest consistent information and are not changing.

Once this command has been run, *mongod* will enqueue all incoming writes. It will not process any further writes until it has been unlocked. Note that this command stops writes to *all* databases (not just the one `db` is connected to).

Once the `fsynclock` command returns, copy all of the files in your data directory to a backup location. On Linux, this can be done with a command such as:

```
$ cp -R /data/db/* /mnt/external-drive/backup
```

Make sure that you copy absolutely every file and folder from the data directory to the backup location. Excluding files or directories may make the backup unusable or corrupt.

Once you have finished copying the data, unlock the database to allow it to take writes again:

```
> db.fsyncUnlock()
```

Your database will begin handling writes again normally.

Note that there are some locking issues with authentication and `fsynclock`. If you are using authentication, do not close the shell between calling `fsyncLock()` and `fsyncUnlock()`. If you disconnect, you may be unable to reconnect and have to restart *mongod*. The *fsyncLock()* setting does not persist between restarts, *mongod* will always start up unlocked.

As an alternative to `fsynclocking`, you can instead shut down *mongod*, copy the files, and then start *mongod* back up again. Shutting down *mongod* effectively flushes all changes to disk and prevents new writes from occurring during the backup.

To restore from data directory copies, ensure that *mongod* is not running and that the data directory you want to restore into is empty. Copy the backed-up data files to the data directory, and then start *mongod*. For example, the following command would restore the files backed up with the command shown earlier:

```
$ cp -R /mnt/external-drive/backup/* /data/db/
$ mongod -f mongod.conf
```

Despite the warnings about partial data directory copies, you can use this method to backup individual databases if you know what to copy. To back up an individual database (called, say, *"myDB"*), copy all of the *myDB.** files (including the *.ns* file) to backup. If you are using the `--directoryperdb` option, copy the entire *myDB* directory.

You can restore specific databases by copying just the files with the correct database name into your data directory. You must be starting from a clean shutdown to restore piecemeal like this. If you had a crash or a hard shutdown, do not attempt to restore a single database from backup: replace the entire directory from backup and start the *mongod* to allow the journal files to be replayed.

> Never use `fsyncLock` in conjunction with *mongodump*. Depending on what else your database is doing, *mongodump* may hang forever if the database is locked.

Using mongodump

The final way of taking a backup is to use *mongodump*. *mongodump* is mentioned last because it has some downsides. It is slower (both to get the backup and restore from it) and it has some issues with replica sets which are discussed in "Backing Up a Replica Set" on page 361. However, it also has some benefits: it is a good way to backup individual databases, collections, and even subsets of collections.

mongodump has a variety of options that you can see by running *mongodump --help*. Here, we will focus on the most useful ones to use for backup.

To backup all databases, simply run *mongodump*. If you are running *mongodump* on the same machine as the *mongod*, you can simply specify the port *mongod* is running on:

```
$ mongodump -p 31000
```

mongodump will create a *dump* directory in the current directory, which contains a dump of all of your data. This *dump* directory is organized by database and collection into folders and subfolders. The actual data is stored in *.bson* files, which merely contain every document in a collection in BSON, concatenated together. You can examine *.bson* files using the *bsondump* tool, which comes with MongoDB.

You do not even need to have a server running to use *mongodump*: you can use the `--dbpath` option to specify your data directory and *mongodump* will use the data files to copy data:

```
$ mongodump --dbpath /data/db
```

You should not use `--dbpath` if *mongod* is running.

One issue with *mongodump* is that it is not an instantaneous backup: the system may be taking writes while the backup occurs. Thus, someone might begin a backup that causes *mongodump* to dump the database *A*. While *mongodump* is dumping *B*, someone drops *A*. However, *mongodump* has already dumped it, so you'll end up with a snapshot of the data in a state it never existed in on the original server.

To avoid this, if you are running *mongod* with `--replSet`, you can use *mongodump*'s `--oplog` option. This will keep track of all operations that occur on the server while the dump is taking place, so these operations can be replayed when the backup is restored. This gives you a consistent point-in-time snapshot of data from the source server.

If you pass *mongodump* a replica set connection string (e.g., `"setName/seed1,seed2,seed3"`), it will automatically choose a secondary to dump from, if one is available.

To restore from a *mongodump* backup, use the *mongorestore* tool:

```
$ mongorestore -p 31000 --oplogReplay dump/
```

If you used the `--oplog` option to dump the database, you must use the `--oplogReplay` option with *mongorestore* to get the point-in-time snapshot.

If you are replacing data on a running server, you may (or may not) wish to use the --*drop* option, which drops a collection before restoring it.

The behavior of *mongodump* and *mongorestore* has changed over time. To prevent compatibility issues, try to use the same version of both utilities (you can see their versions by running `mongodump --version` and `mongorestore --version`).

Moving collections and databases with mongodump and mongorestore

You can restore into an entirely different database and collection than you dumped from. This can be useful if different environments use different database names (say, *dev* and *prod*) but the same collection names.

To restore a *.bson* file into a specific database and collection, specify the targets on the command line:

```
$ mongorestore --db newDb --collection someOtherColl dump/oldDB/oldColl.bson
```

Administrative complications with unique indexes

If you have a unique index (other than "_id") on any of your collections, you should consider using a different type of backup than *mongodump/mongorestore*. Specifically, unique indexes require that the data does not change in ways that would violate the unique index constraint during the copy. The safest way to do this is to choose a method that "freezes" the data, then take a backup as described in either of the previous two sections.

If you are determined to use *mongodump/mongorestore*, you may need to preprocess your data when you restore from backup.

Backing Up a Replica Set

Generally, you should take backups from a secondary: this keeps load off of the primary and you can lock a secondary without affecting your application (so long as your application isn't sending it read requests). You can use any of the three methods outlined previously to backup a replica set member, but file system snapshot or data file copy are recommended. Either of these techniques can be applied to replica set secondaries with no modification.

mongodump is not quite as simple to use when replication is enabled. First, if you are using *mongodump*, you must take your backups using the `--oplog` option to get a point-in-time snapshot; otherwise the backup's state won't match the state of anyone else in the cluster. You must also create an oplog when you restore from a *mongodump* backup, or the restored member will not know where it was synced to.

To restore a replica set member from a *mongodump* backup, start the target replica set member as a standalone server with an empty data directory. First, run *mongorestore* (as described in the previous section) with the `--oplogReplay` option. Now it should have a complete copy of the data, but it still needs an oplog. Create an oplog using the `createCollection` command:

```
> use local
> db.createCollection("oplog.rs", {"capped" : true, "size" : 10000000})
```

Specify the size of the collection in bytes. See "Resizing the Oplog" on page 220 for advice on oplog sizing.

Now we need to populate the oplog. The easiest way to do this is to restore the *oplog.bson* backup file from the dump into the *local.oplog.rs* collection:

```
$ mongorestore -d local -c oplog.rs dump/oplog.bson
```

Note that this is not a dump of the oplog (*dump/local/oplog.rs.bson*) but rather the oplog operations that occurred during the dump. Once this *mongorestore* is complete, you can restart this server as a replica set member.

Backing Up a Sharded Cluster

Sharded clusters are impossible to "perfectly" back up while active: you can't get a snapshot of the entire state of the cluster at a point in time. However, this limitation is generally sidestepped by the fact that as your cluster gets bigger, it becomes less and less likely that you'd ever have to restore the whole thing from backup. Thus, when dealing with a sharded cluster, we focus on backing up pieces: the config servers and the replica sets individually.

Turn off the balancer before performing any of these operations on a sharded cluster (either backup or restore). You cannot get a consistent snapshot of the world with chunks flying around. See "Balancing Data" on page 289 for instructions on turning the balancer on and off.

Backing Up and Restoring an Entire Cluster

When a cluster is very small or in development, you may want to actually dump and restore the entire thing. You can accomplish this by turning off the balancer and then running *mongodump* through the *mongos*. This creates a backup of all of the shards on whatever machine *mongodump* is running on.

To restore from this type of backup, run *mongorestore* connected to a *mongos*.

After turning off the balancer, you can alternatively take filesystem or data directory backups of each shard and the config servers. However, you will inevitably get copies from each at slightly different times, which may or may not be a problem. Also, as soon as you turn on the balancer and a migrate occurs, some of the data you backed up from one shard will no longer be there.

Backing Up and Restoring a Single Shard

Most often, you'll only need to restore a single shard in a cluster. If you are not too picky, you can restore from a backup of that shard taken using one of the single-server methods just described.

There is one important issue to be aware of: suppose you take a backup of your cluster on Monday. On Thursday, your disk melts down and you have to restore from backup. However, in the intervening days, new chunks may have moved to this shard. Your backup of the shard from Monday will not contain these new chunks. You may be able to use a config server backup to figure out where the disappearing chunks lived on

Monday, but it is a lot more difficult than simply restoring the shard. In most cases, restoring the shard and losing the data in those chunks is the preferable route.

You can connect directly to a shard to restore from backup (instead of going through *mongos*).

Creating Incremental Backups with mongooplog

All of the backup methods outlined must make a full copy of the data, even if very little of it has changed since the last backup. If you have data that is very large relative to the amount that is being written, you may want to look into incremental backups.

Instead of making full copies of the data every day or week, you take one backup and then use the oplog to back up all operations that have happened since the backup. This technique is much more complex than the ones described above, so prefer them unless incremental backups are absolutely necessary.

This technique requires two machines, A and B, running mongod. A is your main machine (probably a secondary) and B is your backup machine:

1. Make a note of the latest optime in A's oplog:

   ```
   > op = db.oplog.rs.find().sort({$natural: -1}).limit(1).next();
   > start = op['ts']['t']/1000
   ```

   Keep this somewhere safe—you'll need it for a later step.

2. Take a backup of your data, using one of the techniques above to get a point-in-time backup. Restore this backup to the data directory on B.

3. Periodically add any operations that have happened on A to B's copy of the data. There is a special tool that comes with MongoDB distributions that makes this easy: *mongooplog* (pronounced *mon-goop-log*) which copies data from the oplog of one server and applies it to the data set on another. On B, run:

   ```
   $ mongooplog --from A --seconds 1234567
   ```

   `--seconds` should be passed the number of seconds between the `start` variable calculated in step 1 and the current time, then add a bit (better to replay operations a second time than miss them).

This keeps your backup relatively up-to-date with your data. This technique is sort of like keeping a secondary up-to-date manually, so you may just want to use a slave-delayed secondary instead.

CHAPTER 23

Deploying MongoDB

This chapter gives recommendations for setting up a server to go into production. In particular, it covers:

- Choosing what hardware to buy and how to set it up
- Using virtualized environments
- Important kernel and disk IO settings
- Network setup: who needs to connect to whom

Designing the System

You generally want to optimize for data safety and as fast access as you can afford. This section discusses the best way to accomplish these goals when choosing disks, RAID configuration, CPU, and other hardware and low-level software components.

Choosing a Storage Medium

In order of preference, we would like to store and retrieve data from:

1. RAM
2. SSD
3. Spinning disk

Unfortunately, most people have limited budgets or enough data that storing everything in RAM is impractical and SSDs are too expensive. Thus, the typical deployment is a small amount of RAM (relative to total data size) and a lot of space on a spinning disk. If you are in this camp, the important thing is that your working set is smaller than RAM and you should be ready to scale out if the working set gets bigger.

If you are able to spend what you like on hardware, buy a lot of RAM and/or SSDs.

Reading data from RAM takes a few nanoseconds (say, 100). Conversely, reading from disk takes a few milliseconds (say, 10). It can be hard to picture the difference between these two numbers, so suppose we scale them up to more relatable numbers: if accessing RAM took 1 second, accessing disk would take over a day!

$$100 \text{ nanoseconds} \times 10{,}000{,}000 = 1 \text{ second}$$

$$10 \text{ milliseconds} \times 10{,}000{,}000 = 1.16 \text{ days}$$

These are very back-of-the-envelope calculations (your disk might be a bit faster or your RAM a bit slower), but the magnitude of this difference doesn't change much. Thus, we want to access disk as seldom as possible.

Fast spinning disks do not cut down disk access time that much, so don't spend lots of money on them. It is more productive to get more memory or SSDs.

An example from the wild

The graphs in Figure 23-1 through Figure 23-6 illustrate some of the advantages of SSDs. These graphs are from a user bringing a new shard online midday on August 8. The user's deployment was previously just spinning disks. He added a new shard backed by SSDs and, in the graphs, was concurrently running one shard with SSDs and one with spinning disks.

As shown in Figure 23-1, the spinning disk peaks at nearly 5,000 queries per second, but generally only handed a few hundred queries per second.

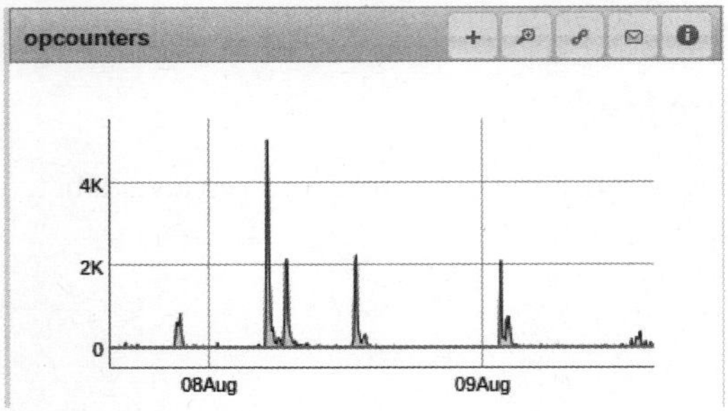

Figure 23-1. Queries on a spinning disk

In comparison, the chart in Figure 23-2 plots queries on the SSD drive. The SSD handles 5,000 queries per second consistently and peaks to 30,000 queries per second! This new shard could essentially handle the entire cluster's load by itself.

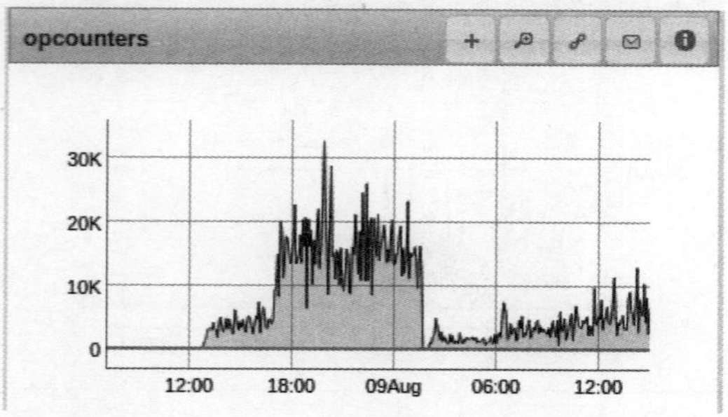

Figure 23-2. Queries on an SSD

The other interesting point to note about SSDs versus spinning disks is the amount of stress these relative loads placed on the system. If we take a look at hardware monitoring on the spinning disk server (Figure 23-3), we can see that the disk is quite busy. The main visible line on the chart is IO wait: the percent of time that the CPU was waiting for disk IO. You can see that the CPU is waiting for disk IO at least 10% of the time and this often spikes to above 50% of the time. This means that the user's workload was essentially being throttled by his disk (which was why he was adding SSDs).

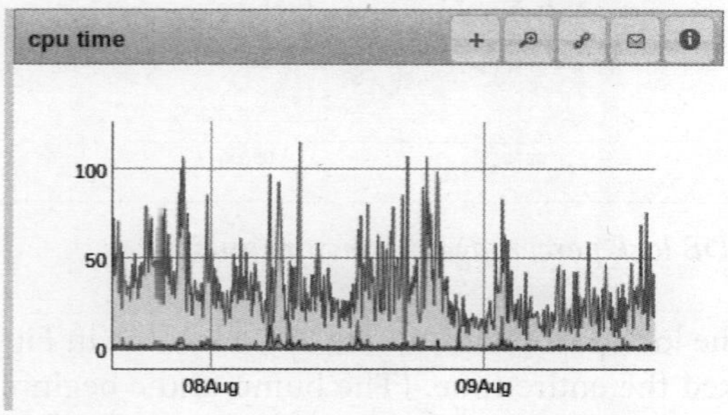

Figure 23-3. CPU usage during the queries

In contrast, Figure 23-4 shows the CPU usage on the SSD machine. IO wait actually isn't even present on this graph: the two visible lines represent system time and user time (the higher and lower lines, respectively). Thus, the limiting factor on this machine is how fast the CPU can run. As the numbers are greater than 100%, this graph also shows that multiple processors were being utilized. Contrast that to the chart in figure Figure 23-3, where not even a single core could be fully utilized due to the lag from disk IO.

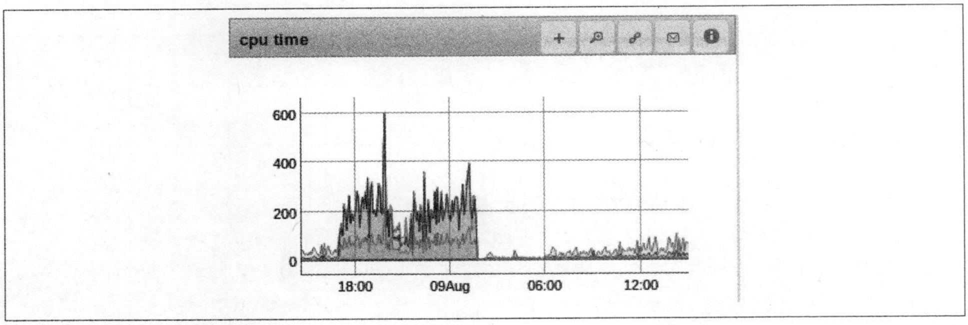

Figure 23-4. CPU usage during the queries

Finally, you can see some of the effect this has on MongoDB by looking at the graphs of lock times in Figure 23-5. On the spinning disk, the database spent between 10% and 25% of the time locked and sometimes spiked to locked 100% of the time.

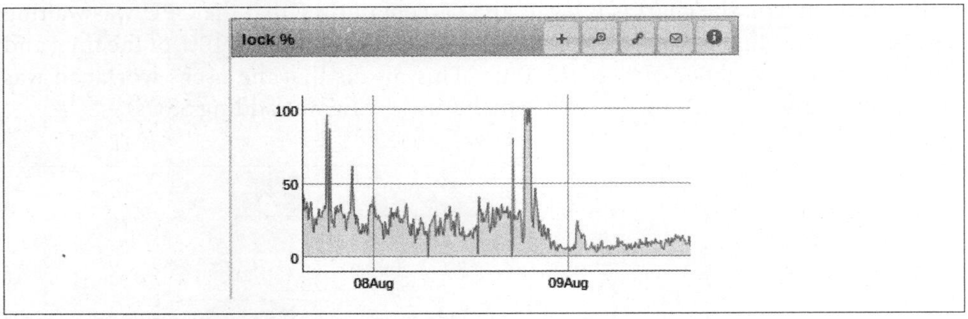

Figure 23-5. MongoDB lock percentage during the queries

Contrast this with the lock percentage on the SSD machine in Figure 23-6. MongoDB is essentially unlocked the entire time. (The bump at the beginning of the chart was from a data-loading operation that he performed before bringing the SSD online.)

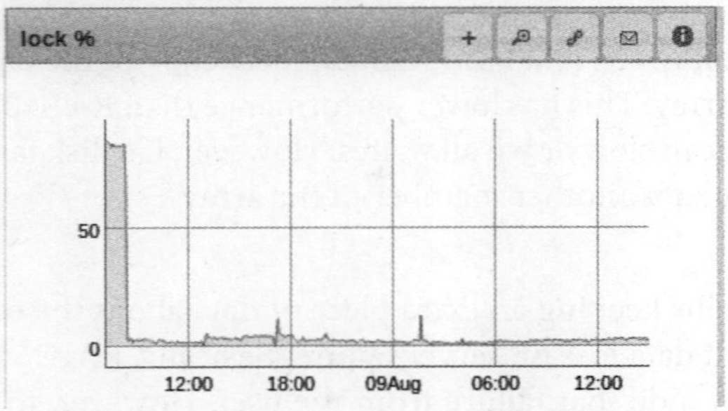

Figure 23-6. Lock percentage on the SSD machine

As you can see, SSDs can shoulder a lot more load than spinning disks, but unfortunately they aren't an option for a lot of deployments. If you can use them, do so. Even if it's not possible to use SSDs for your entire cluster, consider deploying as many as possible and then using the forced hot spot data pattern in Chapter 15 to take advantage of them.

Note that generally you cannot add an SSD to an existing replica set (where the other members have spinning disks). If the SSD machine becomes primary and handles anything close to the load it is capable of, the other members will not be able to replicate from it quickly enough and will fall behind. Thus, it is a good idea to add a new shard to your cluster if you are introducing SSDs.

Note that SSDs are excellent for normal data usage patterns, but spinning disks actually work very well for the journal. Putting the journal on a spinning disk and your data on SSDs can save you SSD space and should have no impact on performance.

Recommended RAID Configurations

RAID is hardware or software that lets you treat multiple disks as though they were a single disk. It can be used for reliability, performance, or both. A set of disks using RAID is referred to as a *RAID array* (somewhat unfortunately, as RAID stands for redundant array of inexpensive disks... array).

There are a number of ways to configure RAID depending on the features you're looking for, generally some combination of speed and fault-tolerance. These are the most common varieties:

RAID0
: Striping disks for improved performance. Each disk holds part of the data, similar to MongoDB's sharding. Because there are multiple underlying disks, lots of data can be written to disk at the same time. This improves throughput on writes. However, if a disk fails and the data is lost, there are no copies of it. It also can cause slow reads (we've particularly seen this on Amazon's Elastic Block Store), as some data volumes may be slower than others.

RAID1

Mirroring for improved reliability. An identical copy of the data is written to each member of the array. This has lower performance than RAID0, as a single member with a slow disk can slow down all writes. However, if a disk fails, you will still have a copy of the data on another member of the array.

RAID5

Striping disks, plus keeping an extra piece of data about the other data that's been stored to prevent data loss on server failure. Basically, RAID5 can handle one disk going down and hide that failure from the user. However, to do this, it is slower than any of the other varieties listed here because it needs to calculate this extra piece of information whenever data is written. This is particularly expensive with MongoDB, as a typical workload does many small writes.

RAID10

A combination of RAID0 and RAID1: data is stripped for speed and mirrored for reliability.

We recommend using RAID10: it is safer than RAID0 and can smooth out performance issues that can occur with RAID1. Some people feel that RAID1 on top of replica sets is overkill and opt for RAID0. It is a matter of personal preference: how much risk are you willing to trade for performance?

Do not use RAID5: it is very, very slow.

CPU

MongoDB tends to be very light on CPU (note Figure 23-3 and Figure 23-4: 10,000 queries per second only uses about two CPU's-worth of processing power). If you have a choice between investing in memory and investing in CPU, go with memory every time. Theoretically, you could max out multiple cores on reads or in-memory sorts, but in practice that's rare. CPU is heavily used for index builds and MapReduces, but as of this writing adding more cores doesn't help either of these cases.

When choosing between speed and number of cores, go with speed. MongoDB is better at taking advantage of more cycles on a single processor than increased parallelization.

Choosing an Operating System

64-bit Linux is the operating system MongoDB runs best on. If possible use some flavor of that. CentOS and RedHat Enterprise Linux are probably the most popular choices, but any flavor should work (Ubuntu and Amazon Linux are also common). Use the most recent stable versions of operating systems because old, buggy packages or kernels can sometimes cause issues.

64-bit Windows is also well supported.

Other flavors of Unix are not as well supported: proceed with caution if you're using Solaris or one of the BSD variants. Builds for these systems have, at least historically, had a lot of issues.

One important note on cross-compatibility: MongoDB uses the same wire protocol and lays out data files identically on all systems, so you can deploy on a combination of operating systems. For example, you could have a *mongos* process running on Windows and the *mongods* that are its shards running on Linux. You can also copy data files from Windows to Linux or visa versa with no compatibility issues.

Do not deploy any data-bearing server on a 32-bit system because this limits you to about 2 GB of data (due to MongoDB using memory-mapped files). Arbiters and *mongos* processes can be run on 32-bit machines. Do not run any other type of MongoDB server on a 32-bit machine.

MongoDB only works with little-endian architectures. Most drivers support both little- and big- endian systems, so you can run clients on either. However, the server must always be run on a little-endian machine.

Swap Space

You should allocate a small amount of swap in case memory limits are reached to prevent the kernel from killing MongoDB. However, MongoDB does not usually use any swap space.

The majority of memory MongoDB uses is "slippery": it'll be flushed to disk and replaced with other memory as soon as the system requests the space for something else. Therefore, database data should never be written to swap space: it'll be flushed back to disk first.

However, occasionally MongoDB will use swap for operations that require ordering data: either building indexes or sorting. It attempts not to use too much memory for these types of operations, but by performing many of them at the same time you may be able to force swapping.

If your application is managing to make MongoDB use swap space, you should look into redesigning your application or reducing load on the swapping server.

Filesystem

For Linux, the ext4 filesystem or XFS are recommended for your data volumes. It is nice to have a filesystem that can do filesystem snapshots for backups, but that's a matter of preference.

ext3 is *not* recommended, as it takes a long time to preallocate data files. MongoDB has to regularly allocate and zero-fill 2 GB data files, which can freeze for minutes at a time on ext3. If ext3 is necessary, there are some hacks around this. However, try to use something else if at all possible.

On Windows, either NTFS or FAT are fine.

> Do not use NFS directly mounted for MongoDB storage. Some client versions lie about flushing, randomly remount and flush the page cache, and do not support exclusive file locking. Using NFS can cause journal corruption and should be avoided at all costs.

Virtualization

Virtualization is a great way to get cheap hardware and be able to expand fast. However, there are some downsides, particularly unpredictable network and disk IO. This section covers virtualization-specific issues.

Turn Off Memory Overcommitting

The memory overcommit setting controls what happens when processes request too much memory from the operating system. Depending on this setting, the kernel may give memory to processes even if that memory is not actually available (in the hopes that it'll become available by the time the process needs it). That's called overcommitting: the kernel promises memory that isn't actually there. This does not work well with MongoDB.

The possible values for `vm.overcommit_memory` are 0 (the kernel guesses about how much to overcommit), 1 (memory allocation always succeeds), or 2 (don't commit more virtual address space than swap space plus a fraction of the overcommit ratio). The value 2 is complicated, but it's the best option available. To set this, run:

```
$ echo 2 > /proc/sys/vm/overcommit_memory
```

You do not need to restart MongoDB after changing this setting.

Mystery Memory

Sometimes the virtualization layer does not handle memory provisioning correctly. Thus, you may have a virtual machine that claims to have 100 GB of RAM available but only ever allows you to access 60 GB of it. Conversely, we've seen people that were supposed to have 20 GB of memory end up being able to fit an entire 100 GB data set into RAM!

Assuming you don't end up on the lucky side, there isn't much you can do. If your readahead is set appropriately and your virtual machine just won't use all the memory it should, you may just have to switch virtual machines.

Handling Network Disk IO Issues

One of the biggest problems with using virtualized hardware is that you are generally sharing a disk with other tenants, which exacerbates the disk slowness mentioned previous because everyone is competing for disk IO. Thus, virtualized disks can have very unpredictable performance: they can work fine while your neighbors aren't busy and suddenly slow down to a crawl if someone else starts hammering the disk.

The other issue is that this storage is often not physically attached to the machine MongoDB is running on, so even when you have a disk all to yourself disk IO will be slower than it would be with a local disk. There is also the unlikely-but-possible scenario of your MongoDB server losing its network connection to your data.

Amazon has what is probably the most widely-used networked block store, called Elastic Block Store (EBS). EBS volumes can be connected to Elastic Cloud (EC2) instances and can give a machine almost any amount of disk immediately. On the plus side, this makes backups very easy (take a snapshot from a secondary, mount the EBS drive on another instance, and start up *mongod*). On the downside, you may encounter very variable performance.

If you require more predictable performance, there are a couple of options. The most straightforward way to guarantee the performance you expect is to not host MongoDB in the cloud. Host it on your own servers and you know no one else is slowing things down. However, that's not an option for a lot of people, so the next-best thing is to get an instance that guarantees a certain number of IOPS (IO Operations Per Second). See *http://docs.mongodb.org* for up-to-date recommendations on hosted offerings.

If you can't pursue either of these options and you need more disk IO than an overloaded EBS volume can sustain, there is a way to hack around it.

Basically, what you can do is to keep monitoring against the volume MongoDB is using. If and when that volume slows down, immediately kill that instance and bring up a new one with a different data volume.

There are a couple of statistics to watch for:

- Spiking IO utilization ("IO wait" on MMS), for obvious reasons.
- Page faults rates spiking. Note that changes in application behavior could also cause working set changes: you should disable this assassination script before deploying new versions of your application.
- The number of lost TCP packets go up (Amazon is particularly bad about this: when performance starts to fall, it drops TCP packets all over the place).
- MongoDB's read and write queues spiking (this can be seen on MMS or in *mongostat*'s `qr`/`qw` column).

If your load varies over the day or week, make sure your script takes that into account: you don't want a rogue cron job killing off all of your instances because of an unusually-heavy Monday morning rush.

This hack relies on you having recent backups or relatively quick-to-sync data sets. If you have each instance holding terabytes of data, you might want to pursue an alternative approach. Also, this is only *likely* to work: if your new volume is also being hammered, it will be just as slow as the old one.

Using Non-Networked Disks

This particular section uses Amazon-specific vocabulary. However, it may apply to other providers.

Ephemeral drives are the actual disks attached to the physical machine your VM is running on, so they don't have a lot of the problems networked storage does. Local disks can still be overloaded by other users on the same box, but with a large box you can be reasonably sure you're not sharing disks with too many others. Even with a smaller instance, often the ephemeral drive will give better performance than a networked drive so long as the other tenants aren't doing tons of IOPS.

The downside is in the name: these disks are ephemeral. If your EC2 instance goes down, there's no guarantee you'll end up on the same box when you restart the instance and then your data will be gone.

Thus, ephemeral drives should be used with care. You should make sure that you do not store any important or unreplicated data on these disks. In particular, do not put the journal on these ephemeral drives or your database on network storage. In general, think of ephemeral drives as a slow cache rather than a fast disk and use them accordingly.

Configuring System Settings

There are several system settings which can help MongoDB run more smoothly and which are mostly related to disk and memory access. This section covers each of these options and how you should tweak it.

Turning Off NUMA

When machines had a single CPU, all RAM was basically the same in terms of access time. As machines started to have more processors, engineers realized that having all memory be equally far from each CPU (as shown in Figure 23-7) was less efficient than having each CPU have some memory that is especially close to it and fast for that particular CPU to access.

This architecture where each CPU has its own "local" memory is called *non-uniform memory architecture* (NUMA), shown in Figure 23-8.

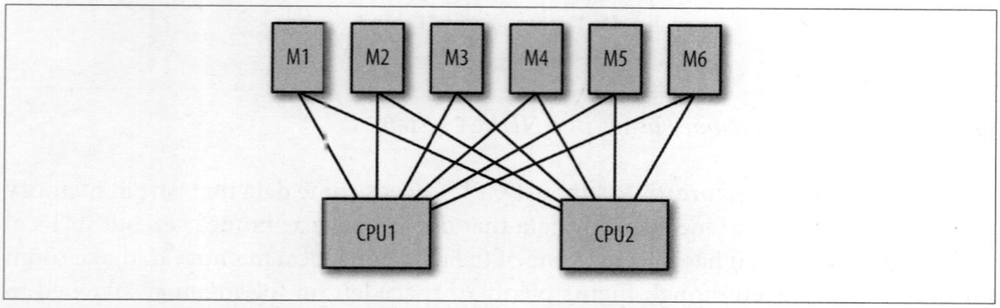

Figure 23-7. Uniform memory architecture: all memory has the same access cost for each CPU

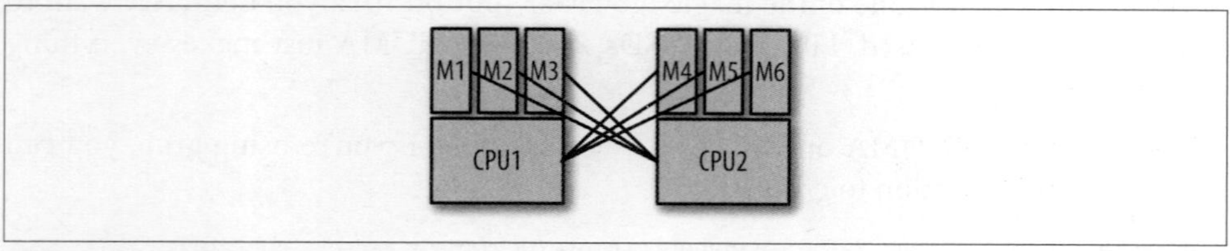

Figure 23-8. Non-Uniform Memory Architecture: certain memory is attached to a CPU, giving the CPU faster access to that particular memory. CPUs can still access other CPUs' memory, but it is more expensive than accessing their own.

For lots of applications, NUMA works well: the processors often need different data because they're running different programs. However, this works terribly for databases in general and MongoDB in particular because databases have such different memory access patterns than other types of applications. MongoDB uses a massive amount of memory and needs to be able to access memory that is "local" to other CPUs. However, the default NUMA settings on many systems makes this difficult.

CPUs favor using the memory that is attached to them and processes tend to favor one CPU over the others. This means that memory often fills up unevenly, leaving you with one processor using 100% of its local memory and the other processors using only a fraction of their memory, as shown in Figure 23-9.

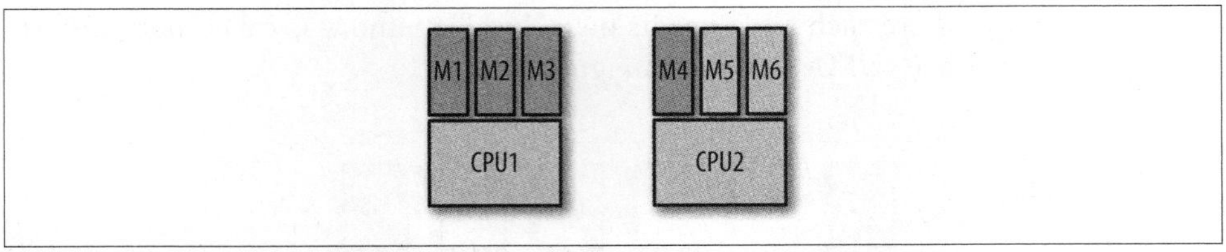

Figure 23-9. Sample memory usage in a NUMA system

In the situation from Figure 23-9, suppose CPU1 needs some data that isn't in memory yet. It must use its local memory for data that doesn't have a "home" yet, but its local memory is full. Thus, it has to evict some of the data in its local memory to make room for the new data, even though there's plenty of space left on the memory attached to CPU2! This process tends to cause MongoDB to run much slower than expected, as it only has a fraction of the memory available that it should have. MongoDB vastly prefers semi-efficient access to more data than extremely efficient access to less data.

Turning off NUMA is one of the magic "go faster" buttons that you definitely want to make sure you've pressed. Like using SSDs, disabling NUMA just makes everything work better.

If possible, disable NUMA on your BIOS. For example, if you're using grub, you can add the `numa=off` option to *grub.cfg*:

```
kernel /boot/vmlinuz-2.6.38-8-generic root=/dev/sda ro quiet numa=off
```

If your system cannot turn it off in BIOS, you'll have to start *mongod* with:

```
$ numactl --interleave=all mongod [options]
```

Add this to any init scripts you use.

Also, turn off `zone_reclaim_mode`. This nasty setting can be thought of as "super NUMA." If it's enabled, whenever a page of memory is accessed by a CPU, it will moved to that CPU's local memory. Thus, if you have a `threadA` on one CPU and `threadB` on another and they're both hitting a page of memory, that page will be copied from one CPU's local memory to the other's on every single access. This is very, very slow.

To disable `zone_reclaim_mode`, run:

```
$ echo 0 > /proc/sys/vm/zone_reclaim_mode
```

You do not have to restart *mongod* for `zone_reclaim_mode` changes to take effect.

If you have NUMA enabled, your hosts will show up in yellow on MMS, as shown in Figure 23-10. You can see the actual warning that's causing it to be yellow by going to the "Last Ping" tab. Figure 23-11 shows the warning you'll see if NUMA is enabled.

Figure 23-10. A host with startup warnings in MMS

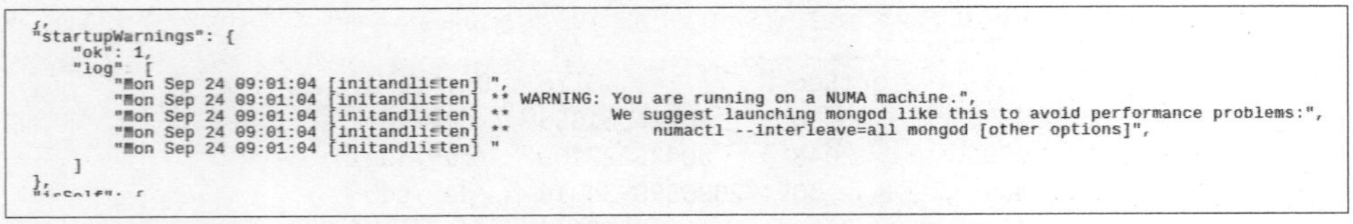

Figure 23-11. Startup warnings about NUMA

Once NUMA has been disabled, MMS will display the host in blue again. (There are several other reasons a host may appear in yellow. Check for other startup warnings, as well.)

Setting a Sane Readahead

Readahead is an optimization where the operating system reads more data from disk than was actually requested. This is useful because most workloads computers handle are sequential: if you load the first 20 MB of a video, you are probably going to want the next couple of megabytes of it. Thus, the system will read more from disk than you actually request and store it in memory, just in case you need it soon.

However, MongoDB is not a typical workload and readahead is a frequent issue on MongoDB systems. MongoDB tends to read many small pieces of data from random places on the disk, so the default system settings do not work very well. If readahead is high, memory gradually fills up with data that MongoDB didn't request, forcing MongoDB to go to disk more often.

For example, if you wanted to read one sector (512 bytes) from disk, the disk controller might actually be instructed to read 256 sectors, on the assumption that you will request them soon, anyway. However, if you are accessing data fairly randomly across the disk, all of those prefetched sectors would be wasted. If memory was contained your working set, 255 sectors of your working set would have to be evicted to make room for these sectors that aren't going to be used. 256 sectors is actually a small readahead, too: some systems default to thousands of sectors of readahead.

Fortunately, there's a fairly easy way to see if your readahead setting is actively hurting you: check the resident set size of MongoDB and compare it to the system's total RAM.

Assuming that your RAM is smaller than your data size, MongoDB's resident set size should be a little lower than your total size of RAM (for example, if you have 50 GB of RAM, MongoDB should be using at least 46 GB). If it is much lower, then your readahead is probably too high.

This technique of comparing resident set size with total memory size works because data that's been "read ahead" from disk is in memory but MongoDB didn't request it, so it isn't included in the calculation of MongoDB's resident memory size.

To see your current readahead settings, use the *blockdev* command:

```
$ sudo blockdev --report
RO    RA   SSZ   BSZ   StartSec            Size   Device
rw   256   512  4096          0     80026361856   /dev/sda
rw   256   512  4096       2048     80025223168   /dev/sda1
rw   256   512  4096          0   2000398934016   /dev/sdb
rw   256   512  1024       2048        98566144   /dev/sdb1
rw   256   512  4096     194560      7999586304   /dev/sdb2
rw   256   512  4096   15818752     19999490048   /dev/sdb3
rw   256   512  4096   54880256   1972300152832   /dev/sdb4
```

This shows you the settings for each of your block devices. Readahead (the `RA` column) is measured in 512-byte sectors. Thus, this system's readahead is set to 128 KB for each device (512 bytes/sector * 256 sectors).

You can change this setting for a device by running this command with the `--setra` option:

```
$ sudo blockdev --setra 16 /dev/sdb3
```

So, what's a good setting for readahead? Between 16 and 256 is recommended. You don't want to set readahead too low, either: you don't want to have to go to disk multiple times to fetch a single document. If you have large documents (greater than a megabyte in size), consider a higher readahead. If your documents are small, stick with something low, like 32. Do not go below 16 even if your documents are tiny, as that will make fetching indexes less efficient (index buckets are 8 KB).

When using RAID, you have to set readahead on everything: the RAID controller and the individual volumes.

Unintuitively, you must restart MongoDB for readahead settings to take effect. You'd think you're setting a disk property, so it should apply to all running programs. Unfortunately, processes make a copy of the readahead value when they start and continue to use that value until terminated.

Disabling Hugepages

Hugepages cause similar issues to high readahead. Do not use hugepages unless:

- All of your data fits into memory and
- You have no plans for it to ever grow beyond memory.

MongoDB needs to page in lots of tiny pieces of memory, so using hugepages can result in more disk IO.

Systems move data from disk to memory and back by the page. Pages are generally a couple of kilobytes (x86 defaults to 4096-byte pages). If a machine has many gigabytes of memory, keeping track of each of these (relatively tiny) pages can be slower than just tracking a few larger-granularity pages, so hugepages allows you to have pages that are up to 256 MB (on ia64 architectures). However, using hugepages means that you are keeping megabytes of data from one section of disk in memory. If your data does not fit in RAM, then swapping in larger pieces from disk will just fill up your memory quickly with data that will need to be swapped out again. Also, flushing any changes to disk will be slower, as the disk must write megabytes of "dirty" data, instead of a few kilobytes.

Note that on Windows this is called Large Pages, not hugepages. Some versions of Windows have it enabled by default and some do not, so check and make sure it is turned off.

Hugepages were actually developed to benefit databases, so this may be surprising to experienced database admins. However, MongoDB tends to do a lot less sequential disk access than relational databases do.

Choosing a Disk Scheduling Algorithm

The disk controller receives requests from the operating system and processes them in an order determined by a scheduling algorithm. Sometimes changing this algorithm can improve disk performance. For other hardware and workloads, it may not make a difference. The best way to decide is to test them out yourself on your workload. Deadline and completely fair queueing (CFQ) both tend to be good choices.

There are a couple of situations where the *noop* scheduler (a contraction of "no-op" is the best choice): if you're in a virtualized environment, use the noop scheduler. The noop scheduler basically passes the operations through to the underlying disk controller as quickly as possible. It is fastest to do this and let the real disk controller handle any reordering that needs to happen.

Similarly, on SSDs, the noop scheduler is generally the best choice. SSDs don't have the same locality issues that spinning disks do.

Finally, if you're using a RAID controller with caching, use noop. The cache behaves like an SSD and will take care of propagating the writes to the disk efficiently.

You can change the scheduling algorithm by setting the `--elevator` option in your boot configuration.

> The option is called *elevator* because the scheduler behaves like an elevator, picking up people (IO requests) from different floors (processes/times) and dropping them off where they want to go in an arguable-optimal way.

Often all of the algorithms work pretty well; you may not see much of a difference between them.

Don't Track Access Time

By default, the system tracks when files were last accessed. As the data files used by MongoDB are very high-traffic, you can get a performance boost by disabling this tracking. You can do this on Linux by changing `atime` to `noatime` in */etc/fstab*:

```
/dev/sda7            /data           ext4            rw,noatime            1  2
```

You must remount the device for the changes to take effect.

`atime` is more of an issue on older kernels (e.g., ext3), as newer ones use `relatime` as a default which is less aggressively updated. Also, be aware that setting `noatime` can affect other programs using the partition, such as *mutt* or backup tools.

Similarly, on Windows you should set the `disablelastaccess` option. To turn off last access time recording, run:

```
C:\> fsutil behavior set disablelastaccess 1
```

You must reboot for this setting to take effect. Setting this may affect the Remote Storage service, but you probably shouldn't be using a service that automatically moves your data to other disks anyway.

Modifying Limits

There are two limits that MongoDB tends to blow by: the number of threads a process is allowed to spawn and the number of file descriptors a process is allowed to open. Both of these should generally be set to unlimited.

Whenever a MongoDB server accepts a connection, it spawns a thread to handle all activity on that connection. Therefore, if you have 3,000 connections to the database, the database will have 3,000 threads running (plus a few other threads for non-client-related tasks). Depending on your application server configuration, your client may spawn anywhere from a dozen to thousands of connections to MongoDB.

If your client will dynamically spawn more child processes as traffic increases (most application servers will do this), it is important to make sure that these child processes are not so numerous that they can max out MongoDB's limits. For example, if you have 20 application servers, each one of which is allowed to spawn 100 child processes and each child process can spawn 10 threads that all connect to MongoDB, that could spawn 20 × 100 × 10 = 20,000 connections at peak traffic. MongoDB is probably not going to be very happy about spawning tens of thousands of threads and, if you run out of threads per process, will simply start refusing new connections.

The other limit to modify is the number of file descriptors MongoDB is allowed to open. Every incoming and outgoing connection uses a file descriptor, so having the client connection storm above would create 20,000 open filehandles (incidentally, the maximum number MongoDB will allow).

mongos in particular tends to create connections to many shards. When a client connects to a *mongos* and makes a request, the *mongos* opens connections to any and all shards necessary to fulfill that request. Thus, if a cluster had 100 shards and a client connects to a *mongos* and tries to query for all of their data, the *mongos* must open 100 connections: one connection to each shard. This can quickly mount in number of connections, as you can imagine from the previous example. Suppose a liberally configured app server made a hundred connections to a *mongos* process. Then this could get translated to 100 inbound connections × 100 shards = 10,000 connections to shards! (This assumes a non-targeted query on each connection, which would be a bad design, so this is a somewhat extreme example).

Thus, there are a couple adjustments to make: many people purposefully configure *mongos* processes to only allow a certain number of incoming connections by using the `maxConns` option. This is a good way to enforce that your client is behaving well.

You should also increase the limit on the number of file descriptors, as the default (generally 1024) is simply too low. Set the max number of file descriptors to unlimited or, if you're nervous about that, 20,000. Each system has a different way of changing these limits, but in general, make sure that you change both the hard and soft limits. A hard limit is enforced by the kernel and can only be changed by an administrator, versus a soft limit, which is user-configurable.

If the number of connections is left at 1024, MMS will warn you by displaying the host in yellow on the host list (as shown in the NUMA example above). If low limits are the issue, the "Last Ping" tab should display a message similar to that shown in Figure 23-12.

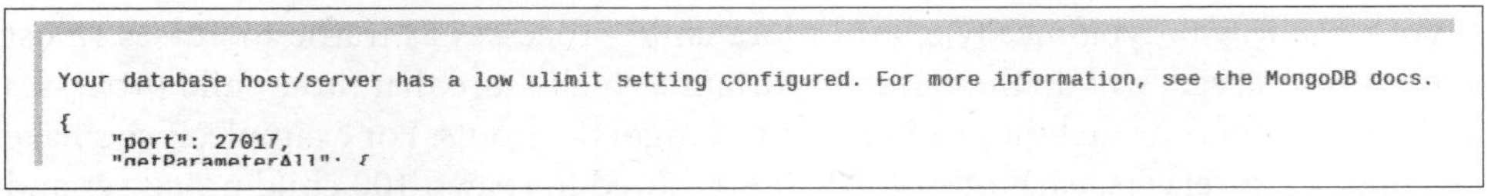

Figure 23-12. MMS low ulimit warning

Even if you have a non-sharded setup and an application that only uses a small number of connections, increase the hard and soft limits to at least 4096. That will stop MongoDB from warning you about them and give you some breathing room, just in case.

Configuring Your Network

This section covers which servers should have connectivity to which other servers. Often, for reasons of network security (and sensibility), you may want to limit the connectivity of MongoDB servers. Note that multiserver MongoDB deployments should handle networks being partitioned or down, but it isn't recommended as a general deployment strategy.

For a standalone server, clients must be able to make connections to the *mongod*.

Members of a replica set must be able to make connections to every other member. Clients must be able to connect to all nonhidden, nonarbiter members. Depending on network configuration, members may also attempt to connect to themselves, so you should allow *mongods* to create connections to themselves.

Sharding is a bit more complicated. There are four components: *mongos* servers, shards, config servers, and clients. Connectivity can be summarized in the following three points:

- A client must be able to connect to a *mongos*.
- A *mongos* must be able to connect to the shards and config servers.
- A shard must be able to connect to the other shards and the config servers.

The full connectivity chart is described in Table 23-1.

Table 23-1. Sharding connectivity

Connectivity	from server type			
to server type	*mongos*	Shard	Config server	Client
mongos	Not required	Not required	Not required	Required
Shard	Required	Required	Not required	Not recommended
Config server	Required	Required	Not required	Not recommended
Client	Not required	Not required	Not required	Not MongoDB-related

There are three possible values in the table: "Required" means that connectivity between these two components is required for sharding to work as designed. MongoDB will attempt to degrade gracefully if it loses these connections due to network issues, but you shouldn't purposely configure it that way.

"Not required" means that these two elements never talk in the direction specified, so no connectivity is needed.

"Not recommended" means that these two elements never talk, but due to user error they could. For example, it is recommended that clients only make connections to the *mongos*, not the shards, so that clients do not inadvertently make requests directly to shards. Similarly, clients should not be able to directly access config servers so that they cannot accidentally modify config data.

Note that *mongos* processes and shards talk to config servers, but config servers don't make connections to anyone even one another.

Shards must communicate during migrates: shards connect to one another directly to transfer data.

As mentioned earlier, replica set members that compose shards should be able to connect to themselves.

System Housekeeping

This section covers some common issues you should be aware of before deploying.

Synchronizing Clocks

In general, it's safest to have your systems' clocks within a second of each other. Replica sets should be able to handle nearly any clock skew. Sharding can handle some skew (if it gets beyond a few minutes, you'll start seeing warnings in the logs), but it's best to minimize. Having in-sync clocks also makes figuring out what's happening from logs easier.

You can keep clocks synchronized using the *w32tm* tool on Windows and the *ntp* daemon on Linux.

The OOM Killer

Very occasionally, MongoDB will allocate enough memory that it will be targeted by the OOM killer (out-of-memory killer). This particularly tends to happen during index builds, as that is one of the only times when MongoDB's resident memory should put any strain on the system.

If your MongoDB process suddenly dies with no errors or exit messages in the logs, check */var/log/messages* (or wherever your kernel logs such things) to see if it has any messages about terminating *mongod*.

If the kernel has killed MongoDB for memory overuse, you should see something like this in the kernel log:

```
kernel: Killed process 2771 (mongod)
kernel: init invoked oom-killer: gfp_mask=0x201d2, order=0, oomkilladj=0
```

If you were running with journaling, you can simply restart *mongod* at this point. If you were not, restore from a backup or resync the data from a replica.

The OOM killer gets particularly nervous if you have no swap space and start running low on memory, so a good way to prevent it from going on a spree is to configure a modest amount of swap. MongoDB should never use it, but it makes the OOM killer happy.

If the OOM killer kills a *mongos*, you can simply restart it.

Turn Off Periodic Tasks

Check that there aren't any cron jobs or daemons that might periodically pop to life and steal resources. One culprit we've seen is package managers' automatic update. These programs will come to life, consume a ton of RAM and CPU, and then disappear. This is not something that you want running on your production server.

APPENDIX A

Installing MongoDB

MongoDB binaries are available for Linux, Mac OS X, Windows, and Solaris. This means that, on most platforms, you can download an archive from *http://www.mongodb.org/downloads*, inflate it, and run the binary.

The MongoDB server requires a directory it can write database files to and a port it can listen for connections on. This section covers the entire install on the two variants of system: Windows and everything else (Linux, Max, Solaris).

When we speak of "installing MongoDB," generally what we are talking about is setting up `mongod`, the core database server. `mongod` can be used as a standalone server or as a member of a replica set. Most of the time, this will be the MongoDB process you are using.

Choosing a Version

MongoDB uses a fairly simple versioning scheme: even-point releases are stable, and odd-point releases are development versions. For example, anything starting with 2.4 is a stable release, such as 2.4.0, 2.4.1, and 2.4.15. Anything starting with 2.5 is a development release, such as 2.5.0, 2.5.2, or 2.5.10. Let's take the 2.4/2.5 release as a sample case to demonstrate how the versioning timeline works:

1. MongoDB 2.4.0 is released. This is a major release and will have an extensive changelog.
2. After the developers start working on the milestones for 2.6 (the next major stable release), they release 2.5.0. This is the new development branch that is fairly similar to 2.4.0 but probably with an extra feature or two and maybe some bugs.
3. As the developers continue to add features, they will release 2.5.1, 2.5.2, and so on. These releases should not be used in production.

4. Some minor bug fixes may be backported to the 2.4 branch, which will cause releases of 2.4.1, 2.4.2, and so on. Developers are conservative about what is backported; few new features are ever added to a stable release. Generally, only bug fixes are ported.
5. After all of the major milestones have been reached for 2.6.0, 2.5.7 (or whatever the latest development release is) will be turned into 2.6.0-rc0.
6. After extensive testing of 2.6.0-rc0, usually there are a couple minor bugs that need to be fixed. Developers fix these bugs and release 2.6.0-rc1.
7. Developers repeat step 6 until no new bugs are apparent, and then 2.6.0-rc2 (or whatever the latest release ended up being) is renamed 2.6.0.
8. Start over from step 1, incrementing all versions by 0.2.

You can see how close a production release is by browsing the core server roadmap on the MongoDB bug tracker.

If you are running in production, you should use a stable release. If you are planning to use a development release in production, ask about it first on the mailing list or IRC to get the developers' advice.

If you are just starting development on a project, using a development release may be a better choice. By the time you deploy to production, there will probably be a stable release with the features you're using (MongoDB attempts to stick to a regular cycle of stable releases every six months). However, you must balance this against the possibility that you would run into server bugs, which can be discouraging to a new user.

Windows Install

To install MongoDB on Windows, download the Windows zip from the MongoDB downloads page. Use the advice in the previous section to choose the correct version of MongoDB. There are 32-bit and 64-bit releases for Windows, so select whichever version you're running. When you click the link, it will download the *.zip*. Use your favorite extraction tool to unzip the archive.

Now you need to make a directory in which MongoDB can write database files. By default, MongoDB tries to use the *\data\db* directory on the current drive as its data directory (for example, if you're running mongod on *C:*, it'll use *C:\data\db*). You can create this directory or any other empty directory anywhere on the filesystem. If you chose to use a directory other than *\data\db*, you'll need to specify the path when you start MongoDB, which is covered in a moment.

Now that you have a data directory, open the command prompt (*cmd.exe*). Navigate to the directory where you unzipped the MongoDB binaries and run the following:

```
$ bin\mongod.exe
```

If you chose a directory other than *C:\data\db*, you'll have to specify it here, with the `--dbpath` argument:

```
$ bin\mongod.exe --dbpath C:\Documents and Settings\Username\My Documents\db
```

See Chapter 20 for more common options, or run `mongod.exe --help` to see all options.

Installing as a Service

MongoDB can also be installed as a service on Windows. To install, simply run with the full path, escape any spaces, and use the `--install` option. For example:

```
$ C:\mongodb-windows-32bit-1.6.0\bin\mongod.exe
    --dbpath "\"C:\Documents and Settings\Username\My Documents\db\"" --install
```

It can then be started and stopped from the Control Panel.

POSIX (Linux, Mac OS X, and Solaris) Install

Choose a version of MongoDB, based on the advice in the section "Choosing a Version" on page 385. Go to the MongoDB downloads page, and select the correct version for your OS.

> If you are using a Mac, check whether you're running 32-bit or 64-bit. Macs are especially picky that you choose the correct build and will refuse to start MongoDB and give confusing error messages if you choose the wrong build. You can check what you're running by clicking the apple in the upper-left corner and selecting the About This Mac option.

You must create a directory for the database to put its files. By default, the database will use */data/db*, although you can specify any other directory. If you create the default directory, make sure it has the correct write permissions. You can create the directory and set the permissions by running the following:

```
$ mkdir -p /data/db
$ chown -R $USER:$USER /data/db
```

`mkdir -p` creates the directory and all its parents, if necessary (i.e., if the */data* directory didn't exist, it will create the `/data` directory and then the */data/db* directory). `chown` changes the ownership of */data/db* so that your user can write to it. Of course, you can also just create a directory in your home folder and specify that MongoDB should use that when you start the database, to avoid any permissions issues.

Decompress the *.tar.gz* file you downloaded from *http://www.mongodb.org*:

```
$ tar zxf mongodb-linux-i686-1.6.0.tar.gz
$ cd mongodb-linux-i686-1.6.0
```

Now you can start the database:

```
$ bin/mongod
```

Or if you'd like to use an alternate database path, specify it with the `--dbpath` option:

```
$ bin/mongod --dbpath ~/db
```

See section TODO for a summary of the most common options, or run `mongod` with `--help` to see all the possible options.

Installing from a Package Manager

On these systems, there are many package managers that can also be used to install MongoDB. If you prefer using one of these, there are official packages for RedHat, Debian, and Ubuntu as well as unofficial packages for many other systems. If you use an unofficial version, make sure it installs a relatively recent version.

On OS X, there are unofficial packages for Homebrew and MacPorts. If you go for the MacPorts version, be forewarned: it takes hours to compile all the Boost libraries, which are MongoDB prerequisites. Start the download and leave it overnight.

Regardless of the package manager you use, it is a good idea to figure out where it is putting the MongoDB log files before you have a problem and need to find them. It's important to make sure they're being saved properly in advance of any possible issues.

APPENDIX B

MongoDB Internals

It is not necessary to understand MongoDB's internals to use it effectively, but it may be of interest to developers who wish to work on tools, contribute, or simply understand what's happening under the hood. This appendix covers some of the basics. The MongoDB source code is available at *https://github.com/mongodb/mongo*.

BSON

Documents in MongoDB are an abstract concept—the concrete representation of a document varies depending on the driver/language being used. Because documents are used extensively for communication in MongoDB, there also needs to be a representation of documents that is shared by all drivers, tools, and processes in the MongoDB ecosystem. That representation is called Binary JSON, or *BSON* (no one knows where the J went).

BSON is a lightweight binary format capable of representing any MongoDB document as a string of bytes. The database understands BSON, and BSON is the format in which documents are saved to disk.

When a driver is given a document to insert, use as a query, and so on, it will encode that document to BSON before sending it to the server. Likewise, documents being returned to the client from the server are sent as BSON strings. This BSON data is decoded by the driver to its native document representation before being returned to the client.

The BSON format has three primary goals:

Efficiency
: BSON is designed to represent data efficiently, without using much extra space. In the worst case BSON is slightly less efficient than JSON; and in the best case (e.g., when storing binary data or large numerics), it is much more efficient.

Traversability
: In some cases, BSON does sacrifice space efficiency to make the format easier to traverse. For example, string values are prefixed with a length rather than relying on a terminator to signify the end of a string. This traversability is useful when the MongoDB server needs to introspect documents.

Performance
: Finally, BSON is designed to be fast to encode to and decode from. It uses C-style representations for types, which are fast to work with in most programming languages.

For the exact BSON specification, see *http://www.bsonspec.org*.

Wire Protocol

Drivers access the MongoDB server using a lightweight TCP/IP wire protocol. The protocol is documented on the MongoDB wiki but basically consists of a thin wrapper around BSON data. For example, an insert message consists of 20 bytes of header data (which includes a code telling the server to perform an insert and the message length), the collection name to insert into, and a list of BSON documents to insert.

Data Files

Inside of the MongoDB data directory, which is */data/db/* by default, there are separate files for each database. Each database has a single *.ns* file and several data files, which have monotonically increasing numeric extensions. So, the database *foo* would be stored in the files *foo.ns*, *foo.0*, *foo.1*, *foo.2*, and so on.

The numeric data files for a database will double in size for each new file, up to a maximum file size of 2 GB. This behavior allows small databases to not waste too much space on disk, while keeping large databases in mostly contiguous regions on disk.

MongoDB also preallocates data files to ensure consistent performance. (This behavior can be disabled using the `--noprealloc` option.) Preallocation happens in the background and is initiated every time that a data file is filled. This means that the MongoDB server will always attempt to keep an extra, empty data file for each database to avoid blocking on file allocation.

Namespaces and Extents

Within its data files, each database is organized into *namespaces*, each storing a specific collection's data. The documents for each collection have their own namespace, as does each index. Metadata for namespaces is stored in the database's *.ns* file.

The data for each namespace is grouped on disk into sections of the data files, called *extents*. In Figure B-1 the *foo* database has three data files, the third of which has been preallocated and is empty. The first two data files have been divided up into extents belonging to several different namespaces.

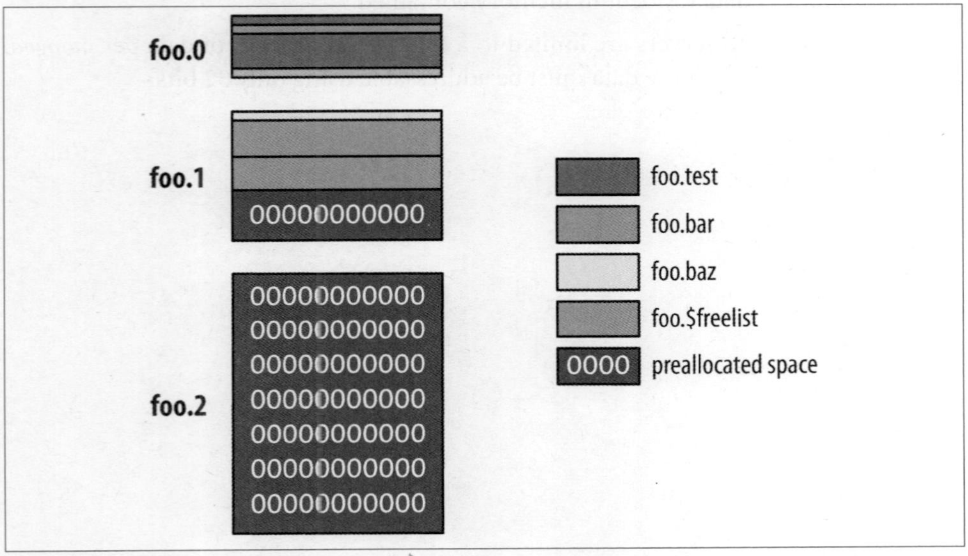

Figure B-1. Namespaces and extents

Figure B-1 shows us several interesting things about namespaces and extents. Each namespace can have several different extents, which are not (necessarily) contiguous on disk. Like data files for a database, extents for a namespace grow in size with each new allocation. This is done to balance wasted space used by a namespace versus the desire to keep data for a namespace mostly contiguous on disk. The figure also shows a special namespace, *$freelist*, which keeps track of extents that are no longer in use (e.g., extents from a dropped collection or index). When a namespace allocates a new extent, it will first search the freelist to see whether an appropriately sized extent is available.

Memory-Mapped Storage Engine

The default storage engine (and only supported storage engine at the time of this writing) for MongoDB is a memory-mapped engine. When the server starts up, it memory maps all its data files. It is then the responsibility of the operating system to manage flushing data to disk and paging data in and out. This storage engine has several important properties:

- MongoDB's code for managing memory is small and clean because most of that work is pushed to the operating system.
- The virtual size of a MongoDB server process is often very large, exceeding the size of the entire data set. This is OK because the operating system will handle keeping the amount of data resident in memory contained.
- 32-bit MongoDB servers are limited to a total of about 2 GB of data per *mongod*. This is because all of the data must be addressable using only 32 bits.

Index

Symbols

A

We'd like to hear your suggestions for improving our indexes. Send email to index@oreilly.com.

D

E

F

G

H

P

S

T

U

About the Author

Kristina Chodorow is a software engineer who worked on the MongoDB core for five years. She led MongoDB's replica set development as well as writing the PHP and Perl drivers. She has given talks on MongoDB at meetups and conferences around the world and maintains a blog on technical topics at *http://www.kchodorow.com*. She currently works at Google.

Colophon

The animal on the cover of *MongoDB: The Definitive Guide, Second Edition* is a mongoose lemur, a member of a highly diverse group of primates endemic to Madagascar. Ancestral lemurs are believed to have inadvertently traveled to Madagascar from Africa (a trip of at least 350 miles) by raft some 65 million years ago. Freed from competition with other African species (such as monkeys and squirrels), lemurs adapted to fill a wide variety of ecological niches, branching into the almost 100 species known today. These animals' otherworldly calls, nocturnal activity, and glowing eyes earned them their name, which comes from the lemures (specters) of Roman myth. Malagasy culture also associates lemurs with the supernatural, variously considering them the souls of ancestors, the source of taboo, or spirits bent on revenge. Some villages identify a particular species of lemur as the ancestor of their group.

Mongoose lemurs (*Eulemur mongoz*) are medium-sized lemurs, about 12 to 18 inches long and 3 to 4 pounds. The bushy tail adds an additional 16 to 25 inches. Females and young lemurs have white beards, while males have red beards and cheeks. Mongoose lemurs eat fruit and flowers and they act as pollinators for some plants; they are particularly fond of the nectar of the kapok tree. They may also eat leaves and insects.

Mongoose lemurs inhabit the dry forests of northwestern Madagascar. One of the two species of lemur found outside of Madagascar, they also live in the Comoros Islands (where they are believed to have been introduced by humans). They have the unusual quality of being cathemeral (alternately wakeful during the day and at night), changing their activity patterns to suit the wet and dry seasons. Mongoose lemurs are threatened by habitat loss and they are classified as a vulnerable species.

The cover image is from Lydekker's *Royal Natural History*. The cover font is Adobe ITC Garamond. The text font is Adobe Minion Pro; the heading font is Adobe Myriad Condensed; and the code font is Dalton Maag's Ubuntu Mono.

O'Reilly Media, Inc.介绍

O'Reilly Media通过图书、杂志、在线服务、调查研究和会议等方式传播创新知识。自1978年开始，O'Reilly一直都是前沿发展的见证者和推动者。超级极客们正在开创着未来，而我们关注真正重要的技术趋势——通过放大那些“细微的信号”来刺激社会对新科技的应用。作为技术社区中活跃的参与者，O'Reilly的发展充满了对创新的倡导、创造和发扬光大。

O'Reilly为软件开发人员带来革命性的“动物书”；创建第一个商业网站（GNN）；组织了影响深远的开放源代码峰会，以至于开源软件运动以此命名；创立了Make杂志，从而成为DIY革命的主要先锋；一如既往地通过多种形式缔结信息与人的纽带。O'Reilly的会议和峰会集聚了众多超级极客和高瞻远瞩的商业领袖，共同描绘出开创新产业的革命性思想。作为技术人士获取信息的选择，O'Reilly现在还将先锋专家的知识传递给普通的计算机用户。无论是书籍出版、在线服务还是面授课程，每一项O'Reilly的产品都反映了公司不可动摇的理念——信息是激发创新的力量。

业界评论

“O'Reilly Radar博客有口皆碑。”

——Wired

“O'Reilly凭借一系列（真希望当初我也想到了）非凡想法建立了数百万美元的业务。”

——Business 2.0

“O'Reilly Conference是聚集关键思想领袖的绝对典范。”

——CRN

“一本O'Reilly的书就代表一个有用、有前途、需要学习的主题。”

——Irish Times

“Tim是位特立独行的商人，他不光放眼于最长远、最广阔的视野，并且切实地按照Yogi Berra的建议去做了：‘如果你在路上遇到岔路口，走小路（岔路）。’回顾过去，Tim似乎每一次都选择了小路，而且有几次都是一闪即逝的机会，尽管大路也不错。”

——Linux Journal

出版说明

随着计算机技术的成熟和广泛应用，人类正在步入一个技术迅猛发展的新时期。计算机技术的发展给人们的工业生产、商业活动和日常生活都带来了巨大的影响。然而，计算机领域的技术更新速度之快也是众所周知的，为了帮助国内技术人员在第一时间了解国外最新的技术，东南大学出版社和美国 O'Reilly Meida, Inc. 达成协议，将陆续引进该公司的代表前沿技术或者在某专项领域享有盛名的著作，以影印版或者简体中文版的形式呈献给读者。其中，影印版书籍力求与国外图书“同步”出版，并且“原汁原味”展现给读者。

我们真诚地希望，所引进的书籍能对国内相关行业的技术人员、科研机构的研究人员和高校师生的学习和工作有所帮助，对国内计算机技术的发展有所促进。也衷心期望读者提出宝贵的意见和建议。

最新出版的影印版图书，包括：

- 《Android 编程 第二版》（影印版）
- 《Python 数据分析》（影印版）
- 《R 语言技术手册 第二版》（影印版）
- 《自然语言标注——用于机器学习》（影印版）
- 《移动 Web 编程 第二版》（影印版）
- 《PHP 编程 第三版》（影印版）
- 《MongoDB 设计模式》（影印版）
- 《Python Cookbok 第三版》（影印版）
- 《学习 Java 第四版》（影印版）
- 《学习 Python 第五版》（影印版）
- 《游戏开发中的物理学 第二版》（影印版）
- 《HTML5 Canvas ——网站本地化交互和动画设计 第二版》（影印版）
- 《学习使用 C 指针》（影印版）
- 《Linux 系统编程 第二版》（影印版）
- 《MongoDB 权威指南 第二版》（影印版）